Safari Salesman

John Harrison

Copyright © 2013 John Harrison
All rights reserved.

ISBN: 1-4791-6687-1
ISBN-13: 9781479166879

Library of Congress Number: 2012915679
CreateSpace Independent Publishing Platform
North Charleston, South Carolina

Authors Note

This book is a true account of my safari; however, for the purposes of the book, my assumed name is John Carter.

The adventures are real, the people are real, but the names of the products have been changed.

chapter

ONE

It was late afternoon, the sun was low in the sky, and warm air was still rising off the endless African savanna. For some time the land had been drying out since earlier rains, and only the unleveled ground that ran down the middle of the red murram road remained wet. However, the camber on each side was greasy and dotted with treacherous water holes.

The short-bladed grass that covered the plain appeared greener as we headed south toward the town of Gulu in northern Uganda. It was only the isolated clumps of borassus palms, with their big orange fruit, that broke up the flat monotony of the grassland.

It had been another tough day. We had been working the dust-ridden trading centers surrounding the northern township of Kitgum, places with such strange-sounding names as Madi Opei, Padibe, Palabek, and Nam-Okora. The sticky ocher dust of the region had settled into everything—our clothes, our food, and our hair. We sat in silence, obsessed with our destination, less than fifty miles down the colorless track. The past four nights had been spent sleeping rough in the confining space of our transit van, and it would be a relief to get to Gulu and have a bed to sleep in.

The sales of our medicinal products had been slow in the sparsely populated region fringing southern Sudan, but we were more than hopeful that this deficit would soon be wiped away in Uganda's rich cotton-growing areas to the south.

The road south had been empty of traffic for some time, and with nothing to grab my attention, I was reduced to watching the shapeless shadow of our van stalking our progress along the level of the land. Every now and then the van would jolt on potholes that lay hidden beneath innocuous pools of dun-brown water. This was nothing more than a minor irritant for Thomas, our African driver, whose keen eye ensured that the wheels remained slotted into the parallel tracks that ran along each side of the road. However, despite generally poor conditions, he managed to keep the vehicle well-balanced while maintaining a cruising speed of forty miles per hour.

A short while later he reduced the speed to thirty miles per hour as we passed through a place called Lagute. There was nothing there for us to see, except for a few mud and wattle huts set behind a bare compound. On the far side of the settlement there was a fenced field planted with finger millet, while alongside was a mixed herd of sheep and goats enclosed by a green cactus hedgerow.

The low clouds began to break up, and it was now possible to make out the far hills that bounded the view. The rain-washed track was all but dry and could be clearly seen for some way ahead as we skimmed the tilted ground. On my side I glimpsed a solitary acacia tree on the sienna-colored plain. Its dark, fan-shaped canopy formed a circle of shade, and parasite creepers were slowly extinguishing the bright golden flowers on the lower branches. However, up higher, and doing well, were the black, hanging hives of the African honeybee.

Sitting on a rumble seat directly behind Thomas was our Indian sales representative, Vinoo Visavadia, who was nearly asleep. He had a unique skill for coaxing large orders for our medical products out of the ubiquitous Asian merchants. He also had the ability at the end of each day to search out nightly accommodation for himself, even in the remotest areas of Africa. Occasionally however he'd fail, and would have to spend the night in the bush with us. I had been informed by our Nairobi office that he preferred to be called by his surname. He felt it made for a more proper tone, although Thomas largely ignored his sensitivity and called him by his first name.

We passed two men wrestling with large black bags of cotton across their shoulders. They moved quickly off the road when they heard a warning blast on the van's horn. Their women were walking behind them. Their breasts were heavy and bare, and they had ample hips rolling under the weight of water-filled calabashes finely balanced on their heads. They were Acholi people and smiled in response to Thomas's slow, low wave from his driving seat. Small flecks of cotton dotted the shoulders of the road like early snow.

"Are we stopping before Gulu?" Thomas queried without taking his eyes off the road.

I pulled the map from under the dashboard.

"Yes," I said, adding, "There's a small place called Oyelomon coming up after we cross the Aswa River."

"Is it far?"

"Not far," I said with a yawn as I studied the map. "It'll be about twenty-five miles, and after Oyelomon we'll go straight through to Gulu, which is another thirteen miles. We won't be stopping anywhere else."

"What's the time?" he asked nonchalantly, with a slight turn of the head in my direction.

I checked the dial on my wristwatch. "It's almost five thirty p.m.," I said as I pressed myself against the back of the passenger seat.

We dropped back into silence. I noticed the speedometer needle had crept up and was now touching forty-five miles per hour, but the road was straight and almost dry; only an occasional patch of mud or a rain pool scarred the tilted surface. Our boxed cargo of medicines had dwindled to a third of the full carrying capacity, and because of this, our speed remained within the recommended safety limits set for these conditions. Even now, despite tiredness, I kept a steady eye on the road ahead.

The laterite surface of the road was always a problem, and after heavy rains, workmen were called out within a day or two to fill in the potholes, flatten ruts, and clear overgrown ditches. The other danger on the road at night came from wildlife. However, in the light of day, it was the turn of domestic animals, such as goats, sheep, and cattle, to wander in search of fresh grazing areas. These flocks were usually under the supervision of a herdsman. Another unexpected hazard during daylight hours was from small children crossing the road. They carted water on their heads or large bundles of firewood on their backs, and due to tiredness, they forgot about the possible dangers from vehicles. The young ones found it difficult to judge their speed as they trekked home across the dusty savanna to outlying settlements and villages. Fortunately the land we were journeying on was relatively flat, but in hilly areas, there was the added danger of sudden bends in the road.

However, despite the generally poor road conditions, we once more picked up speed, and as a result, the van swayed when the rear passenger's side wheel slipped from its groove. There was a resounding thump as a couple of cartons of medicine tumbled down onto the wood floor. Thomas immediately pulled hard on the steering and maneuvered the offending wheel back into its track. This short-lived danger was soon corrected, and once again we relaxed into an easy silence.

Shortly afterward we passed a woman and child walking together along the gritty shoulder, and they stepped aside as we thundered by. I automatically loosed two advertising leaflets from the open door and watched them flutter to the ground through the rearview mirror. The small boy picked up the leaflets and handed one to his mother.

Our three-man crew's basic job was to see that as many people as possible were informed about our two principal products. They were called Herbalex Cough Medicine and Gripe Aid for babies, and both came in 5-ounce bottles, which we carried with us and sold to many wholesalers and retailers along our route. Our 3.5-ton customized transit van came equipped with loudspeakers, microphone, record player, and a tape recorder. We also carried promotional advertising material such as illustrated leaflets, brochures, samples, and metal signs for nailing on shop fronts.

At each and every village we would stop to give a show from the back of the van to crowds that varied in size from a mere handful to a few hundred. We sold directly to the people on the roadside while we played music and advertising tapes, and, in addition, we persuaded shop owners to allow us to nail up tin plates on their doorways. Then, having created a lively demand, we visited the traders and took orders for our products. It proved a very successful routine, and as we were unique—in that we were the only safari team that had penetrated the bush for months on end—the market for our medicines was virtually unchallenged. Every so often we would need to restock the van while on tour, and this would be done with the cooperation of our agents, who had offices in Nairobi, Kampala, Mwanza, and Dar es Salaam.

The deliveries of stock up-country would be done via railway stations or bus depots.

At the same time our head office, otherwise known as Medical & General Exporters of Clapham, London, had an extended range of products that included soaps, cosmetics, lactics, pine and coal tar disinfectants, portable toilets, urinal cleansers, air fresheners, and toilet paper. However, while on safari we concentrated principally on Herbalex Cough Medicine and Gripe Aid for babies, although that's not to say that we weren't on the lookout for orders for our other products from hotels, airports, missions, and mining companies.

***

We had driven on many bad roads in our time, and this one was no better or worse than normal. The worst roads were the no-road routes coming from the Sudan, the Congo, or Southern Tanganyika. At intervals, in the flat openness of this road, we passed pyramid-shaped anthills that stood out like conical sentries; otherwise, the view ahead was monotonous and almost empty of life. It was a warm evening, and it wasn't unusual for us to have both the front doors of the van wide open, and from behind our rear wheels, we relentlessly churned out a dense, billowing cloud of sand-like grit. We were no longer slipping and sliding but were now firmly slotted into the polished tracks on each side of the central ridge.

The declining sun filtered through the fly-splashed windshield, and we became partially dazzled by piercing green and red rays of light. In response we lowered the visors and dropped our speed back to a steady forty miles per hour. Having made these adjustments, we settled back into our seats and continued to bowl along the slanted road in silence.

Then, both Thomas and I leaned forward in unison, eyeing the dark straightness of the brown-and-green shoulders of the road. We each spotted a circular brown patch, the size of a child's bicycle wheel that interrupted the smooth flow of the driver's-side track. Perhaps it was just a small mud puddle isolated on a fast-drying surface, or maybe a freshly heaped pile of dung not yet disturbed by a dor beetle, or even an old piece of coiled rope that had fallen from the back of a passing truck. However, it wasn't any of these, and only a millisecond was left for us to absorb and react to this possible problem.

We strained our eyes through the splattered glass, but it was far too late to take evasive action. After all, it might just have been an innocent surface puddle; but it wasn't. It was a ten-inch-deep, sharp-edged cavity, and our front driver's-side wheel jarred right into its center and the rear of the van was tossed high into the air.

We cart wheeled and crashed onto a broad strip of stony ground that ran parallel to the road, and the van instantly burst into flames and disintegrated into many parts. The shouldering wreckage was spread across a wide area from the point of impact. Yellow flames and a concentrated plume of dirty smoke reached into the darkening sky. I found it very hard to believe that I had been thrown clear and had landed face down on the left side of the road. My back felt warm and sticky, and although in pain, I was able to move my limbs.

The acrid smell of burning rubber and the harsh sound of crackling metal invaded my senses. I figured I was facing north in the opposite direction to our destination point at Gulu. I found it difficult to turn my head or get to my feet, and as a result was cut off from what was going on behind me. I had no idea whether my colleagues had survived the accident.

Our safari had clearly come to an end.

It must have been a good fifteen minutes before I was able to clear my head and think logically. My right arm swung loose, and I was clearly aware of someone moaning. The muffled sound appeared to come from behind me, possibly from the drainage ditch that ran beside the road. However, my eyes were focused on the woman and small boy whom we'd passed earlier and who were now hurrying toward me. The moment she arrived, she lowered herself onto the ground and began swatting at the gray cattle flies that had settled on my wound on my back.

"Please look for my friends," I pleaded. "There are two others besides me, and one of them is behind me."

She tugged at my shirttail and draped it over my back.

"I'll send my boy to get help," she replied as she got to her feet and looked around. Then, with a note of increased urgency, she spoke rapidly in Lwoo to the youngster. It was clear from her Nilotic accent that she belonged to the Ancholi tribe, a warmhearted people.

Two minutes later the young lad was lost in the colorless desert, where the land stretched and faded into the rising distance. The woman started to pace the ground toward the ditch and beyond in search of Thomas and Visavadia.

The sun had settled on the horizon, and large splashes of yellow covered the face of the distant hills. It was then that I sensed the stir of beating wings above the track. I looked upward with some difficulty and saw a flight of black vultures circling the warm thermals. It was far too late for them to be searching for a carcass. Their interest was definitely limited to an inborn instinct of curiosity, and it was a certainty that they would soon be on their way again. Less than a minute later they obliged by flying off in a northwesterly direction, most probably to their nesting site in the Payera Hills.

The sound of moaning had ceased, and I began to think that perhaps the Ancholi woman had abandoned us, having decided that the situation was too much to cope with and that it might be wiser not to get involved. I was still in the same position, facing northward up the road. Being tired of lying down, I attempted to push myself into a sitting position with the hope of getting to my feet. I nearly made it but gave up and lowered myself back onto the road, my head swimming. The thought of yellow-and-white hunting dogs prowling the savanna in darkness would undoubtedly provide me with enough incentive the next time I tried to get to my feet. However, in the meantime I noticed that the fire had more or less extinguished itself on the hard ground and it was fortunate that there was no wind to fan the burning embers.

My doubts about the Ancholi woman were soon disproved as I spotted her striding purposefully down the road toward me. I immediately felt a deep sense of guilt that I had assumed she'd gone for good. I breathed a heavy sigh of relief as she once more sat on the ground and began swatting the flies and mosquitoes that had settled on my back. It was obvious now that she wouldn't have sent her own son off into the darkness of the African bush unless she had been convinced that help was needed. I wished there was a way in which I could make amends, but all I could do was to lamely say *"asante sana,"* or "thank you very much" for her help.

Then, out of the blue, she spoke in a quiet voice: "Your friends are OK. The Asian man has a broken arm and is in pain. He's in a ditch a few yards behind you. The Kenyan has a bad leg and needs treatment for burns on his shoulders and neck."

"Thank you very much for your help," I repeated, and I felt immensely glad that the doors of the van had been wide open when we hit the water hole.

"We'll wait for my boy to come back with help from the village. It will be some time yet." And with those words, she turned her head and silently watched the empty road.

It wasn't long afterward that we heard the distant drone of a car engine. At first the sound was faint and could have been anything. Then it was louder and was coming from the south, from Gulu. As the throb got closer, the Acholi woman shouted *"Iko hapa gharri"* in Swahili and pointed down the track toward an approaching car. I struggled to turn my head and failed, although for a fleeting moment, I sensed the headlights of an oncoming vehicle. The next thing to happen was the sound of brakes and the sliding of wheels on the loose dirt. The car had stopped behind me, and a cloud of gritty dust mushroomed from the ground. I couldn't see a thing as I gulped for a breath of fresh air. This was quickly followed by a blur of garbled voices and the sound of feet on the broken road. Then, seconds later, two car doors banged, the engine roared back into life, and more clouds of dust encompassed the air as the car jerked into reverse, gears grinding, before picking its way around me and accelerating down the tilted road toward the northern town of Kitgum.

The Acholi woman began to run down the track, shouting and yelling, finally sinking helplessly to her knees as the vehicle disappeared into the extended landscape. She beat the warm earth with her fists. *"Mzungu,"* she kept repeating as she struck the ground in angry frustration.

"She's right." It was Thomas's voice, and it echoed from farther down the embanked road. I twisted my head and saw him standing by the shallow ditch some fifty feet away. He began to hobble up the track. "They were Europeans," he confirmed, "a man and a woman." I noticed that Thomas's black hair was caked in blood.

"It doesn't make sense to me," I said in a loud voice.

"Nor to me," he agreed.

I swiveled around on the loose surface and looked up into his face. "Have you seen Visavadia?" I asked, before adding, "I hear he has a fractured arm."

"Vinoo's OK," he replied and started to limp toward me.

"That's good news," I said and smiled. "And what about you?"

"I'm OK, as well."

"Give me a hand up," I asked, and grimaced with pain as Thomas reached for my right arm.

"I reckon your shoulder's out of joint," he said in a flat tone.

Moments later I was at last back on my feet.

"Look what I found," he announced with pride. His face was set as he reached inside his bulging jacket and pulled out our metal cash box. "It's a good thing I caught sight of it," he went on, "because by the morning everything here will be picked clean."

For a few moments we said nothing. There was only the stillness and the low crackle of spent fire as we stared down the middle of the road in silence. All that was left were the orange-colored flames that licked at the remains of the wreckage. In the darkness I was able to pick out the figure of the Acholi woman. She was no longer protesting but sitting quietly on a broken cardboard box.

"Let's go and find Visavadia," I said.

"He's in a ditch over there." Thomas pointed with an index finger as large blobs of sweat trickled down his well-featured face onto his colored shirt. "He was knocked out like you were," he commented.

We soon found him and helped him out of the ditch.

Thomas removed his shirt and made it into a sling for Visavadia, gently raising his arm. "That'll have to do for now," he said, and they looked at each other and smiled.

"When do you think the boy will return?" I asked.

"I've no idea," Thomas responded, and once again stared vaguely up the empty road. "All I know is that the woman lives in a small settlement near the village of Atanga some three miles from here. She told me that her uncle owns an old car and has told her son to insist that he gets back here as soon as possible."

For the next two hours we sat in the road and waited. Eventually we saw the narrow beam of headlights as a car picked its way down the road from the north. It looked unreal in the moonlight. It was a vintage car, circa 1933, painted in funereal black. As it closed I could make out its square windows, flat roof, and gilt buckle-shaped radiator.

An old man with a silver beard sat behind the steering wheel. He clambered down and lent a hand in getting us all packed into his car. The ride to the Mission Hospital near Gulu took an hour. We were slumped against each other in the rear seat, and every now and then there was a groan as the car jarred onto unseen ruts.

It was something of a relief when we made out the steady glow of lights coming from the hospital quarters; everything else was bathed in darkness. The old man carefully slowed the car and followed a stretch of white perimeter walling before turning off the red murram road and going through a pair of open, wrought-iron gates. There seemed to be an air of expectancy as we inched our way down from the graveled driveway toward the front entrance. And to confirm our arrival, a heavy front door was pulled open from inside and a splash of light lit up the vestibule. There was a sudden gust of warm air, and beyond in the blackness, we heard the faint rustle of trees that bounded the open compound.

"Please come in," the nurse beckoned, as we spilled from the car.

This was my chance to thank the old man for his kindness. I gave him two five-pound notes and slipped another fiver to the Acholi woman and asked her to buy the lad something. We then shambled toward the welcoming light.

Once inside, we were blinded by the bright tubular lights that shone harshly from fixtures fitted to the white ceiling. After dark in the bush, we were accustomed to the meager light given off by a paraffin lamp, and it was no surprise to the nurse when we shielded our eyes with the backs of our hands.

The emergency room was empty, and we sat on a wooden bench and waited to be examined.

Ten minutes later two nuns entered the room. They wore white habits, and behind them were three nurses and an orderly wielding an old-fashioned stretcher. Once they realized that Thomas was having trouble staying on his feet, and having briefly examined his burns, a nurse was sent to fetch a wheel chair. He was lifted onto it and then pushed through a pair of swinging doors at the far end of the room. It was now Visavadia's turn to be examined. It was at once confirmed that his arm was fractured, and they led him away to the X-ray department.

"See you soon," he shouted, and then hurriedly added, "At least we'll have a bed to sleep on tonight!"

It was my turn next, and a young nurse led me over to a small cubicle adjoining the reception room. "The doctor won't be long," she said, drawing the railed curtains.

I looked at myself in the walled mirror set behind an arch-backed wicker chair. I was covered in dust, and my deeply tanned face could not hide the pallor and strain of recent events. The khaki jacket around my shoulders was torn, and my shoes and socks were missing. Only my khaki shorts remained more or less intact. I then made a half turn in front of the mirror and peered over my shoulder at the wound on my back. The seepage of blood appeared to have clotted. It would be great to have treatment and to have a night stretched out on a comfortable bed. I took another quick glance into the mirror, half hoping it wasn't as bad as I first thought, and finally sat down on the wicker chair and propped my elbow on the edge of the examination couch. I shut my eyes and waited to be called.

"Ah, there you are," a voice said, adding, "I'm Doctor O'Brien." He was about forty-five and had a vigorous attitude, although the years in Africa had pulled down the corners of his mouth and eyes. He proceeded to hold back the door for a young nurse and an older man in a blue suit. "I understand you have been involved in an accident on the Kitgum Road?"

I climbed up from the chair. "Yes, that's correct," I replied, looking him in the face and giving him a nod of my head.

"Have you been drinking?" the doctor asked pointedly, rolling his eyes and adding, "It's Saturday night, you know."

"No, I haven't."

"Well, it doesn't really matter," he went on. "You see, this is an African hospital run by the Mission for the African people. I'm afraid we can't admit you here." The doctor paused, giving time for his jaundiced opinion to sink in.

"I don't believe what I'm hearing," I protested, and put my hand on the back of the chair for support.

"It's perfectly correct," he said, and then with a waggle of his forefinger he beckoned for the man in the blue suit.

"This is Mr. Makumbi, and as head clerk of this hospital he is in charge of all admissions. He will be happy to confirm to you that what I have said.

I therefore advise you to leave the mission and find alternative treatment." The head clerk shifted awkwardly from one foot to the other, but remained tight-lipped.

"There's no need to make a thing of this," I said, "but surely you can give me some sort of first aid?"

This time it was the clerk who responded. "We can't do that either," he said. "Look, we're wasting valuable time, and we've got nothing more to say. However, I will leave you in the capable hands of Nurse Lettue. She'll phone for a taxi and ensure you leave the premises."

Neither of the two officials seemed prepared to focus on the details of my concerns. "What about my colleague, Visavadia?" I replied. "You've admitted him, and he's an Asian."

"He's native born," the doctor retorted and glanced down at his wristwatch.

"There isn't another doctor for miles," I protested.

"That's not my problem," he countered, "and neither am I going to waste any more time standing here and arguing with you." And with those few short words he opened the cubicle door and walked out, closely stalked by the silent Mr. Makumbi.

"I'm sorry about this," the nurse said quietly.

"It's not your fault," I said with a smile. "But if you have a spare minute, I would really appreciate it if you have a look at my right shoulder. It really hurts."

She ran her hands across my shoulder and down my arm. "No wonder it hurts. It's dislocated," she said hurriedly. "If you want me to, I'll put it back for you."

"Would you?"

I followed Lettue's instructions and lay down on the floor, on the towel she had placed behind my back. She then sat opposite me and put her foot into my armpit, and with both hands tugged my arm parallel to my body and tilted it at right angles. There was a noticeable clunk as the bone dropped back into place. The pain that had been dogging me immediately eased.

"I must get that taxi," she said, as she lifted herself off the floor. "I'm afraid at this time of night it'll have to come from Gulu."

"That's OK by me." I smiled as I scrambled up.

"In that case I'd better call it now."

"One last favor," I said. "Please have a look at my back."

"I'll have to be quick," she said.

I pulled off my torn shirt while she went over to a white wall cabinet emblazoned with a red cross. Then with no time to spare, she cleaned the wound with an antiseptic cloth, and added gauze padding, which she bound with surgical tape.

"Here, you'd better have some of this," she said with a smile, and pulled out a roll of lint, surgical tape, and a pot of antiseptic powder, before reaching to the top shelf to pull out a brown paper bag.

"Thanks for everything."

"You're welcome," she said, and then added with a smile, "and please go before I am shot!"

***

It was past ten o'clock when the taxi dropped me outside the Acholi Inn in Gulu. I paid the fare and limped through the entrance. The hall was cozy and cheerful and brightly illuminated with electric wall lights—a whole world away from the African bush, with our hurricane lamps, paraffin stoves, and makeshift beds. I rang the brass bell on the front desk. I found myself fearful of being refused accommodation on the grounds of being a persona non grata due to my grubby appearance and the fact that the luggage I carried was nothing more than a metal cash box. In these circumstances I was fearful that the landlord would inform me that the Inn was fully booked. I realized that outside this place I had nowhere else to stay the night, and then, as if to press home my predicament, I heard the chimes of the grandfather clock in the hallway strike eleven o'clock.

I heard the muffled sound of feet and the creak of doors opening and shutting before I finally came face-to-face with a middle-aged European woman, and much to my amazement, she offered me a fountain pen with which to complete the register. Under occupation I put "Safari Salesman," for nationality I wrote "English," and I gave my address as Clapham, London, SW9. In the end column, I put the date in as Saturday 24 October 1959. The woman asked no questions and hardly glanced at the book before closing it.

"Theodore," she called down the passageway from the direction she had first come.

"*Ndio Memsaab*," a voice answered, and seconds later a heavily muscled young man appeared in the office. He smiled happily at the woman.

"Show this gentleman to Room Eight," she said quietly, "and if he wants anything to eat or drink, please would you see that he gets it before you close down the kitchen."

"Yes, of course I will," he said as he took the keys from the board and came around to the front of the desk. He hesitated for a moment, and a look of surprise spread across his face as it dawned on him that I had no luggage.

"Please come this way," he said with a smile as he led the way down the corridor and upstairs toward Room Eight.

"That's kind of you," I said and smiled when he carefully placed some clean towels on the ottoman at the bottom end of the bed.

"You don't look well, sir."

"No, I don't feel that good," I replied as I sat down on the edge of the bed, worried that I might stain the lemon-colored blanket. "Where's the bathroom?"

"It's the first door on the left as you leave this room." He paused and walked across to the small washbasin in the corner. "There's running water here too," he added, turning the tap. "Look, if there's anything you need..."

I mentioned to Theodore about the accident and how I was told to leave the hospital. It was a relief to share with someone the recent run of events, and when I had finished I asked if he wouldn't mind putting a fresh dressing on my wound after I had a shower. Not only did he agree to do it, but he also offered to me bring my meals into the room during my stay.

"We have endless items of lost property stacked away in boxes in the attic, and I wondered if you would like to have a fresh pair of pajamas and a pair of size-ten gym shoes?"

"That's great," I said enthusiastically.

"We could fit out an army with the things that people have left behind," he said with a grin.

It was midnight by the time I switched off the bedside light. I was in a pair of lightweight pajama pants and had placed a thick bath towel on the upper part of the bed to protect the sheet. I got into a reasonably comfortable position and within minutes was fast asleep.

Sunday went slowly.

Theodore came in around nine o'clock with my breakfast and handed me a copy of the *Argus* newspaper. Under the late news it mentioned that an accident had taken place early last night on the Gulu/Kitgum road. This brief report was overruled by Theodore, who was a mine of information. He told me that the accident had already been broadcast on the radio that morning. Apparently the report stated that two of the injured were now comfortable in a mission hospital but that the European, believed to be English, had mysteriously disappeared. After finishing my breakfast and reading the paper, I borrowed a pack of cards from the front desk, along with a well-thumbed paperback extolling the virtues of the British film colony in California in the thirties and forties.

In order to pass time I played limitless games of patience, and when finally exhausted, I picked up the biographical book on Hollywood stars, many of whom had spent the war years in isolated safety. Later that afternoon I went for a short walk to take in some fresh air after the stuffiness of my room. All in all, I walked about a mile before turning back to the inn, and on arrival Theodore was there knocking on my door and inquiring if I would like to have tea and sandwiches.

I asked him why there didn't seem to be any other guests, unless like me they too were keeping a low profile. He explained that Gulu was the government headquarters for the Northern Region and many of the foreign staff—some of whom lived on a semipermanent basis at the inn—were glad to escape on the weekends and get away from the oppressive atmosphere of Gulu.

I was pleased with the effort I had put into my walk, I was now fully prepared to take the long trek into town tomorrow morning. I needed to visit the post office and Barclays Bank and shop for some clothes.

***

At last it was Monday morning, and fortunately it was a warm, dry day with the faint touch of a breeze wafting through the leafy crowns of the butternut trees that lined the main boulevard going into town. Before I left the hotel, I decided to borrow a walking stick from the hotel's limitless lost property. The traffic was heavy with cyclists, cars, and overloaded trucks. Every once in a while, a large passenger bus skimmed by, making for the important industrial centers in the south. I was pleased that I felt fitter and was able to cope adequately after yesterday's practice walk. However, not everything went smoothly. There was decidedly more traffic, and I spent a good part of the time dodging on and off the road to avoid local drivers who wanted it all to themselves. I should mention that pedestrians had nowhere to walk, except on stony shoulders on the edge of the tarred road. As I made my way toward the center of the town, I noticed that many of the private cars had Europeans at the wheel, and I was on the receiving end of several curious glances. It wasn't long before I passed a row of tightly built Asian shops made of concrete, with corrugated roofs. On the front of each was a weathered signboard with the owner's name etched in large black letters. Behind the stores, on a narrow street running horizontally with the tarmacked road, was a row of warehouses. Each had a warning notice that the street was private and that dogs and their keepers patrolled the premises.

It wasn't long before I spotted a row of African shops; you couldn't miss them with their heavy music pumping out of open doorways. It was good that the Ugandan Africans were establishing a foothold in the retail trade in important towns. However, on the reverse side of the coin, it was almost impossible to find an African store in any up-country town or village. The Asians had control of this territory.

The main trading item in Gulu was cotton. You couldn't fail to notice the hundreds of sacks of freshly picked cotton stacked against the side walls of several of the buildings. Gulu was not only a thriving trading center, it also employed and housed vast numbers of Europeans working in the extensive government administration offices.

I decided to cross over the road and take a closer look at the African-owned shops. They were difficult to describe; perhaps it could be said that they were small wooden structures, housed within dusty compounds. The atmosphere inside was always friendly, and their principal items for sale were set out on long wooden counters with wall-to-wall shelving. They stocked a range of goods, including foods, clothing, portable radios, and the latest forty-five singles topping the charts. In a few short minutes, I had bought a pair of shorts, a vest, and a khaki shirt, and two Mars bars, all of which was parceled up in a brown paper bag.

Outside the local shops life was less prepossessing, and everywhere you walked was a brotherhood of surly dogs, tethered goats awaiting slaughter, and a throng of scraggy chickens that ran helter-skelter all over the place, stopping now and then to scratch feverously at the dirt in the hope of discovering a stray black ant. The odorous smell of open drains and sewage hung in the air, and groups of naked children circled a sluggish standpipe, waiting in line to fill their buckets or tin cans. Everything was covered in dust: the buildings, the open yards, and the traffic. All was one color, beige, and only when a dog stirred and barked, could it be seen as something separate from the bare yard it was guarding.

After the shops the road widened again, leading to a small, grassy roundabout. On the left side was a car repair yard and local cinema. Then straight ahead was the main commercial area with more concrete buildings and solid terraces with wooden pillars supporting cantilevered roofs. In the shade underneath, away from the lingering sun, were more young Africans pedaling sewing machines, skillfully feeding colorful cloth under glinting needles.

At last I found the post office. It was set back from the line of tightly knit buildings, with a space left for cycles and handcarts. The two-story structure was cumbersome and early colonial, with broken concrete steps surrounding an arched doorway. The forecourt was linked with the rear yard by a clay brick tunnel, and two notice boards on blue posts had various sun-bleached information posters pinned to a faded board behind a metal grille. Inside it was sweltering and jammed with people who had been waiting since the early hours for the post office to open its doors for business.

It took thirty minutes to reach the dusty counter, where I handed in my carefully worded telegram to the post office assistant. It simply read: SAFARI CANCELED STOP ALL INJURED IN ROAD ACCIDENT STOP PLEASE CONTACT ACHOLI INN GULU IMMEDIATELY SIGNED JOHN. The message was addressed to our agents in Kampala, namely L.A. Morgan and Sons Limited, colloquially known as Morgans.

After leaving the post office, I made my way farther down toward the center of town. A large, well-maintained roundabout with a fusion of clipped bushes and flowers appeared to be the focal point of the town. I soon spotted a Barclay's Bank on the corner of a wide street. I pulled a "paying in" form from its small wooden stand and deposited the money from the tin box that Thomas had rescued at the time of the accident, making sure I had a sufficient amount to pay for the inn and other necessities. After finding a cashier and getting my copy stamped, I left the building.

On the way back I stumbled on a broken shoulder lining the boulevard, and in a matter of seconds I sensed the warm stickiness of blood against my khaki jacket. There was nothing I could do, but I was inwardly thankful that I wasn't yet wearing my new shirt. I pushed my walking stick hard into the ground and hurried up the incline toward the hotel. All the time the hum of heavy traffic passed within inches of the broken edging. The harsh shadows of the butternut trees provided a shady haven for a herd of assorted goats, and it took time to work my way round them.

An hour later I was lying face down in bed with my head angled on the heavy pillow, and I allowed myself the luxury of introspection. I found it difficult to anticipate what Morgans' reaction might be to the recent run of events, let alone my head office in London. I realized that the survival of Thomas and Visavadia was all- important. My present worries, in comparison, were of lesser consequence, but I couldn't stop myself thinking negatively about everything that had transpired. I began to wonder how Morgans would respond to the telegram. I expected that company managers would make inquiries through the police or call by telephone, but neither had been done, and even the idea of someone flying in by plane no longer applied.

Theodore had kindly brought me my supper, which consisted of consommé soup, chicken and chips, and apple pie and custard. Then later, when he had cleared the dishes and brought me some coffee, I mentioned to him that it was possible I would soon be leaving for Kampala, and I gave him a five-pound tip. This sum was the suggested maximum I was allowed to put down on my expense sheet for entertaining a potential client, and I knew that Theodore would be happy with my gift for services rendered.

It was dark, well past ten o'clock, and the only assumption that I could reasonably come to was that the Morgans people must have decided to come by road. It was then that I fell asleep.

It seemed I had hardly gone to sleep before I heard loud banging on the bedroom door. It was the night watchman. "There's someone here from Kampala to see you," he said, and when he had gone I heard the grandfather clock in the hall striking twelve.

Downstairs in the hall I could see two young men.

"Are you waiting for me?" I asked them.

Safari Salesman

"Head office has received your telegram and instructed us to come and collect you."

"Just give me a few minutes to get ready," I replied, "and I'll be right with you."

The 240-mile journey back to Kampala took seven hours. We traveled through the night and reached the city as dawn broke over the surrounding hills. It had been cramped in the back seat of the small Peugeot, but this was soon offset by a comfortable room in a local hotel that lay just off the main square in the city center. Shortly after breakfast, and much to my relief, I was visited by a local doctor.

It took sixteen stitches to tie the wound together, and I was prescribed a course of antibiotics. For the next nine days I was visited by a young nurse who changed my dressing and checked for signs of infection. The original swelling and bruising on my legs had diminished, and I was now judged fit enough to return to work.

I lost no time in booking a single flight on a BOAC Britannia to the UK via Benghazi and Rome. I phoned Bob Worsley, the local manager of Morgans in Uganda, and told him of my planned departure. On hearing this, he insisted on picking me up at the hotel and driving me the twenty-odd miles to Entebbe Airport.

"Sorry I wasn't able to bring you back from Gulu," Bob apologized, "but I was delayed at our yearly board meeting."

"No problem," I responded. "The guys from the office were more than helpful. They drove four hundred and eighty miles without a break, and I would like you to thank them from me."

"Anyway, I've got some good news," Bob said as looked at me and smiled, "and it comes directly from our Nairobi office. They informed us that both Thomas and Visavadia are doing well and are home with their families in Kenya. Apparently Visavadia had a broken arm, and he is looking forward to getting his plaster off next month."

A half hour later, we had just settled down to a cup of coffee in the airport lounge when the London flight was announced over a crackly speaker.

"Thank you," I said and shook Bob's hand. "I'm sure it won't be long before I see you again." I smiled, then added, "It's my prediction that London won't want to have an unfinished safari on their hands."

The next three months were spent in England. I had four weeks holiday coming and decided to go back home to Gloucestershire. The remainder of the time I worked at our head office in Clapham, catching up with the correspondence that was piled on my in-tray. I also kept a careful check on our export orders coming in from our worldwide markets. I followed up the many calls we had from potential customers interested in our comprehensive range of products. The sales director had been very encouraged by the success we had seen on the last safari—before the accident happened—and with the agreement of Sir Frederick Bell, our chairman, instructions were given for another "in-depth safari" to be undertaken next June with the same crew, if available.

Morgans, back in Nairobi, was consulted on a general itinerary and was given the go-ahead to purchase a new transit van, which was to be customized according to the plans we had already agreed upon. We needed a larger vehicle and settled for a load capacity of 3.5 tons and 550 square feet of storage space. The electrical extras would include external twin speakers, a tape deck, record turntable, and stand-up microphone. Other modifications included fitting sliding doors and putting in steel runners to protect the wood flooring. The installation of a comfortable third seat behind the driver was high on our list of requirements. The one we'd had was a basic, tip-up rumble seat.

I wrote to the four Morgans branch offices in East Africa and requested that they stock up on Herbalex Cough Medicine and Gripe Aid for babies, I suggested that their next order should be above the normal and that we would be including generous shipments of advertising material, such as illustrated pamphlets, tin plates, brochures, and miniature samples.

I had already asked the sales director to approve the design of a plastic pin-on badge showing a picture of a Herbalex bottle with the words *Stop That Cough* circling the edge. I was sure it would be a very popular gimmick and said the launch should be put on the agenda at the next management meeting.

By the end of January, I had caught up with my backlog of work and spent a good part of my time answering letters that had been posted from all parts of Africa inquiring about free booklets and samples. Then one morning I was called into the export manager's office and told that they were ready for me to leave for West Africa on a sales mission. My instructions were to cover the coast from Nigeria up to the Gambia until I was sent word to proceed to Nairobi to commence the new safari.

chapter

TWO

Four months later I received a letter from the head office telling me to move back to Kenya. At the time I was working the market in Monrovia and had been kept busy calling on large American-owned rubber estates and introducing our chemical sanitation units. The following day I drove the few miles to Robertsfield Airport and took a scheduled DC-3 flight on West African Airways to Lagos, spending the night at the Ikeja Arms Hotel before flying east to Nairobi.

Bill Wright, the sales manager for Morgans in Kenya, was waiting to greet me at the Embakasi Airfield when I flew in. "I've got a couple of people I want you to meet," he said with a grin as we strode across the parking lot.

"I don't see anyone," I said, mystified.

"Look over there, behind you," Bill replied.

My eyes followed the direction of his pointing finger, and immediately it rang a bell. I was looking at the new customized transit van, a larger twin of the one before, parked neatly alongside the perimeter fence. The familiar pale yellow panels, the large green speakers, and blue advertising slogans brought back a flood of memories. I could almost smell the bush—the damp, chilly mornings, food cooking over an open fire, the blistering heat of the noonday sun, and the star-filled nights. It was like being in a time tunnel. I was taking a closer look when the passenger door slid open, and much to my surprise, both Thomas and Visavadia climbed out.

"Hey," Thomas said, smiling sheepishly. "How's it going?"

"Fine." I gave him a wide smile. "All I know is that it's great to be back."

We shook hands with a firm clasp and regripped in the African way with elbows pointed down. I then put my arm around Visavadia's back; his serious dark face broke out into a rare smile, showing off his brilliant white teeth. I walked slowly around the new vehicle. It had been all of eight months since we'd had the crash on the road to Gulu, but it seemed like yesterday.

"I reckon you've got things to talk about," Bill said easily, as he put my brown suitcase on the ground. He then turned as if to go. "When do you plan to leave on your safari?"

"Let me see," I said cautiously. "Today's Thursday, June twenty-third, so what about next Monday? Is that OK with you?"

"That's cutting things a bit fine." Bill frowned. "It's only going to give you three days to get things ready." He paused, took a deep breath, and went on. "Don't forget we've got to go over the details of your itinerary, get the van loaded with the correct stock, and that's with a weekend coming up."

"You've got a point," I agreed. "But rush or no rush, we'll get everything done in time, you'll see, and if it's OK by you, I'd like to come by your office tomorrow afternoon, say about two p.m., and finalize the arrangements for the safari."

I noticed that Bill had taken a step backward; I assumed it was a body-language sign that he wanted to get back to his office. I was aware that Morgans had other important agencies besides Medical & General and that there was only so much time he could devote to our cause. So before he slipped away, I took a folded piece of paper out from my back pocket, on which I had jotted down a list of things I needed for the coming safari that I had hoped he would get for me.

"By the by," I began, "there's a range of equipment I've yet to purchase, and unless you tell me otherwise, I need some wiring, fifty feet of rope, two-inch rubber tubing, a flashlight, a camping stove, tin plates, cutlery, frying pan, saucepan, two spades..."

"Hey, wait a minute, John." He laughed. "Why don't you go to Ahmed Stores on Bazaar Street? I'm sure they'll have everything you want there." With those words Bill ran his eyes up and down the parking lot, adding, "Now, where on earth did I leave my car?"

Once he'd gone I turned my attention toward my colleagues. "Look," I said, "it's nearly midday, and you're free to go home to your families, provided you meet me on Saturday morning at Morgans' warehouse, say at eight thirty a.m. I will need your help to check and load the van. It shouldn't take more than three hours at the most."

"Then we get the weekend off, except for the time it takes us to load the van?" Visavadia said cautiously.

"You've got it in one," I said and smiled.

There was a brief pause before I questioned Thomas about the performance of the new van.

"I've given it a test drive," he confirmed, "and as far as I could see, it motored well and there were no unexpected teething problems."

"That's good news," I responded, "but all the same, I think I'd better give it a spin and get the feel of it. Well I guess that just about wraps things up for the time being, except to say that I'll see you both on Saturday, OK?"

I dropped them off in the center of town and then drove northeast on the tarmac road that led to Thika. After a trial run of approximately three miles, I circled and made my way back to Morgans. The road conditions on the short run were ideal, but I was well aware that a long safari would test us—and for that matter, the new customized van—to the very limits. The vehicle, however, would also be our home, our shelter, and our kitchen for the next six months, through good and bad times.

As soon as I arrived at our agent's office in downtown Nairobi, I parked the van in the warehouse and put through an urgent call to Ahmed Stores. The reason I had earlier reeled off a list of essential items to Bill at the airport was that I had hoped he would take the pressure off me by offering to deal with my requirements for the safari, but I had no such luck. Now I had to find the time to sit down and type out a full report on our West African markets.

"This is Sunhil Ahmed speaking," the voice at the other end of the phone said, "and how may I help you?"

I apologized to Mr. Ahmed for the short notice and told him I needed a shipment of items to be ready by two thirty p.m. this same afternoon. "Can you do it?"

"That very much depends on what you want, but we'll do our very best. What is it you require?"

I once again pulled the piece of paper from my back pocket and started to reel off the items from the list. I paused, turned the paper over, and told him that in addition to those items, I needed two walking sticks, two staves, a handsaw, a sheath knife, an ax, a garden rake, two bowls, two buckets, three mugs, a ball of hard-wearing string, and two safari suits, size 40.

"Yes, I can have everything ready for you," Mr. Ahmed confirmed, "but please tell me what color of suits you want. We have khaki, green, or elephant gray."

"I'll take the khaki."

"And your name is?"

"Carter. John Carter."

"Thank you, Mr. Carter."

I put down the receiver and collected my luggage from the van. From there I walked the length of Standard Street toward the city center, hefting my fifty-five-pound suitcase, along with my briefcase stuffed with files and a metal typewriter. It proved a struggle, and I was glad when I finally arrived at Blakes Motors on Muindi Mbingo Street, where I hired a car for the weekend at a cost of twenty pounds; ten pounds for the hire, two pounds for insurance, and an eight-pound deposit for the keys. They also agreed to pick up the car from the Montagu Hotel next Monday morning at eight a.m.

I went in search of a parking place, and it wasn't long before I found a spot in Delamere Avenue. From there I made my way along the crowded pavement toward the New Stanley Hotel. I took a shortcut and went into the side entrance of the famed long bar, avoiding the normally overcrowded lobby of the hotel.

I felt the time had come to relax and soak up the local atmosphere in the crowded bar for the next hour. I found an empty stool in the far corner and had hardly sat down before the barman arrived and asked what I wanted.

"I'll have a pint of bitter, a chicken sandwich, and a bowl of green salad, please," I said.

The bar was a popular meeting place for people from up-country, mainly farmers, who had happened to drop into town for the day to meet old friends, have a laugh, go shopping, or get a check-up with a doctor or dentist. Today was no exception. The chatter and lively banter filled the bar. I noticed that the deeply tanned customers were mainly in their twenties and thirties, and a few were the vintage type of old Kenyans in their fifties or sixties. I was aware that life hadn't been easy for these people in recent years.

A four-year campaign of terror had been waged by the Mau-Mau—mainly made up of Kikuyu tribesmen—against the Europeans. The war had officially ended some thirty months ago in 1957, but the rigid emergency powers had only recently been lifted.

For the settlers who had lived through those days, an air of uncertainty still lingered. For instance if one took a close look around this cross-section of settlers in the bar, it wasn't difficult to pick out the occasional sidearm protruding from the folds of a bush jacket. It was also commonly known that a good many women carried miniature, pearl-handled .22-caliber pistols in their handbags, ever alert to deal with any unexpected assault on them or their children either in the home or on the road.

Despite all else, Kenya was a land of contrasts and had always meant different things to different people. The country straddles the equator and rises to ten thousand feet before dropping down into Lake Victoria. It has lush farmlands of wheat and maize, pedigree cattle, and great rolling expanses of tea and coffee plantations. It is also an Africa of limitless savanna, unchanging ambience, and an abundance of accessible wildlife.

And now approaching on the horizon were a growing number of tourists ready to enjoy the excitement of a live safari, while overnighting at luxurious hunting lodges or traveling to the eastern coastline to swim and sunbathe off unspoiled beaches thickly lined with splendorous palm trees. This land of East Africa was no longer the exclusive haunt of writers, professional hunters, and Hollywood film stars.

The metropolis of Nairobi was known as the city of flowers with its graceful jacaranda trees and red bougainvillaea that lined many of the roads. The setting of the city was largely due to accident rather than design. In 1896, a party of H.M. royal engineers under Captain Sclater were engaged in building a track from Kibwezi through to Lake Victoria. It was essential to establish a staging post for oxen and donkeys, so a Sergeant Ellis chose

Nairobi. The advantage lay in the fresh water from the Uaso Stream and also that this was a flat place before the uplands leading to the escarpment of the Rift Valley. The region was virtually uninhabited, being a no-man's land between the peoples of Masai and Kikuyu. A year later the railway arrived and what with the combination of water and flat plains, it proved an ideal location to construct marshalling yards. And so, out of this, Nairobi was born. The word *Nairobi* translated from Swahili means "a place of cool waters."

***

"We've got your stuff ready, Mr. Carter," the owner of Ahmed's Store said with a smile as I went in. It was exactly two thirty p.m.

The store was divided into two sections. On one side was a gift shop for tourists, filled with skins, ivory carvings, Masai beadwork, spears, grotesque Makonde curios, and a variety of leather goods. The other section was given over to more practical goods for those people venturing up-country. Safari suits in khaki and steel gray were displayed on racks around two walls, along with blankets, while the deep shelves behind the glass counter were crammed with cooking pots, kitchen utensils, enamel plateware, hurricane lamps, and a rich assortment of colorful bedding and camping gear. The glass casing in front held an array of expensive Japanese and German cameras with wide-angle and long lenses. There was a large, gold-framed picture on the far wall of Mr. Ahmed shaking hands with Ernest Hemingway; it was titled *Another Satisfied Customer.*

"You didn't forget the flashlight and spare batteries?" I asked.

"No, it's all there," he assured, adding, "I've put your two safari suits in a carrier bag."

"I'm glad you mentioned that, as I'd better try one on for size."

A few minutes later I took a last look around.

"I hope you don't mind me saying, but I wished you weren't stocking those ivory carvings, such as chess sets, animal sculptures, and bracelets. It makes me sad to see them on display."

"It's not our fault," Mr. Ahmed protested. "It's what tourists ask for, and it's up to the government to pass a law to prohibit their sale."

"Anyway, thanks for everything." I smiled as I made my way slowly toward the door.

"How long are you going for this time?"

"You remember me from last year then?"

"Yes, I do." Mr. Ahmed nodded. "The moment you gave me your name on the phone, it rang a bell, so to speak, and I connected you with that bad road accident last year, near Gulu in Uganda. It's the bush telegraph at work again." He chuckled.

"Well, I'm not certain how long I'll be this time, possibly seven months, but to be honest I'm hoping to get back by Christmas."

"That's going to be some safari." Mr. Ahmed paused for a moment before going on. "It's strange when you come to think about it. You come to Africa, and in the short time you're here, you see more of the place than those of us who spend our lives in the country. Is that not so?"

"Life's never fair," I said and laughed as we walked out of the store and back onto the pavement. My order for dry goods had already been boxed and loaded into the car.

We shook hands.

"By the way," I said, "please send your account to Morgans for settlement."

I drove out of Bazaar Street and along Delamere Avenue with its line of luxury shops on both sides. It had always been the main shopping area for tourists who were willing to pay exorbitant prices for Persian carpets, ornate hand-carved Arab chests, African beaded silver, precious stones and jewelry, all of which was on display in the glass-fronted stores. The road eventually opened out, and I turned into Crauford Street and then home to the Montagu Hotel.

The following day, Friday, I decided to catch up on my paperwork. I wrote out a full market report on Liberia with the help of my new typewriter, checked the invoices covering recent orders, and finely tuned my list of expenses. I put everything into an A4 envelope and pinned a short memo on top, advising I would be leaving for safari on Monday, June 27. I then posted the envelope at the hotel desk.

My mind had now officially switched off West Africa. It had become history, and I was now free to move onto East and Central Africa. However, I was still naturally curious about all fresh sales orders coming in from any territory that I had visited, and no doubt head office would keep me suitably informed on that score.

After having lunch at the hotel, I returned to Morgans to seek out Bill Wright. It was a few minutes past two o'clock when I knocked on his office door. He waved me in, and we soon found ourselves in deep discussion about the itinerary and the quantitative amount of products that needed to be loaded. I also requested two five-gallon jerricans of water and one of gasoline to be included in the shipment. It took more than two hours to settle all the matters relating to the safari.

"In case I don't see you again, good luck," he said.

I climbed into the car, gave a short blast of the horn, and swung out of the driveway onto the main road. My first stop was at a large supermarket where I picked up two bottles of orange squash, a jar of coffee, a box of tea bags, and a two-pound packet of sugar. Also included were other basic items, such as potatoes, tinned meat, beans, spaghetti, Spam, corned beef, soups, macaroni, powdered milk, and a selection of fruit. It wasn't a large shopping trip by any means but enough to see us through the next few days. Once in the bush, we would stock up at Asian shops as we passed through the townships.

***

As arranged, on Saturday morning, I met up with Thomas and Visavadia at the warehouse. The load that I had agreed upon with Bill Wright was laid out neatly on the floor next to the van, including advertising material, the ten gallons of water, and five of gasoline. In addition I bought with me the tea chest that Ahmed Stores had prepared on Thursday and the groceries.

In almost total silence, the three of us began the loading. A balanced cargo was essential—African roads were recalcitrant, as we already knew to our cost. We recognized that we were likely to exceed the load limit by five hundred pounds at the start. We had no option, as our first pickup point was 270 miles away. However, we had the benefit of more room in the cabin section than before. Our maximum load consisted of forty cases of Herbalex Cough Medicine and forty cases of Gripe Aid—each case, or carton, contained seventy-two bottles. We would also be carrying twenty five-gallon drums of pine disinfectant, toilet paper rolls, urinal tablets, a dozen portable toilets, and tins of chemical fluid.

"There's going to be no room for us and our luggage," Thomas complained in his usual dry way.

"In that case the quicker we sell the more space there'll be," I answered positively. Having locked the van, I gave the extra set of keys to Thomas. It had already been arranged for Thomas to collect the van from the warehouse at eight thirty a.m. on Monday.

"Don't forget," I reminded them, "I want you both to meet me at nine a.m. on Monday at the Montagu Hotel, OK?"

After they had gone, I walked over to our agents' offices and said my good-byes to the staff. Unfortunately, Bill was out, so I was glad that we had already said au revoir to each other.

"Please keep me well supplied with the usual products," I pleaded to the assistant sales manager. "There's nothing worse than being stuck in the bush with nothing to sell."

With those words ringing in my mind, my thoughts drifted back to the Acholi Inn in Gulu, where I had nothing to do. Not wanting to be caught out again, I made my way to a stationer in Koinange Street and bought three paperback books and a pack of cards.

***

It was later that Saturday night, in the restaurant section of the Equator Inn that I happened to meet Inga Carlsson. I was sitting at an adjoining table and we started talking. During our conversation she told me that she was an air hostess with the Scandinavian Airlines, and she had just flown in on a DC-7B Clipper.

After dinner we drove into town. The traffic was light but steady. The blooms of red bougainvillea and the blue of jacaranda trees were shining brightly under the fluorescent glow of the street lamps. We turned right onto Standard Street, and at the junction with Wabera Street we slotted into a vacant angled parking place. Two floors up, on the opposite side of the road, was the famed Green Shutters Club with its New Orleans-style swing band. Their rendition of "When the Saints Go Marching In" would usually empty all the tables as people swung to the music on an oblong parquet floor.

At two in the morning, we left the club and motored to the Montagu Hotel with its floodlit forecourt and rock gardens lining the graveled driveway. Then, with little more than four hours' sleep, we took a late and lazy breakfast outside on the veranda. We even found time to wander across the wide lawns to the beer garden. It was now midday and already things were happening. The long horseshoe bar was beginning to fill up with the under thirty-fives. A four-man combo was playing a mix of calypsos and fast meringues beneath a spreading tulip tree that cast deep shadows across a terrazzo floor. "If you were to shut your eyes for a moment, you would never guess you were in deepest Africa," I said and smiled. "The atmosphere is more like the Caribbean."

A cold buffet of meats and spring salads was set on white-clothed tables in the garden adjacent to the open-sided bar. We stayed there for three hours before setting out in the car for a Sunday afternoon drive.

We drove north through Nairobi's rich suburbs onto Banana Hill Road, with its clusters of small shambas on either side. Young muscular Africans stood happily by the broken edges of the road, selling sheepskins, T-shirts, and fruit and vegetables, which they intermittently lofted into the air in open arms. A few miles farther on, we entered a different world of large farms, given over to dairy herds and coffee estates. Still on tarmac, and climbing steadily, we eventually arrived at the Farm Hotel in Limuru and had a cream tea on the veranda.

"I don't ever want to leave," Inga said wistfully, casting her azure blue eyes over the spectacular view. "This time tomorrow I'll wonder if this weekend was all a dream."

In spite of her doubts, she departed early Monday morning for the eight-hundred-mile haul to Stanleyville in the Congo. It seemed she hadn't wanted to wake me, as it would have only made our parting tougher. Instead she pinned a note to the top pocket of my blue shirt, which was hanging on the back of the bedroom door. It said: "It's over before it begins. You and I are nothing more than ships in the night. I'll think of you down there in the bush whenever I fly across Africa—loving you, Inga."

chapter

THREE

On the Monday morning of June 27, 1960—almost eight months to the day since we had the road accident—I met up with Thomas and Visavadia at nine a.m. in the car park of Nairobi's Montagu Hotel.

Blakes Motors had already retrieved its rental car and left my eight-pound deposit with reception, and there was now little for me to do. I walked slowly around the van and gave it a last inspection in the way a pilot checks his aircraft. Then I paused, put on my sunglasses, took a deep breath, and climbed in.

"Let's go," I said, and looked over at Thomas. He pressed the starter button, circled the graveled driveway, and on reaching the exit gates, turned left onto the tarmac road. We were at last on our way. It would be at least six months before we returned to this beautiful city.

The high sky was peppered with gray wisps of cloud that moved swiftly across the pale blue yonder, disintegrating and then reshaping into larger, more ominous, darker forms. It was a cool morning, there was plenty of light, and hopefully it would soon be warm.

We'd gone only a short distance when we heard a loud thump coming from the rear of the van.

"Better pull over," I advised, "and check it out."

Thomas automatically slipped the gear into neutral, put on the handbrake, and jumped out onto the road. "It's Vinoo's wooden case," he shouted from the rear door. "It's slipped off the top of the cartons and landed against the door."

It had only taken a few seconds to put the matter right—nothing more than a pit stop—but the morning traffic was heavy and had quickly formed a tailback. At the same time, I hadn't noticed a police officer until he was suddenly beside me, big and frowning and waving his swagger stick impatiently. "No parking is allowed here," he growled, his face set in a flat stare. "You'll have to move it."

Thomas had by now climbed back into the driving seat. "We're on our way," he said with a smile from the driver's open door. I was more than aware that the last thing we wanted at this early stage of our long journey was a parking ticket.

Thomas eased the van onto the middle of the left lane, and one hundred yards farther down the road we came to a large roundabout. It was bedecked like an English garden with colored flowers that ran between corridors of well-watered grass. We made a full circle, giving us a last glimpse of the New Stanley Hotel, and headed back up Delamere Avenue. For the next quarter of a mile the road was a dual carriageway, lined by trees on each side, with a dividing strip of grass and stunted bushes. We continued through two sets of traffic lights, before curving left onto the Naivasha Road. The crowded pavements of the old colonial city soon receded, and the glamour of cosmopolitan streets now gave way to suburban gardens with detached villas. The road began to climb and follow the contour of the hill. The new tires of the van hissed effortlessly on the smooth tarmac, and the purr of the exhaust gently drowned out the sound of oncoming vehicles. The sight of small African allotments heralded the arrival of open land, and the view soon became more extensive.

The earlier clouds were now black with storm, and the first heavy drops of rain splashed in widening circles on the windshield. We slid the doors shut and quickly rolled up the windows. The view became faint in the rain, and the land dropped away on one side, while the hill and wood on the other side rose sharply upward, screening the road ahead.

Our destination was the town of Nakuru, capital of the White Highlands, not quite a hundred miles from Nairobi and the headquarters for the Rift Valley Province. This distance exceeded our estimated daily average of forty miles. However, our sales team would not work the route we were on, as it was regularly visited by sales representatives from Morgans in Nairobi and formed part of their territory.

I reached across to the shelf under the dashboard. "Let's make this a good safari," I said, opening the day's copy of the *East African Standard* and glancing at the headlines.

"And no crashes this time," Thomas quipped.

The road twisted and climbed and stretched ever nearer the rich uplands that overlooked the flat grasslands of the Great Rift Valley. All the while sheets of rain washed against the windshield. Besides the rain, the only other sound was the constant snapping of wiper blades and the heavy burr of the engine. During this extensive safari our positions on the van remained fairly consistent. Thomas was more often than not driving, with me in the passenger seat and Visavadia behind, sitting sideways on a cushioned rumble seat. At this moment he had his eyes half-closed with a paperback perched unsteadily on his lap.

This whole area was known as Happy Valley and was the focal point, between the two world wars, of a notorious crowd of colonial playboys and aristocrats.

I folded my newspaper and put it back on the shelf under the dash, and with a deep breath, I sank against the brown artificial leather seating. I then lit a cigarette and was soon lost in thought. The word *safari* seemed to dominate our lives. The translation from Swahili means "a long journey" and that just about summed up what we were doing. I began to think back to last October and hoped that this time the safari would turn out to be a success.

We continued to climb upward through red-soiled fields of maize and pyrethrum and lush Kikuyu lands before entering a wide forest area. Then, a few miles beyond the turnoff to Limuru, the road straightened and then rounded a final curve before emerging into more open country. And all of a sudden we found ourselves overlooking one of East Africa's most magnificent sights. It was the breathtaking view of the Great Rift Valley as we approached it from the eastern edge of the escarpment. Thousands of feet below us was the green flatness of the valley floor.

The tropical storm had lessened, and the view now slowly dissolved in a cloud of shimmering haze. Nevertheless, along the sharp edges and beyond, where the land dropped, the gigantic cones of the extinct Suswa and Longonot volcanoes rose unerringly from the flat colorless distance like a moonscape. This colossal, mind-blowing fault in the earth's crust runs from the north of Lake Galilee in Palestine, through the Red Sea, onto East Africa, and eventually disappears into the Indian Ocean at Beira in Mozambique.

We were off the tarmac now, and red pools filled the wheel tracks that scarred the road. The morning traffic was light, and ten minutes later we descended the winding dirt road onto the wet grasslands of the rift floor, and near the bottom we passed a small chapel dedicated to Saint Mary of the Angels on Christmas Day 1943. It was built by Italian war prisoners who also constructed the road. The highway now gradually climbed the shoulder of the two-mile-wide Longonot crater. There was no lava, but rift activity such as hot springs, fumaroles, and steam jets were active beneath the surface. In the distance we could see the freshwaters of Lake Naivasha surrounded by low hills, together with densely crowned thorn trees and cactus-like euphorbias, which were dotted indiscriminately across the valley floor. Once again we snaked down the escarpment and closed with the lake. Hippos lurked behind papyrus plants that skirted the shallow shores. There were small tracks emanating from cliffs that led off to the primeval forest at the lower end of Hell's Gate gorge. The dark lake itself had hot bubbly springs, and an angler, who was walking along the roadside with a full basket, told us that the waters were teeming with black bass.

The groves of yellow-barked acacias with dripping leaves now marked the course of the road around the lake. We passed through the town of Naivasha and headed north to the township of Gilgil, an easy stretch of eighteen miles over a cinder-strewn track. The clouds were less dark than before, and the glint of sun struck the top of our window glass for the first time, while in the valley there was stillness after the rains. The van began to bump uneasily on the drying surface as the road started to seesaw. It was an anxious time, considering we carried a full load on an untested vehicle. After Gilgil we joined up with a tarmac road and ran down the escarpment toward Lake

Nakuru. The shores were bordered in a shimmering pink, as they were home to millions of long-legged flamingos wading in the alkaline waters.

Nakuru was the farming capital of Kenya and center for the pyrethrum industry, a world leader in natural insecticides. The openness of the lake seemed to dominate the town, with its wide double streets and flowering fuchsias.

It was now late afternoon, and the light was beginning to go. The sky was dark blue, and a roadside jacaranda tree with its blue trumpet-shaped flowers and fern-like leaves threw long, black shadows across the dusty shoulders of the road. We spent an hour calling on the local retailers, taking orders for Herbalex and Gripe Aid. We had to work hard to get these orders, and by the time we'd finished our round, it was dark and the street lamps had come on. This late hour left us no time to find accommodation, so we decided to sleep in the van. It wasn't a big problem as we had seen a site about a mile before we entered Nakuru. It was an isolated place in an open field on high ground with a thick hedgerow. The spotting of a location formed part and parcel of our survival instincts. As Kenya was more set out than most other African countries, it made it easier for us to keep to a planned schedule.

Usually, around four o'clock in the afternoon, we would have a word about our sleeping arrangements for the night ahead. Generally speaking, Thomas would want to use the van. This suited him because he could save his nighttime allowance of two pounds, twenty five pence. He was a gregarious sort of person, and, on occasion, would meet up with friends and have a party. It was because of his socializing that I occasionally felt uneasy that the van might be left unprotected at night. However, he had given me his word that it was always safe in his hands.

Visavadia too, wanted to save his allowance, which at the end of a six-month safari would add up to a tidy sum. However, unlike Thomas, he had no need for the van; instead he would rely on the generosity of his kinsman. Extraordinary as it may seem, he sometimes found free accommodation in the remotest of places. As for myself, I was allotted five pounds per night to include room and food at any available hotel. Anything in excess was debited to my personal account. Despite these convoluted arrangements, the three of us would more often than not end up in the bush.

Tonight posed no particular hardship. It was warm, there was no rain, and we had a full larder from which to choose. The only minor problem was the lack of space to sleep.

***

This was an easy going start to our safari. However, before leaving the town in the morning, we delivered five Chemisan portable toilets and six dozen toilet paper rolls to an Asian hardware store. Apparently the manager had received an inquiry from a privately owned campsite catering to an increasing number of bird watchers, or twitchers, who were showing up at the sanctuary around the lake.

Nakuru in Swahili means "the place of swirling dust," and although the sun had already climbed into the sky, there was sufficient movement of both traffic and people in the airless streets to cause a thick coat of dust that hung low over the town.

After playing some African high-life music and passing out leaflets in the bazaar area, we headed west from the town. The large fields of daisy-like pyrethrum plants fell away on each side, and they continued to do so until we reached the edge of the valley floor and began to climb the dirt road that led over the western rim of the rift escarpment. On this side of the ridge, the vegetation was different, more grassy, while the escarpment still absorbed the view but less abruptly than before. In yesterday's rain the colors had been soft, but now, in the sunlight, the greens and yellows were harsh. We drove along the empty road, entering the cattle country of the white highlands. We passed partially fenced fields of wheat and barley, sprinkled with imported pines, Montereys, and cypress trees. We stopped at Njoro to give a show, then continued to Molo and passed more rich farmlands. The view behind became lost in the colorless distance at the point where the sky met the land and where the eye was no longer clearly focused.

A large crowd of dusty people surrounded the van. They listened to tapes and stretched out their hands, eager to catch a leaflet. Then, before closing the show, we nailed a dozen metal signs on timber doorways, and sold a total of six dozen bottles—three of Herbalex and three of Gripe Aid—to the local shopkeepers. It wasn't much, but like a boxer in the ring, we needed to warm up.

We left Molo and motored through several miles of rolling hills and extensive sheep country, reminiscent of the Cotswolds. We then passed Africa's highest golf course at nine thousand feet. It was here that we had the odd glimpse of the Mau escarpment through our open doors, before we curved left at a road junction. We remained on the Kericho Road and followed the level of the land. At Londiani we halted again. The left wheels sank into the soft shoulder, but Thomas had made sure that he kept the driver's side wheels firmly on the hard, stoned track that ran through the center of the town. Five or six shops bordered the street, crooked structures in wood and concrete with corrugated iron roofs. A small but boisterous crowd of adults and children started to beat time to the rhythms of a calypso that rang out between the dust-caked buildings.

Later, after a break for lunch, we continued west on a rutted track. On one side of the road the land was grassed, and on the other side, there were groups of people on pathways that sloped gently between hidden settlements. A line of eucalyptus trees screened the bare compounds from the embanked track that followed the contour of the land. Thick smoke rose straight up from behind the line of trees, and a few miles farther on, we reached the isolated township of Lumbwa, a halting place for the East African Railways. It was here that the road ran beside a trout-filled stream, before it angled over a narrow gauge rail track. The land soon began to fall away in a ripple of low-spreading slopes.

The road was no longer built on an embankment. It had flattened out against the level of the land and curved less often, but it swung gently between the rolling slopes. We slowed down for a heavily laden truck driven by a turbaned Indian, who forced us over onto the scuffed grass shoulder. The road then turned away from the stream, and all the while the sun slanted through the dirty windshield. A short distance ahead we passed the cultivated fields of lush farmlands and great tea estates, with their row upon row of vivid green bushes that glistened in the resplendent rays of the declining sun. The pickers, in colorful rubber aprons, were walking back from the neatly ordered fields, finished for the day. Another truck emerged from a hidden gate onto the road, carting the leaves to the local factory, where they would be dried, crushed, and then fermented, having turned from green to black in the process.

There were now other vehicles on the gritty road, some old cars, cyclists, and an occasional overloaded bus. An imperfect line of telegraph poles ran more or less parallel with the dusty road, and a collection of small stone buildings, in irregular shapes, bordered the route that led the way into the market town of Kericho. It was then that the road widened and there came an abundance of blossoming flowers on each side. Farther on, near the center of the town, there was a paved plaza dotted with frangipani shrubs that were heavy with perfume.

Kericho was not only an important tea center but also home to the Kipsigis tribe, numbering half a million, who spoke in a dialect called Kalenjin. The town was established in 1902 by expatriate farmers, who named it after a local herbal medicine known as "kerichek."

In the main boulevard dim lights showed from grilled windows, and crooked silhouettes of concrete walls and tightly structured shops could be discerned along the uneven pavements. The sound of dogs barking could be heard in the distance. Visavadia took his square wooden case from the rear of the van, smiled good night, and backtracked down the tree-lined road toward the Asian-owned shops near the darkened crossroads.

"OK to have the van?" Thomas chipped in.

"Sure, on the condition that you drop me off at the hotel first," I said with a smile.

"Are we stopping for one or two nights?"

"Two nights," I came back. "We need a whole day for this town, and it's important we have an early morning start for the seventy-mile drive to Kisii on Thursday."

"Fair enough." He nodded and pulled away from the curb.

This was our second night up-country, and we were slowly getting into our stride. Yesterday the lateness of the hour had caught us on the hop. This time there was hotel accommodation, but in remote areas the three of us had a fail-safe system in which we would hunt down a government Rest House, and if there wasn't one available we would simply camp out in the bush.

The lights from the colonial building spread out into the graveled yard, falling on hedges and gardens. The signboard hanging above the pillared entrance simply said The Tea Hotel—Kericho. It began to drizzle as I walked across the driveway; only the shrill noise of crickets beating their leathery wings could be heard.

***

After a day in Kericho we were back on the road early Thursday and had high hopes of completing the seventy-mile drive to Kisii. The road twisted through hilly countryside, and the land on each side was hummocked, which obstructed the view ahead. A motor vehicle hummed in the distance, and then, almost without warning, it rounded a bend and came closer. The sun caught the windshield, and Thomas quickly pulled down the visor. It was a heavy truck, bigger than us, with thick tires slotted firmly into the worn tracks that ran parallel on each side of the central ridge. I then caught sight of people riding on the top.

"He's not going to give way." Thomas cursed as he pulled left, dropped a gear, and pressed hard on the accelerator.

We were already on the passenger-side shoulder, which sloped down toward a sandy shoulder. The approaching vehicle definitely wasn't going to release the center position and was deliberately running us off the trackway. We now faced the prospect of sliding into a wheel-swallowing drainage ditch with gritted edges. I took a glance at the driver and noticed he had glazed eyes. He'd obviously either been drinking pombe or was on drugs. We now, once more, stared into the jaws of another unfinished safari.

From this "wall of death" position—an acceptable hazard on African roads—it was up to Thomas to regain our balance and get us back onto the center. It was the unwritten code of conduct that vehicles involved in passing another should always surrender the center, move over to the left, and slot their driver's-side tires into the remaining line of tracking.

There were only inches to spare as the truck thundered by, forcing us down toward the gaping ditch. We went silent and hoped that the edging would not break up, while we held on tightly to the underside of the seats and Thomas wrestled with the steering. The van shuddered and slithered, and before we knew it we had passed the vehicle and, by some miracle, had bumped back onto the center of the track.

"That was close," Visavadia commented.

We pressed onward along the tortuous road in continued silence. The heat had begun to take its toll, and sweat poured down our necks and onto our shirts, which stuck unevenly to our bodies. Several miles farther on, we stopped at the lonely township of Sotik and gave a roadside show to a crowd of about two hundred people. We then moved on toward our destination of Kisii, having now crossed over into South Nyanza Province. From this point the road continued to climb and drop, and there seemed to be no end in sight. It escaped our notice that we were gradually going lower. Every now and then we stopped at isolated settlements, played popular high-life music, handed out leaflets, and made a few cash sales. Each settlement had its own set of ocherous dusty paths behind mud-bricked houses that marked out the divisions of ownership. These paths were crisscrossed with others running horizontally, and eventually the broken lie of the land became more open and greener. A few miles on we noticed a stone wall, some four feet high, running along each edge of the road. It was out of character in appearance, almost Cotswoldian, but it didn't last long, perhaps fifty yards, until we spotted a pair of low, black ornamental gates under concrete arching on our left side. We had glimpses of trees, and then came another lot of short walling. There was a large signboard that announced: *Kisii Arboretum—Open Every Day—All Trees Labeled.*

Two miles later we arrived on the outskirts of Kisii. There were a number of substantial houses of brick and corrugated iron. A hint of suburban life, but Africa was never far away with its roadside standpipes, backyard vegetable plots, wobbling cyclists, and little children in bare feet standing on the broken edges of the road giving cheerful waves.

Kisii looked sleepy under the yellow rays of the declining sun. The town was well respected throughout Kenya for its soapstone carvings and intricately beaded stools. Its occupants squinted from doorways, looking uncertain as we asked directions for the local hotel. Once again Thomas was happy to have the van, and Visavadia, as almost without fail, found an Asian family to take him in.

***

Thomas picked me up eight thirty a.m. from the Kisii Hotel. Visavadia sat on the rumble seat and, after an exchange of greetings, he dipped his head and carried on reading his paperback. We spent a good part of the morning in town, giving shows, selling to the public, and visiting shopkeepers.

At eleven thirty a.m. exactly, we left town and headed west. Our intended target today lay some thirty miles from Kisii. It was the small fishing port of Homa Bay on the shores of Lake Victoria. It was getting dark when we reached it. For us it had been another tough day, and as usual we had assiduously worked each mile of the road promoting the company's medical products. There was no accommodation in the town, but we soon found an ideal parking place overlooking the lake and cooked a hot meal, which we ate in silence. This time there was no problem about sleeping space, as we had now made enough sales to have lowered the height of the stacked cartons.

South from Homa Bay is the Lambwe Valley Game Reserve. Unfortunately we couldn't visit it as it would have counted as a frivolous trip, and London would somehow have picked this up when checking distances against timing in my weekly report. Anyway, I discovered that the Lambwe Reserve was only forty-six square miles and was home to rare herds of Jackson's hartebeest, roan antelope, topi, and waterbuck. The reserve also enjoyed a rich bird life, including the gray, small-crested cockatiel of Australian ancestry, the red-billed hornbill, the chestnut sand plover, and the go-away bird.

The next day we worked Homa Bay. We covered the town from back to front, giving full thirty-minute shows in the bazaar area, the bus depot, and along the main shopping zone. The sales, both retail and wholesale, were encouraging. People responded to the lively music, the promotional broadcasts, and heavy leaflet distribution.

We left early Saturday morning for the seventy-two-mile stretch north to the major eastern port of Kisumu.

The drive was through a typical savanna of open grassland dotted with winter thorn trees. Some rather grubby ostriches looked disdainfully down from a grassy slope, necks twisting, before pacing gravely away from the yellow dust that billowed from the back wheels of the van. At the village of Sondu, we stopped and gave another show. Only two or three shops lined the main street. Once more, we distributed leaflets, played music, and hammered tin signs on the wooden doors along the dust-ridden terracing that fronted the opposite side of the street. This stop took thirty-five minutes before we were on the road leading from the village. We circled a wide-girthed baobab tree that occupied the middle of the street, and once again it was soon open country and the light became stronger. The road was empty but badly rutted and scarred with potholes after the recent rains. The holes had yet to be topped off with a mix of gritty sand and cement. This task was the responsibility of the Public Works Department who, as we well knew, took a long time due to the great distances covered from its depots to the required point. Five miles on we pulled over to the side of the road for a bit of lunch. We ate in silence, sitting on boxed cartons with our metal plates topped with beans and rice, followed by fresh pineapple and mugs of hot tea.

After finishing the meal, we cleaned our plates and climbed back into the van. Thomas donned his dark glasses and started the engine. It wasn't often that he wore his shades, and Visavadia was quick to make a comment. "How much did those cost?" he asked in a flat voice.

Thomas wasn't going to be drawn; instead he looked at me and waited for instructions.

"Let's go," I said with a smile.

The red murram road curved and followed a depression that cut between verdant slopes, and then the track straightened as far as the eye could see. Maybe two hundred yards or so up ahead, we spotted movement. At first, it was difficult to discern, but as we closed, we saw two birds, colored black and white, prancing around on the ground. Thomas slowed down, but on hearing our approach, the birds spread their wings, ran down the road at speed, and, once they had gathered enough warm air under their wings, lifted off.

"Secretary birds," Thomas informed. "You can tell that from the quills behind their heads and their gray-and-black plumage."

"I'm impressed," Visavadia responded.

I wasn't sure whether Visavadia was having another go at Thomas. He'd already picked on his sunglasses, and now he was admiring his ornithological knowledge. I decided to take the middle road and kept quiet.

Moments later Thomas braked and peered out of his side door.

"What's going on?" I asked.

"Look," he urged, pointing to the road with an index finger. "We've got a snake right in front of us."

Both Visavadia and I craned forward.

"There's blood on it," Thomas continued.

"I don't see anything," Visavadia said.

"Me neither," I echoed.

"It's gone under the van," Thomas said and sighed.

"We'd better have a look at it," I said.

We all climbed out of the van and stood back.

The last thing we needed this early in the safari was any uncalled-for delay. An hour or two lost here and there could add up to losing as much as a couple of days each month, bearing in mind that we worked a seven-day week.

Thomas crouched on the ground and lowered his head beneath the chassis. Then without warning, he rolled backward and scrambled to his feet. "That was close," he said nervously. "It seems to be wrapped around the brake drum, behind the front driver's-side wheel."

"Is it alive?" Visavadia asked.

"Yes, it's alive," Thomas breathed. "It was those two birds jumping up and down that first made me suspicious that they were trying to kill something, such as a rat, lizard, or snake, all of which form part of their diet." There was a pause, and Visavadia refrained from making any further comment. "Anyway," Thomas continued as he turned toward me, "if it's OK by you, I'll give the van a short run down the road and see if I can shake it off."

"You go ahead," I said with a nod.

A few minutes later, despite Thomas's best efforts, the snake remained firmly coiled around the brake drum. Now it was my turn to crouch down and take a look. It was important to get rid of the snake as soon as possible, because we well might forget it was there in the long-term, and given half a chance it would possibly work its way inside the cabin and snuggle down between the boxes.

In order to identify it, I reached into the pocket of the passenger-side door and retrieved my illustrated book on wildlife. I began to thumb through the section on reptiles. "Well it's certainly not a puff adder or black mamba," I murmured to myself. However, I soon whittled it down to belonging to the cobra family, which were listed as being seriously venomous.

I passed the book to Thomas and asked him for his opinion.

"At first sight, from a distance, I thought it might be a common sand snake," Thomas admitted. "They like basking in the sun and are addicted to eating lizards and small birds."

"Then what do you think it is?"

"It's as you said." He smiled approvingly. "It's this one known as the spitting cobra, which has a black neck. It's exactly the same as the one in this book," he confirmed as he tapped the colored picture with his index finger. He then raised an eye and looked over at Visavadia, almost daring him to make any unwanted comment as he had done earlier about his sunglasses and secretary birds. Then he took long breath and informed Visavadia that he had been out-voted by two to one and his opinion was therefore not required. He gave a rich rumbling laugh and reached for his panga, which he kept wrapped in an oily cloth under the driver's seat.

"Let me jab it with a stick first," I said to Thomas. "This will give it a chance to escape into the long grass. However, if it tries to rewind onto the van, I want you to be ready on the running board and make sure it doesn't. Only as a last resort use your machete, and bear in mind that the snake is already wounded and might well attack. According to my book, it can spray venom up to eight feet.'"

"It's a panga, not a machete," Thomas corrected, his lips smiling but unparted.

A smile settled on Visavadia's face. I turned slowly toward him. "I would like you to stay inside the van and act as backup should Thomas need your help."

"Are there any more questions?"

There was silence.

I moved around to the driver's-side wheel and took a cautious look underneath the chassis. The cobra was still coiled around the axle, and its brown-and-yellow head probed forward at an angle and began to hiss.

"Are you ready?" I asked.

"No, hang on a moment," Thomas replied, and disappeared into the rear of the cabin. He quickly removed a tin plate from an open box.

"What's happening?"

"I'm ready now," he said, "so let's get on with it."

I once more crouched down on my knees and poked it with a stick. I remembered the cautionary words in the wildlife book. It had warned that cobras have a notoriously fast striking speed.

"He's coming your way," I shouted as it unwound itself from the chassis and headed out into the sunlight. I gave it a second prod to speed it on its way and quickly climbed back into the van and slid the door shut.

The diamond-shaped head weaved cautiously from under the chassis and into the bright sunlight. Thomas was motionless on the running board above the point where the cobra was emerging from the shadows. His panga was raised high in his right hand, and the tin advertising plate was held against the left side of his face, while close behind him was Visavadia, anxiety etched on his face.

For ten seconds the situation was stable. The eight-foot snake slid forward and, to all intents and purposes, was making satisfactory progress. However, it became apprehensive and lost interest in crossing the sandy track toward the grass on the other side. Instead, it spun around and began to inflate. The skin around its neck quickly spread into a hood, and the vertical pupils of its eyes were focused directly at Thomas. For a second or two it remained aroused, its erect head wavering slowly in the warm air. It was ready to strike.

But Thomas was ahead of the game. His panga was raised and glinted dangerously in the hot afternoon sun. He swept the plate across his face a nanosecond before the cobra spat its deadly venom. The warm fluid ran between his knuckles, and he immediately lowered the plate and unleashed a powerful downward stroke with his panga, severing the cobra's head in a single sweep. It spun harmlessly onto the powdered track.

An hour later we emerged from the gloom of a forest road and headed downhill toward the openness of the lake town of Kisumu.

chapter FOUR

Kisumu was the fourth largest town in Kenya and the principal port for Lake Victoria. It lies at the head of the Kavirondo Gulf, an eastward-stretching arm of water that is part of the Rift Valley. The town was center for the two million Luo people, the only representatives of the Nilotic tribes from the far-off Nile Valley.

Since settling in this fertile region some four hundred years ago, they have progressed to positions of influence and provide many of Kenya's scientists and doctors. They are cultured in oral tradition, music, and dancing, while in the past they were famed for their elaborate ceremonial clothing of black-and-white colobus skins, hippo teeth, and python bones. Even today their traditions do not allow circumcision, and the less advanced of the tribe knock out their lower front teeth.

The harbor has deep waters and is home to a colorful fishing fleet that plies the lake, which is stocked with over two hundred species of fish, the most important one being the tilapia, a relation of the perch. The boats, including the round-the-lake steamers and train ferries, were built abroad and assembled locally.

One of the major problems related to the climate and sluggish water is that it provides ideal conditions for both bilharzia and malaria. In the case of bilharzia, the illness comes from parasitical worms or blood-flukes, and in malaria the mosquito is the infecting agent. Both illnesses occur through the skin. In spite of this the Luo tribe have multiplied in this environment. The fact is that a good many of them have the red blood pigment known as sickle-cell hemoglobin, which appears to provide some immunity to malaria.

We spent four days in Kisumu, arriving late on Saturday and leaving early on Thursday, July 7, and during our stay we carried out a successful promotional campaign in all areas of the town and surrounding villages. Both our stocks of Herbalex and Gripe Aid had dwindled to less than seventy dozen each before we departed Kisumu, so I cabled Bob Worsley at our agents' offices in Kampala, under whose control we now came, to rail further supplies to the border town of Tororo in Uganda to await our collection.

Late afternoon the day before leaving Kisumu, we took a short trip outside town and visited Hippo Point, a well-known place from which to view Victoria Lake. We found a place to park the van and then walked down to the rocks and thick reed beds that marked the shoreline. The lake in front of us appeared limitless and was as wide as the horizon. The gray and leaden blue of the water was almost indistinguishable from the sky. It was a freshwater sea, unbounded and lacking shape, so that the eye was unable to settle on any one thing as everything dissolved in the sultriness, and all seemed melancholy. The fieriness of the sun at last began to sink beyond the horizon, and the lake waters first darkened as though dusk had arrived, and then brightened as though the twilight was not yet extinguished. This incandescence was nature's own firework show without the sound effects. Then moments later it was closing time, and at last the sun made its exit behind the luminous rim in the western sky, and all that remained was an orange glow that mushroomed across the sky and slowly dispersed.

We left early the next morning and traveled slowly through Kisumu's main streets, before climbing a winding, red murram track in a northeasterly direction toward the hill town of Kapsabet. To begin with we had glimpses of the lake we had recently left, glittering in the harsh light. Then, still going up, we entered the green rolling lands of the Nandi Hills. We lost the view behind us, and the road continued to climb and twist. The ride seemed rougher uphill, and for some time there was no sign of life until we rounded a bend and came across a cluster of huts set back from the potholed road. Men with bows and arrows, Nandi tribesmen, strode purposefully down worn paths as we pulled to a halt on the scuffed shoulders of the road. For the next ten minutes we handed out leaflets and gave Gripe Aid samples to the young mothers who had joined their men at the roadside. We played African high life music over the speakers, and told them about our products before finally ending the show.

It wasn't long before we got underway and settled down to the next stage of our journey. However it was Thomas who broke the silence in the cabin by informing us that we were passing through the area said to be inhabited by Kenya's abominable snowman.

On one side the land stretched all the way to the edge of the escarpment, and on the other the vegetation was different—grassier, with fewer trees to break the view. The higher air had become cool since we crested the slopes, and I leaned forward and slid the passenger door shut. It was cozier now, and the loud hum of the engine fell away.

"I've never heard of an abominable snowman in these parts," I replied. "Are you sure you're not getting mixed up with the one who lives in the Himalayas?"

Thomas weighed my response. He enjoyed giving out tid bits of information, especially about his own country, and seemed undecided whether to take my remark seriously or not. "No, it's true," he said, lifting his eyes off the road for a moment as if to emphasize the point. The sky above was azure blue, and the sun glinted on the fly-splashed windshield. We drove on in silence for another minute, the road swinging from hill to hill along the high plateau. Thomas looked nervously across the front of the van, his face uncertain. "It's called *Nandi Bear*," he said with a weak smile.

It didn't cross my mind that Visavadia had been listening to our conversation. Obviously the paperback that he had been reading earlier no longer held him, because I could hear his muffled laughter coming from the rear seat. "Has anyone ever seen it?" he asked, leaning forward between the seats, his arms resting on the leather tops.

"Fair enough," Thomas growled, shrugging his shoulders. "I won't ever tell you lot anything again."

I nudged Visavadia with my elbow.

We passed another set of farms on our left side, while on the right the escarpment lay blurred, hidden beyond a colorless haze of light. We slowed down for a heavily loaded bus, exchanging blasts on the horn as we inched past on the tilted road. We passed unfenced fields planted with vivid green tea bushes that extended into the distance. We saw people walking on dusty paths and on open land that ran between the estates. Funnels of smoke rose in straight dark plumes from a bunch of solitary huts.

We were now on the Eldoret Road, and after driving a little way, we saw a large yellow signboard on black-and-white striped poles. It was illustrated with a map of Africa. The word *Equator* was inscribed on a red band across the face. At the top was written: "This sign is on the Equator" and underneath, once again in black letters, was the word *Kisumu*. It was official: We were now in the Northern Hemisphere.

At Kapsabet we stopped to give a show. Afterward I checked my map and was surprised to see that we were still in the Rift Valley Province, although we'd been on a straighter road than before. We went through a mixed farming area of fenced pastures and fertile fields of wheat and maize, and stopped briefly at the villages of Mosoriet and Onyoki. They consisted of nothing more than shack settlements with huts in dusty yards. There was a lone shop in each village; both had darkened doorways. The small wooden houses cast deep shadows on the edges of the dirt road. Behind the structures were square-shaped allotments consisting of tangled plots of land, some cultivated with sweet potatoes, beans, and sesame.

Simple road signs gave the name of our destination, pointing northward to Eldoret. The eighty-mile journey from Kisumu was now whittled down to a few miles. The road was still rising, but less and less abruptly, and it had almost flattened out as we approached the town. On both sides were extensive farmlands given over to the growing of wattle trees, the bark substances used primarily for tanning leather and mine props. Patient farming was the name of the game. It can take up to twelve years from the first sprinkling of seeds to the final harvesting.

Sometime later we entered the outskirts of Eldoret. Small concrete buildings were scattered about the main road, and groups of people coming back from the market could be seen walking on the dusty shoulders. Piles of unruly rubbish lay untouched in the side streets. Little children smiled and waved as we slowed for the crossroads. We dropped Visavadia off in front of a large Asian store and then pushed on toward the Lincoln Hotel in the center of town. At the end of the boulevard there was a long stone wall with a horizontal board pointing to the hotel. It was chillier, and the sun had gone behind a bank of gray overcharged clouds and was unlikely to come out again. "We'll stay here all day tomorrow," I said to Thomas, as I took hold of my suitcase, typewriter, and briefcase from the rear of the van, "and we'll leave here early Saturday morning for Kitale."

"See you tomorrow." Thomas smiled as he shifted the gear into second and let the van roll down the incline that bordered the well-kept garden.

***

The weather turned nasty when we left Eldoret and drove northward toward Kitale. There was nothing but rain cascading down, and it drowned the sound of the engine. The road leaving town wasn't built on an embankment but followed the level of the land, and as a consequence water filled the wheel tracks and the potholes soon formed into red pools. Every now and then the van slithered on the greasy surface as the rain splattered remorselessly down, and sheets of water washed over the insect-ridden windshield. The view ahead was all but obscured, and the worsening conditions were making it difficult for the wipers to maintain a clear windshield.

Thomas quickly reached for the duster in the door pocket and wiped the steam off the inside glass. His face was glued against the windshield while he concentrated on the road ahead. He seemed to be in a good mood and chatted to himself while negotiating the water holes. He was wearing his favorite shirt, yellow with short red sleeves, along with khaki trousers, black trainers, and a peaked cap that was forever tilted back on his head. It was an undeniable fact that we had learned our lesson on the last safari when we crashed on the Gulu road. Accordingly, our present speed was reduced to less than 10 mph.

For some miles the road ran beside a railway track, and every so often, the narrow-gauged lines turned across the highway, only to angle back a few hundred yards later. Although the road served the needs of the country villages and settlements, the railroad continued to straddle the route going north. Gradually the rains lessened and the sun broke free from the silvery edge of a gray cloudbank. The green, sloping fields that enclosed both road and railway began to shine and sparkle, and not far ahead was a line of yellow-barked acacia trees that traced the course of a trout stream. Beyond that, the land dissolved and disintegrated in the bright light of an arcing rainbow.

The van bumped again on a railroad crossing. The trees that marked the river still dripped from the earlier rains, and through the green, feathery leaves and flowering branches, we caught our first glimpse of the thirteen-thousand-foot peaks of Mount Elgon, with its misty ridges visible from forty miles away in any direction. The escarpment of banded gray and green sparkled in the reflected light. The mountain sits astride the Kenya/Uganda border, is volcanic, and has a crater stretching five miles across the top. The highest point is the Wagagai Peak which reaches 14,178 feet. The Masai name is *Ol Doinyo Ilgoon,* which means "a mountain shaped like a breast." Its higher slopes were blanketed in yellow giant groundsel along with the scarlet and bright blue flowers of lobelia, both of which bestrode the deep-sided heath. And yet even higher was a broad belt of lichen-covered trees, and lost to the eye were the bamboo forests leading to scrub and coarse tassel grass.

We gave roadside shows at the tiny settlements of Soy, Springfield, and Hoey's Bridge. By now we had become accustomed to the single railway track that had dogged our path since leaving Eldoret, but we sensed a feeling of relief when our route finally divided before reaching Kitale.

After the village of Glanville, we passed several brick-and-timbered farms, European-owned, with lush, beautiful gardens filled with an array of colored flowers. Each house stood at the end of a red-gritted driveway that led away from imposing, black wrought-iron gates that stood half-concealed in dark hedgerows along the road. The rich, fertile lands were blanketed with maize, wheat, and coffee, and everywhere else was covered with the stiff, sharp-pointed, blue-and-green leaves of the sisal plant.

Kitale was similar in appearance to Eldoret. It is an important farming center that was first settled by Arab slavers who originally named it Quitale. The northern section of the East African Railways terminated here, giving easy links with Nairobi, some 240 miles to the south, and beyond, to the port of Mombasa on the Indian Ocean. The tidy thatched houses of the Dutch and British were filled with easy chairs, books, and Persian rugs. Only a few miles north in the Turkana Province the vegetation drastically changed to thorn scrub, sausage trees, and scorched wastelands.

We worked the town area during the weekend, and at noon on Monday, July 11, after a hurried snack in the worn-down lounge bar of the Kitale Hotel, we left for the seventy-mile trip to Tororo in Uganda. The stony road was empty, and all the time the mountains dominated the view, leading our eyes upward as we curved around the southern foothills. It was chilly, and we rolled up the windows against the cold, put on sweaters, and gazed out at the lowland cattle grazing in the fields.

The mountains bristled with dense, dark green forests of African camphors, podos, and pencil cedar trees, and all the time the road followed the rolling contours of the slopes. In the overlapping woods, high up and hidden from view, were leopards, buffalo, red duiker antelopes, and forest elephants. For some time we pushed onward and upward. In due course we passed a ridge of rocks with melting landslides that trickled icy water across the bare road and down into overgrown ditches on the far side. A sun-bleached signboard gave vague, indistinct warnings about falling rocks. The forest was closer now, blurred with bamboo, and we could see the trees covered in those sad lichen trailers. Every now and then, the woods parted and we caught glimpses of the antler-shaped groundsels and the giant rosettes of their cabbage leaves. Then the woods came back, shutting off the fleeting glimpses of the high, open moorlands, with its twisted tree heathers and giant lobelias.

The road began to go down again. The bamboo and coarse ferns dropped slowly away as we made our descent. We waved to a group of road workers in khaki, who were busy filling in potholes after the recent rains, digging into mounds of fresh sand and gritty earth that had been freshly dumped by heavy trucks. We stopped for a short time at the village of Kiminini and played a calypso record to a small audience, selling three bottles of Herbalex, before continuing down the slopes. Again there were fields, terraced hills, and clusters of wooden huts along the grassed-over ridges. The van bumped on the rough dirt road, and we were nearly free of the mountain. However, make no mistake—it was still very much there, rugged and full of high-altitude vegetation, but less challenging. Then farms and fenced fields appeared again.

At the bush village of Kimilili we made our final stop in Kenya. A group of no more than ten or eleven people appeared from little shack settlements, which were screened from the road by tall banana plants. It had been two weeks since we left the tourist-filled streets of Nairobi, and so far it had been an easy run. In Kenya, things were more organized and tended to run smoothly, and so it was no surprise to any one of us that our safari was still fully operational and nothing had come along to disturb our peace. However, the countrified atmosphere would, without doubt, change, and life in Uganda would be more rough and ready.

We switched off the Swahili tape and closed the rear doors of the van. The small crowd politely stood aside.

Our audiences were always curious and watched with unflinching eyes as we said our good-byes and clambered on board the van at the end of a show. There was always a great deal of smiling, laughing, and shaking of hands as we drew away. We would then chuck a final bunch of pamphlets from the open door, and this would invariably start a charge up the empty track, followed by a lot of pushing and shoving as the children would wrestle happily with each other for the printed papers. We had heard, on the grapevine, that some children wrote their homework on the back of the sheet.

We were now making for the border. The sun was high in a cloudless sky; the land was open, and it started to get warm in the van. We passed plantations of papaya and pineapples, closely attended by hordes of fruit-seeking mouse birds darting from plant to plant. On our right we still enjoyed the magnificent view of the blue and green of Mount Elgon, rising from a sunlit plain dotted with rocky slopes. The road curved and followed a leafy line of arching trees, before it dipped and once more ran straight. We gave our first show in the frontier town of Malaba, and on leaving we passed a weathered signboard that simply said: *Uganda*. We pressed on in silence until we reached the town of Tororo and pulled up outside the Rock Hotel. The sun was lower than before, and it made misshapen shadows across the empty street. The signals were all there, and we accepted that it was the end of another day.

***

The next morning, Tuesday July 12, at 8:30, Thomas picked me up at the Rock Hotel. It was a warm, dry day as we eased the van down the main street toward the Asian stores. We passed tight-built neighborhoods, structured in timber, with narrow lanes leading off to backyard compounds. We slowed down as we came across groups of small children waiting patiently at a roadside standpipe for their turn at the water. There were several shops and market stalls lining the streets—each one of which would be visited before leaving the town. At the end of the street was a motor repair yard, and here we turned left into another busy shopping area lined with dark storehouses, selling medicines, textiles, and hardware.

Tororo had the look of a cowboy town. It was just the right sort of place for Hollywood to film a Western. The main highway was a dirt road with parallel lines of adobe buildings on each side painted in green, yellow, and blue. The larger buildings, usually retail stores, had dated verandas and were often fronted with white-painted wood pillars that supported protruding roofs. Everything had a thick layer of dust, and where the cowboys might have ridden through town on their horses, there were cyclists wobbling on bikes, bells tinkling. Under the wooden porches, instead of old men smoking clay pipes, there were young Africans sitting at tables pedaling sewing machines.

We were well aware that Tororo was an important link town with all modern amenities, such as a railroad, airport, and hospital, and with commercial connections spreading out into both Uganda and Kenya. At first sight it had an unsophisticated appearance, but it would have been wrong to have underestimated its importance as a trading center and allow ourselves to be sidetracked from the work that had to be done. We spent the morning giving live shows from the back of the van, using a mixture of music and microphone to persuade our large audiences to insist on Herbalex when suffering from coughs or colds. We would then address the mothers in the crowd and suggest that when they visited their pharmacists to make sure they asked for Gripe Aid the instant their babies suffered from wind or teething problems. We kept on repeating the message, breaking it up with piercing South American music, mambos, meringues, and pasa dobles, and then we'd cut back to the authoritative voice on the tape that spoke in the Luganda vernacular to the swelling crowds that thronged the van.

After that Thomas took an armful of tin advertising plates, and with a hammer and bag of nails, he set off down the road. His job entailed putting up the tin signs on shop doorways or any other prominent position where the potential customer was likely to pass. There was never any trouble getting permission from the *duka* owner, who would give consent with a wave of his hand but remain behind the counter to deal with his customers. Usually in large towns, the doors and shop fronts were fully taken up with a variety of metal signs ranging from advertisements for hot chocolate drinks and cigarettes, right through to aspirins and razor blades.

It wasn't always easy to find a vacant spot to nail up one's own metal sign, and as some of the earlier advertisements had already been robbed of their color by sunlight—leaving only black and pale yellow images—it would prove an unnecessary chore to reenter the dark interior of the shop in order to get further consent to remove the blanched signs. Instead Thomas would suffer no qualms in removing any competitive plates with a twist of the claw hammer before chucking them in a waste bin. Our plates usually ended up in a good position, at eye level when the customer entered the store.

Later, when he had done the rounds, he'd return to the van and take over the cash sales. This would give Visavadia and me the freedom to call on likely stockists and point out the demand we had created with the public. The *duka* owners would be well aware that we were in town, due to the music, leaflet distribution, and Thomas's earlier call. Additionally, we would give them our word that we'd cease retailing from the back of the van should we receive a minimum purchase order for two dozen bottles. Clearly there were times when we failed to obtain an order for the full twenty-four bottles, and on these occasions, our cast-iron guarantee not to trade had not been complied with and we were free to trade. It was strange that members of our audience would invariably insist on buying from us, despite our price being the same as that of their local retailer.

However, on returning to the van, Thomas pointed out that we were down to our last half gross. Being short of stock while on safari was one of our most testing problems. There was nothing worse than having a professional sales team in the bush with nothing left to sell. In this instance we had already estimated that we would require a fresh shipment by the time we reached Tororo. As a consequence, Bob Worsley, Morgans' branch manager for Uganda, had already dispatched this shipment by East African Railways to await our arrival.

It was gone midday when we finished loading the new shipment at the nearby railway station and headed back to Tororo in order to complete our deliveries.

"I'm hungry," Thomas announced.

"Me too," Visavadia chimed in.

"We haven't finished here," I said defensively.

"That's too bad." Thomas grinned from under his peak cap. "You've been out voted by two to one. You, yourself, agreed to majority voting on domestic matters or any other matter that might affect our safety while on safari."

"Fair enough," I caved in. "Chacula it is."

We drove a few hundred yards down the road and pulled into an empty spot that had all the makings of a rest area. It was flat land covered in sandy grit and was ideal for stopping over as it was secluded by a line of wild gardenia bushes. We knew from experience that there was nothing worse than eating a meal with a gaggle of children staring at our every mouthful. They weren't hungry, no way, just curious. After all it wasn't every day that a sales van's international crew was seen eating food on the roadside where they lived.

We emptied a tin of asparagus soup into a pan and waited for it to simmer. While waiting I shared out a packet of sandwiches that I had bought at the Rock Hotel and filled our mugs with water from the jerrican. We ate in silence and watched as Visavadia put a kettle on the stove for coffee and I passed around a large tin of mixed biscuits. When we finished the meal, we spread ourselves on the ground for a catnap.

Twenty minutes later we returned to Tororo, completed our deliveries, and started working the bazaar area before moving into the suburbs. Then, having exhausted all possible outlets, we left town and traveled four miles to a place called Sukulu. The mining of local limestone had led to the building of a giant cement factory, and we spent another two hours distributing leaflets to the workers as they came out of the gates.

Then, for the third time, we headed back to Tororo, and en route called at scattered settlements to play music and hand out leaflets. The narrow pathways between shacks were strewn with layers of rotten plantain leaves, which exuded a heavy smell. The sunlight played on the thick green fronds of the banana plants and made harsh shadows that arrowed across the ground. We could hear dogs barking from both sides of the compound and sensed their aggression, so we kept the van's doors shut and waited while they approached. They soon turned away, growling and resentful, when opposed by an army of small children wielding sticks and throwing well-aimed stones. We then climbed from the vehicle, gave the children free samples, and commenced visiting mud-and-wattle houses in the locality. By the time we returned to the compound, there was a growing crowd of potential customers, and all the time we'd called on the houses we were closely followed by the same children who, at the start, had beaten off the dogs. They were jostling each other and gave us wide smiles every time we turned to talk to them.

In a neighboring field we watched as a young man drummed rapidly on a plank that lay on the ground. He sat cross-legged, and all he wore was a shredded pair of beige shorts and a limp T-shirt that was heavily stained.

Thomas told me that the rhythmic beat of the sticks would sound like the heavy rat-tat-tat of rain to the millions of white termites that nested in the spongy soil. It was true, as a few minutes later we saw the initial signs of activity; swarms of termites surfaced and began to fly in confused circles inches above the ground. The young man continued to drum on the board as his head hung down and rotated while he bit hard on his lower lip. There was now a thick cloud of insects, and their bewilderment over the lack of rain was obvious. They tumbled around in ever-decreasing circles. We hadn't long to wait for their inescapable metamorphosis to take place. Their minute gossamer wings started to break away and swirl gently to the ground. The termites, disoriented and no longer luminous, now formed an opaque blackness and were ready to be harvested. The drummer, who by now was dripping wet, dropped his sticks on the grass and reached over for an empty sack. He went forward on his knees, shook the sack open, and scooped handfuls of insects from the pyramid-shaped mound and stuffed them inside. And finally, when the sack was full, he tied up the end with a piece of sisal, got up, and swung the bag across one of his shoulders.

"What's going to happen to those insects?" I asked. It was a stupid question, and I immediately regretted having said anything. I knew the answer, but perhaps I wanted to hear different. It seemed sad that people had to eat such things, but in up-country Africa everything was geared to survival. I watched humbly as the man trudged wearily over the short-grassed field. He looked drained, and yet he exchanged greetings with Thomas as he passed. As the gap between them widened they hummed in turn until the moment that each one could no longer hear the other.

"He'll fry them in sunflower oil," Thomas said dryly, "and then he'll sell them as a delicacy in the local market."

"Not to me, he won't," Visavadia piped up.

I got back to the Rock Hotel at the very moment they were banging the dinner gong. I took a quick shower, and, with my hair still damp, I sat down at a table for two and started off by asking for a lager. After dinner I went back to my room and got out the gray portable typewriter. Sitting down on the edge of the bed I pulled a barley sugar from my jacket pocket, put it in my mouth, and began to write my weekly report to London, giving them the latest sales figures.

***

At nine o'clock the next day, Wednesday, July 13, Thomas picked me up at the hotel. We drove into town and parked outside the local branch of Barclays Bank. We found Visavadia sitting patiently on his wooden case reading an Asian paperback. He glanced at his big wristwatch with a shining steel strap and smiled. "Right on time," he said, and folded his book.

"That's clever of you to notice," Thomas replied dryly. "I thought you wore that watch just for decoration."

"Come on, you two," I intervened. "We can do some work while we wait for the bank to open."

The streets were crowded, and the people were making their way toward the market, either on foot or by bicycle. Traffic was generally light, and only the occasional bus or heavy truck pounded by, gears grinding as they double-declutched before coming to the corner. Once negotiated, they picked up speed and became faint as they distanced themselves from the urban area. All the while we played soft island music from our speakers, which drifted lazily into the warm air. Small groups of people began to mill around, seeking samples and leaflets.

It wasn't long before the bank opened its doors. I noticed the look of anxiety that was thrown in our direction as the official secured the doors on brass-fitted hooks before stepping back inside. It may have had to do with the music—perhaps it stopped them from concentrating—or did we look suspicious in our rumpled clothes? I wasn't sure. Before going inside I made a final check on the money in the cash box, making sure it balanced against the stock sales sheets. I signed the copies of the credit slips and added today's date at the top. I climbed down from the van, went into the bank, and handed everything over to an obliging cashier who ensured that the monies were paid into our agent's account.

The eighty-one-mile route west-southwest to Jinja was reasonably easy. By noon we had covered the bush villages of Bugiri and Busesa, reaching the township of Iganga, which was set at the main crossroads. Now the highway ran north from Lake Victoria. It would be here, at this point, that we would have to return after completing work in Kampala, and from here we would then strike north for the Lango Province.

After taking the main street out of Iganga, the highway opened up for miles ahead. We settled easily back into our seats as Thomas increased the speed to a steady forty miles per hour. The sky was azure blue, dappled with little wispy white clouds, and the early afternoon sun streaked across the windshield. The strong rays were reflected on the myriad of insects that had splashed onto the glass, and this detraction had pushed us into lowering the visors. But farther along, some five miles perhaps, we noticed a string of soaring mvuli trees, tall and solitary like sentinels. Their dark foliage hung over the dusty track, breaking up the sunlight and throwing off darker shadows. Every now and then we noticed that these trees were ringed with the trailing open mouths of wild ipomoea.

We stopped a few miles farther on at a place called Wanya. There was nothing there save a few thatched huts screened from the road by pawpaw fruits growing on high bushes. Then, ten minutes later, we rolled back out onto the powdery road and set course for Jinja. The view soon became more extensive as we emerged from a wooded slope shrouded by gigantic fan palms.

This time the road had been built on an embankment of yellow laterite clay, smooth and bare, flattened by the passing of heavy vehicles. Small pale mounds of sandy earth dotted the edges, blown there from the sides of the sloping track. The green land had become more broken; fields appeared, seemingly boundless and unfenced, and filled with maize, cassava, and cotton. We were in the Busoga Province, a rich agricultural region farmed by the industrious Baganda people—owners of Uganda's chocolate acres that circled Kampala to the north and the west.

The fields presently yielded to the hedgeless rectangles of sugarcane, which stretched endlessly toward the wide horizon. The cutters were in the fields wielding silver-coated pangas. We threw out a stream of leaflets from the doorway that caught the warm air and billowed upward. The moment we saw the workers running toward us we decided to stop the van and give an impromptu show. Visavadia, without delay, put on a fiesty Latin number. Our music was always a certain winner with the people. We opened the rear doors and set up shop. The spontaneous reaction to our unplanned stop took us totally unawares. I suggested that a free sample should be given to everyone and that no sales pressure was to be used. For ten minutes our roadside party was ticking over nicely until a foreman appeared and ordered everyone to return to work.

The wide view was going, and small well-trodden paths rose toward the high embankment, which was set on each side of the hot, thin road. It was narrower now and had begun to curve. I noticed that Thomas had leaned forward, closer to the steering, and had begun to mutter words of encouragement as he negotiated the shuttered road. He was no longer his bouncy self but seemed on the lookout for anything that might interrupt our steady progress.

"Are you OK?" I asked.

"Yes," he said, "but for some reason I got to thinking about that road to Gulu. We had been going well, and then our world changed. I don't know why, but I got that same sort of feeling just now. Maybe I've been spooked."

"Would you like to change over?"

"I wouldn't mind," he replied, and touched the brake pedal, bringing the van to a halt.

A mile later we came out of the densely packed woodlands into the open. We glimpsed people moving about on the bare paths that ran between the richly planted fields, and not long afterward, we passed a convoy of five heavily laden madhvanis trucks heading for the grain mills. Their engines drowned out our voices as we tilted ten degrees to the left side of the track. Once there it was essential that our driver's-side wheels bit into the groove near the shoulder. I used every ounce of my strength to maintain that position for the next hundred yards or so before we regained the center. It was like riding a roller coaster.

Farther along the road there was a mixture of billboards by the roadside with pictures of smiling people. A solitary sign pointed the way to Jinja, and the highway was now tarred. We soon passed a park filled with spectators watching a football game, after which we motored by a block of high-rise concrete buildings made into flats. The road on each side was lined with telephone poles, and at each crossroads, dirt tracks came to meet the embanked highway. We slowed down to a precautionary speed of less than ten miles per hour due to the concentration of cyclists and cars, and then negotiated a drab-looking roundabout before proceeding straight ahead past an expanse of railway yards and the smoke-filled industrial area with its copper smelting, steel rolling, and sawmills.

Jinja was the second-largest city in Uganda and was the headquarters for the Busoga District. It lay on the east bank of the River Nile. We pushed slowly through the town's center; traffic was bumper to bumper, and groups of workers poured from the factories. We bypassed a brewery and threaded our way toward the western fringes of the town, where the highway widened into a dual carriageway. It was lighter again, more yellow, and the slanted shadows from the trees and tall structures were getting longer in the declining sun.

The road started to slope gently upward, curving slightly, and without any expectation, we suddenly found ourselves crossing the magnificent Owen Falls. The thunder of the waters in the dam drowned all else. A thin spray, more like a heavy mist, clung to the warm air. The view was extensive on both sides. The deep roar of the water was like giving birth to the River Nile.

The wide road bridged the top of the dam in spectacular fashion. Stone parapets guarded the sides. The old Ripon Falls had long gone, and the water levels had risen, making Lake Victoria the largest reservoir in the world. It is from this hydroelectric station that power is supplied to Kampala and eastern Uganda; even Nairobi, some four hundred miles away, is also connected to this grid. The din of the water from the Owen Falls could be heard long after we reached the west bank. We were in the capital province of Buganda, a settled region with the indigenous people rooted to the humid acres. The climate controlled one's diet, which in turn influenced one's physique. The Bagandans were recognizable from their round faces and fleshy bodies. They were an intelligent and handsome people.

We continued along the highway and sighted a grove of African olive trees that spread early evening shadows across the tarmac. The sky above was pale blue, and the light was beginning to go. The road in front of us was once again filled with cyclists. After leaving the main street, we turned toward the river, going slowly through a large commercial area of shops, offices, and foreign banks. It was here that Visavadia tapped me on the shoulder. I braked and pulled up on the broken edges of the asphalt, just opposite a large Asian store with the name Patel painted across the timbered front.

"I'll meet you here tomorrow at eight thirty a.m.," I shouted from the doorway as I pulled back onto the road.

"Good night," Visavadia bellowed above the noise of the traffic, and I signaled my acknowledgement with a wave of my right arm.

It was here that we once again exchanged seats, and I passed control of the van back to Thomas.

"Where do you want to go?" he asked.

"Ripon Falls Hotel," I said. "It's somewhere farther along this road, and then you cut back toward the river on a left-hand curve." My eyes followed the line of the street map that was laid out on my lap.

It was dusk when we arrived at the hotel. I got out of the vehicle and checked the reception desk for accommodation. I went back outside, got hold of my suitcase, briefcase, and typewriter from the van, turned around under a cantilevered doorway, and gave a thumbs-up. I watched as Thomas slipped the heavy van into second and let it slowly roll down the graveled driveway between the neatly cut lawn.

***

After three days of hard work we left Jinja on Sunday, July 17, and headed due west for Kampala. It was an easy trip of exactly fifty miles with only a few stopovers along the route. Open fields of maize and starch-producing manioc were soon replaced by huge sugar estates. The concrete buildings of the sugar-refining factory could clearly be seen from the road. Near the village of Lugazi the highway opened up; the villages were now set back from the main road. Traffic to the capital was light but steady.

We began to pick up speed, touching fifty, and passed simple mileage signs pointing to Kampala—thirty, twenty, and ten miles away. The land became less open. Only the hiss of tires on the metallic surface and the unbroken drone of the engine could be heard.

The road ran beside a succession of fenced-in compounds, and limp African house dogs could be seen lying on dusty wooden verandas, unstirring and yet incessantly alert. Some smaller huts remained hidden by the tall greenness of plantain. There were square-shaped allotments of sweet potatoes, sesame, and beans, irregular plots of tobacco, and solitary breadfruit trees with their farina podules suspended from low, leafy branches. We passed more timbered huts, closer together than before, and gradually reduced our speed in the market areas, where there were rows of rickety-structured shops and more people backtracking along the scuffed edges of the road.

Shortly we entered the eastern outskirts of Kampala, the Mukono Road gradually losing its identity as the maze of city streets absorbed the highway. We worked our way through the tightly built neighborhoods, emerging on the northern fringe of the city. Every now and then we snatched glimpses of residential villas with their yellow vetia hedges and white jasmine shrubs. Beyond the neat gardens were small, pretty orchards of avocado and lemon. From here, we curved in a leisurely arc, going left and merging with Parliament Avenue. The scent of vanilla essence wafted from the pale tropical mallows that grew in the rich herbaceous beds that bordered the road. Tall, waving palms also stood erect alongside the pavements. We turned left again and began to climb, passing glass-fronted shops, a cinema showing Indian films, and blocks of modern office buildings. Out of the blue I suddenly noticed the small hotel where I recuperated from the road accident outside Gulu, and not saying anything, we continued up the road, forking right, following the contours of the central reservation, which broadened onto the city's main square. A solitary, purple-flowered jacaranda broke up the gray flatness on the far side as we entered the central square of the city. It was dominated by the Imperial Hotel.

Thomas pulled the van to the curb. "What about tomorrow?" he said, tightening the handbrake.

"I'll meet you both at Morgans' offices at eight thirty a.m.," I replied, as I set foot on the pavement and reached for my suitcase and other clothing from inside the cab.

"See you." Thomas smiled.

"See you," Visavadia chipped in.

It seemed strange to be back in this beautiful city, which, like Rome, is set among seven hills. This was the center for the ancient kingdom of the Baganda people, Africa's oldest culture, reaching back to the fifteenth century. Today it is a contrast of old and new—the ancient tombs of the Kabakas at Kasubi, three miles northwest, with the new buildings in the city center. Kampala is a fascinating blend of the past and the present.

Three hours went by before I left my bedroom. I had showered and shaved, written some letters, and completed my reports to the head office. It was a warm, humid night, and I donned my blue lightweight suit, conforming to the standards set by three-star hotels. I took the elevator down to the ground floor, crossed the red-carpeted lobby, and entered the spacious dining room. It was filled with smart Sunday night people sitting around polished tables. The hum of low voices and the clink of cutlery permeated the crowded room. An empty table, hidden against the far wall, was pointed out to me by a waiter in a red tunic. I made my own way through the labyrinth of dining chairs, and sat down with my back to the wood-paneled walling. It was a straightforward menu, and I chose a pineapple and crab cocktail for an appetizer, trout meuniere, and roast ribs of beef with Yorkshire pudding.

There was a hubbub of conversation sweeping across the crowded room. The table directly to my right, separated by a narrow aisle, led into the kitchens. It was occupied by a party of eight tourists. They were talking excitedly and obviously having a good time. Every so often the word *safari* would pop into the conversation, and interesting color slides were being passed round. Then, between mouthfuls, they would hold a transparency up to the tubular lights that ringed the ceiling, before returning to their food. It was my guess that they had come back from a five-day conducted safari at the Queen Elizabeth National Park in western Uganda—a sort of Monday-to-Friday adventure—probably staying at the luxurious Mweya Safari Lodge. No doubt, when they got home, they would tell exciting stories about their time in Africa to close friends, and back this up by projecting their 35mm colorslides onto a screen. The word *safari* would fall off lips like confetti at a wedding, and the proof of the dangers faced would be all too apparent in the snarling close-ups of a lion or yawning hippo. However, if your photo collection was incomplete at the end of your safari, it was possible to obtain all the slides you could want from any shop catering to tourists, either in town or at the airport. The paradox of most game-oriented exploits in Africa is that the wild animals invariably move away from the approach of humans unless they have a good reason not to do so.

Other tables in the dining hall were taken up with colorful groups of Africans, mainly Bagandans and their wives, and a sprinkling of expatriate

Europeans, either businessmen or settlers from the rural areas. The Bagandan women were dressed in their traditional ankle-length busiti gowns of saffron and magenta with butterfly sleeves and a loose sash; heads were covered in bulky turbans. The men were in flowing robes, the cloth twisted round their hips and thrown casually over the right shoulder. In spite of the yards of material used, the men were indeed more exposed than their women; bare legs in sandals, half-naked chests, shoulders, and arms.

From my table I watched the coming and going of waiters through the swing doors. My first course of pineapple and crab seemed long overdue. I noticed a foursome who had come in after me was now being served by the same young waiter who had originally taken my order. Some moments later I was approached by a tall, solemn-looking man, again in a red tunic but with polished brass buttons and a purple sash running diagonally across his chest. It occurred to me that he might be the wine waiter, and I was ready to ask him for a bottle of red Bordeaux, preferably Pomerol.

He had the fine features of a Sudanic man from Uganda's northwest region. "I'm afraid I have to tell you that we can't serve you dinner," he said.

"What's wrong?" I asked in puzzlement.

"You are not wearing a tie," he replied, adding, "You'll find that a copy of the hotel rules can be found in every room. It is usually pinned to the side of the clothes cupboard or to the back of the door. Just the same, I have a duty to take notice of any reasonable complaint, and in my capacity as maître d'hôtel, I have no alternative but to act on it."

"Fair enough," I said, getting up from my seat. "But it seems strange that some people are allowed in here with bare chests, while I have to leave because the top button of my shirt is undone, even though I'm in a suit."

"As soon as you come back..."

"Forget it," I cut in. "It's all too much hassle."

The tourists at the next table began to look round, sensing that something was going on.

"It's your choice, sir." The maître d'hôtel stood back to let me through. It was at times like this that I wished I was deep in the bush. I felt uneasy in large towns and longed for the freedom of Africa, away from the pettiness of day-to-day life. Not more than a few hundred yards from the hotel, beyond the city streets, lay the real Uganda—about one hundred thousand square miles of fantastic scenery covering each side of the equator, three-quarters of it land area and one-quarter under water or swamp. The country lies on an unseen plateau, ranging from two thousand to three thousand feet in the north and northwest, and about a thousand in the hilly regions around Lake Victoria.

I stood up and started my ignominious walk of shame from the dining hall, weaving among tables, into the richly carpeted lobby of the hotel. I carried images in my mind of thorn trees, borassus palms, thick mountainous forests, and long elephant grass. I wished I could be anywhere but here. But more flashes of the real Uganda invaded my subconscious mind, such as the cool highland lakes and soaring mvuli trees with their dark tresses of dense foliage, and, last but not least, the wonderful people.

At last I reached the street and walked over to the far end of the square. I turned down an unlit street and went toward the main boulevard. I was alert once more and took enjoyment from having an unexpected evening stroll in this lovely city. I looked at the crooked silhouettes of buildings that shimmered in the moonlight, and for an unexpected moment the empty streets became seriously dark as a blanket of black cloud raced across the sky. A dim light showed in a house and a dog barked. Not long afterward I passed the market, which was closed except for a solitary stallholder who was open for business outside the locked gates. He was busily frying some grasshoppers in a shallow pan while his customers waited in silence under the deep shadows of a naked bulb. Every now and then he would shake red pepper into the pan, followed by a liberal sprinkling of salt. Besides grasshoppers, the food stall offered little oily heaps of flying ants laid out on pieces of old newspaper. There were also different kinds of fat grubs wriggling in enamel bowls and crispy orange-colored caterpillars with bulging eyes. I carved my way forward and finally reached the bright lights of a boulevard.

I began to relax. It had been a long time since I had visited Harry's Bar and Restaurant. I used to go in there after the accident, when they had brought me back to Kampala. Everything was like yesterday. I crossed the road and went in.

chapter

FIVE

The real purpose behind our sales safari was simply that we could reach all regions of East Africa, promoting and advertising products directly to the consumer. Our van was fully equipped for this purpose, and we were well prepared to go deep into the African bush for weeks at a time. In fact, during all the time we made incursions into the deep bush, we never came across any similar long-range sales units. There was no competition, which, in a way, made our safari unique. Now and then we came across smaller promotional vans pushing aspirins, cigarettes, and cola drinks. They were limited to three or four days on the road before returning to base. We had heard that countries such as Nigeria, on Africa's west coast, and Malaya in the Far East, had companies that employed the use of vehicles to advertise their products in remote regions, but unlike us, they didn't have the freedom to cross and recross frontiers for extended periods. Perhaps, if parallels are to be made, then our direct ancestors were the hawkers of patent medicine in America's old West at the turn of the century, living and working from those splendid covered wagons. It's possible with the coming of total independence that this safari would be the last of its kind in Africa.

Our first day in Kampala, on Monday, July 18, we had used our time to pay courtesy calls on the large Asian wholesalers. We told them about our intended work up-country and hoped they would give sizable orders to our agents once the demand filtered in from the towns and villages. They all listened to our requests, and like Asian shop owners everywhere in Africa, they were always hospitable, offering us hot rice buns, sweetmeats, and large bowls of spicy, orange-looking tea.

On our second day we had set off on a tour of the southwest, along the lake road toward the historic town of Masaka, passing large sugar refineries, textile factories, and coffee warehouses on the way out of the city. Once clear of the tightly built-up areas, we reentered another section of rich, fertile acres farmed by the Bagandans. Twenty-foot banana plants, tapioca shrubs, wild dates, green pawpaws, and mango trees all cut off the open view from the curving road. The olive-brown vervet monkey was no longer around; its little black face framed on blue had been driven away. It had plagued the crops for many years before the long-suffering farmers took action. The reason we went on this road was to link up with Masaka, which we would be approaching from a different direction in approximately six weeks time, after reaching Mbarara.

And on Wednesday we had checked our general itinerary with Bob Worsley at Morgan and Sons' downtown offices. The van had been in for a service at Coopers Motors before being loaded with a fresh consignment of Herbalex, Gripe Aid, and other items of advertising material. I also arranged for a further eighty cases to be dispatched, along with drums of disinfectant and portable toilets, to Gulu by train to await our arrival.

We had now completed our work in Kampala, and although our contribution of three days was infinitesimal when compared with the size of the market, our head office had taken into account the regular work plan carried out by Morgans themselves, who ran their own mobile sales units; not only did they cover the immediate area but also the up-country markets and trade outlets within a fifty-mile radius of the city.

There was now nothing left to do but wait for tomorrow's sunrise.

Having got everything in place I decided I had earned the right to a night out. I started my evening at a bijou restaurant near Mweya Street, and on leaving I took a short walk to a place called City Bar in the heart of the town. I had been told by a friend that the place had become a popular watering hole with expatriates and was worth a visit if you were in the mood for a pint or two.

The bar was tucked discreetly across one corner of the dimly lit room. The place was almost empty, but the nine o'clock shown on my watch was somewhat early for the sophisticated people. I ordered a Scotch and Coke and settled down on one of the red-covered stools. And not far from where I sat, around a candlelit table, was a lively group of young, attractive Bagandan girls in brightly patterned gowns, spiky hairdos, and glossy mauve lips. The sound of their voices, along with bursts of excited laughter, was drowned when one of them put a shilling in a multicolored jukebox and pressed some buttons. The low throbbing rhythms of highlife music filled the bar.

The room gradually began to get more crowded. There were now English voices asking for pints of draft beer. The music changed on the jukebox, less rhythmic, more flowing, and couples took to the floor and swayed from side to side. The mood in the room was no longer stolid but had become more romantic. I turned my attention back to the bar and asked for another drink. I hadn't realized that a young girl, maybe twenty-one or -two, had squeezed her way to the counter, waving a green twenty shilling note, wanting similar attention at the same time as me. She ordered two vodkas and tonic and a packet of Crown Bird cigarettes.

The barman smiled: "Who goes first?" he said, looking from the girl to me.

"The young lady first," I said easily.

"That's good of you," she replied, and gave a lovely smile when the barman went to get her drinks.

The jukebox was now playing an inviting slow number.

"Do you have time for a dance," I asked with a smile.

"Well, maybe I do," she said hesitantly.

Once we were on the dance floor, she told me her name was Carol Gray and that she worked as a nurse at the Government Hospital.

"My name's John Carter," I said, and asked, "What brings you here tonight?"

"It's my day off," she said, "and tomorrow I start nights."

I could feel her body against mine, and as the music began to fade I realized that there was a distinct possibility that at any moment this lovely girl would step out of my life. I reckoned I had nothing to lose by asking her an upfront question.

"Are you with anyone special tonight?"

"Just my girlfriend." Carol smiled and paused for a moment before going on. "Look, we're going to a party at a friend's house shortly, and if you're doing nothing, would you like to join us?"

An hour later I was dancing with Carol at her friend's house. The party went on until two. Then people started to drift away, most grumbling about it being a working day and having to go back to their banks, insurance companies, garages, and farms.

We were together on a couch in the corner of the lounge. "As you know, I am going away tomorrow," I breathed gently into her ear, half-hidden behind her long, ash-blond hair. "In four weeks I'll be back for a two-day stopover." I paused to let the facts sink in. "I would like to see you again."

The room was all but empty. Carol was in a bright patterned skirt, an embroidered white short-sleeved blouse, and a pair of high-heeled black patent shoes. There was a gold chain around her neck, and she also wore a pair of dangly earrings. She slid closer to me and lifted her face for a kiss. Her pink mouth was soft and warm. After a few moments she let her head fall on my shoulder. "It's gone all quiet," she said softly.

"Yes," I said, as she lifted her face to mine, but this time our lips were more demanding.

She pressed herself harder against me. "Stay here with me," she said, opening her mouth slightly and responding to my kiss. Her small patent clutch bag fell from her lap.

"Whose house is this anyway?" I asked.

"It belongs to my friend Stella," Carol said in a heavy breath, leaning over to pick up the black bag from the floor. "She's on duty tonight at the hospital. She won't mind us being here, I promise." She placed her forefinger smoothly over my lips. "Stop worrying," she said with a laugh.

***

The very next morning, Thursday, July 21, I met Thomas and Visavadia outside the Imperial Hotel at nine a.m. On leaving the city in a northeasterly direction, we retraced our route back to Iganga. We covered the

Safari Salesman

seventy-four miles in a little less than three hours, and this left us sufficient time to head farther north through the cotton townships of Busembatia and Namutumba in order to arrive at Terinyi before dark.

The last time we touched Iganga was eight days ago, but today our safari started in earnest as we motored up the greasy cotton soil tracks toward the open plateaus of northern Uganda. The soft, easy days in Kenya were now a thing of the past, and we were both glad and excited to be back in the real Africa.

We worked the road for thirty miles, reaching the Terinyi Ferry at four o'clock. The crossing of Mpologoma River—a tributary of Lake Kyoga on the Victoria Nile—took a full thirty minutes. It was raining when we finally drove off the ferry onto the far bank. The clouds had grown swiftly from the merest wisps, reshaping and becoming black and silver with storm, and all this happened within five minutes of arriving. The rain washed down the sides of the van, and we slithered on the flooded track. There was no longer a view; there was only the rain drowning the noise of the engine. Another hour went by. We had hardly done four miles since leaving the ferry. Somewhere in front was the bush village of Kibuku. It was nearly dark when we decided to call it a day. We pulled off the road onto higher ground under the spreading canopy of a large yellow-barked acacia tree. It was cozy in the van, and we started to prepare a hot meal and lay out our beds.

Luckily, during the night, the rains had thinned. There was less drumming on the roof, and when we woke there was just the drip-drip from the branches of the tree. The sun had already started its climb, and we could feel its warmth.

"We've got a problem," Thomas began, brushing aside his usual spirited good-morning greeting. He'd been first out of the van, toothbrush, razor, towel, and toilet roll in his hand, and when he made his accustomed jump from the rear doors, his legs were quickly sucked into a quagmire—the sort of shock one gets when taking a step too many on a staircase. Apparently, in spite of the higher ground, the van had sunk through the porous soil to the level of the chassis.

"Let's have breakfast first," I grunted as I surveyed the damage. It did indeed look as though we were seriously stuck in the mud and stranded.

It took over two hours to dig the wheels out and put down a carpet of heavy foliage before we were able to free the van and get it back on the road.

However, our troubles were by no means over. We were caked in mud, and the track leading to Mbale was now difficult to follow. No longer did the road run true, and what with the movement of heavy vehicles plying their way between cotton fields and ginneries, the sand-like soil had been squashed into a mud bank. The deep wheel tracks about a central ridge had obliterated the furrows, and the road had become almost unusable. It was misshapen, unlined, and glutinous, and we slithered and squelched our way along a narrow depression between dark slopes. Finally, after another two hours, the road leveled out.

It was noon when we arrived in the township of Pallisa. We stayed for about an hour and gave a show at each end of the town. Then, on leaving, we turned due east and headed for the strangely named settlement of Iki Iki, where we played some soft music and handed out leaflets and some samples and sold two bottles each of Gripe Aid and Herbalex. When our show was over, we turned southwest for a seven-mile trip on a narrow stone pathway and emerged at the important cotton town of Budaka. This would be our final stopping point before going east to Mbale.

Three miles farther on from Budaka, we passed a sizable area of open hummocked land that spread away into the distance on both sides of the road. This spoke of recent forests that had been stripped of trees and the ground made bare. The unnatural setting had not been carried out in an act of wanton destruction, to either make furniture for the West or to turn into charcoal for home consumption, but had been ordered to combat the tsetse fly that had ravaged the large herds of cattle that had previously inhabited the region. The scenery had taken on the look of a Martian landscape.

Thirty minutes and six miles later, we reached the outskirts of Mbale. We drove past the local golf course at a sedately twenty miles per hour on a smooth, tarmacked road. We saw attractive villas with gardens of frangipani, climbing jasmine, and brightly colored bougainvillea. It was like a dream after the mud of the bush. It was no more than a matter of minutes before we found ourselves in the town center. On the main corner of the main street, Visavadia's sharp eyes spotted a friendly Asian store, and, clutching his battered wooden case, he jumped from the van. The last thing I said was for him to meet up at nine thirty a.m. tomorrow at the Mount Elgon Hotel. I had added an extra hour off to compensate for the mud and grime of today's trip. I also agreed to pay them out of the cash box to get their clothes laundered.

Then it was my turn to go, and I watched as Thomas gave a big wave and drove off down the road.

I was caked in slow-drying mud, and with a good deal of trepidation, I walked across the lobby of the hotel to sign the register. I felt like a convict on the run and at any minute expected the thud of a hand on my shoulder. Instead I quickly made my way along the blue carpeted corridor to my room, and it was with a sigh of relief that I closed the door behind me. The room had an open fireplace—more for decoration than for use—and white walls reaching to a half-timbered ceiling. It appeared that the hotel was built in the early days of colonialism, Tudor style, with a homely ambiance to reassure the first settlers; from its small framed windows there was a clear view of the mountains, washed clean by the declining sun.

Mbale is overshadowed by the towering, western slopes of Mount Elgon. The town is the headquarters for the whole of the Bugisu Region, a rich agricultural area with arabica coffee estates and wide, spreading cotton plantations. Farther north, and still on the slopes of the mountain, a rough road winds through hillside coffee shambas, opening out onto steep, grassy meadows scattered with large magnolia tulip trees of green and yellow. Beyond this idyllic scene, and even farther north, lie the harsh semideserts of the Karamoja scrubland, along with its thornbushes and wandering herds of dusty, disheveled cattle.

***

We worked throughout the weekend, leaving Mbale on Monday, July 25, and headed northwest for Soroti, a journey of exactly eighty miles. Outside the town we crossed the Namatale River. However, due to the recent rains the Namatale had broadened in many places from a shallow channel of sand and pebbles to that of a natural river. We then entered Bugwere Province. There were low, spreading hills on both sides, scattered with thorn trees over short tufts of grass. Dark lines of trees in the distance marked the course of more rivers and streams. It was a warm day, and the air rushed through the open doors of the van. It wasn't long before we left the mountains, and all we could see of them were glimpses of green and blue in our driving mirrors as they rose sharply from a sun-drenched plateau.

For some time there wouldn't be any more towns of Mbale's size to delay our progress. The savanna opened up, becoming drier and hotter in the northern areas and less populated than before. Ten miles after the bush village of Kachumbala, we entered yet another province. This time it was Teso, the ethnic territory of the Nilo-Hamatic people. There were groups of naked men idling with their cattle, dark bodies made dry by the constant stir of dust. This was our first sight of the Karamojans, cattle stealers extraordinaire, trespassing beyond their own borders.

The road started to rise to the high embankment of the highway, and at Kumi it curved left and continued straight as an arrow. The land, flat with scrub, stretched in every direction, and ended in the distant haze. The sun was high and glittered on the windshield. We passed small mud and wattle settlements off each side of the road. Now and then we stopped to give out leaflets and play music, always moving on, obsessed with our next destination. Five miles later, but before reaching the township of Ngora, the see of the bishop of the Upper Nile, we came to the tiny halt of Nyero with its prehistoric rock paintings.

After Kyere we turned sharp right and headed due north, eventually reaching the headquarters town of Soroti, an important trading center with several parallel streets lined on both sides that had dark, tight-fitting Indian stores shaded by densely crowned butternut trees. Banks, shops, and offices were also to be found, a sure sign of prosperity when up-country, while young African boys pedaled dutifully on sewing machines along the rickety wooden terraces. We dropped Visavadia at the corner of the main boulevard and motored toward the outskirts of the town. We passed smart-looking bungalows and isolated villas set in tangled gardens, and finally arrived at the government rest house. It was screened from the road by eucalyptus trees. It was getting dark, and lights had come on in the dusty street. Thomas by now had decided not to use the van, and instead agreed to share the only habitable room in the house.

The next morning we worked the Asian stores, and backed up these visits with a strong promotional advertising campaign in different parts of the town. Then, after a light midday meal, we departed from Soroti and set out on a seventy-five-mile trip to Lira in Lango Province. We soon left the main shopping area and drove through the untidy suburbs with their cramped, rectangular buildings. The land then opened up, and the road became wider as we motored through the smarter residential district area with parallel lines of detached housing on each side of the road. The road then narrowed as we approached a grass roundabout dotted with dwarf shrubbery. It was here that we turned right and headed off in a northwesterly direction. There were timber shacks in dusty yards and two or three African shops. There was little traffic, and only an occasional car or truck sped by on the dirt road. It wasn't long before we reached our first isolated, sun-parched village, where a grime-spattered bus had pulled up on the far side to pick up passengers heading for the center of Soroti.

From Tiriri and Orongo in Teso Province, we crossed over into Lango District. It was even emptier and drier, but when we pulled over at a place called Alebtongo, there was no one there. It was just a point on the map with a few scattered houses of ocher and red with thatched roofs. They were clustered on one side of the dirt road and dusty pathways crisscrossed open compounds among the low structures.

Once Visavadia had put the music on, and we had set up shop in the rear of the van. We managed to draw a small but interested audience. The people were Nilotics and didn't understand the Bantu tapes that were played after the music died. Our audience was obviously confused and began to laugh and chat among themselves, and, like all tribes of Acholi and Lango districts, they spoke only in the Lwoo dialect. Normally, English can be used as a connecting language, but in these out-of-the-way places that wasn't always possible. In the end we reached a compromise and changed the tape to Kiswehili and played it at a slower speed. The paintings on the side of the van and our metal signs and leaflets—all of which were self-explanatory—were enough to turn the tide and give us the opening to make a few brisk sales. All of our advertising materials depicted either mothers happily spooning Gripe Aid to their babies, or young athletic men pictured sneezing into handkerchiefs while reaching for the nearest bottle of Herbalex. We had similar crowds at the little villages of Aloi and Bar, and, by giving extra care and attention to the needs of our customers, we were able to make a number of sales.

By the time we got to Lira, the light was beginning to go. It was yellower, and shadows were less abrupt. The dirt road leading into the center of town was full of pedestrians and cyclists coming from the market. After passing a small, gray-looking railway station, we slowed down for a large gasoline tanker, which swerved unannounced onto the main thoroughfare.

Not long afterward we pulled to a halt outside the local police post. We not only needed directions for getting to the government rest house, but we also had to find out if they held the key, or could tell us who did. We were tired and dim lights began to show from houses. The quick dusk had gone, and the dark violet of the sky became dotted with stars. This time Visavadia admitted defeat in his search for accommodation and decided to spend the night with us in the rest house.

***

By noon the next day we'd finished working Lira and continued our thrust northwest to the cotton town of Aboki. Here we gave a full show before we changed direction and took a parallel road running eastward to a place called Ogur. Once again we gave a thirty-minute show and then moved onward down the highway that went due north to Kitgum.

On one side of the road we saw a herd of giraffes browsing among the topmost branches of incense-smelling gum arabic trees. They tugged ceaselessly at the small, thorny leaves with their sinuous black tongues, and only a short distance from them was another herd of fat roan antelope that had stopped grazing. They all turned to watch as we motored by in a thick cloud of layered dust that ballooned out from our rear wheels. All the time the view became wider, and the light hurt as it skimmed off the unending savanna.

The scenery changed little, dry steppes interspersed with thorn trees and low scrub. Several miles on we saw dark lines of tall borassus palms marking out the entire length of the Aswa River basin. The view gradually diminished to both left and right, and all that we had been looking at had now been absorbed into the colorless horizon.

Not long afterward we crossed the river and pushed north toward Pajule. The road followed the level of the land, and everything was coated with dust; the air was sticky with warm haze. In the cabin we watched in silence for any tell-tale signs of other vehicles coming our way, almost as though we expected something to happen. We shifted uneasily in our seats, and beads of sweat ran down our faces as the sun penetrated the windshield. Since leaving the river we had entered Chua Province, home of the Acholi people, but just the same we were still in Nilotic tribal territory that formed part of Uganda's northern plateau. It was drier, and signs of life in both villages and settlements were less frequent than before.

Things stayed this way until we reached the little trading center of Pajule. There were two or three stores along one side of the main street, overhung with sun-bleached signboards, while house dogs, tired after a night of prowling, stirred reluctantly from the dusty verandas before barking, chasing, and then turning back. Small children ran out from dark doorways, waving and running forward in pursuit as we drew to a stop in the middle of the street. The music was already on by the time I had struggled from the cab. I felt tired as I picked up my safari jacket, still damp from earlier exertions, and with Visavadia in tow, we called on the two shop owners while Thomas stayed with the van to hand out leaflets to the growing crowd.

The men were dressed alike, khaki trousers and torn singlets; the women wandered about in faded sarongs with heavy bare breasts, while little children, excited and covered in dust, ran naked around the van. Our visit was obviously a treat for the local Acholi. They listened to the Kiswahili tape, and when it was over, they chatted excitedly among themselves. They made signs and gestures, nodding appreciatively as the words of advice floated from the van's twin speakers. When the tape ended, they clapped enthusiastically and made purchases of Herbalex and Gripe Aid from Thomas, who had put down the leaflets and was now engaged with the retail sales side of our business.

At the close of the show, we made a small delivery to each of the two shops. An army of children kept following us, begging for free samples. It appeared that every single child had a pregnant sister and needed Gripe Aid samples. We then closed down, locked up, and did a wide U-turn in the road, retracing our route for twelve miles before making a left turn taking us onto the Patonga throughway. It was the rule of our safari that whatever route we were on we must try to include any village that lay off the beaten track, however inconvenient. At times we became obsessed with reaching the next town, the next village, the next settlement, and this wasn't fair to those who lived in out-of-the-way places. After all, it could be five years or more before a van crew happened this way again, and what with independence around the corner, it might never happen again. At Pajule we had been within thirty miles of our destination, the important link town of Kitgum, but we were now faced with a tortuous dust-ridden track of about 120 miles, with a possible overnight stop in the desert regions running along the western edges of the Karamoja Province.

On this extended route we promoted our products to an untried audience. As far as we were aware, no one had previously visited the area because of its low population count and isolation from other townships. It was already clear that it was unprofitable to trade in this area. An indication that we were the first to explore the region was brought to my attention when Thomas reported that no tin plates had been seen on the doors of the only two shop owners. We never lost sight of the fact that it was our job to advertise in the bush. I would say without hesitation that people enjoyed our visits, and a number of mothers named their *mtotos,* or babies, after our branded products. One pregnant mother told Thomas that she was going to name her baby John after the boss man, who, of course, was me.

This one-off safari was never thought of as a lost cause despite the deserted areas. We relied on the word-of-mouth that would be passed down the family from generation to generation, and with this as our guiding star, we saw our sales program as a wise investment for the future.

The villages along the route were widely separated, perhaps an average of ten miles apart, and because there were so few inhabitants at these places, we found ourselves losing track of time. It seemed our work was now being built on person-to-person contact. We shook hands, smiled, chatted at length, and listened to their problems. On some occasions we needed to use our first aid box or our own personal collection of medicines to treat those with minor ailments such as unhealed cuts, sore throats, bee stings, and abrasions. In truth we weren't able to advise anyone to consult a doctor, as in the first place there weren't any, and secondly such advice was beyond their financial capabilities.

We gave out leaflets, along with samples to those most in need, and invariably were asked to play "one more" record before we finally departed down the sandy road. Sometimes when giving a show, we put on a number of tunes, and the most popular were goombay, highlife, meringue, calypso, and mambo. Thomas privately reckoned that we could make more money by giving dances. By the time we had covered the villages of Paicham and Lira Palwo, it was becoming dark and overcast. Eventually, after much searching, we pulled off the dirt road a few hundred yards before the village of Patonga, located in the southeast corner of the Chua District.

We were tempted to make camp on the dry riverbed that ran at a right angle to the stony road. The place was marked by a distinctive baobab tree that had defied the passage of time. Its trunk was clothed in tattered bark, and one side of its wilted roots lay exposed on the ground. The secret of this tree is that it can store up to 450 liters of water and its seeds can be roasted and eaten or used to make necklaces, and finally the trunk can be hollowed out and be made into a house. The Aguga River was not only bone-dry but also afforded natural cover, giving concealment from across the endless plateau. However, we sensibly decided against using the riverbed as a parking place as we certainly didn't fancy being swept away in a rush of water in the middle of the night, although that was unlikely in the month of July.

We were now running two days behind our schedule, and it slowly dawned on me that with the present rate of progress in this isolated region, we well might have to spend a second night in the open before finally getting to Kitgum. This would undoubtedly cause hiccups with Morgans, which in turn would reverberate all the way back to London. As strange as it may seem, there were still intelligent people who seriously believed that the conditions under which we traveled varied little from a jaunt up the motorway to Scotland. They saw no excuse for failing to keep to a strict timetable.

In the morning we forged our way eastward and spent two hours at Patonga before moving to a small village called Adilang. From here the road swung north, running parallel with the desolate borders of Karamoja Province. The land was flat and destitute. The short-bladed grass had been eaten down or heavily trampled by searching herds of long horn cattle. Everything shimmered under the harsh rays of the sun. It was because of this intense heat that the nomadic tribesmen wore flowing robes similar to the galabiyah found in Egypt. They looked like moving tents as they herded their cattle. Small children could be heard yelling obscenities, beating the animals with long sticks as they strove to clear the track in front of our vehicle. There were older women with pendulous breasts following dutifully behind, carrying large clay pots and bedding on their heads, while young, innocent girls smiled sweetly, their shapely legs and firm breasts intermittently visible between the folds of brightly colored cloth. The day slipped by, and it was almost dusk when we finally reached the tiny village of Naam Okora. Again our progress was slow, and we still hadn't reached Kitgum.

chapter

SIX

On waking the next morning, it was already warm. The sky above was azure blue and hallmarked with the swiftly rising sun. Nature had signaled its message of unrelenting heat to come. Large black cattle flies swarmed about us while we had breakfast. It was a simple meal of paw-paw, fried eggs on bread, and two mugs of tea. We ate in silence, draping towels over our heads, a vain attempt to ward off both sun and flies. After we had finished, I left Thomas to clear up and get the van ready for the final assault on Kitgum, which lay some thirty miles west of our position along an empty dirt road.

I climbed back into the van and asked Visavadia to join me. It was stifling hot inside, and thick with flies that ceaselessly bit uncovered flesh. It was disconcerting, but there was little we could do, and we carried on regardless with a thorough stock check and audit. We tried to establish a routine whereby every last Friday of the month both Visavadia and I did a thorough check. However, as we dug deeper into the heart of Africa, it wasn't always possible as life became less predictable. We checked the cash in the black metal box and filled out the bank credit slips, and I made a start on the weekly report. Finally, before moving back onto the road, I wrote in my diary the entry for the day, Friday, July 29. It was simple and to the point: "We broke camp at Naam Okora at eight o'clock this morning."

Five miles farther down the track we pulled into the isolated village of Omiya Anyma. The atmosphere here was more down-to-earth. There were two or three shops, crooked wooden structures with a dozen or so mud and wattle houses circling a large, dusty compound hedged by green cacti. As usual, our music soon aroused the local populace. Children were first to come running from doorways, quickly followed by their mothers. We noticed with instinctive satisfaction that the shop owners peered from their stores once the tapes had started.

I went over and offered them the opportunity of buying Herbalex or Gripe Aid, making it clear that we would soon be retailing from the van if they decided against making a reasonable purchase—say a dozen bottles of each product. However, we would be happy to send our customers over to their shops the instant they wanted to make a purchase. We would also give them free advertising by broadcasting their shop's name as appointed stockists. We usually obtained an order for our products because the profit was guaranteed.

"Mr. Carter," Thomas said, as he walked toward me, "there's a girl who wants a lift to Kitgum. I said I would have to ask you."

"Where is she?"

"She's by the van."

"I'll be right over as soon as I've finished here," I said, ducking under the doorway of the third shop.

Everyone I met was covered in yellow dust. It was, therefore, something of a shock to the system to see someone who looked as if she had just stepped out from a shower. This girl did. She was standing by the front door of the van with a small suitcase propped against her legs. She appeared frightened, perhaps uncertain of herself, smiling nervously. "Please," she said breathlessly, "would you give me a ride to Kitgum?"

"I don't see why not," I said.

"You mean you will?" The girl seemed relieved and went on to explain, "I have a sister in Kitgum who works in a restaurant called the Star Inn, and there's a vacancy for me."

The girl was no more than eighteen or nineteen, about five foot seven inches tall, very attractive, with sweeping almond eyes and high cheekbones.

Her dark hair was rolled under at the ends. Everything spoke of the proud Sudanic people who lived in this northern-most region of Uganda.

"What's your name?" I asked gently.

"Nyka."

"Mine's John." I went forward and shook her hand. "When do you start your job in Kitgum?"

"On Monday," she replied. "You see, my sister wants me to come as soon as possible so that I can settle in and learn how they run things."

"You understand we have to work the route. It's about twenty miles to Kitgum from here, so the trip shouldn't take much more than two hours or so."

She picked up her case and gave a low wave to a couple who had been standing across the road from where we were parked. She then climbed into the back of the van.

"Those are my parents," she announced proudly, while making herself comfortable on some boxes of Gripe Aid.

Nyka didn't seem to fit the normal patterns of socially accepted behavior to be found in this empty region. One could clearly see that her parents were deeply affected by her departure as we pulled away toward Kitgum. As with all girls from the north, she was cherished and loved by her family. They were an investment, rather the same as coffee is to the Bagandans from the south, and their virginity was carefully guarded until the moment of marriage. A bride price was then paid by the groom to the girl's parents, and the seal over the wedding would now be firmly set. There was little chance of the marriage ever breaking up because the husband couldn't afford a second wife, and fortunately for the girl's parents, the bride being a virgin meant that they would not have to refund any money themselves. Nyka was obviously a modern girl not bound by tribal traditions. She was following in the footsteps of her sister by accepting a sophisticated job in a large market town. Even the way she was dressed—leather sandals, blue trousers, and a cream cheesecloth shirt—declared to the world her independence and unfettered femininity.

Less than two hours later we arrived in the dusty town of Kitgum. It had the same parched look of those isolated places in America's old West seen on so many TV movies. It was as though we had an audience as we drove through the heavily rutted main street. Groups of people loitered at corners or leaned on wood balustrades from the dark shade of long verandas. The

Safari Salesman

deep throb of music could be heard coming from juke boxes on one side of the road. And just as a cowboy might have tied his horse to a post and nonchalantly dismounted, we came to a halt in front of the bar and restaurant, otherwise known as the Star Inn, and clambered out of the sticky interior of the van.

"That's where I am going to work." Nyka pointed with pride. The blistering heat from the midday sun beat down, leaving no shadow to shelter under. "When you've finished whatever you're doing in Kitgum," she went on, "please come and see me."

"Sure," I said and smiled. "I'll drop by later."

"See you." She smiled back and turned to cross the road.

Later, after lunch, we began an intensive promotional campaign throughout the Kitgum area. We gave shows from one end of the main street to the other, and in so doing we covered the bus depot, the main shopping plaza, and the marketplace. We were well aware that sales had fallen off during the past week, so while Thomas worked the van, Visavadia and I made the rounds of the Asian stores, armed with leaflets, metal signs, and samples, looking for cash orders to fill the sales book.

It was only when the light began to fade that we finally called a halt to our operation. There was hardly a person left in the town who hadn't heard of Herbalex and Gripe Aid.

"Where are we going tomorrow?" Visavadia asked, scratching at the stubble on his face.

"We'll cover the villages north of here."

"So we're staying two nights?" Visavadia climbed out of the van with his heavy wooden case. It was getting near dusk. "Where will you pick me up?" he asked.

"Outside the Star Inn, where Nyka works," I said.

"That's handy," Thomas cut in.

"Why did you say that?"

Thomas shook his head in amusement. "Only that I'm fixed up with a room on the opposite side of the road. I met some friends from Nairobi during my lunch break. They run a bed-and-breakfast place with a bar downstairs. It's called Casuals."

"That leaves me on my own," I said.

"I'll drive you down to the police station to see about the key to the rest house," Thomas suggested.

"Yes, I'd appreciate that."

Twenty minutes later the key was safely in my pocket, and it was dark by the time we returned to Kitgum. I dropped off Thomas and found myself alone in the van. It was a decidedly rare occasion, and I was torn between joining Nyka at the Star Inn, where I would get something to eat and drink, or going straight back to the rest house and getting my weekly report done. I came to the conclusion that it was highly likely that the place would be inhabitable due to its remoteness, and I didn't fancy doing my report under a lantern with "things" running around in the semi dark.

In the end I decided on a mixture of the options, and with this in mind I drove to the end of the main street, made a circle, and found a place to park outside a defunct bakery, about a hundred yards down from the Star Inn. I quickly switched off the headlights and put on the cabin lights, placed my portable typewriter on a stack of cartons, and went to work on the report, beginning with the words: "Dear Sirs, I am pleased to report that our sales," etc., etc....

An hour later I strolled down the middle of Kitgum's main street and breathed in the night air. It was relaxing, a panacea to pressure, as at last I was doing nothing—no selling, no traveling, no writing, and no camping. I saw the glow of a lantern from under the eaves of a veranda. A group of Asian lads were sitting cross-legged on reed mats playing cards. They broke off from their game when I walked by and exchanged greetings. Here, up-country, the traders would stay close to their homes to avoid feeling isolated and vulnerable.

"Hello." Nyka smiled as I entered the inn. She got up from a table near the doorway and came over to the bar. "Have you had anything to eat?" she inquired.

"That's nice of you to ask," I said, "but all I need at the moment is a drink and a cheese sandwich."

"What would you like to drink?"

"I'll have a Scotch and Coke please."

Nyka went to the other side of the counter. "This is Lathelia, my sister," she said as she reached for a bottle of whiskey on the shelf behind her.

"I've heard all about you," Lathelia said with a laugh as she went to the end of the bar to serve an impatient customer who was tapping on the counter with the edge of a shilling coin.

"If you want," Nyka began, "I can come to the rest house with you." She lowered her eyes and smiled sweetly. "I'm off duty until Monday, and maybe I can give you some help with the cooking?"

"That sounds all right to me," I said, "but first I must pay for my refreshments."

A short while later we drove out of town and turned left at the far end of the main street. We followed a weather-beaten signboard that pointed up a narrow laterite track. About half a mile later the isolated rest house showed up in the penetrating beam of the van's headlamps.

Inside there were two sparsely furnished bedrooms, a small bathroom with paint flaking off the walls, and a bare kitchen with some plastic shelves and a rusty sink unit. "Could be worse," I commented as I watched a raggedy line of cockroaches scurry across the broken floor and disappear under a corner cupboard.

I didn't want to dishearten Nyka's more positive mood, so I put an arm around her waist and pulled her toward me and added: "It's better than a lot of places I've been in!" The light from the hurricane lamp cast a long shadow on the wall, blending us into a single silhouette. I could feel her breasts pressing against me through her thin striped shirt as she lifted her face, wanting to be kissed.

***

It was Saturday, July 30, and after breakfast Nyka and I drove the same route back to Kitgum.

"In spite of no running water, no electricity and plenty of bugs," Nyka said with a laugh, "we seemed to have managed alright last night." She ran her hand along my leg. "What time will you be back?"

"I can't give you an exact time," I said.

"No problem." She smiled, and as she climbed down onto terra firma, she added, "I'll see you later anyway."

Thomas and Visavadia had been sitting on their suitcases outside the restaurant waiting for me to arrive. They both had wide grins on their faces.

Thomas couldn't resist a dig as he clambered into the van and exchanged places with me. "It's all right for some," he said, loud enough for Nyka to hear.

The dust flew everywhere as we motored north toward the Sudan border, making our first stop at the little marketing center of Palabek, some twenty-five miles from Kitgum. There were only a few timbered structures. Seated on the terrace outside an Asian store were two young Africans hard at work, pedalling their sewing machines while threading bright patterned cloth under sharp needles. Thirty minutes later we worked our way northeastward, heading directly toward Paloga, which was dominated by the Lamwa Mountain to the west. After a ten-minute stopover, we made our way toward Padibe through the soulless tracts of unending land. The flatness was broken only by the scattered scrub of green cactus or the odd acacia tree. After retailing a few bottles from the back of the van, we departed for Madi Opei. The rugged slopes of the Lolibai Mountains stretched ad infinitum along the border.

The trading center of Madi Opei is the northernmost cornerstone for motorized traffic. It was an empty, desolate place in the far lands of Acholi Province. The township is encircled by a range of gigantic mountains that fringe the Sudanese border some twenty miles to the north. They bounded the view and led the eye upward across the shimmering wastelands, while closer in, and more sharply defined, was the Madi Opei Mountain itself. A farther eight miles to the north was the tiny settlement of Agoro. We made inquiries from a local man who told us that the route was impassable. He said it was made up of deep-layered sand and that our van would sink. "Camels can get through," the man informed, and added that a friend of his brother could arrange the trip if we were prepared to wait for a couple of hours. I thanked him profusely and explained we weren't that desperate to go to Agoro.

The only subsistence crop to survive in this arid region was finger millet, both drought resistant and tolerant to poor soils. The grains store well and do not come under attack from beetles. The ear of the seeds form six separate spikes, known as fingers, and provide a good source of starch, besides being used in the manufacture of beer. The leaves of the plant are fed to the large herds of nomadic cattle that roam the endless plateau.

Only a handful of local tribesmen gathered in the sweltering heat to listen to our Bantu-speaking tapes, initially wooed from their cattle tending by the lilt of Caribbean music. After the show we continued our journey on the sandy loams, curving south, back toward Kitgum, some forty-three miles distant. It was a slow, time-consuming process over narrow tracks swirling with sand and grit. Every now and then we had to stop when the track was blocked by mounds of heaped sand, and we then took turns to flatten the piles with our shovel.

At the village of Musini we halted again, handing out leaflets to a group of dusty, naked people gathered under a cluster of borassus palms, their fan-shaped leaves giving shade from the blazing sun. Five minutes later we crossed the dry, shallow bed of the Aringa River and covered the remaining miles of this deserted route, all of which was on a greasy cotton soil track. We reached Kitgum as the sun declined over the colorless horizon.

I dropped Thomas and Visavadia in the town center and drove the last mile back to the isolated rest house. The encroaching darkness had now changed into early night, and bright crisp stars flickered in the leaden sky.

"John," Nyka shouted as she rushed from the house, her warm smile full of promise. "I heard you coming up the lane," and with those words of welcome she jumped into the passenger seat.

"Tell me your news," I said. "And tell me all about your new job?" I asked as I kissed her on her glossy pink lips.

"Everything is wonderful," she cooed, "and I love my job. It's nice working with my sister." She paused for a moment and asked me if I was hungry.

"Yes, I am."

Nyka cuddled even closer. "Well, I'm getting the food ready for supper."

"Sounds great," I said with a smile.

For a few moments there was silence. "You go tomorrow and I'm already sad," she remarked without preamble, and tilted her head, adding, "We've had fun together, haven't we?" She stared hard into my eyes, her body trembling as she sunk against me. "I'm frightened, John." She stayed silent for a minute wrapped in my arms.

"Stop worrying," I whispered into her ear. "We're lucky to be with each other."

"You're right," she said, pulling herself backward and looking me up and down. "You look filthy in your clothes." She laughed. "Guess what I've done?"

"You tell me."

"I've had water put in the bath especially for you."

"Water in the bath." I smiled. "What next?"

"I paid a boy to bring the water from the well at the bottom of the garden," she explained. "I thought you would like it."

"You shouldn't have done that." I smiled and pulled her toward me.

"I've enjoyed getting things ready for you," she said on a breath, her mouth brushing mine as she spoke, adding, "Nothing's too much trouble, please understand."

"Anyway, let's not worry about tomorrow, promise me?"

"Yes, you're right," she agreed with a wide smile.

"I'd better go and have that bath then."

"I've boiled two pans of water that you can use to warm up the bath."

We strolled toward the rear of the house, and, on reaching a paved patio area, we stopped and stood silently under a lone jacaranda tree that was covered in blue blossom. The embers of a charcoal fire were on the wane; Nyka swiftly knelt down, puffed, and in no time at all lambent flames began to lick upward. Close by, on the edge of the paving, stood a saucepan of rice, a small tin of corned beef, and another pan of fresh yellow maize in clear water. Lying apart, on a flat wooden board, was a sliced loaf of brown bread.

Leaving Nyka to get on with the cooking, I went to the bedroom, opened my suitcase, and probed the lining with my fingers until I found a small package wrapped in tissue paper. It was a simple bead necklace of green jade. I took it out of the paper and laid it down on the old dressing table beyond the bed. The stones were almost luminous in the dimly lit room.

A minute later I poured the hot water from the pans, holding them with my towel, and then plunged into the bath. This definitely was an unknown luxury while in the bush, and I couldn't resist thinking that it was as close as one could get to spending a night at the Ritz. I had been lazing in the bath for nearly ten minutes when Nyka rushed in and announced that supper would be ready in ten minutes.

Safari Salesman

The meal was set on a small table close to the fire, and above our heads was a lantern hanging from a low branch of the jacaranda tree. A swarm of insects twirled around in its pool of light.

"Here's something for you," I said, sitting down at the table.

Nyka opened the small packet and gently pulled out the jade necklace. "It's lovely," she gasped. "It will always remind me of you." She held it up to the light, turning it carefully over in her slender hands. "Please put it on for me," she murmured.

Much later, after the meal was over, we wandered slowly back to the bedroom and lay down on the straw mattress that covered the old iron bedstead. Big shafts of moonlight slanted into the room through the unlined curtains. However, we were already in another world making furious love, and neither the obtrusive light nor shortage of time was of any importance.

***

"John, it's nearly eight o'clock," Nyka whispered into my ear. "It's time to wake up." She shook my shoulder and added, "I've brought you a cup of tea."

"What's the date?" I asked, trying to get my bearings.

"It's Sunday, July 31," she said in amusement, "and perhaps you want me to give you a weather forecast as well?"

I opened my eyes and blinked against the morning light. The chintz curtains were still drawn, giving seclusion, but still too thin to ward off the early sun.

"And hello to you." I smiled.

"I hate today," she said.

I sipped at the hot tea and put the cup down on the bedside table. "Let's look on the bright side, we've had the good luck of meeting one another, and I'll be writing to you when I get back to England. I can't do more."

Loud knocking on the front door interrupted our chat.

"Go and see who it is, please,' I asked Nyka as I reached for my clothes.

A few seconds later she reappeared. "It's a small boy," she whispered across the room, "and he wants to talk with you."

The boy, about twelve years old, was standing in the garden near the flower beds. A bicycle lay on the ground by his feet, and he looked nervously toward me as I stepped outside onto the veranda. He began to explain that he had come from Padibe, nineteen miles to the north, journeying by bus to Kitgum with his bicycle strapped to the roof rack. He told me that he was a pupil at the mission school run by the Catholic fathers and they were interested in buying some portable toilets. Apparently they had heard about our visit yesterday through the bush telegraph.

"What's your name?" I asked and smiled.

"Samson, sir," the boy responded.

"You must be hungry, Samson, after all that traveling," I said quietly. "You'd better come with me." I led him to the rear of the house, where Nyka was busy making breakfast. "We've got a guest," I told her, "and I think he's hungry and thirsty."

"No problem," she said quizzically.

"And what's more it seems I'll be spending another night here."

Nyka immediately broke away from cooking and ran wildly into my arms. "That's great," she screamed and tugged at my shirt.

"How come?" she asked.

I explained my change in plans, and thirty minutes later after breakfast, with Samson and his bike on board, I drove down to the center of Kitgum and picked up Thomas and Visavadia, who were once more sitting on the restaurant stairs. They were already packed for the journey south and were surprised to learn about the change in plans. They knew that the possible sale of six portables was not something to be treated lightly, while the opportunity to gain space in the cabin was unmissable.

While they were getting settled down, I dashed inside and left a message with the barman to tell Lathelia that Nyka would be back tomorrow, Monday morning, around nine.

On our way out of Kitgum, driving north, we passed an orchard clustered with butternut trees. Their dense crowns were covered with green plum-like fruit, and their leaves cast pools of shade onto the hot, flat terrain. It took less than an hour to complete the short journey to Padibe.

On arrival at the township, young Samson, who had been sitting in the rear of the van, directed us along a dusty path to the mission. The fathers gave us a courteous welcome, and after a cup of coffee and biscuits, they listened carefully while we answered their questions on the operation of the chemical toilets. They studied the illustrated brochures we had handed to

Safari Salesman

them that depicted the different colored models that were available in the portable toilet range.

After showing us the outbuilding to be utilized as a pupils' lavatory and examining a portable that we had unpacked, they gave us a firm order for six units and twenty-four gallons of chemical fluid.

We had hardly started our trip back to Kitgum when we were flagged down by a flustered Asian man standing on the sandy edge of the powdery road on the outskirts of Padibe. This time we were asked for twelve dozen bottles of Herbalex. He explained that people from the locality had been besieging his store asking for our products. "I've never known anything like it," he said. Unfortunately we had to tell him we could spare only two dozen but would take his order for the balance and pass it on to our agents in Kampala. It would then be up to them to ship the balance by bus once they had received confirmation from his bank. We followed him into his store to complete the sale.

While waiting at the worn counter for our money, I noticed a couple of swarthy Lebanese customers and a European-looking man. They were grouped in the corner of the store, by the hardware section, examining some pick handles. The big European left the corner and came over. "You the Medicine Man?" He smiled sociably.

"I guess you could call me that," I said, and added, "What are you doing here?"

He turned his head, pointing to the hills along the distant horizon. "My business is out there," he replied. The guttural tones of the thick Afrikaner voice, sharp and precise, seeped into the words.

"And what's out there?" I asked, looking through the open doorway from the shop front.

"Diamonds." He laughed loudly.

"You reckon there's diamonds out there?" I quizzed.

"Well, we've been prospecting in southern Tanganyika for over a year and found nothing and…"

"The Williamsons Mines have already covered that region," I interrupted.

"Yes, that's true, but the geological features are similar here, and what's more, there is a high carbon content in the ground."

"You shouldn't be telling me all this," I said and laughed.

"It's the back of beyond here. I don't have a problem with talking about our expedition. After all, we've found nothing yet."

"My name's John," I said, "and the best of luck to you."

"Mine's Jan."

We shook hands.

chapter

SEVEN

The heat could be seen rising off the parched scrub as we drove south to Gulu. It was very dry, and the yellow dust billowed like bonfire smoke. Old memories stirred in the mind, right back to the road accident that so nearly ended in tragedy some nine months ago on this self-same route. Today, Monday, August 1, we hoped our luck would be better. This time there were no earlier rains to muddy the track and leave deadly water-topped sinkholes.

After we passed through the empty trading center of Lagute, Thomas slowed the van and cast a hesitant glance in my direction. He then turned his attention back to the road and the endless savanna.

The gray shadows from a cluster of borassus palms gave temporary cover to a motley herd of goats and sheep. They chewed mindlessly on the desiccated vegetation, and for a moment the watchful eye of their shepherd boy stole a look at us as we dropped a Herbalex leaflet.

A few miles later, Thomas broke his long silence. "It was about here it happened," he said flatly. He slowed the van down to a crawl. Visavadia got up from his seat, not asleep this time, but alert, and leaned forward and looked through the fly-encrusted windshield. He said nothing as we passed the spot. There was nothing to be seen anyway. No sign of anything to interrupt our steady progress. No scarred road shoulders, no pieces of metalwork. Only the monotonous line of the red murram road. It was as though we had never come this way.

"Let's go," I said, and in response Thomas pressed his foot down on the accelerator and double-declutched into a higher gear.

We stopped for ten minutes at the sparsely populated village of Oyelomon. We were now only thirteen miles away from Gulu.

It was strange to be back here; only weeks seemed to have separated the visits, not months. Everything about the place was so familiar. The boulevard sprinkled with irregular lines of densely crowned butternut trees; the dusty old post office where I had sent the telegram to Morgans; the sloping street, thick with traffic that had squeezed me onto the stony shoulder, where I had stumbled and caused the wound on my back to open up and stain my khaki shirt.

The front desk at the Acholi Inn was empty. I tapped the brass bell and listened for the hushed sound of approaching feet and the creaking of hinged doors. The landlady soon emerged from the passageway that led from the kitchen. "Haven't I seen you before?" she asked tentatively. A puzzled look creased her forehead.

"Yes," I said, "I had that accident on the Kitgum Road in October last year."

"Now I remember." She smiled. "I always wondered what happened to you. I'm so glad that you are all right. Theodore will be pleased to see you." She leaned back from the pinewood desk and turned toward the darkened corridor. "Come here a moment, Theodore," she called.

"Hey, look who's here," Theodore exclaimed quietly as he entered the hallway. "How're things?" He grinned, shaking my hand in two ways, the African way.

I have watched Africans meet many times; they bow with grace, extend a reverential hand, and begin to talk in low, interested tones that slowly rise in animation. I was deeply proud that Theodore had thus accepted me as a friend, and come to think of it, what more could one want when traveling in the bush?

"I'm great, thanks." I smiled, and then added, "And you don't look so bad yourself."

"Do you remember the nurse who worked at the mission? The one who fixed your shoulder and slipped some bandages is your case?"

"Lettue." I smiled. "I'll never forget her and her kindness."

"Well, she came down here the day after you left for Kampala to find out how you were..."

"And you became good friends," I cut in.

"More than that." Theodore grinned. "We got married, and we're going to be parents in a few months' time."

"Well, how about that?" I said in astonishment. "Congratulations to both of you."

"Thank you."

"Where is she now, as I'd love to say hello?"

"She's got a couple of weeks off and is with her family in Lango Province."

"When you see her, give her my best wishes and tell her not to forget the Gripe Aid."

We both had a good laugh.

After lunch I sauntered into town and met up with Thomas and Visavadia outside the local Gaumont cinema. Gulu hadn't changed, and there was no reason why it should have. The small streets that fell away from the main boulevard were packed with people of many races. It gave the town a cosmopolitan character.

From the cinema we drove to Baggs's Garage, which was a mile out of town. These were the people who had collected what remained of our accident last October. We had received a request from London to visit their premises and determine if there was any worthwhile salvage that could be reclaimed on behalf of the insurers, even though they had long since met our claim. There was nothing there; only pieces of tangled wreckage scarred with broken metal and torn paneling covered in burn marks. Everything was reduced to debris, and the only complete part to survive the crash was the rusting chassis hidden under the thick undergrowth of the owner's backyard. Our visit, needless to say, was a waste of time, and it made one wonder at the naïveté of the person who put forward the idea of such a visit.

After leaving the garage we stopped at the railway depot to load another consignment of stock. The next two hours were spent visiting wholesalers and giving promotional shows in the market. We finished our work before five o'clock, and I decided it might be interesting to call at the golf club. It was like another world, with lush, well-tended gardens with evergreen privet hedges lining the finely graveled driveway. Herbaceous borders ran to meet newly mowed lawns, while cassia plants, redolent of cinnamon, dotted the steep slopes approaching the clubhouse. And in the rich earth beds, circling the building, were a variety of tropical mallows, gardenias, and mauve hibiscus shrubs. It was here that the scent of red jasmine wafted gently from the climbing frangipani that festooned the immaculate, well-pointed brick walls.

The bellboy at the reception desk was quick to inform me that the manager was unavailable at the moment. However, if I would like to wait for a few minutes he would try to contact him.

"Fair enough," I answered and placed my card on a small silver salver he held in his hands. From there I crossed the lobby to the far corner and went into the cocktail lounge. It wasn't long before I fell into conversation with another Englishman, who told me that he used to work as an agricultural adviser in Zanzibar. "And what's your line of country?" he asked, tipping back a large pink gin.

"Patent medicines, chemicals, toiletries, and disinfectants," I said.

"Have you been in these parts before?" he pursued.

"Yes, I was here last October," I responded as I propped my elbow on the bar.

"Here, let me." He smiled, clicking his fingers to attract the barman, who was busy slicing a fresh lemon. "What's yours going to be?"

"Thanks, I'll have a lager." I smiled and added, "By the way, my name is John Carter."

"David Barnes," he said as he leaned forward to shake hands, and then immediately fell silent while the barman filled the glasses.

The cocktail lounge was a long, wide room with two square oak-stained pillars and a row of latticed windows facing out onto the front gardens. Bright rays of sunlight filtered through the windows and formed splashes of magnified light on the polished parquet floor, partially covered in a deep red carpet. The spacious room was pleasantly furnished with comfortable leather armchairs and dark mahogany tables. The oak-paneled side walls were hung with watercolors depicting late eighteenth-century golfing scenes. They hung in a straight line from wood-carved picture rails. A sign in gold lettering indicated a billiards room that led away from the lounge on the far side.

Barnes remained silent, looking thoughtfully into his drink before pulling a pack of Kali cigarettes from the top pocket of his colorful native shirt. "There was a road accident on the Kitgum to Gulu highway around that time," he said thoughtfully. "It caused quite a stir. A truck hit a sinkhole and smashed to pieces...." His voice trailed off as he paused to take a drink.

"Why did it cause a stir?" I asked.

"Well," he began guardedly, shifting his feet, "the accident must have happened about six o'clock on a Saturday evening. A young couple recently arrived from the UK, who happened to be members of this club, had been invited to a dinner party at the District Commissioner's residence near Kitgum. Apparently, so the story goes, they came across the accident, and instead of stopping to help, they drove round the crash, leaving the three people badly injured on the road. We learned on the radio the next morning that one of these chaps was a European, but that was beside the point. The whole thing was a bad show!"

"Perhaps there was a reason for not stopping," I said.

Our stilted conversation began to falter, and I took the opportunity to signal for another round of drinks. A noisy foursome of golfers had now entered the main doorway and took a table in a paneled recess to one side of the lounge. Their laughter slowly died away as a waiter took their order, and then they settled back onto a large red leather settee and matching armchairs.

"It's funny you should say that," Barnes said. "They did have a reason for not stopping. They thought there had been an ambush and they wanted to get away before anything like that happened to them. It was as simple as that. They were young and had never been outside the UK before, you know, fresh blood for the mozzies, that sort of thing. But it did leave a bad taste in the mouth of the old African hands at the time." Barnes stopped talking to offer me a cigarette.

"Thanks." I smiled, inhaling the strong local tobacco.

He put his gold lighter back is his pocket. "The thing is, we all knew about the accident from the broadcast, and quite a few of us had seen a European man limping around town."

"I don't understand the point you are trying to make," I said politely.

"Simply that quite a few of us could have offered help at the time, but as with the young couple from this club, we did nothing. It wouldn't have been too difficult to find out that the chap in the accident was staying at the

Acholi Inn, but he had left by the time we got around to calling." Barnes stubbed his cigarette out in the glass ashtray. "I think people can be frightened by a stranger." He smiled in my direction.

"I wouldn't let it worry you," I assured. "You see, it's my turn to apologize. I feel guilty for letting you go on talking. I just had to listen to you first. I was the European in that accident."

"Oh, my God," he said. "I'm awfully sorry." Barnes jerked forward and moved his feet up onto the brass rail that was bolted to the parquet floor.

"It's all right," I reassured. "It's all forgotten now. I have no bad feelings. It's just one of those things."

"You look well enough, I must say," Barnes said with a look of relief, adding, "What about the other chaps who were with you?"

"They are alright too." I smiled.

A young African waiter came to the bar. "Excuse me, sir," he said, "but the manager will see you in his office now."

"Nice meeting you," I said to Barnes. "You don't have to worry anymore."

***

On Wednesday morning, the third of August, we finally left Gulu for the forty-four-mile drive north to the trading center of Atiak. We motored through extensive cotton-growing areas, the pyramid-shaped cotton plants obscuring any view from the road. After several miles the black, oily tracks gave way to firmer, sandier ground. The rich loam soils supporting cotton had now gone. The new scenery was flat and bleak. The shacks in the isolated settlements were no longer of mud bricks and straw, but were partly made up of old timber and were set back from the road behind prickly cactus hedges. They were circular shaped and set out in clusters, rather like the rondavels in the southern parts of the continent.

We made a short stop at the village of Lamogi and resumed our journey northward at a steady thirty miles per hour. We went through the isolated and almost deserted bush settlements of Pabo and Palaro. An hour later we arrived on the dusty outskirts of Atiak, bypassing the frontier post leading farther north to Nimule in the Sudan. We curved left and drew to a halt outside the only store operating in this remote town. A long white board

Safari Salesman

hung suspended on rusty chains over the open-terraced entrance. The sign, in fat red letters, stated simply Chowdari & Sons—Wholesalers and Retailers.

We clambered out of the van, and with the palm of our hands we banged the dust from our clothes and stretched our legs in the deep orange sand that covered the main street. The temperature was in the low nineties, and the only shade came from a few butternut trees.

Within moments of our arrival, Visavadia had the music going, and as expected in these remote regions, we drew only a small crowd, say of twenty or thirty people. It was while I was talking to a young African mother with her baby tightly bound to her back that I was approached by a uniformed askari in blue shorts and matching shirt. It immediately occurred to me that he was going to object to our loud music, despite the fact that the only complaints we had in the past had come solely from the authorities in the large urbanized towns, and with this in mind I signaled to Visavadia to tone it down.

"I've come from the customs post down the road," the askari explained in serious tones as he dismounted from his bicycle.

"And how can I help you?" I replied cautiously.

"An old man has been taken suddenly ill, and we want to commandeer your truck to transport him back to his home in Nimule. It's about twenty-five miles each way, and then we will give you your truck back." The soldier paused to get his breath as small blobs of sweat ran down his cheeks and dropped onto his neat blue shirt. "This man needs a doctor urgently," he said.

This was a bitter blow, as we were tired and hungry and it was the end of a long, hot day. All we had left to do was to complete the present show, call on the one Indian wholesaler and retailer, namely Chowdari's, and search for a campsite a mile or two up the dirt road. "You leave us no choice," I said, "but there's no need to commandeer our vehicle. We'll take him there ourselves if you can tell us where he is."

"He's at our border post."

"And how are we expected to get into Sudan with no entry documents? I take it that Nimule is in the Sudan?"

"My officer will fix those details for you, and anyway, we have already received word that all formalities will be waived in this instance."

"This man must be quite important," I surmised, brushing away any possible reply. I immediately agreed to run this errand. "Give me ten minutes to wind down things here," I said, "and we'll come straight to the border post."

"Are you quite sure?"

"You've got my word."

"Tell them you've come for Mr. Assad," he said, "and be as quick as you can, as the road is closed to traffic after six p.m."

The red-and-white wooden barrier was down when we arrived a few minutes later at the Ugandan frontier post. A line of people straddled the dusty walkways leading up to a low, concrete building. Tall Arabic men in flowing blue-and-white jibbahs, their heads swathed in loose turbans, stood patiently in line. The women, in yellow robes, waited silently under the heavy canopy of a solitary acacia. They had unwieldy bundles and heavily strapped suitcases bulging open at the sides precariously balanced on their heads.

I got down from the van, eased my way to the front of the line of people, and managed to squeeze myself through the entrance.

"I've come to take a Mr. Assad to Nimule," I shouted to an officer seated at a desk. It was littered with papers, and a thin coat of dust covered everything. "I understand he's been taken ill," I went on.

There was a sudden silence in the stuffy room as the officer scraped back his chair on the concrete floor and stood up. "He's over there," he said in a set face, pointing to the corner of the room. He then opened his top pocket and pulled out a folded piece of paper. "Here, you can have this note and hand it over to my counterpart on the Sudan side."

The journey between the two frontier posts took more than an hour. The sandy road ran narrow, with deep wheel tracks about a central ridge. Our patient, a Mr. Abdul Asaad, was in a semi conscious state for most of the time, but he was well cared for by his two daughters, who had been with him since the moment he was taken ill. Upon our reaching the border post at Nimule, a Sudanese official quickly dispatched a messenger to the home of the local doctor. The old man was laid out on a straw litter, his dark face contorted in pain, as his daughters, shrouded in traditional black, mopped his brow with a damp cloth.

"This has got to be more than a fever," I said to the doctor on his arrival at the customs post.

The doctor knelt down on the floor and began examining the old man. "Probably brucellosis," he said after an interval, weighing up his own diagno-

Safari Salesman

sis and murmuring audibly to himself before coiling up his stethoscope and pushing it into his jacket pocket. "We'd better get Mr. Asaad into my car," he concluded, as he struggled back onto his feet.

"What's brucellosis in layman's terms?" I asked.

The doctor picked up his black medical bag and stopped mumbling long enough to make his reply. "It's an enlarged spleen," he said, looking up at the ceiling, "caused by goat's milk. It brings on that undulating fever, but he'll be alright once we get him home."

The moment they had gone, we said our good-byes to the Sudanese officer and headed back down the narrow dirt road toward Atiak in Uganda. It was dark now, and black, overcharged clouds raced low in the sky. A roadside acacia was momentarily lighted by the moon, and then went dark.

The storm clouds blotted our headlights while sudden gusts stirred the thick sands. We were deep in the desert, and there was nothing but hot wind and choking dust. Then the rain came. It was hard and drummed on the roof, deafening all other sound. There was no longer a view, and we slowed to a mere crawl, our wheels slipping into the heavy sand about the gullies.

"It's no good, Mr. Carter," Thomas chipped in. "We not only have a sandstorm, but a rainstorm too, and what's more it is getting worse by the minute." The glow from the lights on the dashboard shone against his worried face as he hunched over the steering wheel and peered out at the rain washing across the windshield.

"We'll call it a day," I said, and asked Thomas if there was any chance of pulling off the road onto higher ground.

He shook his head. "No way," he replied. "Everywhere is deep in sand, and anyway, this is a prohibited area after dark, so we'll be all right parked on the road."

We watched in silence as a pack of wild dogs, caught short in the storm, their yellow fur matted in grit and sand, loped wearily across the track. They tilted their sodden heads, snarling and baring white teeth directly into the beam of our headlights. But before we were able to absorb their presence they had sloped off into the darkness.

"We'll call on that Indian store tomorrow, and then we'll make for the ferry. Is that all right with both of you?"

"That's OK by me," Visavadia's voice floated from the eerie darkness behind my seat.

"Me too," Thomas agreed.

"Then let's have something to eat," I said, reaching for the portable stove that lay in a box at the back of the passenger seat.

Just over an hour later, we had settled down among the boxes and went to sleep.

chapter

EIGHT

"Mr. Chowdari, I presume?" I said to the old man who stood behind the wooden shop counter. He was possibly little more than fifty-five, but because he eked out an existence in this desolated place, there was already etched a number of deep, premature lines on his leathery face.

The wood counter ran the whole length of one side of the big room. It was stacked with irregular piles of tinned foods. There were open sacks with the torn edges folded down, displaying shapely mounds of rice, maize, lentils, purple eggplants, and starchy fu-fu flour. On the broad shelves behind the counter and over to the left, roll upon roll of imported silk rose vertically to the ceiling. Overhead, suspended from metal hooks in the cross beams, was a spreading forest of cooking pots, pails, pickaxes, spades, and spiky coils of barbed wire—all indiscriminately set out on the timbers, forcing visitors to duck their head to avoid a collision with a stray bucket or ax. Besides the section for hardware, there were other, less obvious areas for tobacco, patent medicines, toiletries, and a colorful array of French perfumes. The shelves on the walls at right angles to the counter were narrower and crammed with unending lines of essential items such as packets of tea, sugar, chocolate powder, salt, and thick glass jars of coffee—and closer to the bare floor were uneven rows of fizzy drinks weighing heavily on bending, white boards.

The shop owner smiled and leaned forward from his chair. "Yes," he responded in a quiet voice. "I am Mr. Chowdari." The smile emphasized the crow's-feet at the corners of his searching eyes.

I shook his hand. "My name is John Carter," I said. "And I want to apologize for not calling yesterday, but we were called away to help a man who had been taken ill."

"Not to worry, Mr. Carter," the owner said reassuringly. "You see, news travels fast here, and I have heard that you gave assistance to Mr. Abu Asaad. He's a good Sudanese customer of mine going back many years, and he's the mayor of Nimule. I am more than grateful you were able to help him. How is he now?"

"It was a sudden fever due to a stomach disorder," I responded, "and the doctor told me that he will soon be alright again now that he's home."

"That's good," Mr. Chowdari replied. "I was concerned that he'd suffered a stroke. Not many of us here live past sixty." He smiled as he got up from his seat and stepped away from the counter. He went over to a curtained doorway and shouted some garbled instructions in rapid-firing Punjabi. He then sat down again in his chair. "I handle most of the trade in this area," he continued, "and since your arrival in Atiak yesterday, I have received a number of inquiries for your products, and I would like to give you an order for six dozen Herbalex, and the same for Gripe Aid.'

"I appreciate that," I said. It was a rarity that I got an order without resorting to sales talk. I opened my briefcase and took out the sales order book and wrote the date across the top of the page. It was Thursday, August 4. I was filling in the details when the beaded curtains that partitioned the shop floor rustled and a young girl came into the room carrying a tray with tea and pastries, which she put on the counter.

Mr. Chowdari patted the girl on the upper arm. "How is my lovely granddaughter?" he said with obvious pride.

She appeared to hesitate for a moment, and instead of making any movement, she stood there holding the empty tray, uncertain of what to do next. Her head was slightly bowed in deference to her grandfather.

"Mr. Carter," the old man said, "this is Nindi." She slowly raised her head and gave a shy smile across the wood counter, projecting friendliness in her warm, sweeping eyes. Then, noiseless in her sandaled feet, she turned to go. I watched her as she strolled back out toward the curtained doorway. There was a glint of gold around her soft brown neck, but it was half-obscured by the provocative swing of her dark, waist-length hair.

"You must be very proud of her," I said openly.

"Yes," he agreed, "she is all I want in a granddaughter. Nobody could wish for more." Mr. Chowdari's expression became more set. "But sometimes I am made to worry about her future, even though she is all that is wonderful."

"Forgive me," I inquired carefully, "but why do you say that?" I didn't want to ask the question and make it look as though I was prying, but I felt irresistibly drawn into this girl's world. However private things might be to the family, it seemed natural to me to want to know more about her.

Mr. Chowdari pressed the tips of his fingers together in silent supplication. "I have a large family," he began at last, "and they all come and go as though this house is running like a hotel. Mind you, I am not complaining. But always Nindi stays home looking after the others—she is sister and aunt, but not a wife—and already she is twenty and promised to no one. She meets no one in this lonely place. The young men of Atiak leave here to find work in the more prosperous south. Naturally, with such a pretty girl, some did ask for her hand in marriage, but she says she must stay and look after the family. I even suggested to Nindi that I would write to my cousins in India to find her a young husband..."

"And what did she say to that?" I interceded.

"Like everything else, she rejected the idea. You see, in spite of what we may seem, Nindi herself has modern ideas. She believes that the right man will one day arrive and sweep her off her feet, so nothing I say will change her mind. This isn't our custom, and I would much prefer to arrange matters for her. All the time she gets older, and no one is ever going to find her in this isolated region and take her away on a white charger," Mr. Chowdari sadly prophesied, before he released his fingers and looked straight into my face with doleful eyes.

"The world is changing for everyone," I replied in worn platitudes. "She's very beautiful. I'm sure it will be alright."

"Tell me, Mr. Carter, are you returning to Gulu today?" The old man smiled, changing the subject.

"No," I said. "We're going on west to Moyo."

"Oh goodness." He seemed surprised. "You obviously haven't heard that the ferry from Umi to Laropi has broken down. I am informed that it definitely won't be running today. In view of this, you must spend the night here as my honored guest."

"That's very kind of you," I said, accepting his invite.

"You'll be most welcome."

Thomas came into the store carrying a carton of six dozen Herbalex. "Where do you want it?" he asked as sweat poured off his face and left dark pools on his T-shirt.

Mr. Chowdari got off his wooden stool and indicated an empty space at the far end of the counter. "Over here," he said with a low sweep of his arm. Thomas dumped the heavy box on top and slid it across.

"Where are your men sleeping?" the old man inquired solicitously as he shuffled toward the till to get the money.

"They'll be all right," I said, putting my mug down and reaching for a cigarette from the open box in front of me. "They've got the motor vehicle, and there's more than enough room for two people. It can sleep three if necessary."

There was silence while Mr. Chowdari counted out the fifteen pounds. I noticed Thomas glance across the room to where I was sitting.

"I would like your men to be my guests as well," he said finally. "It's not often I get the chance to entertain, and it's no trouble. I'm sure my family will be more than pleased to have you all under our roof."

"Thank you very much, sir." Thomas smiled at the old man as I signed the receipt.

The sound of blaring music drifted in from the dusty street. "I must go and do some work," I said.

"What time will you finish?" Mr. Chowdari asked. He pinned the receipt on a vertical nail holder and shut the till drawer.

"About five," I said.

***

Promptly at five o'clock, I re-entered the dark interior of Atiak's only store.

"Ah, there you are," Mr. Chowdari greeted. He was in the process of closing the louver shutters on the windows. "Ask your driver to take the truck around to the back," he said while he walked across the dimmed room. "There'll be someone there to show him where to park it."

I went back toward the door and stepped out onto the wide veranda. "Drive the van around the back," I shouted to Thomas before going back inside the store.

"Would you come with me?" The old man gestured, waiting to bolt the front entrance.

"Of course." I smiled, going back into the store.

After finishing locking up, Mr. Chowdari led me around the counter and through the beaded partition. It opened up onto a darkened storeroom; the only light came from cracks in the corrugated roof. We threaded our way along a narrow passage, bulging with unopened crates and shredded sacks. He pushed open the door at the far end, and we stepped out into a huge courtyard dotted with palms.

There were many small rooms with separate doorways abutting the south wall, and at the far corners, columned pilasters rose above the symmetrical stone turrets, giving off an atmosphere of peace and protection. On the left, beyond the high palms, Indian women in colored saris were busy supervising the cooking over open wood stoves. Two young Africans in white kanzus were brushing the smooth ground with short-stemmed switches.

"This way, Mr. Carter." Mr. Chowdari indicated the way with the open palm of his right hand.

We made our way in silence for a few more steps. "Please sit down." He motioned with another low sweep of his arm. A pair of plain rush mats were laid closely together on the bare ground.

"What can I say?" I gestured toward the surroundings, and then turned slowly back to my host. "It's fantastic."

"I'm happy you like my home." Mr. Chowdari beamed, clapping his dark hands and looking across the big compound. One of the young Africans dropped his broom and ran quickly forward. "Bring tea," he said in a quiet voice.

We talked in idle fashion about the weather and crops, and when the tea came we lapsed into silence. Then there was more plain conversation on business trends and the fears for the future in a politically changed Uganda when the British finally moved out. Mr. Chowdari mentioned the name Idi Amin and told me that this man was holding meetings in the northern region and preaching tribal rule. "He's in the British Army, you know. His home is in Arua, and he comes down here when he gets a weekend off, solely to stir up trouble."

Mr. Chowdari then changed tack and asked about England, cricket, and the royal family. These were precious moments. The sun had now disappeared behind the parapet wall, and all that remained were pale patches of light that tapered and flickered over the sandy courtyard. However, the diminishing light was replaced by the steady glow from burning lanterns that were set at intervals along the wide perimeter.

"In an hour we will be eating," the old man said, getting up from his mat.

"I think I'll go and check that everything is all right with the van," I replied.

Mr. Chowdari rang a handbell and summoned an assistant to show me the way to where it was parked. I was told that Visavadia and Thomas were already being looked after by members of Chowdari's large family. At last alone, I washed, shaved, and changed into a white shirt and a creased pair of light blue acrylic trousers.

"Ah, here you are," Mr. Chowdari greeted me when I returned three-quarters of an hour later.

A knot of people were grouped under the palms, nodding and smiling as the host made the introductions. Then, when I had met everyone, I sat down on a mat between him and his wife, and seconds later, two serving men, their hands bound in cloth to prevent burns, carried out an immense pail of steaming curry, which they planted on the ground in front of the diners.

A metal ladle was then used to fill the plates, and while this was going on, two more servants hurried backwards and forwards with earthenware dishes piled high with chapattis, seasoned vegetables, and naan bread.

Later, when all traces of the curry had gone, we were served a choice of elaborate sweetmeats, and again, more spicy tea. We heard the sound of musical instruments being tuned up, and as the conversation fell away, heads turned expectantly toward a trio of musicians beneath the towering palms.

Safari Salesman

The leader of the group sat cross-legged on a red embroidered carpet of entwined yellow serpents. His instrument was a veena with seven strings—four main and three auxiliary—and along with it was a fretted fingerboard with a pair of dried gourds angled between his knees. Behind him, and over to one side, was a second musician poised over a set of nagara drums; while a third man stood slightly apart, almost aware of his lesser status, and drew large circles in the air with a long ivory flute.

And suddenly, without warning, the fast hypnotic beat of music broke through, instantly shedding the discordant tuning of their instruments. Then, once again without warning, three young girls leaped into the arena from the shadows and, with legs bowed, feet pointing out in the traditional stance of temple dancers, and their hands depicting the legendary lotus blossom, they began to weave, keeping time with the deafening rhythm. The exotic movements gave way to a series of low sweeping passes and the flash of dark upturned eyes. It was only then I realized that Nindi was one of the dancers. It was unexpected, and what with her bright red and gold sari, heavy makeup, and the mark of bindis on her forehead—along with the pounding of the music—made me wonder if this scenario wasn't in reality a Bollywood production. But like all pleasures, it was soon over.

"I hope you enjoyed the evening," Mr. Chowdari said, getting up from his mat.

"Your granddaughter is very talented." I smiled, and with the music still ringing in my ears, I added, "This will be a night to remember."

"I'm glad it went so well," he said. "Anyway, I'm now going to leave you in the good hands of my sister, Jagdish. She will make the arrangements for your sleeping here." He turned and nodded to his relatives before moving away into the shadows on the far side, near to the perimeter wall.

"Please come this way." Jagdish pointed a finger to a line of mats laid out across the center of the courtyard. "It's too hot to sleep indoors this time of the year. You can have this one," she said, indicating a bed.

"Thank you," I said, "but I must first go for a wash."

Some ten minutes later I returned to find Jagdish settled on the next bed to mine. I smiled in her direction, realizing that diplomacy dictated that the sixty-year-old woman, sister of Chowdari, was designated to look after my needs while under his roof. Not wishing to offend her in any way, I lay silently on my back and stared at the stars. Not long afterward I heard rustling coming from the bed on the other side, and thinking it might appear to be rude should I steal a glance at my new neighbor, I closed my eyes.

"Hello," a voice whispered. "Did you like my dance?"

Unbelievably, it was Nindi, her dark upswept eyes tinged with amusement, the thin bedcover pulled close to her chin.

"Yes, I thought you were great."

"It made me happy that you were watching," she said in a hushed voice, before slipping a slender golden-brown arm free of the cover and reaching for my hand.

It was only a matter of minutes before we both fell asleep.

The first bright rays of a yellow sun spread across the big compound. I soon found myself awake, blinking at the morning light, and not totally aware of the strange but hospitable environment. I checked my watch and found it wasn't yet six o'clock. Nindi had loosed my hand during the night and was now well awake. She stretched her arms, extending them in a wide V shape behind her head.

"Did you sleep all right, John?" she asked, propping herself up on an elbow and trying hard to stifle a yawn.

"Yes." I smiled, glancing down at the gentle rise and fall of her breasts under the simple white cotton pajamas. The bed behind me was already empty, and there was no sign of Jagdish, but some of the other beds were still occupied.

"Is there any chance of taking a shower?" I asked.

"Sure." She smiled, showing off an immaculate set of pearl-white teeth, and pointed to a large doorway set in the outer wall beyond the concrete structured houses. "Go through that opening over there, and follow a worn path until you reach a wooden shed. That's the bathhouse for our guests."

"And is there soap and a towel?"

"There's soap there," she replied, "but I'll have to bring you a towel. The shower is worked on an overhead cistern that has to be filled with water from a nearby tank. You'll see what I mean when you get there," she added with a little laugh.

As I left the compound, I noticed that other members of the Chowdari family were now out of their beds and neatly folding the light blankets. I copied what they were doing as I thought it would show that I had the good manners expected from an Englishman.

The directions given by Nindi were easy to follow. The pathway was lined on one side with a spiky thevetia hedgerow that opened out onto level ground circled by green cactus shrubs. The bathhouse stood in the middle and was partially shaded from the swiftly rising sun by a red-flowered flame tree. The water was in a large metal drum, murky looking, and covered in a thin layer of dead insects, which I scooped aside with my hand before dipping the bucket. I had to make eight trips from the drum, climbing a rickety stepladder, before the cistern above the shower unit was finally filled with the dull-colored water. The shed had been built without a roof, and although that allowed for a more hygienic atmosphere in the tropics, it did mean there was an easy entrance for snakes and lizards. I checked the place, but outside a dozen or so green chameleons, better known as two-lined skinks, which had glued themselves onto the tiled walls, as far as I could see there was little else to worry about. I was just testing the cord that released the water through the sprinkler when the door sprang open.

"I've brought you the towel you asked for, and a fresh cup of tea," Nindi said, smiling happily.

"Thanks very much," I replied with a smile.

The tea tasted hot and was spiced and blended with herbs. The feeling of warmth ran down my body.

Nindi hadn't moved from the doorway, so I reached out and put an arm around her waist. "Shouldn't you be going back?" I said quietly.

"What for?" she responded. "Jagdish thinks I'm getting wood for the cooking fire. You don't want me to go, do you?"

"No, of course I don't." I laughed. "I've wanted you since the moment I saw you." I began to undo the buttons on her blue blouse.

"And I you," she gasped. She peeled off the rest of her clothes and stood naked under the shower.

She looked more alluring than any Hollywood star I've ever seen on the screen. Her light brown body glinted in a steady shaft of bright sunlight, and her firm, shapely breasts tilted forward as we came together under the watchful eyes of the two-lined skinks.

chapter

NINE

The road out of Atiak was red and narrow with deep grooves about the central ridge. The rush of warm air through the open doors of the van did little to relieve the stifling heat. Every now and then we crossed flat concrete bridges, spanning shallow rivulets—umbilical cords from the deep-flowing Nile, giving off a network of rivers—their paths traced by dark, solitary trees that wound into the colorless distance.

I closed my eyes against the light and thought of the last few minutes I had alone with Nindi.

After making love we had fooled around in the shower, soaping each other's backs and pulling the frayed cord to let the water sprinkle down from the home-fashioned rose. I remember the long dark tresses that fell about her coffee-brown shoulders, the sound of the water splashing, and the happiness in her laughter. We both knew in those few last minutes in the shower that our time was running out. It was when she tilted her head up wanting to be kissed that I saw a real sadness come into her eyes.

"Please come back one day," she implored.

"I will," I promised.

She ran her long, manicured fingers through my hair. "I'll miss you, John," she whispered. "Always remember that we had this time together...." Her voice trailed away.

"Shush," I breathed, feeling her tremble in my arms. "I won't ever forget you." I looked again into her eyes. "You know," I said, smiling gently, "if we're not careful, Jagdish will send a posse after us."

It was at this point that the van began to shudder on the corrugated road, and without warning Thomas braked and pulled sharply over onto the tufted edging that ran level with the road.

Clearly, my thought processes were set elsewhere, and I had failed to respond to what was going on. For a matter of seconds, I sat immobile on the passenger seat and watched as Thomas leaped out of the van to open the rear doors while Visavadia scrambled over the cartons to put a lively record on the turntable. It was the music that lulled me back to life as it resounded across the desert, and without wasting another second, I climbed down from the cab onto the coarse, sand-like ground and joined Thomas at the back to deal with the first of our customers.

"Where are we?" I asked him.

"At a place called Pakeli," he said.

Fifteen minutes later we were again heading up the track, only to stop at another settlement. Then, at last, we arrived at our destination called Umi, which was situated on the eastern banks of the Albert Nile. We noticed two cyclists sitting on some rocks near the river. Their bikes were spread on the ground next to a pile of boxes that they had been transporting. The news was bad. Apparently a man from the Public Works Department had canoed across from Laropi earlier in the day to say that the ferry was still canceled.

"Nothing until Monday at nine," one cyclist said gloomily.

However, as it was Friday, and as we had a whole weekend in front of us, I gloomily set about typing up a weekly report. My typewriter was the sole means by which I could communicate with the outside world, save for those times when we were fully in touch with our agents at Nairobi, Kampala, Mwanza, and Dar. Of course, I had lost my original typewriter in our crash near Gulu, but my new portable was just as sturdy and had already served me well despite wind, rain, and the odd sandstorm.

When I had finished my report I searched for the pack of cards I had bought at a stationers in Nairobi, and after a good deal of rummaging, finally found them tucked away at the back of the glove compartment. When things like this happened, I always blamed myself for not looking there in the first place. It would have saved so much time. Anyway, after shuffling the cards, I sat down in the back of the van and played several games of patience. In the end I got bored and asked Thomas and Visavadia if they would like to have a game of blackjack with me, and to my surprise, they both answered in the affirmative. We then agreed to use matchsticks in place of money and to settle up at the end of the game. However, I had a gut feeling that Thomas couldn't resist the chance of possibly beating me. A good hour later we ended the game, and I discovered that I was down twelve shillings to him and three shillings and sixpence to Visavadia.

"Never thought I'd beat you," Thomas crowed.

"Somebody had to win." I smiled back at him.

We had lunch on the grassy banks of the Albert Nile. The meal was more about slapping flies and squashing insects than it was about eating. This weekend break in our routine seemed to have brought the best out in both my crewmates. Shortly after finishing the meal they both wandered off, and I soon lost sight of them among the growing crowd of would-be ferry passengers. This left me with nothing to do, and I was glad that I had remembered to buy some paperbacks before leaving Nairobi. Less than a minute later I was sitting on the rumble seat hidden from the sun, and opening a can of lager I started to read.

It wasn't long before I dozed off, and some three hours later I awoke when a mother with a baby on her back knocked on the paneling and asked for a bottle of Gripe Aid. It was quickly getting dark now, and I lit the paraffin lamp. I took a stroll round the van, looking in all directions in the diminishing light. There was no sign of either Thomas or Visavadia. This wasn't a surprise as they were both sociable people, although it seemed that Thomas was the more gregarious while Visavadia was the dark horse and at times was difficult to fathom out. Anyway, I had no doubt that by now they had made new friends among the growing population of would-be passengers.

I decided the time had come to cook myself a meal.

***

By the following morning, the number of people who had arrived at the ferry point had swelled and the first tent had gone up. The overall picture was bleak. It had started to resemble a refugee camp, but that's where the similarity ended. Everyone, and every group, dotted around the ferry terminal acted independently and yet were favorably disposed to each other, and in all four corners of the camp there was an air of bonhomie. After all, we were all in the same boat—well, not yet anyway. Everyone had water, wood for fires, food to tide them over, and blankets for sleeping on. The fact that the ferry wasn't going to operate until Monday morning was immaterial. The invigorating sound of laughter and the chatter of voices bore witness to this mood of optimism. There was hardly any criticism of the ferry operator, just an easy acceptance of the delay.

About seven o'clock, Thomas and a couple of his new friends sought me out and asked if they could put the word about that we would organize a Saturday night dance. In fact what he and his friends really wanted was for us to play music over our loudspeaker system.

"That's not a problem," I assured, and suggested that he find Visavadia and ask him to be the disc jockey. I also made a proviso that the session was to be started and finished with an address in Swahili telling the audience that the program was coming to them by courtesy of Herbalex and Gripe Aid.

"I'll do the announcement live," Thomas volunteered.

"What about Visavadia?"

"I'll get him. He's somewhere over there with his Asian friends." Thomas pointed with forefinger.

Thirty minutes later Thomas made an announcement concerning the excellent quality of our products, which was immediately followed up by the sound of a calypso that drifted invitingly upward in the warm evening air.

On the whole the dance was a great success and was continued without so much as a break for two hours. But before we packed in, Thomas again advertised our two products and informed the listeners that we would conduct sales for two hours tomorrow morning between ten and twelve o'clock.

We considered this approach both subtle and fair. We didn't wish to antagonize our captive audience, nor did we want to incur the displeasure of the head office in London. It had to be acknowledged that they were our paymaster, and it was costing the company's shareholders good money to keep us on the road. But how would they know we weren't up to scratch? Well, it would show up on our daily sales sheets, giving nil returns for Saturday and Sunday. It wouldn't be long before we got a letter asking for an explanation of these non results; and somehow I don't think that Head Office would swallow the story that our ferry had broken down for three days.

Anyway, on Sunday morning we played soft music and did a brisk business, selling a total of five dozen Herbalex and two dozen Gripe Aid.

However, our most memorable moment came in the afternoon when Visavadia landed a three-pound Nile perch from a tributary flowing into Lake Albert. What was so extraordinary was that he borrowed one of our staves for a fishing rod and a length of wire from the van's toolbox to make the line. He then bent a nail, baited it with a mudskipper, and cast it into the fresh waters of the surrounding lake. Unbelievably it was the first time he'd ever attempted to fish, and that night we had fresh fish and chips for dinner.

At a few minutes past nine a.m. on Monday, August 8, the river ferry hove into sight from the opposite bank. Thick black smoke curled upward from its single, yellow-painted stack, and the heavy drone of its engine reverberated as the twin paddles labored against the strong current. A trail of white-capped water frothed and bubbled in the wake, and we watched in silence as the two-man crew manipulated the long, flat-decked ferry into position and secured it to the jetty.

There were more than a hundred people waiting to board. Fortunately, our van was one of the first in line, with about seven or eight other vehicles behind us all perilously loaded. Each of them was resigned to a long wait, as no more than two vehicles could be taken on board at a time. Thomas started the engine and eased the van gently down the steep metal ramp. He was waved on by a lone deckhand. We caught sight of the captain, leaning from the tarnished superstructure, cajoling passengers to move aft and make room for those who were still waiting in line.

We exchanged greetings with the two cyclists. They now had their boxes securely tied with sisal and piled high on the backs of the bikes. Other groups of Arab and Asian traders came on board, probably on their way to the important West Nile town of Arua, and gateway to the rich northeastern region of the Congo. Islamic women in black gowns and masked faces floated slowly across the studded deck and squatted on their haunches. The sharp bleating of half-breed sheep and undernourished goats was heard from the grassy banks beyond the wharf. Unfortunately the high-pitched sound of the flock of unruly sheep and goats was no longer distant; it was suddenly beside us, loud and deafening, their hooves catching on the dimpled metal as they roamed indiscriminately over people and property. It was hot in the van. A group of small boys kept coming up to us and asking for samples and leaflets, always insisting that it was for their friends, until the moment Thomas cracked under the pressure of heat and noise. He shouted at them to go away. He was immediately aware that he had broken the cardinal rule that states: "Thou shall not get stroppy with your customers." He hung his head low and just stood there and said, "I'm sorry." I put an arm around him and told him the incident was already forgotten.

There was more skirmishing when the herdsman suddenly appeared, shouting his face off, brandishing a thin bamboo cane while trying to round up his bleating, unruly animals.

"Come on," the captain shouted as he leaned forward over the rails that circled the superstructure. He then gave two blasts of the ship's siren, before adding. "Let's have you."

"Listen to that," Thomas said in amazement. "We've waited here since Friday afternoon, and now suddenly it's panic stations."

The ferry began to inch away from the shallow edges of the sedge-filled banks. It was good-bye to Umi and hello Laropi. We stared at the glum-looking faces of the people left behind. Some naked children lined the rocky slopes, laughing and joking, seemingly energized by all that was going on, while their parents eyed the departing ferry with a look of deep suspicion. It wasn't long before we reached the far bank; the whole excursion took about thirty minutes. Shortly it was our turn to drive off the ferry and out onto the red murram tracks of the West Nile Province. We went through the tiny village of Laropi and headed seventeen miles northwest toward a place called Moyo.

We hadn't gone much more than a mile down the dusty track when there was a shrill bleat from the back of the cabin. "What's that?" I asked Thomas, and turned around to have a look.

Thomas was bent over the steering wheel and was concentrating on the empty road. He took nothing for granted and small beads of perspiration dotted his forehead. "That's a goat," he replied out of the corner of his mouth.

I climbed from the seat and picked my way to the back of the van. There, standing on thin matted legs, splayed out to ride the bumps, was a shabby, undersized billy goat. He was busily engaged in chewing one of the cartons. "Did you pay for it?" I pressed.

"What do you think?" Thomas said in exasperation, and not waiting for an answer, added, "I gave the man twenty shillings before we boarded the ferry."

"You could have asked me," I said as I returned to my seat.

All I got for my trouble was a noncommittal shrug of the shoulders. By this time Visavadia had put his book down and was ready to add his two cents' worth. "It could be a health hazard, Mr. Carter. The thing is shitting all over the place."

This remark was like food to the hungry as far as Thomas was concerned, and he turned his head from the open road. "You'll be the first person to complain if you don't get your share of curry and rice tonight," he said in a toneless voice, before looking back at the empty road.

The sun was quickly arching into the blueness of the sky, and it left us with nowhere to hide. Its rays had the sting of a hornet, and struck at both the windshield and through the open doors. It could be argued that Visavadia was sitting in the shade, but there were no escapees; it was like an oven inside the van.

"Phew, it's hot," Visavadia exclaimed.

"You ought to try it where I am, and then you'd know you had it easy!" Thomas was never at odds for more than a few seconds. He simply enjoyed the jousting; in fact, it was more banter than joust. He just couldn't resist having the last word.

The rough track had begun to twist and turn, and a mile farther on it straightened out. We bridged a small stream, but it was nothing more than a mere trickle of running water between stony banks. On the far side of the stream we turned left and headed due south, and the wide view across the plateau was no longer there. The land became more broken. We passed huts scattered about the main road, and we saw a few people on bicycles carrying sacks of fresh vegetables. The red ocherous dust swirled from our tires, and it coated everything. It was far too hot to close the doors despite the dust. If we gave a show of hands, we'd prefer the dust to the boiling heat, but the two usually came together.

We soon progressed into the center of Moyo and pulled to a halt outside the town's white-bricked police station with its Union Jack hanging limply from a white flagpole. We picked up the keys to the rest house after we had exchanged the usual pleasantries with the resident officer. We explained to him our raison d'etre for being in Moyo, and gave him a sample of both Herbalex and Gripe Aid. We followed the directions he had given us and pushed onward through the far end of the village until we reached the only crossroads, and then swung left along a deeply rutted pathway, finally emerging onto leveled ground. The rest house stood alone—dilapidated and shabby with a tangled garden of wild canna flowers sprouting red and yellow from grassed-over beds. A small, spreading tonka bean tree, limp and dry looking, gave off a faint scent, its upper branches leaning precariously against the coping stones that lined the lower edges of the red-tiled roof. We watched while Thomas removed the goat from the van and tethered it to the underside of the bean tree—I had been worried that he might have broken one of its rear legs to prevent it straying, but I was happy to see that he hadn't done that. To me, the hobbling of an animal struck me as an extreme form of cruelty. Then, after taking our blankets and suitcases from the van, we trekked through sand toward the rest house. Once inside, the first thing we did was to find a place where we could bed down, and having done that we set about preparing a light midday meal of bread, tinned ham, and fruit, which was to be followed by a pot of fresh chuggan coffee.

When lunch was over, I left Thomas and Visavadia doing the washing up while I popped out to the van and poured some fresh water into a bowl. This was my offering to the goat, which needless to say, lapped it down.

It was after one o'clock when we returned to Moyo, and we spent the remainder of the afternoon giving a series of promotional shows along the main street before we made our usual calls on the African and Asian shops. We used the crossroads as our starting point and worked our way to the center of town.

It was after five o'clock by the time we arrived back at the rest house, and the first thing we did was to make a pot of tea. I had already noticed that there was an outside bathroom linked by a small passageway to the house. The whole place looked as though it had been built in the earlier colonial days and perhaps was once the home of a district commissioner.

I picked up a towel and walked the length of the passage. A musty smell was everywhere. The many doors that led from one room to another were wrinkled with dry rot, and none would close; the same went for the window frames, which were twisted out of position in the angled walls. The bathtub itself was seemingly a relic from the late Victorian days; the ornamental enamel was badly scarred, as were as the brass fittings. The water, when I ran it, gurgled and squirted out in brown-yellow jets. Anyway, it was better than having nothing, and after filling a quarter of the tub, I took a deep breath and launched myself into the syrupy water. I ended up sitting on a thick layer of sand and grit, and I was glad when five minutes later I climbed out, toweled myself clean of sediment, and returned to the bedroom.

Outside, through the open window, I could hear a continuous rasping sound and guessed it was Thomas sharpening his knife. I was not new to this, as Thomas had once before sharpened his knife with a whetstone that he kept in his leather suitcase. However, some moments later there was loud bleating and then total silence.

"It won't be long now," Thomas said, smiling as he walked into his room and threw himself on his bed.

An hour or more had passed since I had returned to my bedroom. "I guess I've been asleep," I said as I blinked against the light of the hurricane lamp that Thomas had placed on a nearby dresser. It was already dark outside, and insects were arriving by the boxful. Nonetheless, on the credit side was the strong smell of a well-seasoned curry that wafted through the warm night air. In the far corner of the room, Visavadia was opening his wooden case and pulling out an Asian paperback.

Thomas looked disappointed and turned toward Visavadia. "Aren't you going to eat with us?" he asked.

"Yes, I'll have some curry," he said in a quiet voice, as he slowly got off his bunk and followed us outside.

"I thought your fish was great last night," I flattered him, and added, "And what with Thomas's meat curry tonight, we're not doing at all badly."

Later, after the meal, we talked across the hot embers of the wood fire. There were pieces of goat's meat hanging from a wire that was stretched between vertical stakes, slowly curing in the rising smoke. Our conversation turned to the question of security. I pointed out to my colleagues that we could be vulnerable in this isolated place. Only the other week a cattle dealer had his throat slit with a panga while asleep in one of the up-country rest houses. He had been traveling south to the cattle areas of Ankole, and when they found his body some days afterward, he no longer had his well-filled wallet.

Our thoughts about placing trip-wires, battening down windows, or temporarily burying the cash box with its four hundred pounds were short-lived. Without warning we were subjected to a systematic attack by king-size mosquitoes. They went for our arms, legs, and necks. Normally their bite would be only a minor irritant or they would leave us alone entirely, our blood no longer having the fresh, sweet taste that they desired. However, this larger, more vociferous type of mosquito must have come here from the harsh arid regions of southern Sudan. Small splashes of blood began to stain our skin as we slapped our bodies. Their sheer size and endless aggression left us in no doubt that we had been carefully targeted, and we rushed into the house and threw the nearest blanket over our heads. Usually sitting close to a fire would keep them away, but there was no longer enough smoke to deter them. Curiously, it was the female of the species, with hairy antennae, that did the most damage. Some of them had already pierced our skin through the blankets in their desire for blood.

"I've had it, "I yelled as another swarm of mammoth insects zoned in. The whole room was alive with angry buzzing.

"It's hopeless," Thomas answered, lowering his blanket while he put a towel around his head, adding, "I'm going back to the fire and build it up. It's not so bad there!"

We followed him back outside and added some of our kitchen waste to the fire in the hope of getting more smoke. However, there was little respite for the rest of the night. At one point when things once more became intolerable, we got up from the roaring fire and went for a walk down to the crossroads and back.

Relief came as the daylight gradually broke across the flat sandy plateau, and the yellow rays of the early sun glinted intermittently among the greenness of the tonka bean tree. Some vultures were already busy unearthing the pitiful remains of the goat that Thomas had half buried beyond the strip of garden that ran parallel with the concrete wall that circled the house. The vultures had the appearance of funereal birds with their bald heads and black plumage. They made short work of the goat's remains by shredding the large pieces with their clawing feet and gulping it down. Every now and then they would jerk spasmodically as they forced the food farther down into their huge, empty crops. We ate our breakfast in silence and ignored the birds.

This was the most northerly point of our entire safari, although Nimule was on an identical longitude.

An hour later we were back on the road and heading southwest along a narrow, red dusty track. It was good to be working again, stopping at isolated trading centers, giving noisy promotional shows, and meeting new people. I was glad that I had that extra bit of sleep before we sat down to supper last night; it meant that I could drive the van while Thomas and Visavadia took catnaps between villages. Our bodies were sore from the hundreds of bites, and what we really needed was an uninterrupted night's sleep.

The places came and went—Koka, Yumbe, Ladonga, and Kaboko. We passed large groups of people tramping along the shoulders to the local markets; men in Moslem caps and white kanzus, the women, tall and majestic, their strong bodies swathed in orange-red gowns with vivid turbans on their heads. And all the time there were more villages. The bazaar area at Maracha, serving the twin townships of Ofude and Omogo, was thick with both buyers and sellers. And not long afterward we arrived in Arua. It was exactly three o'clock.

The town is headquarters for the important West Nile Region, providing a link with Aru, some fourteen miles south in the Congo. In order to mark out the border, there was a Ugandan frontier post at a place called Vurra, and beyond that point was a swath of deforested land, approximately eight acres, which was neutral territory. This no-man's land was acknowledged by charter, and it was here that each country operated a customs post in its half of the neutral zone. Nonetheless, the surrounding forest formed a natural border between the two countries.

We checked at the local police station for the keys to the rest house. The officer smiled when we related the story about our night in Moyo.

A second policeman approached the desk holding the keys. "You'll like the rest house," he assured. "It's partly furnished and regularly looked after by a caretaker."

"We are civilized down here," the other officer mimicked, roaring with laughter.

We left the station and clambered into the van.

"Is there a chance we might call it a day?" Visavadia leaned forward between the seats. "I'm tired," he explained.

"Yes, why not," I agreed. "In fact, let's all have the rest of the day off. It'll do us good."

***

The following two days were taken up with crisscrossing the immediate area surrounding Arua. This didn't prevent us from making a one-off journey to a place called Rhino Camp, some forty miles east and lying on the western banks of the Albert Nile. The town is primarily concerned with the marketing of cotton and forms an important link with other river ports, extending as far as Nimule in the north and Packwach in the south. Fishing, from dug-out canoes, for perch and other freshwater species is skillfully attempted with nets or shallow reed baskets.

On returning from Rhino Camp at the day's end, we passed endless tracts of bush scorched by grass fires. There were clouds of blackened ashes rising from the flat plains, and here and there we saw irregular humps of soot-stained anthills and solitary coral trees, nearly leafless, as flames reached up for the untouched branches like little flares of amber light. The smell of burned wood was everywhere.

Then, on Friday, August 12, we packed our cases and loaded them on the van. Before departing Arua, we returned the keys of the rest house to the police station. There was only one of the original officers on duty. We thanked him and handed over fifteen shillings for the three nights, and with that all done, we returned to the van.

This was a good time, before departure, to refresh my mind on our projected itinerary that had been put forward by London. I unfolded our road map and spread it partly out in front of me. Since leaving the ferry at Laropi, we had driven directly south, and it was now clear that we were to continue south until we reached the trading center of War. Then, ten miles on, we would need to keep our eyes open for a minor road, probably a dusty track, going east to Pakwach via the settlements of Nebi and Ngal. However, I noticed that the road, from start to finish, ran more or less parallel with the eastern side of the Belgium Congo.

"Let's go," I said to Thomas.

"Have we got everything?" he queried.

"We've filled the jerricans with water," I began, "and the gasoline tank is full and..."

"What about provisions?"

"Yes, you're right," I admitted, "I think we need to do a shop."

"Try the Bedi Store," Visavadia chipped in. "I can get a discount there."

"The Bedi Store it is," I said to Thomas.

Seated alone at his desk near the entrance of the store was Mr. Bedi himself. He was occupied in pouring a cup of hot tea into a saucer. "I've got all the Herbalex and Gripe Aid I can handle," he said with a smile as we came through the door into the shop.

"No," I replied and laughed. "It's our turn to buy from you."

"Seen today's paper?" he said, resting an arm across the brass till. "There's plenty of trouble in the Congo."

"Looks nasty," I agreed, glancing at the headline on the front page: STATE OF UPROAR IN THE CONGO.

"Would you like a cup of tea?" Mr. Bedi inquired, sliding a pack of Belgian cigarettes across the counter.

"Yes, please," I said, helping myself to a cigarette and handing a short shopping list to Visavadia.

"Mind if I read this article about the Congo?"

Mr. Bedi spread his arms wide. "Of course not."

It began: *By Henri Mauriac, Brussels Foreign Correspondent in the Congo—Thursday 11 August 1960.*

Units of the Congolese Army are today in a state of mutiny at Thysville, south-west of Leopoldville. It is strongly rumored that in the Oriente Province soldiers have not only mutinied and looted numerous shops, but have raped the wives of Belgian officers. The most serious of the present disturbances are taking place around the town of Watsa.

Our latest communiqué suggested that Europeans are grouping in the outposts of the Oriente and attempting to defend themselves against attack. Elsewhere, forces loyal to the Armed National Congalaise are involved in bitter fighting to win separation of the rich Katanga Province from the rest of southern Congo. These rebellious forces come under the direct control of Moise Tschombe, and it is now feared that the diamond mines at Kasai will soon be under attack.

Meanwhile, the president of the UN, Doug Hammarskjold, is to order the replacement of the Belgian troops by UN detachments at the insistence of Prime Minister Lumumba. The reason behind the present reign of terror in the country is largely due to the pro-Lumumba and anti-European stance of the Kasavubu government forces. At Watsa, entire units of the Force Republique under PM Lumumba's influence are preying on the defenseless population. This has brought the workings of the gold mines to a standstill, and has also put the vast stocks of ivory, warehoused locally, in great danger of being pillaged.

It is understood that Europeans are making desperate bids to escape the region as the mutinous troops of the Congalese Army continue to roam the towns. Watsa itself lies one hundred miles west of the Ugandan border, and cars have been reported abandoned at ferry points. Even hard line Belgian cattlemen are known to be planning escape from the wave of madness in the Oriente Province.

Our Special Reporter, Henri Mauriac, speaks of his last hours in Watsa as its historic buildings and fine stores stand burning in the early evening. He tells of the Arabic heritage and the lush palm and mango trees lining the avenues of this onceproud town; but not only the broad red-graveled boulevards and the architectural brilliance of the private residences need comment, but the red-bricked mission lay smoldering and dying, like everything else in this high, cool, and opulent spa town.

It was several minutes later when Visavadia and I emerged from the dark interior of Bedi's Store. The light hurt now that we were in the open, and I put on my sunglasses. On the other side of the street, standing close to the van, was Thomas. He was busy handing out leaflets, and the moment he caught sight of us, he waved. It was an unusual gesture, and I could only think that something was wrong. I crossed the street.

"Is everything all right?"

Thomas stepped forward. "There's a priest who wants to talk with you," he said uneasily, "and he's sitting in the van."

"Any idea what he wants?"

"No idea." He shrugged. "But he's insisted on speaking with you."

I waited while Visavadia loaded the box of groceries into the van, but the priest had already spotted me and was starting to climb down. "Hullo," I said and smiled.

He was small, almost dapper, and a pair of rimless glasses hung on the nose of his chubby face. His white soutane looked grubby against the harsh light of the lingering sun. "Sorry to bother you," he said in an agitated manner and thereupon extended an arm; we shook hands. Then, together, we walked around to the shady side of the van and waited while he mopped the sweat that was running down his fleshy neck with a linen handkerchief that he carried in his left hand. "I need your help in a rather difficult matter," he confided.

"What kind of help are you talking about?" I said quietly.

"Are you aware of the troubles going on in the Congo?"

On hearing this unexpected question, I leaned against the paneling of the van and considered my options. It's always possible that an in-depth safari loses touch with the outside world. But in the case of the Congo, it was on our doorstep, and besides I had only just read about it in this morning's newspaper. However, I was worried about the possible implications that might be linked to this direct question and what, if anything, I might be letting myself in for. But basically there appeared to be little harm in giving him an affirmative reply. Anyway, I was curious as to what he had in mind.

"Yes, I'm aware of the events in the Congo," I replied.

"In that case, may I introduce myself?" he began gravely. "My name's Father Francis. I'm from the Catholic mission here in Arua, and I will now come straight to the point. There's a group of Belgian refugees, eleven in all, who are hiding in the forest at this very minute, of whom three are youngsters under the age of six. Their exact position is known only to me and my assistant, Jacques. It is enough to say that they are within two hundred yards of the Uganda borderline. This group represents some of the few people who have managed to escape out of Watsa alive. Many others have been caught and murdered, their women raped and then slaughtered, and only heaven knows what has happened to the children!" The priest trembled and crossed himself once more, then turned his head and added almost as an afterthought. "It's like Sodom and Gomorrah over there," and with those words he swept his arm in front of him, looked toward the Congo, and pointed.

"Naturally, I'm very sorry to hear all this, but why are you telling me?"

"Well, this particular group of refugees has been traveling for the last twenty-four hours since leaving Watsa, and they are now exhausted, in fear of death, and waiting to be rescued. Their guide is a Congolese man known as Jacques. He has worked for the last twenty years with a leading gold mine company in Watsa as a messenger and general factotum. He was a trusted man, who has taken it upon himself to save the ex-pat Belgians wherever possible in order to repay the good they have given to him over the years. In view of this, and as he is devoid of income to feed his family, I have employed him as my assistant. We now have a common obligation to bring this group of eleven, and any others, to the safety of this country."

"I don't understand," I broke in. "What's to stop them from walking across the border into Uganda right now?"

"That's not possible," the priest replied. "The border is patrolled by mutinous Simbalese troops, and they will stop at nothing to prevent anyone trying to escape the Congo. They have agents here already, some of whom are dressed in mufti, making it difficult to know whom to trust. As for the refugees, we had already considered bringing them over at night, but Jacques warned that it was too big a risk to take, and it would be dangerous to delay their rescue. It has to be before dark today, and I have agreed with him on that.

"As you can see, this is a matter that needs immediate attention. My plan—and there appears to be no viable alternative—is for you and your men to assist in their escape." The father again took off his rimless glasses and dabbed at his face with the linen handkerchief.

"No way," I said as I shifted my feet uneasily on the ground.

I had to witness the defeated look that spread across the father's face, and for almost thirty seconds neither of us spoke. This uneasy silence was broken by Father Francis, when he said that it was an agony for him to think about those eleven people in the forest, and quoted the adage that things seem to be "so near and yet so far."

"Isn't that what you English say?"

"I'll tell you what," I replied. "Give me the details of your plan, and I'll promise to listen."

"God bless you, my son," he whispered, and took out a map of Arua's streets and pointed to the exact location of the Catholic mission.

"Have a close look and remember this place."

"I've already been in that district," I replied.

"That's good," he said, and paused while he refolded the map and placed it back into the folds of his soutane.

"I watched your activities yesterday and came to the conclusion that with your help, it's possible to save the precious lives of this small group of refugees. It's for that reason that I gave my word to Jacques last night that he was to move them up under cover of darkness to a holding position from which there is no turning back. I staked their lives on my certainty that you and your men would help them in their hour of need."

"It is known that the Ugandan authorities have recently dispatched a contingent of East African Rifles to patrol the area. They are not here to prevent Europeans from entering this country, but are here to intervene should a serious dispute break out on our side of the border. It is likely that in the heat of the moment, mutinous factions of the Force Republique will infiltrate this side of the border and drive back any escapees.

"I want to make it clear," the priest went on, "that I minister not only to those here in Arua but also to those across the border in Aru. That explains why I have the freedom to come and go, and that includes Jacques. And this is where you come into the equation." He paused while he swatted a fly that had settled on his nose.

"If you accept the task that I'm going to put forward, it's vitally important that you listen carefully," Father Francis warned as he pulled another map from his jacket pocket beneath his soutane.

"I'm listening."

"Your first hurdle is to proceed through the Vurra checkpoint which is here." He pointed it out with a forefinger. "It will be manned by a couple of policemen and a dozen soldiers. You must tell one of the policemen that you want to proceed to the customs post about one hundred yards farther down. It's no good looking there, as a twist in the road blocks off the customs post. I am confident that once you have explained the reason for your visit, they will wave you through. Then once past the twist in the road, you will come face-to-face with your second hurdle, H.M. customs and excise post. They, too, will have a barrier spread across the road. You must now politely ask them if you can play quiet music and hand out a few advertising leaflets."

Father Francis paused momentarily and used his free hand to straighten out the crinkles in the map. "It is my belief that the appearance of you and your colleagues in a large transit van with advertisements plastered over the panels will secure their interest. It will be something new in their lives, and their curiosity will be aroused. They might even be slightly amused. If so, this is a positive reaction." The priest paused again and breathed deeply.

"Thirty yards beyond the Ugandan customs post is the Congolese border checkpoint manned by army dissidents, and they won't be amused. You must remember never to look at them. However, once you've explained to our customs the raison d'être behind your mission, I'm hopeful you will get their permission to proceed. This is now the most crucial point of the whole exercise, and once given the nod you must turn right into the large compound that is used by customs for parking vehicles that need to be searched should the officers suspect any vehicle of carrying illegal cargos. This is an ideal place to begin your show, and you'll have the forest running along the south side of the compound.

"This woodland is all part of the same forest that stretches for several miles and forms a natural border between western Uganda and the northern Congo. Once in the compound, you must reverse your truck against the perimeter of the forest, leaving sufficient room for the rear doors to open. This will then provide access for the refugees and shield them from prying eyes. Always remember that the land you are on is legally neutral, but if pressed the Congolese might ignore diplomatic niceties, although so far this hasn't happened." Yet again the father dabbed at his face and looked straight at me and asked, "Are you with me so far?"

"Yes, I reckon so," I replied, although doubts were once again surfacing in my head.

"The moment the group of eleven have boarded, you must shut the rear doors, turn off the music, and cease trading," the father instructed. "You must appear to be in no undue hurry, but of course you are, and that's why it's vital that you don't so much as glance at the people behind the Congolese border post, which is now approximately sixty yards, at two o'clock, from your present position. This rule of 'not looking' also applies to Uganda's H.M. custom post, but if you have to give a wave to the customs men, then for goodness' sake don't take your foot off the accelerator. Just drive toward the Vurra checkpoint, and once you are past the twist in the road, you are over the last fence and home and dry. It's then that I will look forward to meeting you all at my mission in Arua some ten miles up the road."

"You make it sound so easy," I said, "but I must now put the facts to my colleagues and see what they have to say."

"Yes, quite so." The Father nodded, his anxious face there for the world to see as he nervously pulled at his chin. He was in a predicament, and he knew it; eleven lives, now waiting fearfully in the forest, were seriously at risk.

"However," he went on, "I realize there is a risk factor where you and your men are concerned, but if you get stopped insist that you and your colleagues are British citizens, and hopefully that should worry them. And always remember that at the end of the day, you and your men will have saved eleven souls."

Father Francis paused, took a deep breath, and exhaled slowly. He appeared relieved to have finished detailing the procedure, and he removed his rimless glasses, again vigorously mopping the sweat off his brow with his handkerchief.

"I'm not convinced that your plan will work," I said, once again wading in at the deep end. "And I feel we are seriously underestimating the Congolese."

"Of course I understand your worries," the father responded, "but all I'm asking you to do is to demonstrate your products and hand out a few leaflets. It's something you do every hour of the day. It's my suggestion that you place your colleagues about fifteen feet in front of the truck to help fend off anyone who wants to take a closer look. I don't think you will get more than a handful of people, which I'm sure you can cope with." The father paused and put his glasses back on.

"I have two questions that need answering," I said.

"What are they?" the priest said sharply.

"How will the refugees know that we will be coming to pick them up, and how will they know where?"

"That's stupid of me," the Father admitted. "I should have mentioned that Jacques is right now waiting for me at the mission, and he will act as the group's guide."

"I don't understand," I said. "You're telling me he can just pop into the forest at will?"

"Yes, he can," he replied. "He's well-known on this side of border and is looked upon as harmless, but he's something of a character and neither the police nor customs have any problem with him."

"What about the Congolese?"

"They know him too. He's the only passenger who I have in my car that gets waved on. They also know that I've given him some part-time work since he lost his job in Watsa. And if they spot him going into the forest, well everyone does when they get caught short or need wood for their fire."

"My second question is why don't the refugees exit the forest at the graveled compound where we're going to give a show? It's neutral ground, and there'll be no need for us should they do that, so where's the problem?"

"This is a good point," he responded.

"And the answer is?" I pressed.

"If any white person should step out into the open they would be taken back and killed," the priest said. "The first on the scene would be the Force Republique from the border post. They would ignore the neutrality zone and chase our group back into the forest, and as I've said before, they would be killed. You must try to grasp the seriousness of the situation. It only needs a few well-armed insurgents to gain control of the border area, and although the police at the Vurra checkpoint, along with our soldiers, are operational, they can take action only if the insurgents set foot on Ugandan soil."

"I hadn't thought of that," I responded.

"Time is of the essence," the priest concluded, glancing anxiously at his wristwatch. "I want you to be parked in the compound and ready to give a show at exactly eleven forty-five a.m. This will be fifteen minutes before the police change duties at the barriers. This timing will favor you, as the minds of the police and customs officers won't be totally occupied with your activities.'

"You want all this in the next two hours when I've yet to consult with my colleagues?" I asked in astonishment.

"If you want to avoid a *ciyuga*,"—Father Francis used the Swahili word for a bloodbath—"there's no alternative. I warn you, John, that the sight of a Simbalese soldier wielding a machete is enough to strike fear into the bravest man. It might help if you think of the three youngsters who form part of this group of eleven."

The father drew another deep breath and looked down once more. "I suggest we check our watches," he said in a quiet voice.

***

We went past an armed patrol of Ugandan soldiers who were lying in thick vegetation on the approach to the Vurra checkpoint. On arrival we explained to the police officers the purpose of our visit, and they waved us through. So far it had gone exactly as the priest had predicted.

"Alright if we play music and give out leaflets?" I asked the customs officer as he stepped from the guardhouse and took up a position behind the black-and-white barrier. There were two other uniformed Ugandan officers who stood in the doorway and peered at us. However, thirty yards farther on, there were several heavily armed Congalese soldiers who stared coldly in our direction. "We won't be here long," I reassured the officer, and gave him some free samples and illustrated brochures to share with his colleagues.

For several seconds the policeman said nothing but kept turning the miniature bottles around in his large hands in a suspicious manner. He didn't seem at all amused, as Father Francis had forecasted. "All right," he said at last. "You can go on the compound, but I want your truck well clear of the road. Do you understand?"

"I'll go over there on the hard ground and make a turn, OK?"

The policeman grunted and moved back to the barrier. "No more than twenty minutes, mind," he shouted over his shoulder before disappearing into the white-painted guardhouse.

I parked at the arranged spot and turned to Thomas and Visavadia and nodded for them to get out of the van. I had already told them that it would be stupid to limit our activities to the handing out of leaflets and samples; we must also be prepared to deal with cash sales, and with that in mind I gave them an amount of small change. This way they wouldn't need to leave their positions.

"Good luck," I said in a quiet voice.

They had agreed to take part in this venture when they learned that the lives of little children were at risk, and neither of them had asked for anything in return.

They each picked up a packet of leaflets and a box of Herbalex and Gripe Aid, and went forward about twenty paces. Then, without glancing either left or right, they placed their boxes on the ground and waited for their first customer.

By now I had reboarded the van and switched on a calypso tune called "Island Woman." The slow beat drifted lazily into the warm air. It was neither too loud nor too soft. Then, I made my way along the blind side of the vehicle, out of sight of the Congo checkpoint, and cautiously opened the rear doors. The heavy cartons in the van had been stacked in such a way that they

Safari Salesman

formed a wall at each end with a gap on one side. A few loose cartons had been left on the cabin floor to rebuild the gap.

I returned to the front and tried to look casual by putting a leg on the running board. I leaned across and wiped down the windshield. Each second that passed I sensed the hostility of the Congolese burning into my back. I stole a quick look at my watch, and the dial showed it was six minutes to noon. The impending change of soldiers and police would hopefully distract the attention of the Congolese. The inducement of food, cups of hot coffee, and a restful cigarette might well have a peaceful effect.

Shortly afterward I became aware of a soft rustling sound of foliage and the rise and fall of the van on my leg. I immediately started to count, and this up-and-down motion was repeated twelve times, almost like the chimes of a church clock at midnight. For a moment I almost panicked, but at once I remembered that I had forgotten to include Jacques. I was glad that we had taken time to rehearse the routine; otherwise, this whole situation might have then and there blown up in our faces. Instead, without thinking, I automatically went around to the blind side of the van and closed and locked the doors. Then without any loss of momentum, I climbed into the driver's seat, reached back, shut off the music, and started up the engine.

That was the signal for Thomas and Visavadia to pick up their boxes, stroll back to the van, and climb in. The six or seven people who had been circling the sales points broke up and ambled off in different directions.

In a matter of seconds, I drove across the graveled compound and noticed that there was increased activity at both posts. It was the changing of the guard, so to speak, and I quietly turned left down the track and away from both frontier points. It was in my rear view mirror that I spotted a policeman standing by the same black-and-white barrier. He was shading his eyes against the glare of the midday sun, staring hard at us, perhaps vaguely puzzled by our unannounced departure. Beyond the twist in the road, and out of sight of both posts we began to relax, and exchange smiles at a job well done, but no sooner had we settled down than an unseen policeman darted out of the bushes onto the trackside. He held up his right hand and signaled for us to stop.

"I have orders to search all vehicles on this road," he barked, looking at me through the rolled-down window. Then his face suddenly brightened. "I thought I recognized you," he said. "You're the people who are staying at the rest house. Am I right?"

"Yes, that's us," I said and laughed in response. I leaned forward from the seat, smiled, and shook his hand through the window.

He took a step back from the van. "It's nice seeing you all again." He grinned and waved us on.

chapter

TEN

Our route now lay southeast toward Pakwach, a distance of eighty-four miles over narrow, greasy tracks. We went past some isolated settlements, mainly mud and wattle huts set in bare, dusty compounds and screened by dense plantain shrubs.

Arua, and all that happened there, was soon put out of our minds as we fought our way along the black oily track, wheels slipping and sliding every few yards.

When we did find the time to think back about things, it seemed incredible that it was still the same Friday, the twelfth of August, when we set out for the drive south after returning the rest house keys to the police station. And looking even further back, it was as though weeks had melted from the calendar since we drove off the ferry at the village of Laropi on Monday morning.

We had now freed ourselves from all obligations that the father had placed on us. We had safely delivered the refugees to Arua's mission hall. It was odd that the father wasn't there to greet us, so we waited, along with Jacques, in case something had happened. But much to everyone's relief, some five minutes later, he had swept toward us in his beat-up Morris car in a swirl of red dust.

"Sorry I'm late," he had said cheerfully, "but I was called out to visit a parishioner who had been taken ill. It meant I had to wait with the poor man until a doctor arrived." His rubicund face was dripping in sweat, and in a matter of seconds he had shaken hands with the refugees. Then it had been our turn to bid good-bye, and we drove away from a heavily flushed and excited father in the center of a small group of his newly made but tired friends. The dust from our vehicle soon obliterated them all from view.

Now it was back to business again, and we made our first stop at the obscure village of Kango. "It's all go, isn't it?" Thomas joked as we opened the rear doors of the van and once again the music drifted freely from the speakers.

On the far side of the track, there were two women busily leaning over a large metal cooking pot, and steam rose as they stirred the mixture with long, unwieldy sticks. The sour smell of potatoes hung uneasily in the air. "Looks like the witches brew," I commented to Thomas.

"It's better than anything like that," he said and laughed. "It's pombe."

We left Visavadia to deal with the few customers, and crossed the dirt road to where the women were stooping over the cooking fire. They looked up and exchanged the usual African greetings. Inside the communal pot were green bananas wrapped in their own leaves, boiling and giving off a sharp pungency that stung the nose. "Would you like to try some?" one woman asked.

"Come on." Thomas shot a glance in my direction. "You'll be sorry you didn't try it," he added persuasively. We sat down on the ground while the women began to unwrap the hot plantain with the tips of their fingers and let the yellow mash spread slowly across the leaves. Then, from an old tin container, they sprinkled a mixture of ground nuts and strong-smelling spices over the steaming pulp, known as *matoke*.

"Eat it with your fingers the African way," Thomas advised.

It seemed a messy way of doing things, but my worry was soon pushed to the back of my mind by the delicious taste, each mouthful better than the last. As soon as we had finished, the women returned and asked Thomas in Swahili if we wanted some pombe to drink. "You have a choice," Thomas said with a smile as he turned his head toward me. "You can have banana or pineapple flavor."

"I'll stay with the bananas," I said, getting up from the bare ground. I had already been told about the effects of pombe, and the fact that it went on fermenting in the stomach after ingestion, a kind of delayed Molotov cocktail. I had once sampled it at a friend's house in Nairobi. But now, here in the bush, under a baking sun, it was another thing. "No pint glasses in this place," Thomas jested, and handed me a straw reed from which to suck the pombe. A flock of raggedy chickens ran helter-skelter across the compound as we wandered over to a cluster of mud huts on the far side. We went inside the larger of the huts, and it took a few moments to get used to the darkness. We were surprised to find a number of people already there. The men were dressed in kanzu gowns, or short trousers and stained vests, and were standing around in silence. Their women, in ankle-length busutis twisted round their ample hips, sat cross-legged along the edges of the circular floor, some breastfeeding babies, others drowsing or blankly staring into the gloom with seemingly glazed eyes. Not quite in the center, but set back a little, were two huge cauldrons, each resting on a wooden brandeth.

We replied to the greetings and deep vocal hums, and then moved quietly toward the giant-size vessels. "Here goes," Thomas quipped, sinking his straw into the thick liquid. The only light came from the doorway, and every now and then one of the scrawny chickens lingered in the bright entrance, head jerking at searching angles, before pecking with its beak in the warm dust. Thomas made room for me, and I leaned over the pot, sucking deeply on the straw, and felt the smooth banana-flavored liquid, sour yet refreshing, run down into my stomach.

We spent a good thirty minutes in the dark of the hut before we stood up and thanked the women for their hospitality. I gave them a twenty shilling note to share. We blinked in the heavy sun when we left the hut and quickly shielded our eyes with the back of our hands.

Visavadia was waiting for us by the van looking lonely, but he immediately cheered up the moment he caught sight of us. So much so that he placed the big band number "American Patrol" on the turntable. We sometimes used this exciting mood music with its strong brass section as a signal to close down the show. In fact our audiences throughout Central and East

Africa enjoyed our music, and they were sad to see us go, a subdued reaction compared with what we had received in the jungles of West Africa.

Our Bedford van in West Africa was twice as large, some 7.5 tons, manned by a different crew of five. There were audiences of many hundreds when we showed films at night. The people were much more vocal, and should they get so much as a hint that we were getting ready to leave, they would throw stones, puncture tires, or clamber into the vehicle to prevent us from driving away. In Nigeria, Gold Coast, or Sierra Leone, the word would be passed among our salesmen to get ready to leave, and we'd drive away while the movie was still on the screen, which inspired frightening howls of dismay. Of course it couldn't last, and the bush telegraph responded by placing logs at either end of the vehicle on arrival. That way we'd have no option but to negotiate our way out.

It was several miles later, after we had left Kango, that we made another short stop at the oddly named trading center of War. When we were back on the road again, we crossed a tortuous trail that wound its way through the rolling Koro Hills. From there we struck northward to the village of Nebbi. Up until now the road had been relatively empty of traffic, but we began to pass several cyclists lugging large bags of cotton on their backs, and occasionally soft balls of fluff would fall from the lips of the sacks and litter the shoulder of the road with what looked like snow.

By now the banana beer had begun to do its work; I was not only knocked out but was sick too. It was as though I had been to an all-night party. My stomach was now visibly swelling, caused by acids being in ceaseless fermentation since drinking pombe. I glanced at Thomas at the wheel, and he didn't look much better.

"Better pull over for the night," I said, before retching out of the open door.

***

It was late when we broke camp in the morning. It didn't seem like a Saturday, and I was still hung over from the beer. I should have written a weekly report the night before, along with an up-to-date tally of sales, but it would have to wait.

About two miles farther on we drove slowly past a large troop of baboons, some walking deliberately across the road with a haughty air, their tails held high in a drooping curve. Every now and then we were forced to brake. A big male, a mandrill with an all-blue backside, jumped heavily onto the hood and pushed his muzzle against the windshield, barking angrily. The others were less aggressive and sloped off into the nearby woods, searching for hard fruits and insects. Not long afterward we came to the village of Ngal.

From here the road carved its way forward in an easterly direction and narrowed into a single powdered track, with barely enough room for our heavy-duty tires. We bumped and bumped over the stones and steeply sided potholes, and gradually reduced our speed to a crawl. A short time later we became shut in on one side by huge, nine-foot-high, shrub like a cassava plant. The heavy-lobed leaves on low branches slapped and scraped the windshield, before parting and brushing noisily against the van's panels. We slid our doors shut and partially closed the windows to avoid getting scratched. Every so often we would be forced to stop and free our wheels from the heavy rootstock along the scuffed edges of the road. For a time we lost all sense of direction, and now the other side of the track had also become seriously screened by cassava. It was like being in a car wash but with no water. According to the map, we were on an unclassified road that was not maintained by the Public Works Department. You could say that again, and all we could see was intermittent glimpses of sky. Otherwise there was nothing; only the greenness of the plants.

Ten minutes later we emerged from this green tunnel. It was a welcome sight to see the openness and the blue of the sky. We slid back the doors and breathed in the clean air. The view became more extensive with patches of wooded land set against distant slopes. We passed the Tangi River, which had been reduced from several yards wide to mere beds of sand and pebbles, and only lines of borassus palms were left to mark the course of the basin, some of which had already died. It was sad to see their parched and tindery roots sticking out of the sandy ground.

We followed the level of the land, which gently dipped as it neared the ferry crossing over the Albert Nile, and it was there, at the ferry, that we joined a long line of vehicles waiting to make the crossing. We were informed that some of the drivers had been there since yesterday, so we resigned ourselves to spending the night in an open-sided, very large, corrugated iron shed that bordered the river.

It was chilly in the early morning, and we made sure that we claimed our place in the line. There was a large school of wallowing hippos, their mouths yawning wide while limbering up after a night spent searching for food along the riverbanks. Beyond them we could make out the log-shaped forms of Nile crocodiles sunbathing on eroded sands that were bordered with papyrus plants. Only a month ago, a twelve-year-old boy from a nearby village who was fetching fresh water was dragged into the river. Unfortunately this occurrence was not uncommon, as Nile crocodiles invariably attack humans if they perceive their territory is being encroached.

Then, without warning, we heard the short, sharp blasts of a paddle steamer echoing from some distance away along the river. Later, as we crossed over on the ferry to the east bank, we noticed a huge, oily cloud of thick black smoke coming from the funnel of the lake steamer. It blasted its siren when it spotted us, and all of us watched in fascination as it rounded a dense line of tall reed beds, churning its way upriver from the far-off port of Butiaba. Its present journey would terminate when it arrived at Nimule in the southern Sudan. It was somehow uncanny to witness an ocean-going steamer, deep in the heart of the African continent.

We rolled off the ferry on the far side and headed through the Murchison Falls Game Reserve, 1,500 square miles of low grassland, interspersed with the yellow-barked thorn trees and large herds of elephant and buffalo, with the River Nile forming a natural barrier for the animals. Then, turning south, we worked our way along a narrow laterite track that was not built on an embankment. We had now covered approximately twenty miles since leaving the ferry point, and at last we arrived at a place called Paraa, overlooking the fast-flowing Victoria Nile.

Since leaving Nairobi some forty-eight days ago we had driven a total of 1,562 miles, which gave us a daily average of thirty-three miles, well below our original estimate. This was possibly due to the delays incurred in the tightly grouped towns spanning the Kenyan countryside. We also had to put in extensive work in the industrial lakeside townships in Uganda, and besides that we made a full week's stopover in the capital of Kampala. There was also a lost weekend at the Umi Ferry crossover, where Visavadia landed the perch. Now we lived in the hope that the daily mileage would improve once we moved through the less populated areas of the south.

We made inquiries at the reception desk of the Paraa Safari Lodge about staying for one night, but unfortunately it was fully booked due to the expected arrival of a bus load of tourists. Instead of a guest room, we were offered a tent pitched in the gardens opposite the entrance to the main building. It contained three camp beds and cost thirty shillings inclusive to hire for a single night. Although it was a disappointment not to have accommodation at the lodge, at least it was a step up from being offered a bivouac site, and at any rate we wouldn't have to spend a third night on the trot in the bush. I took the opportunity to question the clerk about the proximity of the river to our campsite, and he reassured me that neither hippos nor elephants had been known to stray into the grounds at night. However, he mentioned that a croc had once come ashore and had been beaten back by the night watchman after he heard the yells of a tourist, and since that time the crocs had moved downstream.

The canvas tent was large and shabby. It was set on a patch of lawn well away from the river and faced the safari lodge across a wide graveled driveway. Nevertheless, it was dwarfed by a cluster of borassus palms that soared upward for a hundred feet, and neither Thomas, Visavadia, nor I fancied getting hit by one of its large, hard, orange-type fruits.

It didn't take long to unload our gear from the van, which was parked nearby, a few feet away from the graveled driveway. We then proceeded to make our beds, which entailed nothing more than throwing a blanket down on any one of the available beds. We agreed, however, to reserve a corner of the tent for kitchen items, such as pots, pans, and stove, along with food and water. We had made ourselves as comfortable as possible and had gotten everything we needed for a single night's stay. Perhaps all we lacked was a wooden signboard staked into the ground with the words *Chez Nous* burned in black lettering across the middle.

After each of us had enjoyed a mug of hot of tea, we watched through the open flap of our tent as the new arrivals disgorged from a large bus. When they had gone we set out for a walk down to the river bank. We soon found a grassy spot to sit on, and with the afternoon sun on our backs, we looked across the Nile at the endless savanna plains beyond the far banks of the river. The grunt of hippos as they poked their mammoth heads through the water was surreal, and an air of stillness spread beyond the river into the distant plains. We turned our attention to a flock of brown-plumaged bitterns as they waded sedately over the marshland that bordered the river to our right. They pecked their way among the thick-growing reeds, while the sound of low booming noises echoed outward from amid the sedge. This hinted at the probability of mothers with chicks sitting on well-hidden nests. Suddenly the birds in the open froze, alarmed by a pair of bush shrikes that circled overhead in search of prey. It wasn't surprising that ornithologists had christened the shrikes "butcher birds" because of their hooked bills and sharp claws.

An hour later, on our return to the tent, we noticed that a number of tourists were now lounging on settees placed equidistant along the open-sided loggia that extended the length of the hotel. They were drinking sundowners, and the soft clink of ice in highball glasses could be clearly heard from across the graveled courtyard; and to the keen eye, the yellows, greens, and golds of daiquiris, grasshoppers, and screwdrivers were visible.

The main tools of any discerning tourist were evident. This included an expensive camera in a leather case and a handy light meter slung loosely around a sunburned neck. The hubbub of their excited talk swelled into the warm air as they compared notes about their day's safari into the nearby game reserve.

It was getting dark, and we were debating what to eat for supper, when we noticed that our tent flap was being tugged vigorously.

"Can we help you?" I asked in a loud voice.

The person then stuck his head inside and said *"Excuse moi"* and went on to explain in broken English that he was the hotel's assistant chef and he had slipped out from the kitchen to bring us a cooked dinner of prime steak and chips for three. He offered us a large parcel, wrapped in grease-proof paper and told us that this was a donation from the cooks, who were worried that we might not have anything proper to eat. He went on to explain in a heavily coated French accent that he had adopted an undercover approach because, and I quote: "I know eets early but the 'ead chef soon come on duty at seis heures et demi, and eets better 'e not know about ze food."

"Thanks very much," we chorused.

An hour later, after Thomas had made a steaming pot of coffee, I walked across the stony driveway toward the hotel entrance. The night had now fallen and there was a suggestion of rain. The glow from the windows, coupled with the brilliance of the floodlights that spread evenly across the frontage, gave off an attractive three-dimensional effect to the handsome red-bricked building.

An American tourist was perched astride a stool in the corner of the well-furnished bar and gave a friendly nod as I entered the room. He was dressed in a smart blue lounge suit, crisp white shirt, and black-stringed necktie with gold aiglets. His pale face was strangely out of place.

"I'll buy you a drink, buddy," he drawled, as he picked an olive out of a side dish and dropped it in his mouth.

"That's kind of you," I said. "I'll have a beer."

"Hey, Mac," the tourist drummed the counter and called to the barman "give this guy a beer, and give me another Jack and Dry."

"It's a warm night," I commented.

He paused and took a deep breath while digesting my opening remark. Then he smiled and said, "Hell, my name's Mel Pinder, and I'm from Brownsville, Texas."

"That's a long way to come," I said.

"Sure is," he said approvingly. "We've been over to the game reserve today. That's really something, I'll tell you. Have you seen it?"

"Not yet. I'm going through tomorrow."

"You'll sure like it. Take my word on that."

Basically, I didn't want to get involved in a conversation about hunting trips and wildlife. I knew that if Mel started probing about what I did, it would quickly lead to another drink. I wanted to be out of there, as I had a report to file, which, if completed tonight, I would be able to get posted at the hotel before leaving in the morning. Mel was definitely a great guy, but I had a schedule to follow, and it was running a week late. In any other circumstances, I would have been pleased to stay and have a chat.

"Have you been to Murchison Falls?" I asked.

The African barman pushed my beer across the Formica-topped counter and, at the same time, popped an orange slice into Mel's drink.

"Going tomorrow," Mel replied. "It's a four-hour trip by boat, you know."

"It's worth the effort," I said, and added, "It's on the Victoria Nile where the waters thunder down a cataract toward the fertile valleys of the

Sudan and Egypt. It's very impressive, and, if my memory serves me right, it was discovered by a Mr. and Mrs. Samuel Baker in April 1864."

"Well I'll be darned!"

"What's more, they were in a dugout canoe."

Mel paused for a moment.

"Say, are you staying at this hotel?"

I drained the beer and smiled. "Not in the true sense. I'm camped outside and I only popped in to get a pack of cigarettes and some cans of beer. It's best I get that now before I forget," I said and laughed.

I then signaled the barman over and asked him for six cans of Tusker beer and two packets of Kali cigarettes.

"Look, please excuse me," I said to Mel, "but I've got some food cooking and must go," I lied.

"What do ya mean?" He smiled incomprehensibly. "They're not serving dinner yet, and anyway, the eight o'clock gong hasn't been rung." He checked his wristwatch. "Am I right, Mac?" He looked over toward the barman.

The barman hadn't been listening to our conversation and frowned as he came forward. "How can I help?" he inquired.

"Just let's forget I ever asked." Mel laughed.

I got up and shook the American's hand. "I'm eating out," I said, "and anyway, I've got to go. Thanks for the drink, and have a good trip up the Nile tomorrow." I walked across the lounge to the lobby.

"Say, buddy, who is that guy?" I distinctly heard Mel fire off the question to the barman as I stepped out onto the veranda.

Back at the tent, Thomas had finished washing the dishes and was reboxing the unused tinned foods. "That's the best supper we've had in a long while," he announced.

"I agree," I said.

I heard a groan coming from Visavadia, who was curled up on his bed reading a book.

"No Patels in Paraa then?" Thomas gibed good-naturedly.

There was no response.

Thomas switched the conversation back to the present. "Do you want these things put back in the van?" he asked as he held up three separate polythene bags of rice, sugar, and coffee.

"No, leave them on top of the packing case," I replied. "The last thing we want is ants coming here."

With that question settled, I lost no time and removed the lid off my portable typewriter and fed in two sheets of A4 paper and a black carbon onto the roller. My mind was now firmly fixed on my weekly report to London, along with the accounts for the past week.

"May I speak?" Thomas asked.

"Yes, of course."

"I had an accident with the sugar." Thomas was back on the subject of food.

I took my eyes off the report and looked at Thomas, who sat on his bed with his legs over the side. "What's the problem?"

"I thought it wise to tell you that the bag burst when I opened it to make coffee. I cleared it up the best I could, but we've got no pan and brush."

"That's no big deal," I assured. "I'll buy another bag at the next town." I then turned my attention back to the report.

Ninety minutes later I completed the paperwork and folded it neatly into a large brown envelope. My colleagues were already fast asleep, and for a few moments I stared idly into the half-light. Then, with a large intake of breath, I picked up my typewriter along with the written work and walked slowly back to the van, depositing my things under the seat. I checked the locks, went back to the tent, and dimmed the paraffin lamp that Thomas had hooked to the center pole.

At last in bed, I listened to the rasping snorts of bullfrogs in the reeds, and the unending grunts of hippos as they emerged from the river banks. It was plain that they were intent on browsing amid the thick, lush vegetation that grew on the marshy banks. Anyway, I wasn't concerned with the possibility of intrusion, as the receptionist on the desk had clearly said it was safe to camp. I must admit, though, that I would have felt safer had I been in the van rather than out here in a flimsy tent. It seemed paradoxical that I should have asked a clerk about the wildlife situation when I had Thomas and Visavadia, both hardened safari men, to consult with at the blink of an eye. Whatever, the final sound I heard before falling asleep was the ululating laugh of a solitary hyena, a sure sign that he had uncovered a wounded animal. This noise was quickly followed by another crackle of howls and then silence.

I must have been asleep for about two hours when I was awoken by the heavy rumble of snoring. At the very beginning I accepted that it was Thomas, and as a result I stirred and became restless. It wasn't unusual for him to snore and keep me awake, but this time it was loud enough to drown my thoughts. I wanted to tell him to shut up but found myself reluctant to disturb him. Instead I shifted my position and pulled the blanket over my head. This didn't work either, so I rolled over onto my back and stared into the darkness. As far as I could discern, Visavadia was still fast asleep, and it made me wonder how he managed to stay like that with all the noise going on.

I then heard a deep, recurring resonant sound, a mix of heavy snoring and repetitive rumbling. For a few moments I failed to identify the sound and even wondered if I was dreaming it, but in my heart of hearts I came to the awful conclusion that we were dealing with an elephant. Something serious would happen unless we vacated the tent pronto. This whole scene from the time I woke to the present moment had taken no more than sixty seconds. I sat bolt upright and felt for my flashlight under the bed, and my fingers fumbled as I tried to find the button to switch it on. Then, suddenly, there was a quake-like vibration, and our pots, pans, and the rest of it went flying to the ground.

"What the hell's going on?" Thomas shouted.

The noise of metal plates, tinned food, and cutlery clattering off a packing case was alarming. By now I had managed to locate the button on the flashlight and was busy scanning the darkness with its penetrating beam.

"Iko hapa tembo," Thomas said in Swahili, this time alarmed as the bottom end of the tent collapsed. It was at this point that the elephant's trunk probed its way inside the tent. Unfortunately for Visavadia he was the first in the elephant's diary of "things to do." It turned his bed over and started to scan his half-naked body with its trunk. Visavadia in a frenzied reflex action scrambled off the floor and shot across to us. Then a giant foot slammed down in the middle of the tent, and everything came down.

"For God's sake, let's get out of here," Thomas yelled.

The three of us were trapped under the heavy canvas and were close to suffocation. All the time we struggled, seeking a way out, but there was none. It was Thomas who reached for his sheath knife, which was kept on his belt day and night, and slashed open the tenting.

Visavadia stayed motionless as Thomas and I crawled through the opening clutching our blankets. By this time it appeared that Visavadia had become frozen with fear and had simply given up the fight to stay alive. He was in deep trouble to say the least, so both Thomas and I, in unison, reached back into the tent and grabbed any part of him that we could get a grip of, and pulled him through the opening. Now, uncertain where we were, we stumbled forward away from the tented area, and finally impacted on the graveled driveway. Once more we got to our feet—still with Visavadia in tow—and raced across the gravel to the relative safety of the hotel veranda. We watched in disbelief as the bull elephant trampled the same ground where we had been asleep just seconds earlier.

In the dark shadows of the hotel perimeter, an old man quietly hobbled toward the wooden terrace. He paused, silhouetted against the light of a downstairs window, and pointed his stick. "That *tembo* is looking for something in your tent," he said bluntly in a deep, sonorous voice. He was clothed in an old army overcoat, which was decorated with half a dozen war medals, and his frizzled white beard was illuminated against the light of the window. But his dark, interesting face was lost in the slanting shadows.

"Do you have *chakula* in your tent?" he persisted.

"Who are you?" I asked quietly.

"I'm the night watchman, and I work here," he replied.

"Yes, of course we've had food in our tent," Thomas snapped. He was in no mood to be cross-examined.

It began to rain, and we sheltered under the eaves of the roof. The old man, the *mzee,* considered the situation in silence, while we turned our attention back to the elephant. It appeared to also have had enough and was beating a retreat through the trees toward the river.

"*Iko sukari na samaki?*" the night watchman persisted after a prolonged silence.

"So, what about sugar or fish?" Thomas rolled his eyes.

"*Chakula* brings animals, especially if sweet or has big smell."

"I suppose you're right," Thomas admitted, and told the *mzee* about the bag of sugar.

"Ah, well," the old man surmised, "that *tembo* would have smelled it on the wind and crossed the river."

We were suddenly taken aback by an ear-piercing screech followed by the sound of trumpeting. It rent the air and came from the direction of the reed banks some two hundred yards down from where we stood. We all agreed it was our elephant and he was letting his extended family know of his triumphant return to the herd. However, this deafening blast had fully wakened most of the heavy sleepers in the hotel, and in a flash all the bedroom lights came on, yellowness fanning out across the upper floor of the hotel, something like a power outage in reverse. The windows were filled with anxious faces peering out into the sodden night. The hum of excitement filtered down into the garden. There was a barrage of inquisitive talk centered on elephant behavior and the reasons why this intrusion had taken place, probably the first in twenty years. These thoughts were uppermost in everyone's mind, and, within a matter of seconds, cameras and binoculars were produced and pointed into the darkness as flashbulbs popped.

"That *tembo* happy now he's gone home," the *mzee* murmured as the excitement died down. "But just you remember," he went on, and turned toward me, "when a *tembo* make trouble, all you need to do is light a small brushwood fire and he'll go fast away, pace pace, you'll see."

He smiled as I grasped his hand. "Thank you for your help," I said, "and have a good night." I turned around and walked across the compound toward the remains of the tent.

We agreed that enough was enough, and we removed what was left of our belongings and spent the remainder of the night in the van. It was lucky for me that I had taken my typewriter there, although I now realized that this whole event could have been avoided had I taken notice of Thomas when he first reported that a bag of sugar had burst in his hands. His emotional gloom over the sugar had been invasive. It wasn't part of his nature to cave in under questioning. He was tired, but it cheered him up no end that, when clearing the tent, Visavadia found a big pile of dung right in the middle of his blanket. We all had a good laugh over that, but it didn't stop us from joining in and giving him a hand by bouncing the muck off. Visavadia had seemed hesitant about using it again, but I suggested that he sleep under the good side of the blanket and that at the first opportunity he should take it to a cleaner for a proper wash, assuring him that he would be reimbursed from the money in the cash box. After all, it was a business expense.

The rain had thinned, but the hills over the Western Nile Province remained faint, and occasionally, when the moon shone, the light penetrated the haziness and gave off a blurred image of the higher slopes of the Padyeri Mountains.

It was close to three o'clock by the time we finally made it back to bed, and as I went to shut the passenger door I noticed the African night watchman was still sheltering under the narrow eaves. The yellow rays from the main door splashed out onto the veranda and illuminated him. There were still trickles of rainwater dripping down from the tiled roof onto globular-headed mimosa plants that skirted the terrace. Then, some moments later, the old man stepped from the dry of the veranda and walked slowly across the loose gravel of the driveway and was soon swallowed up in the darkness. For a moment I wondered about the medals on his coat and what battles he had fought. It was then that I fell asleep.

***

The sky was clear early next morning, and after breakfast I went to reception and bought a book of stamps. I sent my report off to London. However, before leaving Paraa I went over to Thomas and told him to stop worrying about last night. I said I felt responsible as he'd done his best to warn me about the sugar, but I had been too tired and had only wanted to get on with my sales report. I acknowledged that the entire farrago was my fault, and that given the facts, I should have insisted that we sleep in the van. On hearing this Thomas gave me a wide smile, and we hugged in the true African style.

At nine o'clock we left Paraa and crossed the Nile by a chain-linked ferry into Bunyoro Province and began the drive south to the town of Mascindi, a distance of around fifty miles.

The land was flat, and the ocherous scrub was lifeless. The dirt road was empty and reasonably easy to negotiate. We went past an enormous herd of smooth-coated buffalo standing still and staring impassively at us while chewing the cud, their erect ears twitching against the bite of the marauding tsetse fly. No sooner had we lost their picture in the mirror than Thomas had to slam on the brakes as several hundred oryx antelope changed direction and raced across the narrow track. It was their distinctive black-and-white faces that caught the eye. They are a brave animal, just one of a handful in the continent of Africa that would stay their ground and fight a lion to the death.

Gradually we moved away from the game reserve. There were now hills in the distance with dark trees along the rivers and streams. The land was becoming more broken, and the dusty road curved more often. We splashed across the Sembiye River, a mere six inches deep, and passed people on bicycles and others on bare feet walking the paths that led to settlements. Long puffs of smoke could be seen rising straight up from hutted areas, and then allotments and small, timbered shops. We had arrived at a little village, and yet, according to the road map, it didn't exist. Perhaps it had only recently been constructed. Anyway, we stopped and gave it a full thirty-minute show.

Some fifteen miles later, and going south, we arrived at the large, spreading town of Mascindi, an important marketing center at the crossroads of Uganda.

We spent three days here and covered a wide area that included the headquarters town of Hoima to the southwest and the port of Butiaba on the northern shore of Lake Albert.

It was here at Butiaba, some six years before, that Ernest Hemingway, the writer, had arrived by boat after his aircraft had crashed near Murchison Falls. The plane had dived under a large flock of Ibis birds and as a consequence tangled with telegraph wires. The press already had him dead, but he survived along with his wife, Mary, and together they pressed on and chartered a boat going south to the port of Butiaba, from where they had planned to drive by road to Kampala. Instead they thumbed a lift on an H-89 de Havilland Rapide that was flying to Kampala, but the craft failed to maintain height after taking off from Butiaba's poor runway and became violently unstable. It too crashed, and both the Hemingways were badly hurt. They ended up taking an agonizing fifty-mile car ride east to Mascindi, where they rested overnight, and the following morning they completed their road journey by taxi northward to Entebbe, and then back to Kampala.

On Thursday, August 18, we left Mascindi and headed south-southeast for Kampala, a distance of 133 miles. We exited the Bunyoro Region, where the road bridged the fast-flowing Kafu River. And there, beyond the village of Kibangya, was a bright forest extending back to the horizon. The air was thick with the long-tailed black bee-eater birds, with slender beaks swooping low in search of insects, their contrasting blue wings matching the blue of the sky.

We came out of the woods, and once more the view became extensive. The ride was less rough. The embanked road was smooth and bare and cut a path through the surrounding marshlands of the upper Mengo Region. A short while later we were held up by a road barrier, and a squad of khaki-clad workers sprayed our van with a strong dosage of tsetse fly repellent. After a brief halt at the trading center of Nakasongola, we pushed southward on an empty road through the widening swamplands toward Bombo, a mere twenty-three miles from Kampala itself.

We were soon out of the swamps, and in their place were big, spreading farms with well-drained fields of green-stemmed sesame plants. Their seeds are called by different names, such as sim-sim, benniseed, or gingelly. The plant is a quick grower—a cash crop if ever there was one—and can be utilized for making of margarine, fats, and soap, or fed to cattle and pigs after they have been pressed for oil.

We stopped every now and then to give shows to plantation workers and to shack settlements, each with its own tall, gangling banana plants and rich, well-drained vegetable plods. As we passed by, the people, both adults and children, would wave and smile, and in return we would do the same and also drop leaflets.

It wasn't long before we found ourselves on a black tarmac road that glistened in our lights from the recent rains. We traveled slowly toward Kampala's city center, and the first thing we did was to drop Visavadia off in Visram Street, home of a consortium of large Asian wholesalers, Uganda's lifeline, before continuing across town to the Speke Hotel.

"Take the van to Coopers Motors tomorrow morning for its midway service," I said as I climbed down onto the van's running board.

"They might not be able to book us in at short notice."

"In that case tell them it's a rush job and we need the van for the twenty-mile trip to Entebbe tomorrow morning, and what's more, remind them of the amount of business that Morgans throws their way."

"I'll see what I can do."

"And I also want you to pick me up at ten sharp, OK?"

"I'll do my best, but I can't give you a guarantee."

I moved my suitcase, typewriter, and briefcase before stepping back onto the pavement carpeted in red. I gave Thomas a low wave as he skimmed around the driveway and turned onto the main road. The rhythmic noise of the engine gradually receded and was soon lost in the drone of the night traffic.

I took a deep breath, turned in a half circle, and made my way between two potted plants into the hotel foyer.

chapter

ELEVEN

The Speke, a businessman's hotel, provided me with my first comfortable night between clean sheets after four weeks of tough travel in Uganda's northern regions. The luxury of a hot shower and a served meal gave a heightened sense of euphoria.

The next morning, after breakfast, I phoned the number that Carol had jotted down for me on a scrap of paper. I pulled a cigarette from the open pack lying on the bedside table and listened to the dull, monotonous, purring tones over the earpiece.

"Hello," a girl's voice came on the line.

"Is that Carol?" I asked, lighting the cigarette with my free hand and inhaling the strong, locally grown tobacco.

"No, sorry, my name's Lorraine," the voice replied cautiously. "She's already left for work."

"I thought she worked nights," I said.

"Would you like to leave a message with me?"

"That would be great," I answered. "Perhaps you would tell her that John called, and I'll ring again at six tonight."

"John?" the girl said guardedly, pausing for a few moments. "Are you the guy that's on safari?"

"Yes, I guess I am."

"Oh, dear," she said in a gloomy voice. "I've just remembered that Carol's going straight to a birthday party from work tonight. It's someone's twenty-first, and there's no way I can get hold of her as I'll be going out before she gets back."

"Not to worry," I said. "Perhaps you could leave her a note saying I am at Room 316 of the Speke Hotel, and would she be good enough to call me anytime she gets home?"

"Of course I'll leave her a note," she confirmed.

"I'm only here tonight," I added, "so I don't want to miss the chance of having a chat. However, if all else fails, I'll leave a letter for her at the hotel's desk."

"Is there any chance of your returning to Kampala in the near future?" Lorraine asked.

"No, not really, but I can always fly over when I get back to Nairobi about Christmas time. Thanks anyway for your help."

"Bye-bye," she breathed down the phone.

"Bye now." I put the receiver back in the cradle and stubbed out the cigarette into a large glass ashtray.

***

It was ten a.m. and the hotel lobby was crowded with people. I walked past the main reception desk and took up a position near the wide, glass-fronted entrance bounded by a pair of potted palms on each side of a long red carpet leading out from the hall and running the whole way across the pavement to the concrete curb, affording a bit of luxury for cars and taxis when letting their passengers down. Overhead, flapping gently in the warm morning breeze, was a green-and-white-striped canopy stretching beyond the curb and giving protection from both the rain and the glare of the sun.

Then, minutes later, rolling serenely down the gentle slope of the graveled driveway, making a tight circular turn before levelling out along the concrete curb, came our van with all its emblems colorfully displayed. Thomas inched slowly under the canopy and drew to a rest alongside the red carpeting. "Door-to-door service," he said enthusiastically. He would have been quite happy to park the van at the entrance to government house, but it was at times like these that I felt a bit self-conscious to be seen climbing into the cab of a commercial vehicle with the eyes of the posh hotel guests boring into my back. There was a strong smell of fresh oil and carbolic soap circulating inside when I sat down in the leather-styled passenger seat.

"You're bang on time." I smiled at Thomas and then leaned back to my right to greet Visavadia.

In front of us, there was a large green limousine with its engine ticking over and the passenger door hanging open. The liveried chauffeur stood waiting hesitantly on the driver's side while his smartly dressed passengers were locked in conversation under the hotel's portico, and they appeared in no great hurry to break off from their chat. "I'm not waiting any longer," Thomas said flatly, and swung the van through the narrow gap between the car and the concrete walling that bounded the hotel. The chauffeur gave a furious look as he pressed himself against the green coachwork.

Ten minutes later we stopped off at Morgans' warehouse and loaded the fresh stock that had been set aside. The inventory sheets showed that there were a hundred cases of medicine to be put in—an all-time record. In addition there were numerous packages of advertising material, including a gigantic tea chest containing seventy-five plastic badges promoting our Herbalex cough medicine, not to mention a shipment of eight hundred tin advertising plates.

"Nowhere to sleep tonight," Thomas grumbled.

Then, before leaving Morgans, I walked over to the office section to call on my friend Bob Worsley. I wanted to get his final agreement to the proposed itinerary for the southwestern region of Uganda. He would continue to exercise authority over our safari until as such time that we come under the control of Dar es Salaam.

"Hi, John," Bob greeted me as I entered his office. He got up from behind his desk to shake hands. "I saw your van out there earlier, and I was just coming over when the phone rang. I wouldn't let you leave without first having a word. How are you?"

"I'm fine," I said. "But I'm not sure about the van."

"Why, is something wrong with it?"

"No." I smiled. "It's only that you've given us a lot of stock and advertising material to carry. Those tin plates are a dead weight, they're right up to the roof, and there's going to be no room to sleep should we be caught short in the bush."

Bob pushed his chair back from the desk. "Your sales have been tremendous on this safari," he said in satisfied tones, and added, "You can't be telling me you won't be able to sell a few dozen by nightfall to ease the situation?

"Anyway," he went on, "I've got you marked down as doing Entebbe today before leaving here tomorrow, so there's no problem about where to sleep."

The door to Bob's office swung open, and a young girl brought in a tray of coffee and biscuits.

"You're right," I agreed. "I guess I'm worried about the weight the van's carrying. I've got an excellent crew, and they'll do anything for me, and that's the way I want to keep it. However, I don't want to have to go on asking them for more, until they've nothing left to give."

Bob poured the coffee and looked across the desk. "Anyway, while we're on this subject. I've worked out that you'll need to boost your stock of Herbalex and Gripe Aid when you get to Mbarara in about two weeks. In view of this, I'm sending a shipment of forty cases of each to the bus depot to await your arrival."

"That's all right by me," I said, and jotted down the detail in my notebook. "It's depressing to run low in the bush and have to turn customers away, but at the same time there's a limit to what we can carry, especially if the roads turn nasty."

"Did you see the plastic buttons for Herbalex?" Bob leaned over the desk and handed me a cup of coffee.

"Yes," I nodded. "I like them. I told the Export Department in London that we ought to have these badges. I'm glad they've done something about it."

"Good." Bob smiled. "That seems to cover everything. How was the last section of your safari? Any excitements?"

"Nothing much," I said, "but someday I'll write a book about my time in Africa. I put the notebook back into my briefcase, finished my coffee, and stood up. "It's time for me to go, I guess." I leaned over and shook his hand.

"See you again," Bob said with a smile.

Outside, in the yard, near the perimeter fence, I spotted Thomas. He was sitting in the driving seat of the van thoughtfully scratching his unshaven chin. His peaked khaki hat was, as usual, pushed back on his head. "I've only just managed to get the stock on board," he commented. "I've had to put four cartons in the front. Visavadia has just about enough room to squeeze in sideways. It's up to you how you get in."

***

Entebbe is the administrative HQ of the Ugandan government. It lies twenty miles south of Kampala, and its busy international airport is linked up with the heart of Africa and the world outside, while good road communications and port facilities on Lake Victoria's northwest shore give the town an air of gentle sophistication. Skirting the lakeside are the world-famous Botanical Gardens.

Pretty pink-and-white bungalows with red-tiled roofs nestled inconspicuously on the lush green slopes that dipped gracefully into the rippling lake waters. The alluring scent of red jasmine wafted lightly from scattered frangipani shrubs, and the yellow and white of the gardenia added to the hedonistic atmosphere. Expensive yachts skipped along the blue surface of the lake like paper darts. The sultry heat beat down from clear skies as fishermen, dotted along the wooden pier, cast lines from gnarled rods. The tawny yellow of the thick reed beds, where land met water, was home to countless waterbirds and amphibians. It was taken for granted that such a place was a haven, but it wasn't so long ago that I read an article in a local newspaper that someone had fallen asleep on the grassy slopes near to the reed bank and died when a bull frog had jumped onto this unfortunate man's face and smothered him.

For a moment I was distracted by a swarm of angry black flies rising from the lakeside. I could hear the buzz as they winged upward like a dark storm cloud.

But on the brighter side was a flight of soft-plumaged sunbirds, attracted by trailing ipomoea that bloomed in Entebbe's landscaped gardens. The flowering lobes, both in purple and white mallow, tempted the hovering, whirring, dinky-sized birds to sink their long, downward-curved beaks into the flora, busily searching for nectar, while never ceasing to flash their green and red metallic feathers as they flew off to another waiting plant.

We covered the market areas, played the usual mix of music, and handed out leaflets, and, for the first time, we pinned the new plastic buttons onto tops. Shortly afterward we moved into the commercial center and called upon large Asian stores. At noon we looked for a suitable parking place to pass the lunch hour, and finding none, we settled for a vacant space in the visitors' car park at the airport buildings. A grassy bank lined with white wood railings ran in a curving arc around the borders of the parking lot, which, in turn, was bounded by the main east/west boulevard. The hum of passing traffic was occasionally interrupted by the angry blast of a car horn from the road behind us. We spread ourselves out on the coarse grass that bordered asphalt and got ready to cook a midday meal.

Thirty minutes later we had finished eating and were waiting for the kettle to boil when the sound of approaching feet on the gravel made me turn my head. It was most likely someone on the way to pick up a car.

"Hi, you guys." A man of middle age squeezed his way between the parked vehicles. "My name's Larry Martin," he introduced himself, "and I'm on the foreign news service of Life Magazine. I expect you've heard of us," he said, stopping to smile. "I wonder if I may sit down and talk with you." He smiled some more and handed me his card.

"Sure," I said. "Would you like some coffee?" I glanced at the card with his name in black type. In the bottom corner, it read: Chief of Correspondents, New York Bureau of Life magazine. It was a monthly that appeared on every news stand throughout the world, and it seemed unreal to be brewing coffee near a dusty yellow sidewalk for a man in a blue worsted suit, complete with white shirt and a blue silk tie.

"Yeah, that would be just fine." He grinned amiably.

"How can we help you?" I asked, passing the mug of steaming coffee, adding, "I'm John Carter, and these are my two colleagues, Thomas and Visavadia."

"Well," he began thoughtfully, "it's like this. I'm over here to cover the situation in the Congo." He sipped at the coffee. "Jeez," he continued, "they've only been independent for six weeks and have already gotten themselves into one unholy mess. Anyway, I've been trying to get into the country, but the borders are sealed, and all I can do is to hang around the goddamn airport and hope that one of our stringers can find a way into the country and file an up-to-date report. I grant you I've got myself into a pretty negative situation."

"If you want to get nearer the action," I said, "fly to Arua. It's all happening there."

"I've been there," he said. "It seemed all quiet to me."

"Try Father Francis of the Catholic mission," I suggested, then asked, "What's this got to do with us, anyway?"

Larry Martin started writing in his notebook. "The thing is," he said, looking up, "I was downtown this morning in the local bazaar and saw you guys operating your sales pitch. It reminded me of the old days out west when itinerants used to hawk from the back of a covered wagon. I seriously think there's a story that can be written up here about you lot," he mused. "But I would like you to fill me in on some details of your work."

"What we do here is very different from the image you've conjured up," I said.

He ignored my comment. "Do you operate from Kampala?"

"Not really,"I said. "We're on a possible six to seven month safari covering all parts of East Africa and the borders of central Africa."

"Jeez," he whistled between his teeth. "There's got to be a story in this. Do others do it besides you?"

"We haven't seen anybody." I looked at Thomas and Visavadia, who shook their heads. "I've heard of one or two vans operating on the west coast, but they weren't very successful, although it's possible, here in East Africa, to operate a sales campaign with a fleet of smaller vans in order to cover the villages and towns within a certain distance of Kampala and Nairobi. But, in answer to your question, no one does it like us. I imagine this will be the last big safari before independence, and I'm pretty certain that no one else has ever launched a safari on this scale."

"I would sure like to come along with you guys for a couple of weeks. You could get good publicity out of it, and it wouldn't cost you a nickel. What do you say?"

"I'm sorry Larry, it can't be done," I said, "My company is reluctant to pass on our sales methods. We don't want to be copied. At present we've got the market clear to ourselves."

"If you change your mind, John," he said in miffed tones, "call our Nairobi desk as soon as you can." He got up from the grass and shook hands. "That was great coffee," he said and smiled.

A couple of hours later we slipped back into Kampala on a smooth tarmac road. We'd passed green banana gardens broken up by red tunnel-like paths. There were groups of workers making their way home after toiling in the fields. They walked along the dust-ridden edges of the road, but there was no spring in their steps. And besides them there were hordes of school children backtracking for home, some with their textbooks and even inkpots balanced on their heads.

***

The telephone on the bedside table began to jangle. I struggled from a heavy sleep, bleary-eyed, and grappled with the receiver. My eyes blinked from the bright yellow light of the lampshade that I had just switched on.

"Yes," I murmured.

"Is that Room 316?" A disgruntled voice filtered down the line.

"Yes." The face on my wristwatch showed it was a few minutes past three. I wondered who it could be phoning at this unearthly hour.

"This is the hall porter, sir," the voice droned on. "I have a lady on the other end of the line, and I wish to know if you want to take her call at such a late hour. She insists it will be alright and gives her name is Miss Gray?"

There was a pause while I dug deep into my mind. Then it suddenly dawned on me that the Miss Gray was indeed Carol. The use of first names had made our surnames superfluous. "Yes, put her on, please." My request was followed by a click and then an ominous buzz. I tapped the horizontal bar on the receiver.

"It's all right, sir," the porter assured, "I'm putting you through now."

"Hello," I said, my finger still hovered above the bar.

"John, are you there?"

It was Carol's voice this time.

"Yes, it's me."

"I hope you don't mind me calling," she began, "but I've just this minute gotten back from a party and received your note. It said call anytime."

"Of course it's OK," I said, adding, "It must have been a good party."

"It was great," Carol breathed down the phone, "but I missed you."

"Listen," I said quietly. "I'm leaving tomorrow, and it would be quite something to see you before I go. Are you free to meet me in the morning? Can we have breakfast somewhere together?"

"I'm free until tomorrow evening. My nightshift begins at six o'clock. I'd love to see you, John."

"Tomorrow evening," I repeated slowly. "Do you mean Sunday?"

"Yes, my rota begins on Sunday," Carol answered, slightly mystified by the question. "Why do you ask?"

"How would you like to come to Mubende with my safari team? You know what we do. I've told you all about our work. I'll make sure you'll get you back to Kampala in time for your night shift."

"That'll be great. I can always get a girlfriend to fill in for me at the hospital if I'm late on Sunday—so there's no problem." The rise and fall of her breath came whispering down the line.

"Then that's settled." I smiled as I pushed a pillow behind my back to get comfortable. "Can you make it to the hotel by ten, or is that rushing you?"

"I'll be there."

"I can't wait to see you again." I pulled a cigarette from a pack of Kali lying on the bedside table. "I bet you look great now."

"After being out all night, you must be joking." Her laughter peeled down the line like a carillon of bells. "Just the same. I must admit I've got on a rather glamorous red-and-white strappy dress," she said coyly, "and a pair of red high-heeled sandals and a white linen jacket..."

"And what else?" I teased, as her voice faded.

"There's no more," she breathed happily, "except a gold bracelet, ruby ring, and a touch of perfume."

"And all packaged in that smooth golden tanned skin," I quipped. "By the way, do you still have the gold chain around your neck?"

"Yes I always wear it."

"I'm going to say good-bye now, as you must be tired."

"You're right," she agreed. "See you at ten."

"Good night."

The phone clicked into a silent purr. I put down the receiver, stubbed out my cigarette into a glass ashtray, and switched off the light.

**

It was Saturday morning and shoppers overflowed the city's sidewalks. The bumper-to-bumper traffic was reduced to a crawl. More and more cars choked the central areas as they emerged from a web of narrow, sloping side streets. The high sun struck the top of the clean windshield, glinting on glass and metal. The baking heat was oppressive despite the side doors being open.

"You OK?" I smiled at Carol, who was sitting on some boxes in the back of the van.

Below Lugards Hill we made a detour, turning left at the roundabout. Then going straight, we followed the main boulevard, which was lined with red hibiscus and senna-leaved cassia dwarfed by waving palms. We then forked right near Namirembe Hill before emerging onto the Mubende Road. The capital, with its seven hills, slowly receded, half-hidden behind a curtain of shimmering haze. The scent of cassia was now a memory. It was sticky in the van. We passed suburban gardens with yellow-horned thevetia hedgerows, potato trees, and white jasmine, plus an occasional villa. Gradually we gathered speed, passing open-air barbers and green banana shambas. The handsome, round-faced Bagandan women in busuti gowns, hips rolling, heads straining under heavy loads, were making their way to market at Mityana.

The road was built on an embankment, and for some time it ran straight, dipping occasionally, while we followed the contour of the marshlands. Now and then the van bumped on the rutted surface, and not far ahead of us was a line of eucalyptus trees, leather-leaved and green, that marked the course of a stream. Beyond, the land stayed flat, widening into a yellow haze of unsettled light, becoming indistinguishable from sky. At noon we stopped for lunch by Lake Wamala, sanctuary for the many birds that inhabited the swamplands. The brilliant green-and-red plumage of the ibis could be easily seen wading across the spongy reed beds, their long, curving beaks probing the tall papyrus grass and their metallic wings glinting in the harsh sun.

Another hour went by and we were again back on the dirt road, leaving behind the endless trail of freshwater marshes in Mengo Province. We soon entered the straw-colored lands of the Mubende Region, rich in cotton, coffee, and bananas, along with its scattered deposits of tungsten, beryl, and rare, white tantalum. Near a place called Kitenga, we came to the deep-flowing Nabakazi River and slowed for the old wooden bridge that barely rose above the waters. On the other side, we turned away from the river and entered open savanna. Several miles later the road ran between fields of corn.

We passed a lone man in a scarlet fez and spiraling puttees, walking obliviously along the scuffed shoulder, perhaps a waiter or night watchman going to work. We wrapped a Herbalex sample in a booklet and dropped it in front of him, pointing at it, making sure he saw it, and then, when we had gone past, he disappeared from sight, lost in the mass of billowing clouds coming from the rear wheels of our van.

We traveled on the center of the track, wheels firmly positioned on the hard, shallow grooves that ran parallel on each side of the crown. The sloping sides from the apex of the road to the shoulders were angled at about fifteen degrees. Every now and then the security of the crown position would have to be relinquished when faced with an oncoming vehicle. It's at that point that the difficulty of keeping stability much depends on the severity of the slant, its condition, and the weight and stability of the cargo carried. It's possible when steering into a tilted position that the vehicle might oscillate, but as long as speed is maintained, and the offside wheels are slotted into the groove, the danger of an uncontrollable sway can be avoided. Unfortunately overturned vehicles can often be sighted along the roadside amid overgrown weeds and brambles, and in some ways they have become their own memorial. Occasionally one was confronted with a driver who wouldn't relinquish the crown. Perhaps he was high on pombe or had kamikaze tendencies, but either way spelled certain disaster. The road we were on continued to be shut in by fields of tall corn.

Thomas was a professional driver, and his driving license was proof of it. He was well aware of the dangers on an African road, and he never let up on giving full concentration while driving. He not only used his eyes, but his ears too, always half expecting to see another vehicle coming straight at him from nowhere. But now the track was empty and all was quiet.

"There's something on the road," he said seconds later. He had spotted a billowing cloud of thick dust rising above the corn. It was some distance away, but closing rapidly as its exhaust sound grew louder. Then, without warning, a heavily packed single-deck bus swung from a bend and sped angrily toward us. There was a slogan in huge black letters above the windshield. It simply said Lady Luck. It looked dangerous and overcrowded, and it had broken doors. There were several people riding on the roof, and we could see their faces. It was closing by the second.

We quickly moved over to the left slope, maintaining speed, our driver's side wheels catching successfully into the upper groove. "He's not giving way. He wants the road," I shouted across to Thomas.

"I know. I'm not blind," he yelled in frustration.

There were less than a dozen yards between the vehicles. "Hold tight everyone," I shouted as I turned toward Visavadia and Carol in the back.

Thomas had read the situation. He wrestled with the steering, trying hard to release the slotted right wheels from the deeply rutted groove. We could see the glazed ganja eyes of the oncoming driver. He was grinning and was leaning from his cab, a leg pressed against the outside fender in case he had to jump for it. We barely avoided a head-on collision; only inches separated us. Our van slipped its hold on the road and went hell for leather down the muddy slope, bucking and lurching all the way, until it thumped against an embankment and spun forward into an overgrown ditch. We had heard the taunting voice of the bus driver echoing across the track before he was lost behind his own cloud of rising red dust.

"That was close," Thomas remarked, mopping his brow with a cloth. "It's a good thing we didn't turn over."

"It could have been much worse," I said. "It could have been Gulu all over again."

"Why did you say that?" Thomas turned and looked hard into my face.

"I'm sorry," I said. "I didn't mean to."

I turned round and looked into the packed cabin. I had heard voices but wasn't sure if that was a good sign, but at least it was promising.

"Are you all right in the back?"

"A bit shaken," Carol replied, behind a stack of cartons.

"I'm OK," Visavadia confirmed.

It took nearly two hours to dig our way out of the ground and back onto the middle of the road. All the while Carol had said nothing, but each time one of us broke off for a drink of water, she would take the spade and start digging.

Outside the hotel, before we left Kampala, Carol had agreed that the safari came first. She had spent this first leg of our journey in the back of the van studying the literature on Herbalex and Gripe Aid, rather like an actress learning her lines, and then, at villages and settlements along way, she had talked with the young mothers in the audiences.

It was still light when we entered the market town of Mubende. At the entrance to the local cotton ginnery, we were directed by an askari to the home of the village chief. We found him sitting on a stone slab by his doorway. He quickly sent one of his wives to fetch the key to the rest house, and while we waited, I negotiated the price for one of his chickens.

The stony track on the way to the rest house cut steeply through a forest of blue gum trees and firs. All the time we climbed upward, driving around hairpin bends and spitting out a medley of stones, chippings, and cones from under our wheels. At times, only inches spared us from a precipitous drop on the passenger side, but little by little we progressed up the incline and at last began to level out. The dark, oblong shape of a large bungalow could be glimpsed through the scattered woodland.

"Gosh, doesn't it look beautiful." Carol sighed as she peeked out of the open doorway, her blond hair playing in the warm breeze.

The grass lawns fell away on three sides, and huge evergreen firs dotted the perimeter fence. Beyond the trees, it was the real Africa. The cement walls of the house were painted white, and the large thatched roof draped over the sides, forming eaves; it was supported by hardwood posts set at intervals along the terrace.

"It's all right here, isn't it, John?" Carol squeezed closer, seeking assurance; everything was so new to her.

It was getting dark, and stars began to crowd the steel blue sky. The house looked almost lonely on top of the wooded slopes. I took Carol's hand and said, "Of course it's all right. We rarely get such a nice place as this." I unlocked the door and went inside. The main hallway was spacious with a large built-in fireplace, along with a pair of decorative metal firedogs for the wood. Three doors led off to bedrooms, one door to a musty bathroom.

"Is there electricity?" she whispered.

"I'm afraid not, and there's no running water either." I smiled as I twisted the tap in the bath. Several cockroaches scurried across the tiled floor and disappeared under the splintered skirting board. I went back into the hallway and ran the beam of my flashlight around the walls and ceilings. I put an arm round Carol. "Not to worry," I said. "We have two paraffin lamps, and I'll put water in the toilet from a large rain barrel outside." It seemed that all that was left to make things homely would be a log fire in the hearth, and the ax we had in the back of the van would now come in handy.

We pushed open another door and looked cautiously inside. The room was sparsely furnished. There was an oak-stained dressing table with broken mirror; a badly scarred Victorian cupboard; two straight-backed chairs, one with a broken leg; and, dominating the room, a large Victorian wood-framed bed with a badly stained mattress.

"Not bad," I said, switching off the torch and taking Carol in my arms.

"It seems ages since we were last together," Carol breathed in my ear, "and I want you so much."

"We'll be alone tonight."

The shrill squawk of a chicken echoed from the main room. "Mr. Carter, are you there?" Thomas called aloud.

"Just a moment," I shouted, as I crossed the room and opened the door.

"This chicken," Thomas queried, waving it by the legs, "is it too late to cook now, do you think?"

"We'll have it for lunch tomorrow," I said, and added, "You'd better give it some water and put it in a box." I looked around the hallway and poked my head through a couple of doors. "Where's Visavadia?" I asked.

"He's gone to get wood for the fire." Thomas went over to the big window. "Shall I start to get supper ready?"

"Yes, that would be great."

"No problem."

I walked with Carol to the front door, and turned back toward Thomas. "Carol will give you a helping hand with the cooking as soon as we've got our cases from the van."

We stepped out onto the terrace. The moon was unsettled, half-hidden behind wispy cirrus clouds that raced across the empty sky. The cackle of hoopoes and noisy francolins could be heard from the woods.

"It's going to rain soon," I said.

"Let's hope not," she replied as she pulled her small weekend case from the back of the van. For a brief moment she looked up at the sky and the dark clouds.

Visavadia had returned with a supply of freshly chopped wood and was already lighting the fire. The soft patter of rain splashed against the window.

It wasn't long before the meal was ready. The four of us sat on a blanket in front of a log fire with plates of spaghetti bolognaise on our laps. Later, it was Carol who made the coffee and handed around some digestive biscuits from a hexagonal tin. It was now our turn to kick in, and Carol and I washed up and cleared the room ready for the morning.

"Look what I've found," Carol exclaimed. She was standing by the mantelpiece on the far wall opposite to the fireplace. "It's a visitor's book!" She took a deep breath and blew the dust from the cover. The last entry was for a Mr. George Hayes, assistant district commissioner of Toro Province, dated August 2, almost three weeks before.

"Let's put our names in," she added excitedly. She knelt on the floor, book on lap, and slowly wrote down our names as I spelled them out to her. They were Thomas Mambui, Vinoo Visavadia, John Carter, and Carol Gray, and under the appropriate column we gave our occupation as Safari Salesmen and Woman and put the date in as Saturday, August 20, 1960. "It'll be a record forever, won't it, John?"

"Yes, that's for sure," I agreed, "although Africa has a way of wiping out all that goes before it, and as time goes by only memories remain, and then, nothing." I walked across the hall and opened a window. The tropical storm had moved away, and the house was now decidedly stuffy.

"Talk about being cheerful," Carol goaded.

It was then that Thomas and Visavadia said good night and went off to their rooms.

"It was cruel of you to say that," Carol pursued.

"I didn't mean to be," I said, and then went on to explain that I was guided by a quote I had read in a magazine that I had picked off a pile in a doctor's waiting room. I had breezed through its pages and got caught up with an article on Greek philosophers. I was taken by surprise when I read a succinct quotation on life that said, "Things are as they are, and will end as they must," and I thought about that for a long time afterward and reckoned the saying deserved a gold medal.

I put my arm around her shoulders as she buried her head against my chest. "I'm sorry that I was negative," I said, "and I didn't mean to hurt you. The truth is that I'm proud to have my name next to yours in the visitors' book. Probably in years to come someone will wonder who we were, and what with our different surnames, be curious about our night in this government rest house."

"It's just that I need to be with you," Carol explained, "and I want things to be special between us." She paused for a moment or two while she brushed a mosquito off her leg. "You know, what I'm trying to say, it's us being here alone in the middle of Africa. It means so much to me, and I hope that we'll see each other again after this night in Mubende is over."

"And I you," I whispered, "and what's more, I'll come and look you up, wherever you are, and nothing will stop me."

We fell silent and struggled up from the hard floor and crossed over to the bedroom.

Carol had made the bed with the two blankets we kept in the van. She started to undress, neatly folding her clothes to use for a pillow. "You don't think any creepy crawlies will get in here?"

"Not a chance," I said as I pulled the dowdy cotton curtains across the latticed window. "Come and look at this." A solitary anteater with a long, thin head and bushy tail was moving silently across the grass from the woods. It was spot lighted by the moon and was making its way to the tall termite mounds beyond the firs, well knowing that after heavy rains the white ants leave their red pyramids in large, suicidal swarms.

For a few minutes we stayed still, not talking, and gazed out of the window, absorbed the magnificence of Africa. We then turned away and lay down on the bed. Her firm, tanned body rolled against me.

"You, me, and Africa," she gasped, offering her warm and abandoned love.

***

The morning sunlight was already beating against the cotton curtains. My watch showed the time was eight o'clock, and Carol was still fast asleep. I rolled quietly from the bed, stretched, picked up my wash things, and left the room.

"Look at this," Thomas rounded on me as I opened the door and stepped into the hall. An inch-thick layer of white termites carpeted the floor. "You left the window open last night," he said.

"It was the wood fire that first attracted them," I said.

"Yes, maybe so, but you could argue that none of this would have happened had it not rained in the first place."

The stale air was clouded with whirls of dead insects, and Thomas, with a thin slat of wood in each hand, scooped them up into a large box as they fell to the floor.

"It's my fault," I admitted.

It was then that Visavadia came through the front door carrying an empty box. He dropped it on the coated floor and took an old broom that was propped against the dusty mantelpiece and began sweeping the termites into irregular piles.

"When you've finished," I said, "I would be grateful if you would do me a favor."

"What's that?" Visavadia smiled, leaning on the broom.

"After breakfast, would you go down to Mubende and see if any of your friends are going to Kampala this afternoon? If so, perhaps they would give Carol a lift back. Otherwise, try and find out whether anyone has a taxi for hire. You can go down into town with Thomas, but please try and be back before eleven o'clock."

"Shouldn't be too difficult," Visavadia agreed, arching his dark eyebrow as he went back to his sweeping.

Less than an hour later we sat grouped on the freshly cleaned floor eating breakfast of paw paw, ham and eggs, and mugs of steaming coffee. When we had finished Thomas and Visavadia departed for the village of Mubende, which lay not more than a mile from the bottom end of the narrow winding track that we negotiated last night.

Carol went outside to the garden to catch a breath of fresh air. "This is a fabulous view," she exclaimed as I approached, "even better than when the moon illuminated the hills last night."

Then, everything was mysterious and magnificent, but now overwhelming, with a landscape stretching all the way back to the northern horizon. The land appeared to drop and drop into the colorless distance and eventually dissolved into a mix of cloud and haze.

We walked hand in hand across the drying grass and stopped by the trees that bordered the lawn. We took a last look at the panorama before we wandered across a trodden path that hugged the perimeter, which was dotted with wild pink bougainvillaea. We then made our way toward the woods on the southern side of the house.

A jagged row of several cinchona trees—the barkcloth redolent of quinine—hedged the darkened woodland while many thousands of straw-colored bats hung like bunches of uncooked sausages from tangled boughs.

Carol quickened her pace. "I hate bats," she said nervously. The pungent odor from the fouled leaves rose up from the ground. There was a quarrel going on among a small group of these nocturnal mammals, seemingly agitated as they fluttered their membranes. However, the vast majority remained motionless, hanging upside down from hind limbs to cool off until nightfall.

We entered the woods farther down, and only the crunch of our feet on parched twigs broke the eerie silence. The trees were now indiscriminate, some tall, some short, each one jostling for its own space while the larger ones pressed upward for their special place in the sky. They had exotic names, such as pencil cedars, red ironwoods, kokroduas, greenhearts, and spruces.

Although spoiled for choice, I was searching for one particular tree that hadn't a name. It was known as the giant of Mubende, mentioned briefly in some forgotten guide book. Apparently it had a girth as wide as a baobab tree and was as nearly as high as a sequoia.

Then, twenty minutes later, after keeping to a trodden path, I squeezed Carol's hand. "Look at this," I said. The enormous tree was only a few yards in front of us. It blocked the view in every direction. The thirty-foot girth, ribbed and scarred, rose majestically upward for nearly 250 feet. Its heavy branches drooped and got tangled with neighboring trees, causing all those other trees to lean away, acknowledging its superiority. "This is the Witch Tree," I murmured, and turned to look into Carol's pale blue eyes, and added, "Isn't it fantastic?"

"Wow," she breathed. "It's unbelievable."

She quickly sat down on one of the many silver-gray buttresses that rooted down from the lower section of the thickly barked trunk. "It's a spirit tree," I said, and paused as I pulled a pack of Kali cigarettes from my jacket pocket and lit one. "The tree is feared by the local tribes because it whispers and cries at night." I was silent for a moment while I inhaled the tobacco. "It's said that if you so much as touch the tree and fail to show proper respect, you will inherit an incurable disease or catalyze others in your family."

"I wished you'd said something before I sat on its roots," Carol said fearfully. "It seems to me that I should have asked for some sort of permission or bowed my head or something?" She was trembling as she rose from the abutment and moved silently away with her head down. "I feel cold," she said, and reached out for my hand. "Please take me away from here."

"I'm sorry," I said, "but I'm sure you'll be OK. Do remember, you didn't actually touch the tree trunk." We walked back toward the house, passing the slimy leaf mounds under the cinchona trees, and out across the grass.

"I didn't hear any crying last night," Carol said in a low voice as she pressed herself against me.

"You seem to believe in these myths."

"Yes, I do," she said emphatically. "They have been passed down from generation to generation, although I must admit that I didn't hear any whispering either last night."

"We were making love." I smiled.

She was dressed in a gray noniron safari suit with button-down pockets on the jacket. Her sleeves were rolled up; there was a small gold watch on her left wrist. Her arms were golden brown and strong. The gold necklace glinted in the light. She looked even taller than her five feet seven inches in the outfit.

"Make love to me now," she whispered as we stepped across the veranda, through the hall, and into the bedroom.

Thirty minutes later we heard the monotonous grind of the van laboring up the stony track with its hairpin bends. I looked at Carol on the bed, her perfect body relaxed and yielding, lips pink and inviting. "I'm going to miss you so much," I said.

"And I you," she sighed helplessly.

By the time the van came to rest outside the house, I was dressed and Carol was watching me from under a blanket as I made for the door. "See you in a few minutes," I said.

I waited on the terrace while Thomas and Visavadia clambered down and shut the sliding doors.

"Have you any news?" I asked as I walked across the lawn toward them.

"Yes, I've fixed it, Visavadia confirmed, adding, "My friend from the Patel Store is leaving for Kampala at two o'clock, and he'll come and fetch Carol before he goes."

"That's kind of him," I said.

"He was going anyway because he wants to visit the wholesalers first thing on Monday when the fresh shipments of cloth arrive from India. He's very anxious to place an order for the best bolts before other buyers get there," Visavadia explained, and added, "He'll be glad to have the company of a nice English lady."

I turned to Thomas. "Did you do any business this morning?"

He pushed the peaked cap to the back of his head. "Yes, I did about four dozen each of Herbalex and Gripe Aid."

"That's good work," I said.

We strolled back toward the rest house. "Better get started on that chicken for lunch," I suggested. "You can grill it on a spit. I'll get some wood for the fire."

The most difficult thing I experienced on the safari was to turn my back on the blue metallic car that carried Carol home to Kampala. She leaned from the passenger window waving a brown hand, her blond hair blowing in the wind as the car disappeared down the narrow track hidden by tilting trees. I stood for a moment in silence. The car was noisy, rattling, low gears grinding, twisting down the bumpy, narrow track to the gray-green valley below. And then there was no more sound, only the sharp hammering of tufted barbet birds flying from nest holes in the deserted woods fringing the empty lawn.

***

Thirty minutes after she'd gone, we followed the same route down the rock-strewn track, turning right at the bottom, heading in the direction of Fort Portal. The barking of overfed dogs and the wild calls of yellow-billed plantain eaters fell away as Mubende receded in the afternoon haze. The road flattened out and was now smooth and bare. The landscape was without trees, and we were able to see for some distance ahead. It was two thirty p.m., and it was a late start. However, I was glad that we were leaving Mubende.

Another night in Mubende would have proved too much for me to contemplate, and departure was the only logical answer. After a few miles, we reached the bush village of Bagedza and made a short stop before heading along a dirt road to Toro Province. The night had fallen. A dim light from

Safari Salesman

someone's lantern flicked from a mud hut in the center of a small stockade. There was a narrow path going up a slope, crossing other paths that zigzagged into the darkness. Our headlights no longer followed the contour of the road, which swept away between rising grounds. Thomas's chiseled face was illuminated by an array of panel lights as he leaned forward and concentrated on the driving. The earlier bank of gray clouds now darkened the moon, and moments later we entered the abandoned trading center of Kyegsgwa.

A lone figure stood hunched in front of a wood fence that circled the now-defunct cattle market as the rain began to bucket down. The man's hat was soon soaked, and what with his patched khaki trousers, sagging jacket, and torn greatcoat, he presented a forlorn picture. He came forward as we pulled onto the shoulder of the muddy road, which was fast turning into a quagmire.

"Where's the rest house? " Thomas inquired as he wound down the side window.

The man eyed us curiously while he removed a two-foot bamboo cane from under his coat and started to point the way. He was talking rapidly in Swahili, and I caught the words *apana mzuri nyumba mkubwa,* which roughly translates into "the big house is no good."

"What's he saying? " I asked Thomas as the old man shuffled away into the gloom.

The roof of the van was aloud with the drumming of rain, and Thomas had to raise his voice in order to be heard. "The old man says the rest house is in bad condition and warns that it has neither windows nor doors, besides which it's alive with rats and flies." Thomas broke off, lit a cigarette, and inhaled deeply. He looked washed out.

"Are you OK?" I asked.

"Yes, I'm all right," he answered, "just tired."

"I'm sorry," I said quietly, "but we'll have to spend another night in the bush."

The following morning the skies had cleared, and after an early breakfast consisting of pineapple juice, toast with marmalade, and a cup of instant coffee, we set off westward in the direction of Fort Portal. Unfortunately we took a wrong turn and ended up on a muddy track that led toward an area of dense forest. There seemed to be nowhere where we could make a U-turn, and because of this we had no alternative but to motor on and penetrate even deeper into the woods. Eventually we found a place to make a turn, and it was a good hour before we were able to find our way back and rejoin the original route marked on our map. It appeared that we had mistakenly forked right and had driven onto a road frequented by heavy transporters belonging to a logging company. It only goes to show how easily we had become inured to the poor standard of Africa's unmarked bush roads. What had seemed a typical road to us was nothing more than that of a mud trail.

After we left the woods we entered a region of open countryside and increased our speed, to offset our earlier delay. It wasn't long before we motored through the middle of an agricultural belt consisting of several wide fields that were either dotted with bonfires burning off crop waste or the blaze of crackling stubble. Palls of heavy smoke lingered over the entire area. It was clear that the earth was being made ready for plowing and seeding, and maybe the next crop would be of maize, finger millet, cassava, sugar cane, or cotton.

Farther down the road we passed groups of women working on extensive plots of arable land. Those in the lead were busy hoeing and weeding, while those behind were sowing the seeds. These proud women of Toro Province toiled unceasingly beneath an unforgiving sun, and yet surprisingly were dressed in bright voluminous clothes, and wrap-around headdresses. When they stooped, their hips stayed still, while their upper bodies moved in a synchronized swing, and all the time their babies (*mtotos*) remained tightly bound to their backs and without exception were sound asleep.

We continued to follow the level of the land along the rainwashed track, and gradually the bush began to open up and there was little to see but limitless savanna, blanketed in coarse, white-flowered elephant grass. Here and there were isolated acacia trees whose leafy foliage afforded circles of shade for discerning wildlife. We had to reduce our speed to avoid skidding on the oozy carotene-colored surface.

It seemed an age before we reached the outskirts of our next stop. On each side of the street were rows of small, detached red ocher houses and a scattering of modern brick and tiled bungalows, but finally we entered the center of Butiti Township. By now the weather had turned nasty, with thunder, lightning, and a glowering sky. Suddenly there was nothing but rain, inches of it, pelting down toward a network of ditches.

People tried in vain to cover their heads as they skipped from shop awning to shop awning, and then, when these sun blinds ran out, they raced frantically up the street, anxious to make it home. However, many others held newspapers over their heads and strode bravely down the side of the road. There was only an occasional umbrella to be seen, but despite these protective measures, most of the people ended up dripping wet. It was at this particular moment that our heavy-duty windshield wipers packed in, and there was next to nothing we could do about it. We were driving almost blind.

A short while later we drew slowly into a garage that was situated on our route through town. An attendant in a pair of oily blue dungarees sauntered solemnly toward us from the dry of his timber shelter. "What can I do for you?" he asked.

We told him about the wipers and asked him to check the tires and fill the tank.

"Come back in an hour and it'll be ready," he responded. The one certain thing about dropping into an African garage is the mechanic's willingness to fix most problems right away. Anywhere else you would be told to ring back in a week to see if the parts had arrived and then arrange a booking.

It was decided that Thomas and I would leave Visavadia "to mind the shop." We put on our waterproof jackets and visited the retailers up and down the main street who were most likely to place an order for our products. However, without the backing of music, it made our job doubly difficult. But in the end, our endeavors were rewarded. An Indian grocery store placed an order for two dozen bottles of Gripe Aid and a dozen of Herbalex. We also passed out leaflets in the shelter of projecting roofs, and several potential customers followed us back to the van in order to make their purchases. All of this bustle didn't go down too well with the mechanic who was working on the van.

We left town the moment the vehicle was declared roadworthy by the same mechanic, and headed westward for the seventeen-mile journey to Fort Portal. The incessant rain had turned into a deluge and had muffled any desire we might have had to chat. An hour or so later we reached the outskirts of the town and reduced our speed to walking pace through the heavily populated bazaar area. The shops and warehouses were already closed for the day. We noticed that buildings in the heart of the town were pressed together in a chaotic way, each vying for space.

The main street was narrow; it dipped away from the marketplace and ran beside a wide concrete gully filled with rushing water. Eventually it widened onto a dual carriageway that was lined with fuchsia shrubs and their cerise flowers were drooping sadly in the rain. A couple of hundred yards later the tarmac petered out and the countryside took over. The rising road threaded its way between green slopes, and every now and then we caught sight of snow-capped peaks that climbed above the rains and reached into the sky.

Finally we arrived on level ground at the famed Mountains of the Moon Hotel.

Fort Portal lies at the foot of the northern spur of the Ruwenzori Mountains. It forms the backdrop of the Portal Peaks—a rugged chain of rocks—that block off the main glaciers behind them. The town itself houses the government headquarters for the entire western region of Uganda.

For three days we worked the surrounding district, and on Thursday, August 25, we made ready to leave this lovely town. After breakfast I wrote to Carol at a table in my room, and on completion I came downstairs with my luggage and handed the letter in at the reception desk for onward mailing. Then, at the same time, I settled my account with the hotel and purchased a morning paper. On the way out of the office I picked up a brochure lying on a rosewood table in the hallway. It was entitled "The Ruwenzoris." It was these mountains that would form the background of our itinerary in the coming week, and I thought it wise to get some detailed information on them now that I had time to spare. I found an empty leather chair in the bay-windowed lounge and ordered a pot of high-quality local coffee grown on the flat terraces near Kigezi. The waiter who took my order was attired in a white kanzu and a purple tasseled fez.

I put the morning paper on the nearby table and began to look through the illustrated brochure. There was a colored picture of a group of pygmies outside an adobe tree house. The article explained that the pygmies inhabited the Ituri Forest, which extended across the Uganda/Congo border on the northern foothills not far from Fort Portal. There was another colored picture of the eye-dazzling animal called the okapi. It has a smooth purple and red coat and was adorned with white stripes on its hind quarters. Apparently this shy and solitary animal was being hunted to extinction in the forest regions by the selfsame pygmies.

The Ruwenzoris, the brochure explained, straddled the border for a distance of a hundred miles from Lake Albert to Lake Edward in the south. An uptilted mass of nonvolcanic granite was built on tectonic plates and formed the western rift. It was Henry Morton Stanley who first sighted them on January 8, 1876, from the southeast corner of Lake George. He originally called them the Gordon Bennett Mountains, after his employer, who owned the *New York Herald Tribune.* Subsequently the name was changed to the Ruwenzoris. This is a random description of the word *ru,* which means "high," and *Wenzori,* which was a translation of the local tribe's name, the Nssoro. In any case the name given by the Bagandan people was *Gambaragara,* meaning, "My eyes smart from the glistening snow." The glacier peaks attain heights of sixteen thousand feet in many places along the length of the range.

chapter

TWELVE

The van swung easily onto the dusty driveway that was partly screened from the road by a line of leafy trees and burgeoning thevetvia shrubs. It slowly drew to a halt in front of the hotel entrance. The familiar note of the engine had caused me to glance out of the lounge window. I saw Thomas climb from the cab and lean nonchalantly against the bonnet, having first propped himself up with an elbow, while his peak cap was tilted at a jaunty angle. He was soon engaged in conversation with an old gardener who was trimming around the edges of a hibiscus bed. The bright morning sunlight fell on the hedges and gardens.

I finished my coffee, got to my feet, and folded my copy of today's *Standard* newspaper, which I slid into the pocket of my safari jacket for reading on the journey. I then left the comfort of a red leather chair, picked up my trappings, and walked out of the lounge toward the main entrance and into the outside glare.

"Let's go." I smiled at both my colleagues and hoisted my case into the rear of the vehicle and put on my shades.

"Kasese?" Thomas asked, kicking the starter button.

"You've got it," I responded, and leaned back against the seat.

The vehicle began to move over the graveled driveway. Thomas tooted the horn at the aged gardener, who was bent over the flowers, and gave him a friendly wave. He then turned the van down the narrow slope that opened out onto the dual carriageway. The wide concrete gully that ran alongside the highway was no longer filled with rushing water, but was now dry and cool. We pushed slowly down the main street, lined with colorful Asian shops and tall imported palms, and circled the grassed-over roundabout, where the streetlamps ended and the dirt road started. We slowly made our way through the bumpy lanes of the African market, stalls already busy, smoke hanging faint in the fresh morning air, and headed south on a flat, bush-hemmed track for the forty-five-mile stretch to Kasese. It was still sticky in patches from the recent rains, and Thomas kept a careful watch on the wheels and made sure they were firmly placed in the grooves about the softness of the central ridge. The play of sunlight on the scrub was intermittently broken by gray trunks and thick green foliage of roadside trees, all of which cast harsh shadows across the track. Everything in the van had become coated in a thick layer of dust.

We stopped six or seven times at isolated settlements; a usual pattern of small groups of brown, tin, and timber huts, set at crossroads, all having bare compounds surrounded by little fields, and broken wire fences guarding the plots of sweet potatoes, maize, and beans. Our audiences were limited, but for what they lacked in size, we compensated by giving more personal attention to the individual. It was nearly five o'clock when we reached Kasese, our target for the day, and soon found accommodation at the only place in the village, the Magherita Hotel.

The next morning, Friday, August 26, we set out for the copper-cobalt mines at Kilembe, situated deep in the picturesque Nyamwamba Valley. It was a short eight-mile trip from the hotel, skirting the north edge of Queen Elizabeth Park, some eight hundred square miles of scrub. We saw large herds of red and blue duiker antelopes, and plains-loving, glossy brown topi. Then, unexpectedly, around a hidden curve in the track, we were stopped by a zebra-striped barrier manned by a lone guard. The official questioned the reason for our visit before calling through to administration for clearance. We could hear him talking on the extension relayed from his white guard post at the side of the road.

"OK," he said while raising the barrier. "The supplies manager will see you. It's Block F-6, straight on down on the left."

We drove through the gate past a series of low concrete buildings giving way to a modern glass-fronted shopping complex, then more faceless blocks, blurred images of people behind the tinted windows, a church and commissariat, along with a grassy plot of land set aside with swings and slides, obviously a children's playground. The people we saw were either clothed in gray cottons and white tops or blue boiler suits with tin helmets and yellow identification labels. They either walked alone or formed groups of both sexes going from block to block in silence, unsmiling but purposeful. The whole scene could have been taken out of a space movie; it was bizarre, and it was difficult to piece everything together. I almost forgot that the wild expanses of Africa lay only a few hundred yards away behind the zebra-striped road barrier.

A small twin-engine plane flew in low, wheels down, angling slightly as it descended on a hidden runway behind the row of unbroken buildings. We soon found Block F-6 from small white-painted signboards at the corner of the intersection that crisscrossed the flattened area. Every now and then large yellow dump trucks loaded with soft pyramids of reddish-brown mineral deposits hissed by on heavy industrial tires, coming from the workings in the mines, which were obscured from view by dust and shimmering haze.

I was ushered into a comfortable office by a smiling secretary.

"Thank you for coming," the manager said, before adding, "Now what is it we can do for you?" He sprung the tips of his fingers together as he leaned across his immaculate desk. He seemed cheerful and normal and far removed from the clockwork person I had anticipated. However, the whole environment appeared unnatural, and it shocked me to realize that the bush had preconditioned both my physical appearance and my mind. I wasn't alone because Thomas and Visavadia felt the same apprehension while we were locked into this huge organized complex. We simply felt out of place and only wanted to escape back to Africa.

Some thirty minutes later we left the mining area, the supplies manager having signed an order for five hundred gallons of pine and two hundred of coal tar disinfectants, twelve gross of toilet paper, and two gross of urinal tablets, all of which would be shipped from our manufacturers in Clapham, London.

It was another Friday night, which meant I had to spend an hour or more after supper making out a weekly report together with a roundup of our daily sales, and an expense account for the week, which amounted to twenty seven pounds, ten shillings, and sixpence.

The next morning we departed Kasese on a narrow dirt track and went via the Queen Elizabeth Park. The majestic, 13,682-foot, snow-capped Watamagufu Peak of the Ruwenzori Range towered over us on our right, but down on earth, the swampy marsh lands reached out from the gray metallic flats of Lake George . The northern edge of the lake was choked with papyrus reeds binding the soil to fight erosion. The 150 square miles of the freshwater lake is an outlet for Lake Edward via the Kazinga Channel. In these nine-foot-deep waters the tilapia is fished in considerable quantities—netted from dugout canoes—and taken to the main fisheries depot at Kasenyi on the northern shore. And here it is processed into smoked or frozen fish fillets. The tilapia breeds well, and it carries the eggs and larvae in its mouth. It weighs approximately two pounds when caught.

We drove on southward across the park, tilting and bumping on the dirt road, always following the level of the land. A vast herd of black buffalo stared blindly at us as they browsed impassively among the sedge grasses, some wallowing in the mud pools. The tall reeds obscured the oppressive grayness of the lake beyond. The Kitandara Valley came into view, its rolling slopes dotted with hypericum trees, then it dipped gently away into the haze of the southernmost banks, unmasking momentarily the low hill from which Stanley first saw the Ruwenzori Mountains as he gazed across these flat, marshy plains in 1876.

From the van we caught glimpses of anthills scattered about the far-off plains; red obscene cones that reached heights of more than twenty feet. Then, out of the blue, a swarm of large blue cattle flies entered our dust-ridden cabin and hungrily bit at our skin. The scent from an occasional broken bottle of Gripe Aid attracted flies, and, unless we were meticulous in wiping clean any mess, the aroma was strong enough to attract both insects and wildlife. It took several minutes before we finally rid ourselves of them. It passed my mind that perhaps the black-plumaged shoulder kites that hovered overhead might prove a useful ally. After all, they were riding the thermals and scavenging for insects and stray rodents. We slowed to watch a young leopard, high up on the parched branches of a solitary fig tree, wrestling with a carcass that its mother had hunted.

Almost unnoticed was a faded metal sign on the roadway. For a third time we had traversed the equator, and, as I was in the driving seat, I couldn't resist putting my foot onto the brake.

"What's happening?" Visavadia asked from behind.

"It's the equator," I said, "and it's time we took some photos of ourselves that we could show to our grandchildren in the years to come." We took four pictures and a fun one of me with a leg in the Northern Hemisphere and one in the Southern.

It was Thomas in the driver's seat now, and, although the road was easy and empty, we faced the sun head-on and automatically pulled down the visors to escape the dazzle. The heat was unrelenting and hot air wafted through the open doors of the vehicle. It was like putting the fan heater on at full blow. By now the sharp, needle-like stings from the cattle flies had turned into nasty rash-like pools of damp sweat, and our clothes rubbed on them and made them sore.

On the passenger side we motored past a copse of collapsed trees rotting in the tall clumps of tawny grass. Then, without warning, and some distance in front, we came upon a herd of gray and brown elephants of all shapes and sizes—from the seven-thousand-kilo bulls right down to the young, perfectly miniature calves, sheltering under their mothers' legs. The herd was spread about the track and showed no inclination to move away. They carried on browsing placidly from the acacia trees, their rope-like tails whipping at the flies. Every now and then one of the females would move to a different tree and her young one would race after her. A flock of black secretary birds descended from the sky, angling down and landing among the herd, searching for rats or the hissing snakes that might have been forced into the open by the tramping of the elephants on their lairs.

"All this is going to make us late tonight," Thomas said.

He had stopped the vehicle two hundred yards short of the herd, and he had shown his frustration by thumping the steering wheel with the palms of his hands.

"You'll have something to really worry about if they stop eating," Visavadia chipped in from the back seat.

"He's right," I said. "There's nothing we can do."

An hour went slowly by, and we used the time to brew a pot of tea. I passed around a cake tin with a packet of tuna sandwiches inside, which I had added to the bill at the Magherita Hotel. It was baking hot in the van, and the doors were wide open. The temperature was touching 100 degrees Fahrenheit, and what with 100 percent humidity, we were drenched and our clothes clung to us. It was like being inside a cooker with the heat turned on.

From time to time an elephant would look up before returning to eat. There was little or no movement among the animals, only the ripping of bark and plant, and those watchful stares now coming at shorter intervals. No ground was given although some was taken. The females with their young were much closer to the van than before. The secretary birds made short fluttery steps, skipping sideways to avoid the heavy legs of the herd as they circled the trees.

Thomas was the first to spot the danger. "They're ringing us," he warned ominously.

I leaned out from the door and looked backward. I was hoping he was wrong. But it was true. Several of the elephants had taken up positions at the rear, facing inward, no longer chewing, closing in step by step, and then pausing awhile. Their proboscises hung limply in a near-vertical curve.

At this unwelcome attention, the words of the night watchman at Paraa shot through my mind. "Get the paraffin can," I shouted, and opened the glove compartment and reached in for a box of matches. Thomas was already waiting. He had chosen a mound of esparto grass some twenty feet in front of the van, and he shook a cupful of paraffin over it. I then rushed up and dropped a match into the middle of it, and at once a bunch of yellow flames licked upward. We went to the rear and lit another fire.

Thomas picked up assorted leafage and covered the two fires. For a few moments, the herd stood their ground and stared at our fires. The tinder softly crackled under the growing heat, and the smoke started to billow in thick circles.

It took us by surprise when the warm air was filled with the harsh, banshee sounds of trumpeting, and we watched in silence as the herd of elephants turned around and lolloped away, heading for an isolated copse of tangled scrub.

"It would have saved time if we'd remembered to do this at the beginning," Thomas observed.

"I know," I answered, "but I had clean forgotten what the *mzee* had said back at Paraa. Anyway, thanks to him it's done the trick, and at the end of the day that's all that matters."

We stamped out the fire and splashed some of our drinking water on the embers.

It was dusk now, and we pressed on southward along the stony track, gearing down to meet the wooden bridge that forded the Kazinga Channel that connected Lake George with Lake Edward. Our destination was the Plough Inn at Kichwamba. We were already tired, and a glance at the map was enough to tell us we had a battle on our hands.

The van bounced, rumbled and strained as we made the mile crossing. The flat blackness of the water that flowed beneath us ran in silence for the whole twenty-three miles that separated the lakes. On the right we picked out the widening shores of Lake Edward, an immense mirror of shining water, bright under the strong moon, a virtual sea without salt. Every now and then the eroded banks opened up to form deserted beaches and grass valleys, while in the foreground, half-hidden by sedge, were the more melancholy swamps and marshes that fed off the Lake Nyamisigeri.

The far bank of the channel loomed toward us, a good thirty feet high, and threatening. The van's engine began to pitch as we toiled against the uneven boards of the bridge, bumping, jerking, and wheels spinning perilously close to the unguarded edges. The gleam of brown reeds in our headlights helped show the way as we picked out the good ground ahead. By and large it had turned darker, and the road was steeper than before. The gruff snorts of hippopotami could be heard, no doubt clambering up the steep mud banks in search of nighttime grazing. The moon shed a brilliant light and uncovered the endless watery plains of the lake flats set in a vast amphitheater bounded by the Ruwezzori and Busoagora mountains. Gradually we struggled up the final few yards of the rising bridge, the stink of the sedge beds filling our nostrils, to emerge on the comparative safety of the sloping lands of Ankole Province. A few hundred yards up the rocky track we pulled in at the isolated village of Katunguru, music playing from the speakers as we handed out leaflets by the light of the moon.

A quarter of an hour later, we were back on the winding dirt road, destination Kichwamba.

"I'm tired," Visavadia complained.

"We won't be long now," I replied.

I honestly didn't blame him for having a moan. Thomas and I usually had some sort of idea about where we were going and how long it might take. But Visavadia, in the back seat, heard only snatches of conversation on which to form a rough picture of our itinerary. However, he was free to ask at anytime, but tonight's late trip was out of the ordinary.

It was another eight miles up the rocky slopes, and we made full use of both our headlights and the moon to light the way. The climb steepened as it twisted and turned. Stones spewed backward into the silent night. An unending wall of smooth black rocks jutted dangerously from the sides, while over our heads were shredded overhangs of roots and earth. And again we were confronted with sharp curves that came advancing toward us from the narrowing road, and all the while the wheels slipped and spun on blind corners to within inches of the dark precipice. Over on our right, and coming into view, was the olive green blanketing of the Maragambo Forest, which sloped gently downward into the unseen valley, It was luminous, almost metallic, under the shining moon.

"Look," Thomas breathed, peering through the tainted glass, "there's a light." His face was screwed up against the steady glow of the dashboard. I pressed forward in the passenger seat and stared upward in the general direction of the summit. Stars flickered, and then, where the sky met the earth, I spotted a soft, off-white fluorescent glow along the high rim. In spite of the light's poor output, it remained constant and unerring. It had the appearance of a lone beacon on which we could hold direction.

And once more the land fell away on one side, and the van continued to roar its discontent as it grinded away in low gear.

"Yes, that's the Plough Inn." I confirmed as I focused my binoculars.

The silence was all pervading as we climbed up an unending slope. Then, at last, we rounded a final bend and the yellowish-beige light was now within our grasp. This lodestar had been glowing from an upstairs window of the inn. We turned from the harsh track onto a circle of level ground behind the isolated house. It was eight o'clock, and it had taken us eleven hours to travel the thirty-four miles from Kasese.

The door of the inn opened and a pool of yellow light fanned out onto the yard. Two lonely figures stood silhouetted in the glow of a lantern below a cantilevered concrete slab. They smiled warmly as we crossed from the motor vehicle.

"We have rooms and a meal waiting for you all," the lady said, reaching forward to shake hands. "I'm Lucy Reeves and this is my husband, Jim."

"John Carter," I replied with a smile, "and these are my two colleagues, Thomas and Visavadia." There was a short pause while we shook hands.

"Tell me," I said. "How on earth did you know we were coming?"

"We saw you crossing the lower end of the canal over an hour ago," Jim replied, "although I must admit we lost you for a bit in Katunguru...."

"That's eight miles away," I said incredulously.

"It was my wife who saw your headlamps reappear from the village, so she put a lantern in the upstairs window to help guide you. In actual fact, I used my binoculars, so we had a clear view of you all the way," he smiled generously "except for that blip at Katunguru. You see, there's nowhere else for you to come to. At the end of the day, Kichwamba is only a point on the map, and there's nothing here except this hotel and some fabulous views."

"Thanks for the welcome," I said.

"Not at all," Lucy purred. "Now, let me show you to your rooms, and then we can find something for you all to eat." She moved toward the door. "Are you staying the one night?"

"Two nights if that's possible," I replied.

It was Sunday tomorrow and I saw no need to hurry away from this idyllic place. On hearing my words, both Thomas and Visavadia brightened up. They quickly chose to share a room in the annex of the hotel that bordered the yard, and, in so doing, they kept their expenses below the level of the daily allowance and would be able to save a few shillings in addition to having their pay automatically banked in Nairobi.

"Two nights it is," she confirmed, and added, "There are no other guests staying here at present, so you have the place to yourselves."

Although the Plough Inn had no main electricity, hence the use of lanterns where necessary, it did have a noisy generator that supplied hot water, and from a traveler's point of view, hot water was the ultimate in luxury.

Before supper, while having a wash and shave in the only bathroom at the end of the upstairs corridor, I thought it strange, or perhaps a coincidence, that each Saturday night seemed to bring our safari to an isolated residence in the bush. My mind flashed back to the previous week when I shared a room with Carol at Mubende, and the Saturday before that when we camped out in a tent at Paraa Lodge.

Downstairs, in the hall, both Thomas and Visavadia had already asked to have their meal in the kitchen with the staff, with whom they had already made friends. The menu was made up of vegetable soup, cottage pie, and black treacle pudding. For my part, I ate in the dining room around a large wood table, and afterward had coffee in the lounge by a roaring log fire. It wasn't long before I decided to call it a day.

"Good night, *bwana*." The hall porter smiled, his perfect white teeth gleaming in the half-light. "If you want anything during the night, I'll be downstairs by the desk."

"Thanks."

I crossed the hallway and turned down a narrow corridor toward the red-carpeted staircase. Once upstairs, and in my room, I was hit by a sense of loneliness. The feeling of confinement and restriction gathered around me. Perhaps it was a mild attack of claustrophobia after being used to wide open spaces. Who knows?

Anyway, I got undressed, put on a pair of pajama bottoms, and crossed the room to where there was a wood-trestled washstand with a white jug and matching bowl. I brushed my teeth and rinsed my mouth, before recrossing in an easy two paces and drawing back the light chintz curtains that ran on an old-fashioned hooped rail.

It was as though I had unveiled the roof of the world. The timeless, flawed Rift Valley was illuminated like day under the brightness of a clear moon and a star-studded indigo sky. The view through this square-cut dormer window was nothing less than simply spectacular. The Lake George Flats were bordered by the jagged, snow-covered peaks of the Ruwenzori Mountains—the source of the Nile—which provided an amazing backdrop. The sheer size and beauty of the landscape was beyond description. Africa had indeed played its trump card, and my eyes became lost in the wide distance.

Large herds of game roamed silently across the grassy flats. The giant hippos had already climbed on the banks to graze, while elephant, zebra, black buffalo, and buck roamed in segregated groups. And above, in the violet sky, were black-and-white fiscal shrikes—butcher birds with hooked bills and sharp claws—sitting upright on thorny trees, ready to swoop down into the ground to catch lizards, insects, and small birds. Having caught their prey, they'd carry them back to the tree and impale them on the thorns in order to tear at the warm, succulent flesh. And sometimes, in their excitement, they too might pin themselves on the branches and become a victim.

This was the vast eternity where no roads, no cultivation, no human habitation existed. It was like being born again to witness such beauty. The very stillness and tranquility was hypnotic, and after spending the best part of an hour at the window, I reluctantly moved away and tumbled into bed. It was no wonder that Churchill in his 1908 book titled *African Journey* described Uganda as "that paradise on earth."

***

On Monday, August 29, we left Kichwamba and climbed steeply up a stony zigzag track toward the isolated trading center of Rubirizi. During the climb we enjoyed intermittent glimpses of the craggy slopes of the distant Ruwenzoris that pierced the cloud line and reached into the sky.

We continued our journey upward and went past a lone wide-trunked baobab with its upside-down rooting and an array of edible fruits. It was clearly home to a pair of matching touracos birds perched together on a high branch, their colorful crimson-and-green plumage glinting proudly in the morning sun.

The eight miles to Rubirizi was proving to be a hard grind and a challenge to Thomas's driving skill as he wrestled with the controls. Without let up the wheels spat out a mix of sand and stones only inches from the unguarded precipice on the passenger side. Every so often we passed irregular rocky outcrops jutting from the edge of the dirt road. However, despite the difficult conditions, we maintained steady progress. The sound of our vehicle laboring up the incline would no doubt have alerted the people of Rubirizi that we were on our way.

On arrival we were greeted by the village chief and about forty of his people. The audience was made up of all age groups. At first they appeared nervous—who could blame them in this isolated place?—so to break the ice we put on a recording of "Blue Suede Shoes." We followed this up by handing out copies of leaflets and miniature samples. We left fifteen minutes later to a sea of smiles all round.

Safari Salesman

The oppressive heat shimmered off worn tracks, and little places came and went—Nadele, Lutoto, Bushenyi, Butoro—and all the time we kept pressing onward to our destination—the important town of Mbarara some sixty-nine miles to the south. The smell of smoke drifted in the air as farmers burnt off coarse grass, preparing the poor soil for finger millet, cassava, and maize. The sustenance of the people was derived from these grains.

The pass began to twist sharply, and without warning the engine spluttered and steam rose from the front. This was followed by a sharp backfire from the exhaust, loud like a gunshot, which ricocheted through the thin mountainous air before getting lost in the valley. The van then lurched from side to side and slid backward down the road.

Thomas pumped the accelerator with his right foot, "The power's gone," he said as he pulled hard on the handbrake and brought the van to a stop.

The moment the engine died, I felt a sense of guilt that my instruction to Thomas when we left Kichwamba this morning was to press forward between villages. The idea was to reach Mbarara before nightfall. But this now appeared to be a bad mistake and had unwittingly contributed to the breakdown in this inhospitable environment. Usually, on a rough road, I'd keep an eye on the clock and odometer to ensure we were running on time with the day's planned itinerary. Unfortunately the temperature gauge was out of sight from where I sat, and Thomas was fully occupied and therefore unable to warn that the engine was overheating.

He leaned back against the seat and blew out a lungful of powdered air, while beads of sweat trickled down his sand-coated face and ran along his neck, before seeping into his shirt collar. He said nothing, and in slow motion lifted himself off the driver's seat, clambered down onto the track, and wrapped his right hand in a greasy towel before raising the hood.

It was unarguably a sweltering-hot day, touching 40 Celsius, and it was more than possible that we might be in for a long stay. Luckily we had pulled up a yard from the precipice, and as if to emphasize the point, a further rush of stones broke away from the edging as Visavadia and I made our way around the van. The sound of them rattling down the scree into the empty valley below was chilling.

"I've started checking," Thomas said as he wiped his hands on the towel, "and you'll be pleased to know that both the radiator and fan belt are OK."

"And the battery?" I stepped in.

"I'm checking the self-starter right now," he breathed, and took a length of insulating wire from the tool kit and made a connection between the terminal on the coil and the engine. There was crackling and a series of sparks, which verified the ignition switch was in working order.

"Is this going to be a long job?" I turned to Thomas.

"Can't say," he said quietly, "but at present I'm eliminating all possible faults."

"I'm making tea," Visavadia called as he reached back into the van for the primus.

"Make mine a mug of water," Thomas shouted as he scrambled under the chassis.

This place was desolate and uncompromising. The silence was broken only by the hushed sounds of our own voices. Every now and then more stones clattered down the rockfall. However, the far side of the roadway was more or less level, and beyond the gritty track was a solitary, flat-topped acacia tree with suspended grass nests—home to the yellow weaver—and a lone, large beehive woven into a topmost branch.

Ten minutes later Thomas emerged from beneath the chassis. "I've checked everything," he informed. "At first I thought it might have been a worn gasket and we were burning oil, but there has been no earlier loss of pressure on the gauge and neither is there any sign of oil. There is, however, a smell of gasoline, which I haven't yet investigated. So I reckon I'm right in saying that the trouble lies with the fuel pipe and carburetor." He paused to wipe his hands on an oily rag and reached over for his mug of water, which he gulped down.

"How long do you think it will take?" I repeated, offering him a cigarette from the pack that I kept in my shirt pocket.

"I wouldn't know," he answered. "We'll have to wait and see. There are a couple of more tests I need to carry out."

We moved away from the van and paused while Thomas leaned forward and took a light from a match cupped in my hand and inhaled. "If it's a case of having to strip down the carburetor to check the jets and float, then we'll not be ready to go before midday tomorrow. It's difficult working in this heat."

For a minute or so the three of us stood around in a rough circle and said nothing.

Both Visavadia and I recognized that Thomas was a first-class mechanic, and we felt confident that there would be a successful outcome to our present predicament. In fact he was an all-round safari man who also worked as translator, driver, and wildlife informant.

Despite the setback, I vented my frustration by throwing a rock into the abyss.

"We couldn't have chosen a worse place to break down," I despaired.

It was getting close to three o'clock, and I left it to Visavadia to set up camp and start preparing for an early evening meal. Thomas, meanwhile, had decided not to dismantle the carburetor and fuel pipe until tomorrow. "I'm going to use the remainder of the day to carry out a general service of the van. It needs attention," he said.

This timing gave me the chance to catch up with my written work in the flickering shade of the nearby acacia. I began by typing out a lengthy report covering the past week of our travels. This included our time in Fort Portal, Kasese, and the copper mines at Kilembe. I attached our large order for pine and coal tar disinfectants. What I didn't tell them about was the scrape we'd had with the elephants; the management would have found that irresponsible behaviour.

After completing the written work, and leaving the accounts for another time, I took my second paperback out of the briefcase and started to read. It wasn't long before the sun began to dip, and I picked up my things and walked slowly back to the van.

"Food's ready," Visavadia announced.

The next day, Tuesday, August 30, we did little different. I finished my paperback under the tree while Thomas started work in earnest on the blocked fuel line and carburetor. Visavadia sat on a couple of cartons, half-hidden from view on the shady side of the van. Life was virtually at a standstill, and I was becoming worried about our drinking water. We had approximately six pints left, and all the time the merciless African sun was beating down from a cloudless sky.

I had no wish to start on my final paperback, and instead I stared out across the savanna into the vast emptiness. I watched as Thomas methodically stripped, cleaned, and reassembled all the piping and the carburetor. It was when he broke off for another drink of water, followed quickly by Visavadia, that I realized that our supply had rapidly dwindled to less than four pints. It was a serious situation, and I introduced rationing immediately. The nearest garage was thirty miles to the southeast at Mbarara, and should the van fail to start, then it would be up to two of us to trek the three miles back under a grueling sun to the village of Butoro in search of water, leaving one of us here with the van. All this would seriously delay the safari and undoubtedly would be picked upon by London.

It was four o'clock when Thomas restarted the engine, and an overwhelming sense of relief swept through our camp. It was already too late to travel on. During the two days we'd been here, no vehicle had come by, nor had we seen anyone except for a solitary shepherd, and the moment he stumbled across us he ran off in fright down the track, chased by his flock of bleating goats and scrawny sheep.

It wasn't long before my staring into space paid off. I heard a soft whirring sound and spotted a small brown-and-gray feathered bird that landed near the edge of the dirt road. It was half-hidden by a clump of groundsel and appeared to be lying immobile except for a twitching wing stretched out across the ground. When I went over to see what was wrong, it instantly stirred and flew away, making a strange hooting noise. I watched carefully and noticed it had once more landed on a patch of braken a few feet away from the tree.

"Don't bother to look for it," Thomas shouted from across the road. "He's after that beehive in the acacia tree." He pointed upward with his forefinger. "He's hoping a ratel—an African badger—will give him a hand and raid the hive and share out the honey." Thomas left the van and strode toward the braken and clapped his hands. Immediately the honeyguide bird flew off.

"What's that weird sound it makes when flying?" I asked.

"He does it with the rush of air on his plumage," he answered.

chapter THIRTEEN

As daylight struck on Wednesday morning, August 31, we at last quit this place without a name and headed southeast via the township of Kibongo. At noon we arrived at Mbarara, the governmental headquarters for the Ankole Region.

"How long are we going to be here?" Visavadia asked after we found a parking place outside the Ankole Hotel.

"Let's first have a look at the map," I said, and reached into the glove compartment.

Mbarara was strategically placed at an important crossroad and linked all the areas leading to southern Uganda. "It's hard to say, really," I replied. "It's vital that we cover the Masaka District on the western shores of Lake Victoria, and then we'll have to double-back through Mbarara to take in the extreme southwest of Kigezi Province. I think we'll need to spend two nights here for starters before we leave for Masaka."

"Don't forget we've got a shipment of Herbalex and Gripe Aid waiting to be collected at the bus depot," Visavadia reminded me.

I glanced over my shoulder at the cartons neatly stacked in the rear cabin. "We'll pick up the consignment on our route back through Mbarara." I pulled my suitcase from the back and climbed down onto the roadside. "In the meantime, please get the jerrican filled with fresh drinking water. Now, is that everything?" I asked.

"Not quite," Thomas answered. "What time do you want us to report?" He restarted the engine and blipped the accelerator pedal.

"Well, it's lunchtime right now, and we've been roasting in the bush for two days, but thanks to you we're now back in the land of the living. For that reason I reckon we all deserve a break, so let's say we meet again tomorrow morning at around eight o'clock."

"Great." Thomas grinned.

"It's all right for you," I joked. "I've still got some work to do on the accounts."

"That's too bad." He laughed and let out the clutch and drove off in a cloud of ocherous dust.

By my reckoning, it was the first time that Visavadia hadn't been first in line in order to be dropped off at the end of our working day.

The Ankole Hotel stood in its own grounds on the fringes of town. It was English owned and popular among the local ex-pats. In the garden was a pair of green monkeys tethered by a long, rattling chain. They jumped and chattered as they scampered about looking for scraps of food fed to them from the kitchen window. Also patrolling for food was a motley group of bald-headed vultures, flustered and nervous. They sprung back from the doorway as I walked down the narrow pathway toward the hotel. This melee was soon interrupted by a large marabou stork, apparently a house pet, which barged between the vultures and started to peck at the scraps.

The outside walls, painted in a faded pink emulsion, were badly flaked and splashed with mud stains along the bottom edges. The owner's wife saw me coming from the front window and retreated behind the hall desk.

"What can I do for you?" she asked and smiled.

"I would like to book a room for two nights, please."

"No problem," she replied and swiveled the register around for me to fill in the appropriate details.

Later, after lunch, I went up to my room to finish off my paperwork. It took no more than an hour to balance the books and write a cover letter to include the earlier report I had written while stranded outside Rubirizi, and which I had yet to post.

The room was stuffy, and when I had finally addressed an envelope and licked it down, I was free to take a short walk down to the post office to mail the letter. It was especially good as I could enjoy the fresh air and the welcome peace of not having to play music and sell to a gathering crowd.

I bought some stamps for my envelope and handed it over to the clerk at the post office counter. I then had to produce some form of identification when I asked him to check the *poste restante* box to see if I had any mail. I showed him my UK driver's license and in return he produced three letters, all of which were imprinted with the words *To Await Arrival.*

Back at the hotel, I found an empty but well-worn sofa in the sitting room. The first letter I opened was from Head Office and was postmarked Clapham, London, SW9. They mentioned the good results from increased orders that had been relayed back to the factory. At the same time, they queried my laundry expenses during July, and complained that I had failed to keep properly in touch with Morgans and themselves while on tour.

The second letter I opened came from our associate company, Chemisan. It informed me that they had received a very interesting inquiry in connection with our range of portable lavatories from a Mr. Crispin Netuwa of Kibondo in western Tanganyika. In the top left-hand corner of the embossed writing paper was a red sticker with the word *Important.* This thrust was followed up with a strong suggestion that I give this matter immediate attention and send in a full report. I smiled to myself as I folded the letter and put it back in the envelope. The reason for my amusement was that there was no way I could reach Kibondo for at least six weeks. As the crow flies, it lay nearly five hundred miles to the south, but the itinerary that had been agreed in London for this particular area covered a thousand miles of dirt roads and a prolonged two-week stay over in the important port of Mwanza on the southern shores of Lake Victoria.

The one other letter was from Morgan and Sons in Kampala, and it enclosed a dispatch note detailing the shipment of sixty cases of pharmaceutical products to the bus depot at Mbarara.

Later, after supper that night, I went over to the bar for a drink. It was full of local people enjoying a good night out. The owner and his wife were settled back at a nearby table with a bottle of whiskey. They nodded, smiling, as I eased through the crowd toward the counter. The shabby, skin-covered stools were already occupied by three or four local girls, all heavily made up and looking for a partner.

***

The following day, Thursday, September 1, we proceeded to give saturation coverage not only in Mbarara but also the surrounding area, up to a distance of ten miles. The next day, on Friday, we again worked the center of the town, and included a spate of calls on large trading houses. By now there was hardly a person who hadn't heard of our products, and the orders came tumbling in. But because of the extra work involved, we left the town early on Saturday morning, a day behind our original schedule, and headed eighty-six miles east to Masaka.

For the first few miles the route was fringed with small compounds surrounded by bananas and scarlet canna flowers decorating the space in front. As usual, between green gardens, there were narrow red paths leading away from the road. We followed the level of the land past more plots of sweet potatoes, sesame, and beans. The small farms of the local shamba owners finally gave way to open fields and fences of plantain and finger millet.

We worked our way past uncropped fields, and in time the terrain changed. There were now square-shaped plantations of tobacco stretching into infinity on each side of the murram road. I watched from the open cab as the workers stooped to pluck the lower and upper leaves, while others carted the cumbersome bundles to wire lines, hanging them in the sun until they ultimately took them into the drying sheds. Although I could no longer see the procedure, I understood that they would spread the leaves onto racks to be cured over smoking fires, and at first the leaves would turn yellow, and then red and brown, before finally being graded.

After a total of twenty-two miles, we eventually arrived at the trading center of Sanga. During our promotional show, we were approached by one of the village elders. He asked us several solicitous questions about Herbalex, explaining that the workers in his fields suffered from coughing bouts due to the strong aroma of nicotine that drifted across the curing sheds. After much consultation, and the giving of samples and booklets, he made a cash purchase of twelve dozen Herbalex.

Once more, we pressed on eastward, through open grass savanna toward Masaka, and slowed down for a herd of long-horned Ankole cattle, along with some raggedy sheep and goats, most of which had strayed into the middle of the dirt road, and who could have blamed them? One or two grass fires had been lit along the road to keep the tsetse flies off the herd. However, it took a while to work our way through the cattle.

Darkness fell as we entered Masaka, and we drove slowly down the main street and heard loud high life music blasting from well-lighted bars and open doorways. We passed groups of Asians who stood huddled on shop-front terraces casting watchful glances at us. Every now and then house dogs sprang angrily to their feet and chased our van down the middle of the road, as small children scampered out of the way to the safety of wood-fenced shacks along the narrow side roads. At the top end the road divided. The wider of the two routes, curving to the right, hugged the northwest shoreline of Lake Victoria for the eighty-mile stretch to Kampala. We turned onto the minor road, and after a half mile we located the signboard that pointed the way to the Tropic Inn.

We stayed three days in Masaka, working the many bush villages in the area, including a fifty-mile return trip to the tiny port of Bukakata situated on the thick, sedge-ridden shoreline of the lake. After completing the promotional work at the port, we took the van down to the lakeside in order to wash the grime off the panels. We soon found an accessible place where we could run the van into the shallow waters near to a timbered pier head. For thirty minutes we paddled around, wielding buckets, sloshing water, wiping dirt with odd pieces of rags, and when finished, Thomas drove the van back onto level ground, close to the landing stage, and rubbed it down.

We were in no hurry to return to the inn at Masaka, so instead we strolled down the length of the old pier to a point where two anglers were sitting on the broken wood edges with their legs dangling in the air; each of them clasped a homemade rod. A small catch of fish, mainly spine-backed perch and their close relative, tilapia, lay in an untidy pile on the worn boards. One of the men was sucking on an old clay pipe. He turned around at our approach and smiled quietly, brushing a bony hand across the deep-smelling fish to drive the flies away. The other man stared disconsolately out at his empty line with his chin almost resting on the stained undershirt that stretched across his large frame. In the distance, from the south, there was the sound of a light aircraft. It was a faint sound, coming steadily toward us on the warm lake air.

Thomas put a hand on my arm. "They've caught something," he said in my ear, and raised a hand to point out the line that had gone taut. It belonged to the second fisherman with the worn shirt. The first man quickly lost interest in his own line and stuffed the clay pipe behind his trouser belt and watched in silence as his friend reeled the fish toward the pier. Some moments later it broke the surface and struggled in what was a losing battle, before plunging back into the sluggish water. The man then skillfully pulled in the slack and hauled the fish clear of the lake, landing it on uneven timbers; he picked up a short, heavy stick and battered it over the head.

"Do you know what that is?" I said.

"Could be anything." Thomas shrugged.

We both stared down at the odd-looking fish with its narrow head and long pre-hensile snout. Thomas turned toward one of the fishermen. "What kind of fish is that?" he asked in Swahili.

The clear vibrations of the airplane were now vanishing to the north. The man with the pipe who had been stooping over his line straightened up and shook his head, smiling quietly again, as he took in Thomas's Kenyan accent. "We call it an elephant-nose fish," he said at last, pushing at it with his bare foot.

***

On Wednesday, September 7, after an early breakfast, we left the cramped lobby of the Tropic Inn, driving through the center of Masaka, and for some distance we ran parallel with a minor road. The town itself was no more than two blocks deep on both sides, and its many cross streets led nowhere, ending only in vacant lots and piles of rat-infested rubbish. Once past the town we motored down a bush-lined road that took us to a wide, grassed-over roundabout, and from there we chose the route that would take us the ninety-two miles west, back to Mbarara.

The stony edges of the road began to widen, and we passed a large shop below a great tree. On the veranda a barber was at work with comb and safety razor, scraping hair, while his client held a mirror before his face and watched the work being done. At the end of the boulevard, with its broad

Safari Salesman

spiked palms, we turned onto the Mbarara Road and began a fast non-stop journey toward our destination at Mbarara—a rare luxury for us. Several miles later we went through the villages of Mbirizi and Lyantondo, reentering the Ankole Province with its wide expanses of open-grass savanna. We overtook a line of slow-moving trucks loaded with plantain and charcoal. It was a dicey move, as the commercial vehicles were swaying dangerously, each one of them fighting to keep control and stay on the crown of the road. A lone cyclist laden with sacks of cotton lunged unceremoniously off the road into the bush, frightened by the oncoming traffic.

At Sanga we were flagged down by a young African standing with his arms outspread is the center of the dirt road. "Find out what he wants," I asked Thomas as we drew to a halt.

"*Jambo.*" The boy smiled and greeted Thomas with a handshake.

I watched them while they talked, hoping to pick up the gist of what was said, but I failed to do so.

"What does he want?" I asked. I was impatient to leave and get on with the journey back to Mbarara and re-book a room at the Ankole Hotel. There was nothing worse than searching for a place to spend the night in the bush if it's gone dark.

"Come on," I urged.

"There's no problem." Thomas laughed, peering into the cab through the open door. "You remember that man, the *mzee,* who bought twelve dozen Herbalex in this village?"

"Yeah, the village elder." I nodded. Don't tell me he wants us to buy it all back."

"No way," Thomas replied. "Apparently all the women who work in the tobacco fields were each given a dose of Herbalex, and it's done them a power of good, so much so that production in the field has gone up.

"You won't believe this," he continued and laughed again.

"Try me," I challenged.

"He wants another gross of Herbalex."

"That's what I like to hear." I smiled. "But why the laughter?"

"It's because they're using Herbalex for backache problems," Thomas replied, "not coughs and colds."

"Backache," I repeated unbelievingly. "Look, tell the young boy that we will only sell the medicine to the chief providing we can talk with him and explain that Herbalex is for coughs."

"The chief apparently knows all about that, as the *mzee* showed him the literature," Thomas said slowly. "Don't forget the label on the bottle is in Swahili, English, and Bantu, so he's quite clear about the usage. The chief's not stupid, Mr. Carter."

"That's an unfair comment to make," I growled. "I've neither said nor thought he was. All I'm doing is trying to get to the bottom of this matter. I'm fully aware that the chief guessed rightly that we were coming back on this road from Masaka and that's why he sent his messenger to stop us. That's all part and parcel of the bush telegraph. However, I do realize he knows exactly what he's talking about."

"OK I'm sorry, but it's my duty to make sure that the chief is under no misassumption, and, as far as I'm concerned, the only way to resolve this matter is to go and visit him." I signaled for the boy to step aboard the van and show us the way.

Ten minutes later we were standing in an open compound, and grouped around the chief's hut. He sat on an ornate chair that had been carved from a wooden log. Through an interpreter it was explained that our medicine was for coughs and colds, not for backaches. For several seconds there was total silence in the compound while the chief beat off the flies with his horse-tailed switch. "Is there a law that prevents me from giving your medicine to my people for backaches?" he roared.

"No, there's no law," I said with a smile, "and at the end of the day the customer is always right."

By the time we completed the negotiations the compound was crowded with people from neighboring huts, all eager to see what was going on. The chief, fly-swatter in hand, was enjoying every minute. Every now and then he consulted his interpreter, making sure that he was kept fully informed on all that we sold, not only to him but to the others.

"The chief wants to know," the interpreter began, "if you and your friends would wish to spend the night in his village. He is honored that a *bwana* from London has come here, and will put one of his houses at your disposal. He says that his wives will prepare good *chakula,* and you will be well looked after during your stay."

"Please tell the chief that we are most grateful for his kind invitation," I told the interpreter, "but we are several days late on our safari and must be back in Mbarara tonight."

The interpreter leaned over from his stool and translated the words into the Bantu dialect. The chief listened attentively before he finally made his reply. "The chief asks me," the interpreter said with a smile, "whether you would kindly play some music from your truck before you leave. He quite understands that you cannot stay the night, but if you ever come back this way the invitation remains on hold. You will always be welcome in his village."

"Of course I will play music." I smiled. "What would you like to hear? We have rock, mambo, highlife, calypso…"

After another exchange of words, the interpreter said the chief would like music for his people to dance to, something African.

"Put on some highlife," I said to Visavadia.

Then, moments later, the vibrant tones of West African music drifted across the compound. The deep, seductive beat of the Mensahs Tempo Band playing *Kratchi* was enough to trigger the villagers. The chief smiled, nodding approval as his people swayed seductively to the earthy rhythm.

***

Next morning, Thursday, September 8, we loaded the shipment of Herbalex and Gripe Aid that had been waiting for us at Mbarara's downtown bus depot and departed on the southwest road for Kabale. Once again we had to put up with another torrential downpour, which not only hindered progress but made it exceptionally difficult to carry out effective selling along the route. Our journey southwest would clearly take longer than the single day we had originally estimated.

The blur of cultivated plots slipped by as we stared out from the splattered windows. The earth roads had now churned into a deep, oily mud. The many shamba owners along the way sat morosely in doorways, waiting for the rain to cease, while those caught outside sheltered under large banana fronds that bordered the edges of the road. Some miles later we emerged into open savanna, sadly stripped of trees to combat the tsetse flies. The green prairies were now used for grazing by large herds of long-horned Ankole cattle. We stopped briefly at the trading center of Kinoni. The rain had lessened, and we shortly left the ranching areas behind and pressed onward down a tilted, dark earthen track that was bordered on each side by thickly wooded slopes.

We climbed, slithered, and swung on the mud. At times we lost power and the van slewed right and then left. The road darkened from the overhang of both trees and bushes, and several points on the map came and went in slow monotony—Ndeizha, Ruhanga, and Ntungamo—until we were prevented from going farther by the wide, flooded banks of the Rufua River. The concrete crossing that linked us with the far bank was submerged in the rushing waters, and we had no alternative but to wait for the flood to subside, which was likely to take quite a time. In view of this, we pulled over onto higher ground and made camp for the night.

By morning the conditions had changed drastically. The sky was blue and serene. The floods had diminished, and all that remained was the soft, lazy lap of water against the concrete buttresses of the bridge. I watched as grassy clumps of fast-seeding hyacinth flowed eastward, while thick tangles of floating vegetation formed little islands, their rubbery vines and stalk-like masts clogging the wide course of the river.

After a breakfast of maize porridge and hot coffee, we crossed the bridge and stopped briefly at Lubale—a small thatched settlement hidden in dense undergrowth—and then carried on along a greasy track that was fast drying. A lone group of khaki-clad road workers paused momentarily from their labors to allow us through. They returned our wave and quickly raced across the road to retrieve the samples and leaflets we had thrown out from the passenger-side window.

A mile later we passed from the wooden savanna lands into open fields of corn, finger millet, and sorghum. The road narrowed before finally curving onto a gentle slope that led into the township of Lwentobo.

Five miles farther on, and climbing, we entered the Kigezi Region, the remote corner of western Uganda. The climb became steeper, and we were soon well into the mountains. It was cooler and greener now, and the dark earth road switched back through pine forested slopes. We watched as swarms of purplefeathered starlings lined the grass between the roadway and woods, and all the time there were open patches of smooth, bare ground that were followed by dense lines of towering blue gum trees, smelling of eucalyptus, with black beehives suspended from the high branches.

The road started to twist as it climbed and eventually reached an altitude of six thousand feet, and among the higher open ridges we caught sight of people from the Bakiga tribe tending their crops of tea and coffee. These strips of intensively cultivated land stretched above the clouds to the very top of the Rukiga Mountains. Eventually we reached the market center of Kabale, headquarters for the Kigezi District. It was not quite dusk, and the red glow of weed bonfires were irregularly spaced on the steep slopes that encircled the isolated town. It is said that these fiery beacons can be seen from over the border in the Congo.

We drove slowly past a golf course screened by imported spruce, and caught glimpses of green turf and red earth worms. A signpost pointed up a stony track. It signaled the White Horse Inn, with its rose bushes and cypress hedges.

chapter

FOURTEEN

Two days later, on Sunday September 11, after we had finished working the area, we left Kabale and headed west on a circuitous mountain route, making for the remote border town of Kisoro. The overall distance between the two points was exactly fifty miles. It was to prove a whole day's run due to the hazardous driving conditions prevailing in this isolated region.

Green coniferous trees lined the main boulevard, casting dark, funereal shadows through the chill of the early morning haze. The jagged Biruaga Mountains rose majestically above the mist to heights of more than eight thousand feet, providing an unending backdrop of rounded peaks curving across the pale blue sky. We passed further groups of long-horn cattle grazing solemnly on patches of coarse apple-green grass. On the fragrant senna leaves of the cassia plants were hundreds of fluttery burnet butterflies, with sepia wings and brown trailer legs. And suddenly, without notice, as if an unknown signal had been received, they flew up the steep slopes in their endless search for other aromatic flowers.

And we too kept climbing, and every so often we had glimpses of the high plain that we had recently left. Through the lifting haze there were warnings on signboards of land falling away on both sides of the track. Farther on, around sharp cuttings, we drove past scattered gangs of raggedy children sitting on the dusty shoulders and hawking Belgium cigarettes, a clear sign that we were once again hugging the Congo border.

Every now and then the laterite road flattened and straightened, giving temporary relief, before once again curving dangerously upward. We stopped at the tiny market center of Rubanda, but there was nothing there, only a few Kigezian natives. The men were tall with thin Hamitic noses and full Watusi-like lips, while their women with fattened hips and dark vestal faces, were shy and fearful as we handed out the leaflets. They stayed huddled near a wide-trunked tree close to the roadside, and, after working the area for twenty minutes, we moved on. Around the next sharp bend we were hampered by a nomadic herd of piebald cattle. The blocked track was soon opened by two small boys, wielding long sticks, who screamed and shouted at the animals.

The van's low gears ground monotonously as we twisted and turned toward the Kanaba Gap—the pass through the Birunga Mountains that leads to Toro—on the western limb of the Rift Valley. After four more miles, we halted briefly at a place called Maziba. The van's radiator was again steaming, and we were close to calling it a day. Instead we continued the journey in silence.

"According to the map there's a rest house somewhere nearby," I commented.

"We're only nine miles from Kisoro," Visavadia informed.

It was unusual for Visavadia to air an opinion.

"Makes no difference," Thomas chipped in. "It's best we stop somewhere for the night before the radiator starts to boil."

A few minutes later we spotted the rest house up a steep track, off the side of the road. Almost every government-built rest house had an empty, shabby look. It took us a further ten minutes to locate the key holder, who lived in a wood shack nearby. We paid him four shillings for a night's sojourn, and with Thomas at the wheel, Visavadia and I helped push the van up the stony incline.

***

The next morning, after breakfast, Thomas set about servicing the van. He had asked for an extra hour at the start of the day to carry out checks, so I decided to use the time to catch up with outstanding paperwork. It was left to Visavadia to clear up the rest house, load the van with our belongings, and make us all a fresh cup of coffee.

The rest house was perched on a rocky outcrop fifty yards from the main road up the steep pathway we negotiated on arrival. It was overgrown with alpine weeds. The view from the terrace was fantastic; the Birunga Mountains stretched endlessly across the far horizon from the northwest. The peaks of Muhavura, Mgahinga, and Sabinio dominated the far left, while in the center was the majestic, 14,750-foot Karisimbi Peak, terminating in the southwest with the active volcanoes of Niragongo and Namlagira.

Beyond the rough roads that led to the coffee shambas, the slopes were covered in steep grass meadows dotted with green-and-yellow tulip trees. Above, on higher ground, were pine forests encrusted with lichen trailers, and then came twisted tree heathers and bamboo thickets that sprouted aimlessly in the tawny scrub. And beyond were the upper moorlands sprinkled with coarse tufted grass, yellow grounsels, and giant lobelia, their stems filled with creamy latex, while their blue-and-yellow flowers hid insects upon which the tiny malachite birds fed.

An hour later the van was ready and we lost no time in forging westward toward Kisoro. A damp mist shrouded the forests along the high ridges. We caught occasional glimpses of the Mufumbiro Mountains transversing the Kanaba Gap. This vast range, combined with the Biruaga Mountains, is shared among the Congo, Rwanda, and Burundi.

In the high forests of this region, it's possible to find the rare mountain gorillas moving about in groups along the bamboo thickets. Unfortunately we were on a sales safari and hadn't the free time to go on a search. However, I did meet up with someone who had seen the gorillas close up, and he said he was mesmerized by the size of their black hands and long thumbs, and how they picked ponderously at the plant material growing on the slopes. These dense forests and entwining undergrowth are the sole habitat of man's closest relation, whose life span is estimated at thirty-five years.

Before we entered the town of Kisoro, we had to go through the custom and immigration post. There were several policemen in brown capes asking questions, and all they wanted to establish was whether it was our

Safari Salesman

intention to enter the Congo or Rwanda. They raised the zebra-striped wood barrier on learning that we would be working in the town. We eased the van under the heavy pole and climbed the sloping street that led through the main shopping area. Two-story concrete buildings ran in parallel lines up and down the narrow street, giving off an air of claustrophobia, and outside the shops people sat idly on cane chairs drinking sweetly spiced tea. Women peered out of open windows, impassively watching as we handed out leaflets and pinned badges, the music drifting loudly down the road.

After visiting the shops, we drove out of town to the local hotel known as the Travelers Rest. The lush garden of the inn was ringed with African thatched huts, known as rondavels, which serve as the guest rooms. The fragrant aroma of herbaceous flowers planted in the rich earth beds wafted gently through the thin cool air.

"So you've not come to see the gorillas?" the owner asked in puzzled tones. I was sitting on a bar stool in the cocktail lounge drinking Rwanda beer.

Not really," I replied. "I'm a safari salesman."

"As soon as people arrive in Kisoro," the owner said tetchily, "they seem to automatically think they can stay here."

"Surely there's nothing wrong in that," I said, "but if you want me to go?"

"No, of course you can stay here." He smiled. "I was just sharing a few thoughts with you. He offered me a kali cigarette from his pack. "It's these types that come here from all over the world in order to see the gorillas in the jungle. They feel cheated and humiliated if they fail to find them." He paused to light the cigarette. "Then what do you think they do?"

"I've no idea," I said. "Perhaps they buy some color slides from a Nairobi gift shop to show their friends back home."

"Yes, they may well do that, but while they're here they vent their frustrations on this pub," he complained bitterly. "They'll swill beer, break my furniture, and trash their rooms, and to cap it all they expect unlimited credit."

The dinner gong echoed loudly from the hallway.

***

Early next morning I was awakened by a light tapping on the split-timbered door of my mud and wattle guest house. "Come in," I shouted, thinking it was a waiter with a cup of tea.

"Excuse me," a voice said, "but if you've got a minute. I would like to show you something interesting. Would you come, please?"

I lifted my head off the pillow and rubbed my eyes. "Who are you?" I asked in amazement.

He was a forest pygmy, barely four feet tall and about fifty years old. He stood unwaveringly at my bedside. He wore an old army coat decorated with two full rows of shining campaign medals. A bow was clutched loosely in his left hand, and a bunch of arrows were poking out of an okapi-skin sheath, which in turn was draped over his shoulder.

"It's all right," he assured, beckoning with his right hand. "They know me at the hotel, so please come."

My curiosity got the better of me, and I donned a pair of khaki shorts, T-shirt and, a V-neck sweater, as I guessed it was going to be cold outside. "What's your name?" I asked as I followed him into the garden.

"My name is Pierre," he said emphatically. The war medals on his chest clinked against each other as he took off his coat. "These I got with the Belgium Army in the last war," he added proudly. "You watch and listen." He neatly folded his coat and placed it on the grass, the bow and arrows balanced on top. The only clothes he now wore were knee-length khaki shorts and a torn singlet. Then very slowly he began to weave his body from side to side, his tiny hips undulating while bare feet repeatedly stamped the coarse, patchy grass. It seemed at this stage that Pierre was reenacting some form of primitive dance of his tribal ancestors in the Congo forests. What else could it be? As each minute passed I became more and more aware of his feet stomping the ground. They were overlarge when compared with his other features. The continual thumping seemed to drain the mind of any reasonable thought. I was standing about twelve feet away from Pierre and noticed that his rolling eyes were now half-closed, and his dark face lacked all expression. All the time his legs continued to beat up and down in piston like rotation.

The ground began to quiver and shake. My eyes became fixed on the whirring feet, hypnotized by their endless pounding. I had now become his captive satellite. It stayed like that for another long minute as the seconds ticked by, one by one, and my head blurred as he went on stamping the dry ground. I thought I was mistaken when I began to hear the first imperceptible rumbling sounds emanating from the earth itself, but any doubts were soon wiped away as the vibrations rose and fell, all the time growing in intensity like a musical crescendo. The very ground beneath me was now moving, and the rising wave of reverberations wiped out the senses, then, as though a switch had been thrown, the drumming died away and the ground suddenly stilled. It was quiet again. The little dark body of the pygmy was bathed in sweat, and he slid slowly forward onto his knees, arms outspread, back bowed, until the top of his tiny head came to rest on the patchy grass. It seemed as if someone had come along and removed his supporting stick and he had crumbled like a raggedy doll.

"Are you all right?" I asked uneasily.

I bent over his elfinlike body, and in doing so lost my balance and fell to the ground alongside him. My head throbbed as though on fire, and my senses were numbed.

Pierre slowly raised his head. "Takes a bit out of me," he conceded, grasping my hand and panting in short bursts. "What did you think of it?" He was trembling violently as he got off his knees onto his feet.

"Fantastic," I said. I put my hand back on his arm. "Take it easy," I added gently. "Tell me, does the ground really hum and move, or is it all in my mind?"

He raised his hands slowly. "I've got a confession to make." He smiled. "If I want to, I can make the ground talk to me." He reached forward and picked up his coat. His face was flushed with sweat.

"Thank you, Pierre," I said, and pulled an orange-and-black five-shilling note from the back pocket of my khaki shorts.

He had stopped shaking by now. "I'm very happy you enjoyed my show," he said enthusiastically, leaning forward to retrieve his bow and sheath of arrows. *"Kwaheri,"* he said in farewell. A hint of a smile etched the corner of his mouth, and then he walked across the grass and down a pathway, and for a few seconds he was partly obscured by the tall flower beds before disappearing behind the main building. He had gone before I had time to acknowledge his good-bye.

In the distance I could hear barks and high-pitched screams coming from the lower end of the forest. I took it to be a troop of chimpanzees getting psyched up for the morning ahead, and top of their list of wants would be food.

***

Just after ten that morning we left the Travelers Rest Hotel. It was Ruben, the chef, who waved good-bye to us from the back of the kitchens, and not long afterward we headed back through the fertile lava plain onto the sweeping mountainous route that cut into the thick forests leading to Kabale. We stared out from the van's doorways and windshield as streaks of white lightning illuminated the deep, crested fumaroles that topped the Mufumbiro volcanoes. The rain began to fall in large blobs, and it wasn't long before the woods and bamboo thickets of the Kanaba Gap were hidden behind a curtain of grayness—the majestic pines, satinwoods, and irokos along the Birungas literally disappeared before our eyes.

"Where did you guys sleep last night?" It was a question I seldom ever asked, as it was none of my business, unless of course, they volunteered to talk about it. However, in this case, it was a particularly difficult overnight stop, and I couldn't resist asking them.

"We were given a staff bungalow around the back, same as the one you got," Visavadia said and smiled.

"Ah," I said with a grin, "along with a free dinner and breakfast."

"What's wrong with that?"

"Nothing," I said. "I was just curious, as chefs don't often wave us good-bye."

"Very funny," Thomas said, but he couldn't hide behind a straight face for long and joined in the laughter.

We continued our journey east-northeast, retracing yesterday's itinerary until we reached the township of Lubale, some seventy-five miles from Kisoro. It was here that we forked right for the mining town of Kikagati, some thirty miles farther on. Once more we recrossed the Rufua River, but this time there was no threat of rising waters. We had left the rains behind, and we went over at a point lower down.

The road could now be seen for some way ahead. The escarpment still bounded the view behind, but the land in front was getting lower and greener. We stopped for a short time at Mwirasandu on the fringes of the tin-mining area, which had a power line running to the hydro-electric station at Kikagati, an additional twenty-two miles east on the Uganda/Tanganyika border. Our maps showed that a Catholic mission operated in the vicinity, about two miles up a dirt road from the highway, but we decided that we were pushed for time and it wasn't worth making a call, as the mother superior would more than likely refer us back to her head office in Geneva.

The open scrub gave way to cotton fields and cultivated plots of sesame and finger millet, while dark trees in the distance hinted at rivers and streams. The mountains beyond the flat valley were less and less abrupt, almost faint in the rising haze, and close to the road were acres of hummocked land, which spoke of recent wooded savannas that were now planted with the large, green matoke bananas. After another ten miles we came to rest at a village called Chitwe. It was a small settlement of thatched mud huts set back from the road, but because there was a funeral taking place, we moved a couple of hundred yards farther down the road.

It was now well past two o'clock, and we took our first break of the day. We had a light snack of beans and potatoes, ripe mango, and a glass of beer, and afterward, while having coffee and a cigarette, we played some calypso music over the speakers but kept our doors shut until we were finally ready to give a show.

Thomas took a bunch of leaflets and sauntered across to the dusty collection of mud and wattle huts, while Visavadia opened up the rear doors and set up a display of Herbalex and Gripe Aid bottles on the edge of the platform. A crowd soon formed round the van—small laughing children, cyclists, and young women with water drums or bundles of washing balanced on their heads. Both men and women, mainly from outlying villages, listened intently as the Luanda tapes automatically cut in and a toneless Bantu voice extolled the virtues of the two medicines. It was a familiar scene we repeated a hundred times each week, along with the clatter of coins dropped into the metal cash box, the clamor of the crowds circling the van, the unending heat and dust, and the unvarying sound of music drifting loudly from the twin speakers above our heads.

I was sitting in the passenger seat, usually occupied by Visavadia, and was doing the accounts, when the passenger-side front door slid open. It was Thomas. I presumed he had returned to pick up some more leaflets and badges. "How's it going?" I asked.

"We've got a problem," he replied.

"What sort of problem?"

"Well, while I was handing out leaflets, I was approached by a young girl of about seventeen," Thomas began. "She was limping badly and told me that last week she went to the local witch doctor, the *mundumugu,* about a minor pain in her ankle, which happened when she fell out of a tree and…"

"And what did he prescribe?" I asked with a trace of cynicism. I turned down the volume on the record player, dimming the crooner's mellow voice, so that I could hear his answer.

"You've got to be joking," Thomas flared. "The bastard tried to rape her and then took a lump hammer and told her to put her foot on a nearby rock and then he beat it into a bloody pulp."

"Oh, my God," I exclaimed.

"It's true."

"Why in the hell did he do that?"

"The usual reasons," Thomas replied. "It was to give him the power he needed so that he could drive out her evil spirits."

"Why are you telling me this?"

"The girl has come to us for help."

"I don't see what we can do," I said, switching off the tape and putting on the closing 78-rpm record with its medley of American military music. The moment it went on, Visavadia would have checked with me—in this case he would have seen that I was in close conversation with Thomas—and would have proceeded with closing down the show by shutting the rear doors and generally tidying up the bottles and open boxes. However, he would have made sure that all last-minute customers were properly served, and last but not least, he would have locked the cash box and brought me the key.

"We could dress and bandage the wound," I added.

"She needs hospital treatment," Thomas said sternly. "If she doesn't get some professional help, gangrene will set in. That's my opinion, and don't say I didn't warn you, Mr. Carter."

Thomas, without fail, always reverted to my surname when he wanted to stress a point—good or bad—and we sat in silence for the next minute. I put the paperwork that I was doing back into its folder and watched as Visavadia repacked the bottles he had put on display at the rear of the cabin.

The heat inside the van was over 100 degrees Fahrenheit, and I moved away from the rear seat into the front section. "Where's my map?" I asked, searching the shelf underneath the dashboard.

"It's over here," Thomas replied, and pulled it out from the door pocket next to the driver. The well-worn map was frayed about the edges and breaking apart at the creases.

"Just as I thought." I paused and nodded my head. "There's a Catholic mission at Mwirasandu. It means we'll have to double-back for about twelve miles. Now, where's the girl?"

"I'll go and fetch her," Thomas volunteered. "She'll be waiting for me at her home," and with those words he jumped out of the van and half ran down the road toward the settlement.

"How did we do here?" I asked Visavadia.

"About a dozen of each," he replied easily as he handed me the key to the cash box.

I explained to him about our change of arrangements, as it appeared that we were committed to taking this girl to the mission as quickly as possible. "It will probably mean we will stop over at a different place tonight. Have you made arrangements?" I asked.

"No way." He smiled. "How am I to know where we'll end the day?"

"You've got a point."

"I should warn you, Mr. Carter, that Thomas has a thing about the *mundumugus*," Visavadia went on. "It's because his father died while in the hands of one."

"I didn't know that, but Thomas is from the city," I reminded him, "and these old traditions are still a way of life in the country."

We stared down the dusty road as Thomas emerged from a pathway with the young girl he had spoken about, and they slowly made their way toward us. She winced in pain every time her foot touched the ground. Thomas was supporting her by the arm.

"This is Kamore," Thomas said as he helped her onto the passenger seat. Her foot was red with blood and had been roughly bound in a banana frond tied with a dirty rag.

"Tell this *bwana* what happened to you," Thomas said uneasily.

"It's like this," Kamore began nervously, and she bit into her lower lip. "About a week ago, my young brother and I went to the fields at the back of the village where there are some palm trees. We wanted to collect the coconuts that were ripe. I was half way down the tree when I slipped and fell to the ground, twisting my foot on one of the coconuts that was lying around under the tree. The pain never left me. So on the fourth day I consulted with the *mundumugu*. He told me that there was an evil spirit inside my foot...." The young girl's voice began to quaver.

"Go on," I said quietly.

Kamore leaned forward and wiped a tear from her cheek with the back of her hand. "Anyway, the *mundumugu* first tried to rape me, and I fought him off. He then told me that I would never marry unless the bad spirit was driven from my foot."

"He used the sacred mugabe beans from his medicine bag," Thomas interjected. "Those ones they use for divining." He paused to get his breath. "And after the attempted rape, he then smashed her foot with a lump hammer. Kamore has told me where he lives and has pointed out the mud hut, which is sited at the rear of the compound. It's the one that has an overhanging avocado tree. I want to go and see this man."

"Steady on," I said. "The first thing we must do is to take Kamore to the mission at Mwirasandu as quickly as possible."

A small cloud of gray-winged cattle flies swarmed into the van through the open door, buzzed around, and finally settled on Kamore's foot. From behind, Visavadia poured some clean water into a large mug, leaned forward between the uprights, and splashed the wound. He then passed me a spare towel, which I wrapped around her foot.

"Let's go," I said.

Forty-five minutes later we arrived outside the mission gates and rang the bell. Two minutes later a priest came marching down the driveway. "My name's Father Michael," he said. "How can I be of help to you?"

He listened sympathetically to our story, and after carrying out an examination of her foot agreed to admit her to the hospital wing of the mission. "She'll need specialist treatment, and without raising too many hopes, it's possible that our surgeon may be able to save Kamore's foot. Anyway, he'll do his best," the father assured. "It was so important that you brought her here as quickly as possible."

With that note of optimism we watched in silence as Father Michael escorted her away from the van and across the graveled drive to the front entrance. Then, before going in, they stopped by the large oak-stained front door, turned around, and waved. They made an odd couple, he clothed in a red soutane, with his bald head burned chestnut brown by the sun, while Kamore, a lovely 17-year-old with lustrous wavy black hair, wore a simple flowered dress. Then they were gone.

We motored back down the dirt road for two miles and then turned right toward Chitwe.

"I want Visavadia to use his whip," Thomas fumed.

"Two wrongs don't make a right," I said angrily.

I knew about Visavadia's whip because Thomas reported it to me a few days after we had left Nairobi. I had given my word to Thomas that I wouldn't say a thing as long as it was kept hidden. I was loath to upset Visavadia at the outset of a major safari. Thomas went on to tell me that Visavadia had brought it on board for his own security and would use it only in dire circumstances. Apparently the recent but now-defunct activities of the Mau Mau in the country areas of Kenya had unnerved him, but this was nonsense as the Asian community was never the target. I understood that he was skilled when it came to using the whip and that he could take a cigarette out of someone's mouth at ten feet.

On the outskirts of Chitwe, where the settlement ended and open country began, Thomas pulled the van off the road. "This is where the *mundumugu* lives," he said, and pointed an accusing index finger at the man's thatched-roof house.

"Come on," Thomas urged, "let's teach the bastard a lesson he won't forget." He was about to boil over, and nothing in this world was going to stop him from what lay ahead.

However, I had to make a protest and barred him from leaving the van and begged him to cool down. I explained that we would take down the man's details and lodge an official report with the police when we reached Mbarara. But Thomas wasn't listening, and instead he simply turned and made his way out of the other door. I raced around the front of the van and grabbed him by the arms and asked him not to stain the good name of our safari. While I was imploring him I completely lost sight of Visavadia, who had been rummaging among the cartons in the back of the van.

The *mundumugu* was squatting in front of his shamba at the rear end of the compound. He was preoccupied and appeared to be about to administer a *thahu,* or curse. From his medicine bag he took a pair of bushbuck horns and dipped them into a leaf-lined hole that was filled with murky water. A circle of elders waited patiently under a fig tree. The loud bleating of a billy goat struggling in the arms of a small boy disturbed the calm.

In spite of the warm sun, the witch doctor looked cold and stiff, although wrapped in a monkey cloak with his skull covered in gray wool. His stretched earlobes contained cylinders of wood, and a long, fine-linked chain dangled from his scrawny neck. He reached into his tattered cloak and brought out a clay flask stoppered with a long cow tail, before once again dipping into his medicine bag, speaking all the time of crops and weather. In the palms of his hands, he shuffled a set of black mugabe beans and began arranging them in separate piles. These shiny beans were sacrosanct when divining was about to take place.

"Did you rape and then hammer a young girl's foot into a bloody mess?" Thomas shouted in Swahili at the witch doctor while ignoring the incantation that was going on.

The *mundumugu* looked up from his drowsiness, seemingly unaware and not understanding the threat that was unfolding in front of his glazed, rheumy eyes. He was high on pombe, and his mind was fixed on the ceremony at hand. He picked at his black-and-white colobus jacket with skinny fingers in an effort to reshape the cloak that hung too loosely around his shoulders and was about to slip off. The men in the circle stayed silent. The only noise came from a sharp, pistol-like crack that cut through the air. Visavadia had been among the crowd and had stepped quickly forward while Thomas berated the man. Then with a minimum of movement, he swung his right arm and the hippo-hide lash landed across the witch doctor's face, opening the cheek, and blood splashed onto the colobus cloak that had now slipped to the floor. The man's expression changed from one of stupor to that of unhidden fear, and the small crowd moved backward.

"Let that be a lesson for you." Thomas stood over the bewildered man and stabbed the air with an index finger. "This is payment for what you did to Kamore," he raged.

"Come on," I said, pulling Thomas by the arm. "Let's go before the situation get's worse."

The men in the *boma* all stood aside as we threaded a path between the thatched wattle huts back to our van, and in a matter of seconds we were speeding down the road toward the tin-mining center of Kikagati.

"If either of you do anything like this again," I fumed, "I'll drop you both off at the nearest bus station and you'll be unemployed. Is that understood? I am especially shocked at you, Visavadia, and perhaps you would remember that two wrongs don't make a right. I feel you two have let me down, and don't think for one minute that I can't manage without you, because I'll get two replacements from Nairobi within three days."

I felt bad that I had rounded on my friends, because I knew they liked me and would do anything for me. However, at the end of the day, I blamed myself for losing control of a festering situation.

Our next stop was Kikagati, a featureless trading center with no shops or accommodation for the traveler, and by the time we'd arrived there, it was already dark, so we pulled into an empty side street.

"I wouldn't like to have you guys as enemies," I said dryly, hunched over a plate of rice and beans.

"It had to be done," Thomas responded, and eyed me as he poured himself a cup of tea. "It wouldn't have been right if that man had gotten away with his crime?"

"I know that you both acted in the heat of the moment, and there's nothing more to say, so let's forget it and move on." We sat in silence in the flickering light of the hurricane lamp.

For me, it was a situation steeped in conflict. Visavadia, normally mild mannered, knowingly a pacifist, had armed himself with a lethal leather whip. His argument was similar to what Thomas had told me. He said he needed some form of defense when traveling in the bush, and made a point that both Thomas and I carried sheath knives under the tails of our bush jackets, while his *kiboko,* or whip, was locked in a cow's leather case and not readily available. It seemed that his viewpoint was a paradox based on an unfounded premise. For instance, our knives were used for cooking, cutting rope and wood, opening heavy-duty cartons, and to save our lives when we had to cut our way out of the canvas tent, about to be trodden down by a furious elephant as happened at Paraa Lodge.

We spent an uncomfortable night in cramped conditions near a dozen timber shacks, just a few yards from the main street. In the morning we awoke to a crowd of small boys peering noisily through the front windows. We passed out some leaflets and pinned a few badges before starting the engine and driving out of town in search of somewhere to have breakfast.

"It's our last day in Uganda," I remarked, slicing a pineapple with my knife.

"How long do you reckon we've been here?" Thomas asked as he prepared a bowl of cereal.

"It's been about ten weeks since we crossed into Uganda from Kenya at the border town of Tororo," I responded.

"And our daily mileage, what's that?" Thomas asked as he dug vigorously into his posho with a metal spoon.

"It's gone up to forty-three miles," I replied. "That's ten more since we left Paraa." I pulled out the note book from my top pocket and studied the figures. "In a nutshell we've done three thousand four hundred and twenty-three miles in eighty days." With that said, I slipped the book back into my jacket pocket and passed round the pineapple.

"Not quite around the world," Visavadia quipped

I was taken aback by his comment, because he usually stayed quiet at the best of times. "Maybe not," I said with a smile, "but it seems like it!"

***

After two hours promotional work in Kikagati, we called on the manager of Kikagati's major tin-mining complex. "You ought to have come here last night," he grinned, signing an order for fifty gallons of pine disinfectant, after he had learned we had slept out.

"We hardly ever get visitors from the outside world, and my wife would have been delighted to have you all to stay," he went on.

"Next time we're in the neighborhood, we'll keep you to your kind offer." I smiled, and at the same time confirmed that his order would be shipped from London within the next three to four weeks.

We left the tin mine and went east through open scrub land toward Nsongezi. The twelve-mile stretch ran parallel with the Kagera River across a flat valley.

The last few miles of Uganda unrolled across cattle plains. There were repetitious dirt paths leading to isolated settlements from the main road. Traffic was nonexistent. We slowed down for a zebra-striped barrier erected across the road. This was Nsongezi, and it was nothing more than another name on the map. There was nothing here, only a tsetse fly post and a ferry point crossing to Tanganyika.

A health inspector boarded the van and caught a few flies with some muslin netting and popped them into a jam jar. "I'm afraid you'll have to get out," he said. "The van will have to be sprayed."

Another man was waiting outside. His face was partially covered in a gauze mask, and he held a metal bucket filled with an acrid yellow fluid. He climbed into the cab in heavy Wellington boots and inserted a stirrup pump into the pungent liquid.

"Hey," I shouted at the inspector, "what about my stock?"

"It'll be OK," he assured. "This is a very fine spray and it won't cloy on the boxes, and anyway, I've looked at a couple of your bottles and they are all capped and sealed. There won't be any contamination to worry about, that's for sure, and all you will need to do is to wait for fifteen minutes while the gas clears."

"It seems a lot of work for a few flies," I said, biting my tongue at my stupid remark.

He shook the jam jar full of flies lying in heaps on the bottom. "They carry parasites that can cause sleepy sickness in people. They can make farm life impossible; the cattle will suffer from weight loss, debility, and low milk counts. The tsetse is our greatest enemy, you see!"

We walked through the shallow trough of impregnated netting and wandered along the eroded banks of the river. The hot savanna lands of Tanganyika dissolved in every direction in the yellowy distances beyond the ocherous reed banks. In the center of the slow-flowing river were little islands of matted grass being carried a hundred miles eastward toward Lake Victoria, and every now and then there were clumps of water hyacinths with their stalk-like masts topped with violet lilacs.

A young boy was sitting in a slouched position on a wood jetty while flies walked unhindered on his face. A pair of catfish and an ugly lungfish lay heaped by his side. We pinned a Herbalex badge on his shabby vest. And, as he was alone, we took two shillings from the cash box. He gave us a brilliant smile, and that more than made up for the incident with the *mundumugu*.

The car ferry was getting loaded on the far shore and was half-hidden by the tall reed beds encasing its hull. The warble of sedge birds as they darted from stem to stem was clearly heard. Then came a splash in midriver, followed by a series of grunts and barks, and a group of shiny black heads swam toward the marshy backs below us. It was the herbivorous dugong searching for weeds amid the anonymity of the water plants.

"Let's go," I said, and we trailed back to the van and drove slowly down the rutted slope onto the gently rolling log ferry. The boy on the jetty opened an eye against the sun to watch our departure. We waved to him from the ferry as we floated across the Kagera River. Tanganyika loomed toward us.

chapter

FIFTEEN

It was Wednesday, September 14, when we crossed over the River Kagera into Tanganyika. It was the late afternoon. The sun was behind our backs, and the endless savanna was spread in front. We headed east toward the important lakeside town of Bukoba, which lies midway on the west coast of Lake Victoria, some 115 miles north of the major trading center of Biharamulo.

The dry central plateau fell away on each side of the dirt road. The flatness was broken only by the occasional acacia tree, its dark canopy thrusting up from a blanket of low, sandy vegetation. The temperature fell dramatically as the evening approached, perhaps touching 21 degrees Celsius as a few clouds gathered in the gray-blue skies. We pulled over from the road, having driven twenty miles since we left the ferry. We were tired, thirsty, and hungry, and very much needed to set up a camp before the darkness arrived.

Next morning, with the sun beating down from an azure sky, we continued our journey along the same road that followed the course of the river. We had left the tungsten quarries and tin mines of the Karagwe Province behind us and arrived at the trading center of Kyaka. For another time we had to recross the Kagera River on a second, but smaller, road ferry. It took no more than twelve minutes to make the trip. We now made our approach on the final sector, heading toward the port of Bukoba, and thirty miles to the north of this route lay the invisible line of the Uganda/Tanganyika border.

Green, lush hills screened the area around Bukoba, with acres of robusta coffee on well-drained slopes. We reduced our speed and dipped down into this richly soiled valley of seven rolling hills, seeking accommodation at the Coffee Tree Inn.

We spent the next day doing promotional work in the town before leaving in a southerly direction for Muhutwe. A few miles after leaving the town, we made a right fork off the main highway in order to visit an arc of villages that lay hidden in the low bush areas. The deep red and black earth narrowed to a single track, and as custom dictated, we slotted our wheels into the grooves that ran on each side of the central ridge.

After a brief stop at a place called Ibuga, we pressed forward on a curving course toward our next stopover as shown on the map. A troop of baboons was foraging in a thicket circling a group of flame trees. They were unpredictable animals with their dog-like snouts and gray, wiry hair. They communicated by using the narrowing of the eyes and the smacking of lips, and they meticulously obeyed their leader's instructions without question.

Our attention was suddenly diverted when we heard a loud rattling noise coming from underneath the vehicle.

"Sounds like the exhaust has come adrift," Thomas diagnosed in his easy, unconcerned way.

"I'll have a look," I said, taking a length of wire from the box under my seat. I climbed down and spread myself under the chassis and swept the earth away from the middle of the track, using my arm as a brush. The deep camber in the road had fractured the exhaust pipe, and it was dragging on the surface. I started to wire it up when I heard the distant drone of another vehicle, all the time coming closer. I turned my head around in the confined space and saw its front wheels draw to a halt in front of us. The track at this point was too narrow to attempt a pass, and the embankment on each side sloped into a ditch of sand and rubble.

I cursed my luck that this should happen, and the only way to solve this impasse would be for one of us to back up the track to a wider section. But if my memory served me right, the track had been narrow for at least a mile or more on my side. This thought was going through my head as I tried to tighten the wire on the exhaust. However, the drumming of the other vehicle's diesel engine was generating a lot of heat, and I soon found it difficult to breathe. I was about to complete fixing the exhaust when the driver of the vehicle switched off the engine and everything went quiet.

It didn't last long. "Hey, you guys," a voice boomed out, "get that thing out of the way."

Rivulets of sweat poured off my forehead and into my eyes as I eased the end of the wire over the support and twisted it tight with a pair of pliers. All the time I was well aware of Visavadia's voice as he tried to explain to someone that we were carrying out repairs and it shouldn't be long before his *bwana* sorted things out.

"Just get it off the road," the same man shouted. "Otherwise I will have it pushed off the road. Do you understand what I'm saying?"

The pipe was now firmly fixed on the vertical bracket, and I wriggled backward from under the chassis. Thomas was waiting for me at the rear, which was out of sight of the other van.

"What's going on?" I asked, brushing the sand off my clothes and wiping my face with a cloth.

"It's a hunting party in one of those safari wagons," he said tersely. "There are about six white people and the same number of askaris."

"That figures," I said. "The Rumanyiko Game Reserve is about eighty miles west in the Kishanda Valley. It's my bet that they have licenses to shoot any rhino that wanders outside the rain forests that cover the surrounding mountains."

"Let's go and help Vinoo," Thomas suggested.

"Leave this one to me." I put a restraining hand on him, and added, "I'll do the talking, and we'll keep it cool."

"What's the problem?" I asked as I emerged from the rear of our van and walked toward the man who was sitting in the passenger seat next to the askari driver.

"You're in the way," the man retorted as he leaned out from the open vehicle.

I reckoned that he was the one who had been vocal from the outset. He was wearing a fresh safari suit along with a hunter's hat that bore a two-inch-wide strip of leopard skin laced around the brim.

"There's no need to shout at my man," I said, finding it difficult to control my anger, "and anyway, who appointed you spokesman?"

"You are blocking the way," he responded while he glanced over his shoulder and sought support from his colleagues.

"No more than you are," I said, "and to be frank, it makes no difference to me whether we spend a week here or not."

The hunter's face was red from the sun, and I surmised that he'd arrived in Nairobi less than a week ago and had flown to Biharamulo, here in Tanganyika, before joining a ten-day packaged safari.

"I find that hard to believe," he said.

"It could happen unless you stop shouting, and just in case you don't know it, this is Africa, where time is of no consequence."

The heavy sound of a second vehicle could be heard approaching from the same direction. It grew louder as it negotiated the thick-coated track. It then halted right behind the hunting wagon. We now had two vehicles blocking the way.

"It's getting like Piccadilly here," I mused.

"Pardon me?"

"Nothing," I said with a shrug.

"This'll be our supplies jeep," the hunter said in a less hostile voice, "and perhaps it'll help if you have a word with him. His name's Bill Baylis." I was about to leave when the hunter held out his hand and apologized for his aggressive behavior.

"That's OK by me," I said, shaking his hand, "but I would also like you to apologize to my salesman. His name is Visavadia," and with that said, I trudged over to the back-up jeep.

The askaris had already moved out of the wagon, preferring to sit down on the edges of the track. The tourists, however, stayed inside and were shaded by its flat roof. They talked among themselves and seemed nervous about setting foot onto African soil.

"My name's Carter." I smiled. "John Carter."

"I'm Bill Baylis."

"You can no doubt see for yourself that we have a problem here," I began with a sweep of my arm, "and I'm pretty certain, as far as I can recall, the track has stayed narrow for at least the last mile."

"Me too," Bill said as he unfolded his survey map and spread it out on the jeep's hood. He lowered his head and said nothing for a moment or two. "My map gives this route as an unclassified track that lasts for three miles, and by my estimation we have met more or less at the middle."

"In that case it rules out any thought of reversing."

"I agree."

"To be honest, I think it's up to you to drive round my van for two reasons. The first is that we only have one vehicle, so any work that has to be done to the embankment is cut in half. And secondly I'm not going to ask my men to unload and reload the van in this humidity. We have approximately forty-five cartons on board, each weighing forty-two pounds, and moving these onto the ground and back again into the van in this heat would most likely cause dehydration followed by exhaustion. What's more, we only have seven pints of drinking water left."

"I'm not totally convinced," Bill demurred, "that I can get past you without first fortifying the embankment, and even then the curvature of the road might force us into the ditch." He paused for a moment as though lost in thought. "Tell me, John, do you have any spades on board?"

"I've got two."

"That's good, and I've got four."

He then paused for a second time before going on. "It's my suggestion that we cut two furrows, running parallel, say four inches deep by ten wide, on each side of the central ridge. We would then be able to slot our driver's-side wheels into their respective grooves. What do you say?"

"Yes, that's feasible, but you haven't yet said where the grooves are to be placed?"

"I'd say they should be twelve inches from the center of the camber, which should give our vehicles a gap of about four inches in which to pass. What do you say?"

"Yes, I'll agree to that, but I still want both banks stabilized at the base with a mix of stones, grit, and soil."

"So do I," Bill said with a laugh.

It took ninety minutes for us and the askaris to finish cutting the grooves and fortifying the embankment, before cleaning our spades and stowing them away. It was now the turn of the tourists to get down from the wagon. There was a lot of excited chatter going on among them as they automatically reached for their cameras. I wondered how they would explain our presence, deep in the bush, to their friends back in the United States.

When everything was ready, the wheels of the safari wagon were carefully nursed into the groove, followed by the customized jeep. There were no hitches, and we took this as a good sign, as Thomas confidently slotted our driver's-side wheels into the improvised groove. They then passed us and pulled back onto the center of the track. However, the safari wagon did have a near miss in that the base of the embankment began to crumble under its passenger-side wheels. For a moment it lost impetus, and we all gave it a final push. The tires obligingly took a last bite out of the broken track, lurched forward, and landed onto the center of the track, firmly embedded in the original grooves.

"See you, John," Bill hollered from his jeep as Thomas got us back onto the middle of the track, "and don't forget to give me a ring when you get back to Nairobi and we'll have a pint at the Stanley!" He then gave a big wave, and the dust coming from the jeep swallowed him up.

After they had gone, we pushed on eastward through the bush villages of Nshamba and Muleba. The African cedars, or sapeles, covered the surrounding Karambi Mountain Range and cast deep shadows across the unbounded valley. The late-afternoon sun was arching slowly behind the distant bare ridges, a sign that chilled air would soon invade the empty slopes. After several more miles on the dirt road, we turned south and at once realized that we had little chance of reaching our destination before nightfall. It therefore made good sense to pull off the road while we were still able to see the ground. We soon found a small copse a few yards away from the main road and parked for the night.

Later, after our tea, we sat around a log fire and drank canned beer. "Is something wrong with your foot?" Visavadia asked me. It seemed he had spotted me wince when I leaned forward to give it a rub.

"It's bothering me," I admitted.

"I saw you limp too," Thomas added.

"Thanks for your concern." I smiled. "It's probably nothing more than a sprained ankle when we pushed that safari wagon."

I got up from the fireside and walked over to the van and breathed in the fresh evening air. At night a traveler can get used to different animal noises, such as the grunt of hippos getting out of a river; the harsh croak of bullfrog in the sedge; the howl of a scavenging hyena; the short, distinctive panting of lion; and the barking of zebra feeding on the plains. All these sounds and many others depended on where you were camped, but right now I clearly heard a spate of screams and hoots coming from the forest about a thousand yards from where I stood. This was surely the call of chimpanzees, and yet I was puzzled that they were awake at this time. I turned to Thomas, who was usually a mine of information about Africa's wildlife, and asked him what he thought about this excitement in the woods.

Thomas threw his empty lager tin into our rubbish box. "That's a troop of Gombe chimps,' he informed, "and they easily get excited over nothing. It's possible they had been disturbed by a snake or monitor lizard. However, a one-hundred-pound chimp is all muscle and four times more powerful than man. It's the one with rounded head, big ears, pink hands, and..."

"That's common knowledge," I broke in.

"Anyway," Thomas started again, "you remember the chef at the Travelers Rest in Kisoro? Well, he told me something interesting, and it didn't make for nice listening."

"I remember him," I replied. "His name was Ruben." It seemed that my earlier question had touched a button, and Thomas was ready to share his thoughts with me.

"That's him," Thomas responded, but before expanding on the subject, he delved into a box and pulled out another lager. "It was early in the morning on the day we left the inn. I was having breakfast in the kitchen when I heard screaming and hooting going on. The noise was coming from the foot of the forest. I knew it was a chimpanzee just like you have done now."

"Anyway, this got us talking, and Ruben told me that over a period of time he's gotten to know many different personalities who have stayed at the inn. One such person was a German biologist who had studied the chimps' eating and social habits. Naturally, people like you and I assume that their diet is restricted to plants, leaves, flowers, nuts...all that sort of thing, but that's not always the case. Sometimes they kill and eat their country cousins—colobus, for example, who are leaf eaters and live atop trees. We know about this and accept that the chimp is an occasional meat eater. But what we don't know is what the professor told Ruben, and that is the chimp has developed a taste for domestic chickens, lowland birds, and little children."

"I can't believe that," I said in amazement.

"That's what I thought too," Thomas replied, and in saying that he opened his can of lager and took two or three gulps.

"Can this be proved with a film or photos?"

"No, the professor has got nothing to prove it, and nor has he witnessed such an atrocity himself. You see these rare incidents take place close to forests. The chimp will run out and snatch a toddler and disappear back into the forest in a blink of an eye. The proof lies with the farmers and their wives who have suffered under this form of attack. One such person says his year-old daughter was snatched outside his dwelling not so long ago and has never been seen since. He said his wife saw the chimp, but there was nothing she could have done to prevent this from happening. The others in the settlement have spoken of chimps hanging around on the edge of the forest, and they've heard that it has happened before. However, no one in government has listened to their story and offered any sort of sympathy, except for the German professor. After all, these people are just simple farmers."

"There's no easy answer, is there?"

***

Next morning, Sunday, September 18, we left our campsite at Muleba. The wilderness enveloped us as we drove slowly along the narrow track. It then widened as we approached the main road, and in the openness we could now see for some way ahead. The northerly end of the Miambo woodland was bordered by 450 square miles of the Biharamulo Game Reserve. It marked the limit to which protected animals could safely roam. The reserve stretched into the colorless distance, ending up near the dull waters of Lake Victoria. A herd of sable antelope attached themselves to us and raced alongside until they reached a thick line of eucalyptus trees. They then stopped and stared straight back at us, as though expecting to see one of their numbers being swallowed up by our van. But they had misjudged us—we were no lion.

From the direction of the woods came a pack of spotted hyenas. They trundled across the hard scrub, and every now and then their leader would draw to a halt, twist its head, sniff the air, and with its broad jaw agape, show off a powerful array of white teeth that could chew and eat bones. He, along with the rest of the pack, loped off in awkward strides, their large front legs stabbing at the ground until they picked up enough speed to become a perfectly synchronized hunting animal. Their yellow-and-gray fur, when set against the harsh sunlight of faded greens and browns, provided a useful camouflage. They were known as the refuse cleaners of the savanna.

Beyond the reserve we at last had arrived at the trading center of Biharamulo. There was little of consequence here to detain the traveler, just a few straggly shops with half-empty shelves and shamba owners with partially fenced fields of maize and sorghum, along with the usual mud-brick houses, capped with corrugated roofing, and open compounds leading up from narrow, potholed, twisty paths. The importance of this town is based on its position at the bottom left-hand corner of Lake Victoria. It forms a true compass point that leads away in every direction.

We checked in at the local rest house and, after grabbing something to eat, spent the remainder of the day organizing shows along the dusty roadsides.

The next morning, Monday, September 19, we set course due east, on an eighty-one-mile trip to the gold-mining region of Geita. The road was generally easy, although the soft shoulders had been churned up by heavy-duty trucks during the earlier rains. A lonely group of roadside workers was busy filling in pot-holes and ruts from mounds of dumped sand. We pressed on, crossing the soft green underbelly of Lake Victoria. There were knots of women in bright clothes at work in the well-watered fields, planting rice stalks, while mud-splashed children stood still and watched as we thundered by in the van. I was at the wheel, so it was Thomas's turn to throw out leaflets and the odd sample.

Directly north of the road and tucked into a shallow corner of the lake was the famed Rubondo Island, both a zoo and a nature reserve. About fifty game species inhabited this sanctuary, from elephants right down the size scale to a variety of tropical birds. The vast majority of the birds were September migrants with exotic names, such as shovelers, stints, puffs, storks, greenshanks, and yellow wagtails.

On arrival at Geita we called on the principal gold mine. We were escorted into the office of the supplies manager by an affable security guard. The floor was covered in heavy-duty green carpet, and the furniture was principally made up of antique reproduction items from the late-Victorian period. The manager was sunk into a dark leather armchair behind a giant rosewood desk. A series of prints in gold frames hung in perfect lines along the walls. The theme was hunting scenes in England from the late nineteenth century to the 1950s.

After due consideration of our products, the manager gave us a worthwhile order of 250 gallons of pine disinfectant in five-gallon drums.

We took a further order for one hundred gallons of coal tar and two gross of disinfectant tablets for the toilets. However, he declined to take any of our carbolic soap in four-ounce blocks.

The following day, Tuesday, September 20, we departed Geita and made the rest of our way along a narrow dirt road to Mwanza. Simple road signs on metal posts gave the distances at irregular intervals. There were several large hoardings of smiling Africans, smoking, drinking, or taking medicine. Traffic was light and the track sloped gradually downward between hummocked fields until we came to the main crossroad. A sun-bleached sign pointed toward the Busisi ferry for those people intent on going east or wishing to take the shortcut across the gulf to the major port of Mwanza on the far bank.

It was a few minutes after noon when we arrived at the pier head and took our place in the line. It was a four-hour wait before it was our turn to drive onto the ferry for the fifteen-minute ride across the Mwanza Gulf. We disembarked and motored along a dusty tarmac road that led to the center of the town. We passed piles of festered rubbish, rats running in and out, untidy allotments, and a collection of tin shacks on each side before the road widened onto unnamed cross streets. There were one or two tired-looking villas set in large, unkempt gardens, and then we came to a dull green roundabout. The street broadened once again as it neared the town center. A few minutes afterward, we passed several low, off-white concrete and corrugated sheds. We guessed that they were Asian warehouses. We'd seen such buildings before in other towns, and they had a way of condensing the road and giving off an air of modernization. Then finally we made our way through a network of well-ordered streets in the city center, all dotted with blue fluorescent street lamps, dim, yet clearly visible in the darkening light.

We dropped Visavadia off at the main shopping area. He waved and gave us a broad smile as we drove away. He had his shabby wooden suitcase faithfully at his side. It was then Thomas's turn. He had already told me that he had no use for the van, as he had relatives in the town and wanted to look them up.

Safari Salesman

"And where will you be staying?" he asked me in a deliberate sort of way as we drove slowly along the main boulevard, congested with early evening traffic.

"I'm going to try the Lake Hotel."

"Do you know it?"

"No," I said as I folded the guidebook on the shelf under the dashboard. "But I like the sound of the name."

Thomas was in a happy mood as he pulled out his old leather suitcase from the back of the van. He was humming a popular song that was on top of the African hits list and was regularly heard on the radio.

I was driving alone now and had next to no idea as to where I was going. I usually guided Thomas from the passenger seat with a street map on my lap, but he'd gone. My prayers for help were soon answered when I spotted a police officer on a street corner. I stopped and leaned out of the cab; and asked him for directions to the Lake Hotel.

***

Mwanza is the largest port and railway terminal on the southern shores of Lake Victoria. The entire region, fanning south and east, is saturated with townships, trading centers and bush villages—a virtual nightmare for our sales safari team to tackle successfully.

I spent Wednesday morning at Morgans' Mwanza office, discussing and planning the advertising campaign for the next section of the safari with the manager, Lal Prasanna.

"Incidentally, John," Lal began ominously as we strolled down the corridor at the end of our talks, "I've received a memorandum from your head office complaining that you don't keep close enough contact. They feel out of touch with what's going on and suggest you write reports to them on a weekly basis." We went through a set of glass swinging doors at the end of the passageway onto the paved terrace in front of the building.

"You know Africa as well as I do," I said to Lal and turned my palms upward in a gesture of life's unavoidable drawbacks. "Sometimes we're lucky to find a post office to take a letter, and besides, we work in difficult conditions. All three of us get tired and hungry by the time the sun goes down, and I only have a paraffin lamp to help me type my reports in the back of the van. It's difficult to maintain a businessman's schedule."

"I know." Lal smiled. "But I've got to mention it to you." He paused before going on. "And anyway, there's another problem that needs your attention. They want an explanation as to why you haven't filed a report on Mr. Crispin Netuwa and his inquiry concerning Chemisan portable closets."

"I suppose," I said with a chuckle, "because I haven't been there yet. It's as simple as that. This Mr. Netuwa lives in Kibondo, and unless I hire a helicopter there's no way of reaching him," I elaborated.

"What shall I tell your head office?"

"That when I get to Kibondo, I will find this bloke, dead or alive, and file a report," I said. "It'll take about four or five weeks before the itinerary goes through that area near the Burundi border, but I'll give you my written guarantee that he won't buy a thing and it will be all a waste of time and money."

"I can't say that to your directors." Lal laughed.

"Look," I said with a smile, "we have people writing to us in London simply to improve their written English. They like to get letters back. Some mothers write and ask to name their babies after our products. Then there's the students who inquire about working conditions in Britain and send pieces of dried monkey skin in torn envelopes to bring us good luck, but all it brings us is a foul smell up our noses. I get these letters to deal with when I'm back in London, and I spend half my time chasing people who have no intention of buying anything in the first place. We're operating nothing more than a pen pal service!"

"You mean you reply to all these letters?"

"Every single one," I told him, "and we send samples and literature. It costs a small fortune. However, it keeps the name of our products up front and our would-be customers happy."

***

After having a break for lunch, I joined Thomas and Visavadia in the parking garage of the Lake Hotel, and from there we drove through the garden suburbs of Mwanza, stopping at Kisessa and Kisabo before arriving at Kagehi on the southeastern shores of Lake Victoria. It was from the cliff tops that we were able to view a local landmark, known as the Bismark Rocks, named after Germany's iron chancellor. The huge boulders jutted out from the shoreline, and it was here that Lake Victoria blended with the Speke Gulf, which formed part of the east/west tectonic fault. It was John Hanning Speke, the explorer, who took sixteen days to trek here from Tabora, 230 miles to the south, and, in doing so, he had to leave behind his compatriot, Richard Burton, who was unwell at the time. The records show that Speke was the first white man to set foot on the shores of Lake Victoria, on August 3, 1858, but he had little idea of its extent. Nevertheless, seventeen years later, it was Henry Morton Stanley who laid claim to discovering the lakes of Tanganyika and Victoria.

"Before we move on," I said, "let's take a break for tea and discuss our schedule over the coming days." I unfolded the map and spread it out on the ground. "Mwanza is going to be our base for at least the next fortnight."

The three of us sat in the shade of a sausage tree. Its pendulous fruit swayed gently over our heads in the warm, tropical air. The grassy cliffside where we took our tea overlooked the shining wet rocks that fell away into the gray metallic waters of the lake. The view afforded no curves or contours; it just led the eye forward across the flat, limitless haze covering 26,828 square miles of water. We were indeed looking at the third-largest inland sea after the Caspian Sea and Lake Superior. It has a deep point of almost 300 feet.

"Before we leave here, I'm going to take a short walk to a place called Lutongo Point," I informed. "It's just a point on the map where there's a rocky outcrop that thrusts into the lake." I paused and took a last drink of tea before refolding the map. "It's not much more than a half mile from here, so which one of you wants to come with me?"

"But there's nothing either here or there of interest," Thomas said in puzzlement as he flicked over the pages of a Tanganyikan guide book.

"I'm not looking to sell anything," I said with a laugh, "if that's what you are suggesting. All I want to do is to check on something. It's of historical interest. We've got at least another hour before we need to make tracks for Mwanza, and this is an opportunity too good to miss. The way I look at it is that not one of us will ever be here again."

I glanced down at my wristwatch and started to walk across the scrubby grassland. "I'll see you both later," I said over my shoulder as I made my way toward the cliff edge.

"Wait for me," Visavadia volunteered, his curiosity having got the better of him.

I paused and waited for him to catch up. From where I stood, the only sign of human habitation was a pair of dugout canoes beached on the reed-lined shores. However, in the distance I spotted a small group of men, women, and children busy unfurling black nets from which they hoped to scoop a catch of tilapia fish.

Thomas remained behind to guard the van while we tramped off in a westerly direction. We followed the ridge that ran along the cliff top. Two hundred yards farther on, the track opened out onto an uneven slope dotted with stunted plants and bright yellow flowers.

We halted for a few minutes on the cliff and took in the astonishing view of the coast and beyond. To our left was the might of Lake Victoria, and to the right was Speke's Gulf. "You could smell history here," I said, and with this comment I explained to Visavadia the purpose behind the walk we were taking. I told him in more detail about Frederick Barker and Edward Pocock, explorers who were both young and brave. "The two men had joined Stanley's east/west expedition in 1874," I explained, "and I've heard that there's a large, smooth stone overlooking the lake in Barker's commemoration that has his initials inscribed on it." After giving Visavadia the reason for us being here, we began to search for the stone among the long grass that flanked each side of the steep downward path.

Close to thirty minutes later, I signaled to him that it was time to get back. We were bitten, tired, and thirsty, but to my amazement he shouted that he that he had found the stone.

"It's here," he repeated excitedly, as I hurried over to where he was standing.

"Unbelievable," I gasped as I swept back the overgrown plant life with my arm to get a clearer view. I then carefully leaned forward over the exposed gray stone. There was no mistaking the roughly carved initials, FB.

"Is Mr. Barker actually buried here?" Visavadia asked, assuming that we had stumbled on his gravestone.

"It's not his grave," I said, "but rather it's in memory of his death in 1875. It is rumored that these initials were carved by Stanley himself. As far as I know, he was buried near a place called Kagei under a cairn of stones put there by his good friend Pocock. Sadly, a few months later Pocock himself drowned in a canoe while negotiating fast-flowing rapids near a village called Zinga, somewhere in the Congo."

"What did Barker die of?" Visavadia pursued.

"I'm not sure," I said, "but the records say he went very cold in the morning, shaking badly, and was given a brandy by Pocock, together with a hot stone for his feet. But none of this helped, and he started to foam at the mouth and died a short while later. It could have been anything, perhaps malaria, bilharzia, or sleeping sickness. All these diseases are endemic to this region. Odd thing was that he was only a humble clerk working at the Langham Hotel in London when he approached Stanley and begged him for a place on his next expedition into Africa."

We walked back toward the van, but before we got there we heard the soft lilt of island calypso music drifting in the warm air. There were half a dozen children, boys and girls, sporting Herbalex badges and jostling around. Goodness knows where they had come from. It was anyone's guess, but there was nothing like the bush telegraph for spreading news. They glanced nervously in our direction as we approached, and I was aware that I might prove to be the first white man they had ever seen, and, in that case, it was up to me to break the ice. I quickly came up with some words of greeting in Swahili, and there were soon smiles all around.

"You can see I've been busy." Thomas grinned, and everyone had a good laugh.

Shortly afterward we started back to Mwanza. It was only twelve miles, and we had time to stop at both Ihale and Lllemera, where we made a few cash sales. The sun had now started to dip behind the horizon, and in its place was a fan-shaped red-and-gold canvas. This color mix splashed gloriously across the rim of our sighted world, and was soon to dissolve in every direction.

"Are there any questions?" I asked, as we drew into the graveled parking lot of the Lake Hotel.

"What tapes do we use in this region?" Visavadia scratched the stubble on his chin.

"Our agents say that the Swahili tape will be OK. The people are essentially Bantu speaking, although they can well understand Swahili. The local dialect is known as 'Sukuma,' but we haven't been able to produce a recording because the language has no writing standards."

"It doesn't matter about the language," Thomas quipped, "we can always sell."

"See you guys tomorrow." I laughed and walked back across the yard and entered the Lake Hotel.

chapter

SIXTEEN

Exactly three weeks later, on Tuesday, October 11, we left Mwanza on completion of our work in the vast territorial region of the southern lake area. We headed south toward the parched plateau of central Tanganyika. Our destination for this section of the safari was Tabora, some 227 miles along a hot, dusty road. The van was once again filled to the hilt with forty-five cases each of Herbalex and Gripe Aid. We also carried ten gallons of water and five gallons of gasoline in sealed containers.

We said our good-byes to Lal and his staff and clambered into the van. It was good to be on safari again, the open roads, new scenery, and fresh destinations. We were no longer prisoners of a large town. We had worked hard in Mwanza, and several times we yo-yoed over the same ground—it couldn't have been avoided—like a donkey on a treadmill.

Village settlements came and went with their repetitive farms of sweet potatoes and beans and square-shaped fields fringed by shallow, overgrown ditches. The dirt road followed the level of the land between these ditches, flat and open, without the usual sloping embankments. It appeared to stretch all the way across the unbounded plateau, the clear view broken only by yellows and greens of small plantations with crops of sesame, plantain, and sorghum taking turns. It all added up to nothing more than a scratching of earth in these huge, open plains.

Late in the afternoon we arrived at the busy trading center of Shinyanga, an exact hundred miles south of Mwanza. It had been good for us to be back on the road and shake off any rustiness. We had daily destinations now, no longer circling around in suburban districts. Today we had worked the bush villages, settlements, and townships in temperatures soaring toward the upper nineties, but it was even more satisfying to call it a day and check into the local Diamond Fields Hotel at the top end of the main square and take a cool shower. It was almost unbelievable to find such a facility in upcountry regions.

Shinyanga was a large, square-shaped town with timber and concrete buildings. The main street at the north end was lined with pink and brown terraced shops that ran alongside rutted tracks. The whole place was coated in dust and looked shabby under the falling sun.

The next morning, Wednesday, October 12, we left the hotel around nine o'clock and traveled eight miles on a narrow, unmarked track to the diamond mines at Mwadui. Security at the gates was tight. You know the sort of thing—armed guards, patrol dogs, and high perimeter fences. The two guards at the checkpoint telephoned through to the main office. We heard some garbled words behind a thick glass partition, and then the guard replaced the receiver and informed us that the chief purchasing officer could see visitors only by appointment.

"I don't think he likes the look of the van," Thomas said dryly. "He just keeps staring at it."

The high-pitched sound of a small aircraft droned overhead, wings tilting as it angled down and disappeared behind the concrete buildings beyond the wire.

I climbed back into the overwarm cabin and reversed down the dirt road until I found a suitable place to turn around. "Let's face it," I said with a laugh, "if either of you had a diamond mine, I doubt if you would have let in a dirty van with a motley crew like us." I took a last backward glimpse from the open door. The guard was standing by his pinewood hut, hands on hips, squinting hard against the sun as he watched us depart.

Safari Salesman

After leaving the diamond mine, we decided to work the outlying bush villages. It was a hot day, and the sun was beating down relentlessly from a cloudless African sky. Ahead of us was a curtain of shimmering heat rising from an isolated settlement.

At a place called Unanyembe—it was nothing more than a dot on the map—were a few grass shacks and a medium-size wood-built hardware and grocery store. A sunburned signboard was nailed precariously across the doorway. It read: Haddad's Dry Goods and Provisions, and underneath was the Arabic transcription. A small boy ran across the bare compound in front of the huts as we drew to a halt. It would seem he was making for the safety of his house but changed his mind after a moment's hesitation, deciding to slow down and come to a stop. It was Thomas, ever vigilant, who won him over when he stepped out from the van and crouched down and offered the youth a Herbalex badge, which he proceeded to pin onto his tattered undershirt. He was just getting used to our presence, guessing we posed no threat, when Visavadia, unseen in the van, switched on the record player and the booming sound of a South American mambo swamped the neighborhood. In an act of self-preservation, the boy darted back toward his original target and peered anxiously from a darkened doorway. To him, it must have seemed as though a world war had broken out.

Instantaneously I leaned into the van. "Visavadia," I shouted, "lower the volume. It's only a small place!"

"I'm sorry," came the muffled reply.

Thomas was quick to heal any hurt with the local community and went over to the Arab shop owner and gave him a large smile. "Can I nail a couple of metal signs on your wall?" he asked as he held up a tin plate in each hand for inspection.

"*Ndio,*" the man agreed in Swahili. He was clothed in a purple, loose-fitting jellaba and was nonchalantly picking at his teeth with a matchstick.

I approached the wood-railed veranda and gave him a brochure. The shop was partially shaded by a leafy, sweet-smelling myrrh tree. "Are you Mr. Haddad?" I asked quietly. A group of villagers ringed the shady area.

"How can I help you?" He smiled as he leaned on the banister and flicked through the booklet. Every now and then he touched his thick beard, slightly tilting his shaven head while he listened to the tape of Latin music coming from the speaker.

"Would you like to buy some of our cough medicine?" I inquired as the tape finished.

"Give me six dozen of Herbalex," he said casually, "and another six dozen of Gripe Aid."

"Six dozen of each," I reiterated, pulling the order book out of my jacket pocket. A twinge of pain shot through my left leg as I stumbled on the wooden steps leading to the veranda.

"Are you OK?" Thomas asked from behind me.

"I'm fine," I said and nodded.

"You should have seen a doctor in Mwanza," he warned.

Mr. Haddad spoke in Arabic to a little girl in bare feet. She was probably his daughter. Anyway, she ran into the store and dashed out moments later with four bottles of cherry cream soda clasped in her arms.

"Have a drink," Mr. Haddad said, handing them round.

"That's a generous order," I remarked as I finished completing the invoice.

"My store is popular," he explained. "I get plenty of business from the workers at the diamond mine. They all live around here and know me, and I like to stock quality products." He pointed an index finger at the wood floor behind him, indicating to Visavadia where he wanted the boxes to be set down.

"How long have you been here then?"

"Many years." He smiled. "It was before the mine was opened anyway."

He took a swallow from his bottle. "Must be over twenty years." He gazed silently up as though inhaling the scented aroma from the myrrh tree and turned his head back in our direction. "In the old days I used to give credit to anyone with a hard-luck story," he reminisced. "You know what I mean. I'd grubstake them." He bent forward and plonked the empty soda bottle down near his sandaled feet. "There was this one guy, and he regularly passed through here with his old donkey, the pair of them disheveled and hungry, overloaded with all the prospector's gear that they could carry between them, you know, things like shallow pans, shovels, picks, sieves, flasks, blankets, oil, and cooking pots. Well, this man knew what he was looking for. He'd crisscrossed the area so many times, insisting that a vein of diamonds would surface somewhere in this Mwagala plateau. He was obsessed with his geological theory and didn't trek outside the region. He was different from the other prospectors who drifted away. I suppose it goes without saying." Mr. Haddad smiled, then added, "He finally found all the diamonds he ever wanted."

"He founded the Mwadui Mines?" I asked.

"Too right." The Arab smiled. "Nothing but unending fields of clear, colorless diamonds. What more could one want? One stone they found—back in 1947—weighed almost fifty-five carats. They gave it to the Queen of England."

"I wish they had given it to me," Thomas quipped.

After a second night at Shinyanga, we proceeded with the drive south, branching left at Jomu, where the road divided for Kahama. We halted briefly at the trading center of Nzega before we struck due south for Tabora. We arrived there in the early afternoon.

Tabora used to lie on the main ivory and slave trade route. The ruins of Arab houses could still be seen in the town. It was the Germans who laid out this important center as capital of Tanganyika. Only three miles south at the village of Kwihara, one could find the restored house where Livingstone used to live. The central line of the East African Railways trisected here, going to Mwanza, Kigoma, and Dar es Salaam—the north, west, and east, respectively.

The Nyamwezi people—the country's second-largest tribe—inhabited the region. They raised vegetables, including pulses such as beans, peas, and lentils, while tobacco and groundnuts formed the basic cash crops.

Before checking in at the Tabora Hotel, we drove down the main avenue and found a parking space outside the rather dusty, oblong-shaped general post office. There were two letters for me awaiting collection, both recently forwarded by Morgans in Mwanza. The first letter, discreetly scented, had Carol's name and address written on the reverse of the pale blue envelope. I slipped it into my top pocket to read later. The second letter was from my employers in London informing me that the chairman of the company, Sir Frederick Bell, would be arriving in Nairobi en route to his holiday destination at Johannesburg. The dates given were the weekend coming up, and he wished to see me.

"That just about does it," I growled, and pressed my back involuntarily against the passenger seat. I knew full well that I couldn't afford to ignore this summons to meet with the chairman. An interruption to our safari at this stage would be likely to upset the rhythm and impact of our work on a psychological level. It had taken weeks to adapt and blend into the style of life in the African bush, and now, with the threat of delays, it would be very difficult to get back into gear again once our work was interrupted from the outside.

Unbelievably, less than an hour later we drove down the narrow red murram track leading to the local airport. The East African Airways official in the town had already confirmed that a few empty seats were available on the three o'clock flight to Entebbe in Uganda. On arrival I would have to change planes to connect with a BOAC Viscount flying down from Benghazi and scheduled for an onward flight to Nairobi at 19:30 hours. This complicated route would mean that I would be flying a nine-hundred-mile journey instead of the 383 miles direct from Tabora to Nairobi, but on the short direct flight there was nothing until noon on Saturday.

On the other hand, looking more on the positive side, this break in the safari should provide a chance to have my left foot examined by a doctor. During the past few days, it had become badly inflamed, and there were raw areas where the skin had rubbed off and were too sensitive to touch. I was beginning to use a walking stick more often than not. It gave me good support and kept the weight off my foot when touching ground. I was caught up in a negative situation and was anxious to get it sorted out.

The sound of an approaching aircraft silenced our conversation. I was in the middle of advising Thomas on a limited itinerary while I was gone. We left the shabby hallway of the airport lounge and went outside.

"Take it easy while I'm away," I said, shaking hands with Thomas and Visavadia. "I should be back on the direct flight on Monday." We ambled through the exit doors onto the concrete terrace and watched the small, single-prop plane make its landing on the grass runway. Suddenly the pitch of the engine changed to a deep-throated roar, and the aircraft veered upward at a steep angle. Seconds afterward two airport workers in blue dungarees rushed across the apron from the direction of the control tower.

"Some ass is grazing his goats on the runway," Thomas said, pointing a finger across the grass from his position on the perimeter fence as the plane circled overhead. There was a mixture of bleating goats, angry gesticulations, and the crackle of the flight announcer's voice over the speaker. Five minutes later the plane landed on the cleared runway, and its engines roared into reverse. "Watch how you go." Thomas smiled and handed me my case and the rest of my stuff.

Four hours later I landed at Entebbe airport, with its newfangled colored lights running in parallel lines down the length of the runway. I had half an hour to kill before my connecting flight to Nairobi and found myself limping across the vinyl-tiled floor of the mezzanine toward the cafeteria. The low ceiling and the bright lights embedded in acoustic panels illuminated the grandiose murals depicting Uganda's heritage on the encircling walls.

I went over to the coffee bar and sat down on a sorrel-colored plastic stool. It was strange to be here, in civilization, after weeks spent in the African bush. I found myself looking at the most mundane things in a state of wonder, almost the way a six-month-old baby takes things in. A thick bank of stainless steel cookers, flat working tops, shining drink dispensers, shelving, and sink units lined the dividing wall behind the polished counter. Some people sat at Formica-topped tables in the restaurant section eating food, talking, drinking, and making sure that their children didn't stray too far while waiting for their flight to be called.

"What would you like?" a waitress in a green overall asked solicitously. She was a Bagandan of middle age, round-faced and fleshy. She began wiping the counter with a cloth.

"Coffee and a ham sandwich, please." I smiled.

There was a hiss of steam as the woman pulled the black handle on the coffee machine. To me everything seemed unreal. It crossed my mind that Larry Martin of Life Magazine might still be pacing the floor downstairs waiting for his stringers to report in, or then again, he might have returned to Arua and looked up Father Francis to get his story on the Congo.

The double glass doors on the far side of the room swung open, and a large party of people trooped into the cafeteria, some settling at the tables, others thronging the counter. The men were in smart dark gray suits, the women in fashionable two-pieces, dark blue skirts and silk blouses in light cream colors. Besides being well dressed, a good many of them carried variedly shaped black cases, which manifestly housed musical instruments. My guess—which wasn't difficult to make—was that they were a working orchestra, possibly traveling from Europe to South Africa.

While finishing my sandwich, I noticed that one or two of them at nearby tables had given me the odd glance as they carried on chatting with their friends. Feeling uneasy, I slipped a five shilling note under the plate, picked up my stick, and walked slowly from the room, back-tracking across the mezzanine and down the wide staircase toward the toilets on the floor below.

I stared at myself in the illuminated mirror that stretched across one of the walls behind the row of identical washbasins. The reflection in the glass took me by surprise. Somehow or another I looked different from the other people in the restaurant. It was hard to explain.

I was unshaven and the khaki safari suit I was wearing was stained and bleached, while particles of sand and reddish dust clung tenaciously to pocket edges and trouser seams. On top of all this, my shoes and socks were caked in lemon yellow laterite clay, and my hair was parched dry by the sun, no longer light brown but yellow and wild. I cursed at my appearance. It wasn't my fault, as all we had in the bush to identify ourselves was the van mirror, which we used to shave in. I took a step or two back, bedazzled by this giant mirror, and paused to look at myself again. If only I had checked into the Tabora Hotel. It was too late now. I leaned over the basin and ran some hot water and, at the same time, I pumped the soap dispenser. I was furious with myself for being so naive.

In the bush nobody would have bothered to take a second look. I was part of the scene, perfectly camouflaged like a two-lined skink chameleon on an adobe wall, but here I was irrevocably out of place, someone to be laughed at.

I dried myself on some paper towels and went and sat in a cubicle to wait the flight announcement. I slowly twirled the brown walking stick between my hands. The rich-colored bark had partially peeled, and the black adhesive tape that Thomas had stuck around the handle was coming off. The stick and I looked out of place, oddly ridiculous, almost Chaplinesque. I was tempted to leave my stick behind, but I needed it now.

"All those on Flight four zero three to Nairobi, please assemble in the departure lounge immediately," the announcer's voice came over the speaker. "This is the BOAC Flight from London, Rome, and Benghazi and is now loading at Gate Three. Thank you."

The twin-engine Vickers Viscount pulled itself smoothly into the dark sky, the whirring blades invisible from the large, square windows. It circled over the bright lights of Kampala and some minutes later leveled off at eight thousand feet before steering a course of southeast by east for the four-hundred-mile trip to Nairobi.

I looked back over the wing at the fading lights of the city and felt sad. Somewhere down there, in the crowded city streets, or in the suburbs, was a dwelling house, hidden behind yellow thevetia hedgerows, where Carol lived. I drew her letter from my jacket pocket and smoothed it flat against my leg.

The cabin sign for seat belts and no smoking had not long been extinguished before an angry streak of lightning flashed across the leaden sky. Seconds later the red warning lights reappeared and passengers nervously began to refix their belts. By now the aircraft was over Lake Victoria, clipping the northeast corner and pushing hard against the increasing turbulence. There was a further mechanical buzz from the pilot's cabin to remind us about seat belts, and the air hostess hastily bent over the double rows as she made her way along the compartment to check that the captain's instructions had been obeyed. The plane began to dip and yaw.

I slit open the envelope and pulled out the letter. Carol's neat feminine handwriting, set on pale, thinly lined blue notepaper, lay spread on my lap.

I took a Crown Bird cigarette from the American style pack, lit it, and inhaled the strong tobacco before settling back against the comfortable damask seat.

The Government Hospital,
Nakasero Hill
Kampala NW
Uganda

Tuesday, 4 Oct 1960

My Darling John,

I have tears running down my face. I have just heard the ghastly news that my dear Daddy has been killed in a road accident in Hampshire. I know you will understand that I am absolutely distraught and am flying home tonight to be with my mother.
I was so terribly happy that weekend in Mubende and so unhappy when we parted. I cannot describe to you what it has been like without you, and now without my father. I only wished I could be in your arms; it would help me in my sorrow.

Please write and tell me that what is happening has nothing to do with that horrible Witch Tree at Mubende. I didn't mean to sit on it, and I can't stop thinking about what you said about 'an incurable sickness.' It can't be true, can it? I feel awful and there isn't a moment that goes by when my mind isn't filled with thoughts about you. Please come back safely from your safari. How can I ever forget the time we shared together at that house on top of the hill? And any letters I write I'll send via your agents in Nairobi and mark them 'Please Forward' to make sure you receive them. At the moment I am totally confused and uncertain about my future, but I must make sure that Mummy is alright before I make any decisions. I'm so helpless without the steadying influence of a man in my life. I need you more than ever now. You would have loved Daddy. He spent several years in Canada before the war studying geology. Please say a prayer for me tonight and write as soon as you can. I've made arrangements with my girlfriend Lorraine, who I share a flat with and like me works at the hospital, to forward all my mail. I miss you so much, lots of love, Carol.

I stubbed my cigarette into the metal ashtray. The buffeting of the craft seemed to have died off as I stared vacantly into the flat darkness, ears popping; as we gradually dropped height over Kenya.

***

The doctor leaned forward on his chair, waiting to examine my foot while he supported it with his left hand and the nurse unwound the sticky bandage. "Nasty mess you've got here," he muttered to himself. The young nurse continued to remove the bandage and picked up the last of the lint with a pair of forceps. The smell from my wound was strong and unpleasant.

"It seems to me," he began again, "you have a severe form of contact dermatitis." He gently lowered my left foot onto a medicated mat placed underneath the chair. "Because no professional treatment has been given, the condition appears to have deteriorated in the past week."

"Can anything be done?" I asked. I had explained to the doctor earlier that I had arrived in Nairobi only last night, and it was important for me to return to Tanganyika as soon as possible.

"I appreciate that you would run into difficulties in getting the proper medical care up-country," he said reading my thoughts, "but your foot is now in a badly ulcerated condition." The doctor stopped his examination and swiveled his chair backward on the metal castors. "Look, Mr. Carter," he said

Safari Salesman

as he peered over the rim of his tortoise shell spectacles, "I can see you have attempted to keep the wound clean and apply dressings, but I'm interested in the original cause." He paused and leaned forward in his swivel chair. "Have you any idea as to how it started?"

I glanced down at the inflamed foot. Pus oozing from the broken skin, and small pyramids of spongy growths, funguslike, dotted across the raw, open wound. "I don't think I've been bitten or scratched," I replied.

"Have you been in any water?" he pursued. "You know, rivers, lakes, swamps—that sort of thing?"

"Well, yes, I suppose I have."

"Lakes?" he shot back.

"Wait a minute." I searched my mind. "Yes, I remember I washed our promotional van in Lake Victoria at a place called Bukakata. It was about six weeks ago."

The doctor shook his head in agreement. "In that case infected water is the cause of your troubles. The lake areas are well-known for malaria, dysentery, and sleeping sickness...." His voice trailed away. "Have you noticed blood in your urine?"

Once more he leaned forward in the chair, alert and ready for my answer.

"No."

"That's good," he observed. "I thought that you might have been infected by a parasite known in our profession as cercariae. It lays eggs in the rectum and penetrates the bladder and intestinal region, carrying the disease of schistosomiasis." The doctor pushed his glasses farther back onto his nose. "That's bilharzia to you." He smiled. "And one last thing, any diarrhea?"

"No," I said again.

The doctor eased his chair nearer the desk and began writing. "The two men traveling with you, do they have any symptoms?" he asked thoughtfully.

"Not to my knowledge."

"I'm going to give you a compound zinc paste of coal tar. This is to be applied twice daily on a fresh lint dressing. The foot must be cleaned with olive oil, no soap and water," he cautioned. "I am also going to put you on a month's course of multivitamins to build you up and a prescription of antibiotic capsules to fight the infection. You must finish the seven-day course." The doctor placed his glasses on the desk top and pushed his chair backward with his feet. "You're lucky the wound isn't on the sole of the foot. Otherwise, you wouldn't be walking now. I would suggest you spend the remainder of the day on your bed at the hotel, give your foot a complete rest, and, in a couple of weeks, you will be fully recovered. Now, if you would like to go out and wait in the main hall, I'll send my nurse with the prescription, and she'll also clean and dress your foot."

I stood up to go. "Thank you very much," I said and smiled.

"Not at all," he replied, "but remember to keep out of lakes."

***

"We are very pleased with the results we are getting from the promotional campaign," Sir Frederick Bell enthused.

"Thank you, Sir."

We were sitting in the galleried lounge of the New Stanley Hotel after enjoying an excellent Saturday night dinner. Coffee and liqueurs were on the table, and Sir Frederick was in an expansive mood. He tilted his balloon-shaped brandy glass to and fro. "I thought it would be a jolly good thing to look you up on my way through Kenya," he reflected. "It lets the shareholders know that we are active in the field." A blob of ash dropped from his cigar onto the red carpeting.

"It's good to know we are not forgotten," I said.

"Quite so." He nodded as he looked at the sculpturing that banded the ceiling. "The directors tell me that you are not keeping in proper touch with London. The agents say they have the same problem and have difficulties in supplying stock, as you don't always adhere to the agreed itinerary."

"The conditions in the bush don't always lend themselves to a strict timetable," I said defensively, "and most managers in Morgans who've been here for more than twenty years have never actually stepped foot in the country areas. And yet, back in the UK, they are considered experts on Africa."

"I understand what you are saying." Sir Frederick put down his glass and wiped his moustache with a linen napkin. "Anyway, what can you tell me about this chap in Kibondo? He's been writing to us about his interest in Chemisan toilets, and, from what I understand, you've yet to file a report on the matter."

"Yes, I know about Crispin Netuwa," I cut in, "and we'll be visiting him as soon as we are in the area."

"Ah, yes." Sir Frederick wavered for a moment, seemingly uncertain of his ground. "The whole point is," he said slowly, "that we asked you to deal with this matter some weeks ago."

"I'll file a report the moment I arrive in Kibondo," I said, and paused for a moment while I finished off my Benedictine liqueur. "It'll take about a week. Will that be all right, sir?"

"Good. I'm glad that's settled," he said amiably, and added, "By the way, we've received an initial inquiry from the works manager of the East African Railways concerning our new range of closets. However, they have asked us not to call on them at the moment, and I suggest that if we've heard nothing by December, you get in touch with them after completion of the safari, and should there be any positive developments in the interim we'll keep you posted."

"Yes, I'll look into it," I said. The sextet that had earlier been playing in the dining hall had now moved onto a carpeted dais in the corner of the lounge. They began to tune their instruments, and a hushed expectancy descended on the crowded room.

The chairman looked tired, and I was relieved that I had built up a rapport with him, which I hoped would soon be reflected in the end-of-year pay reviews. My modest salary of £800 per annum plus expenses wasn't exactly a fortune, but I did avoid income tax, due to being out of the UK for more than six months.

Opposite our table, near a backdrop of velvet curtains, sat a bored but beautiful young girl. She talked spasmodically to her older companion. It was probably her mother because of similar looks. Every now and then she'd glance across the tables, a hint of a smile on her lovely pink lips.

Discussing the merits of chemical sanitation on a Saturday night wasn't exactly up my street, and I felt that at any moment my conversation with Sir Frederick would delve into the qualities of our range of lavatory papers.

"I understand you are going down to your daughter's wedding in Jo'burg," I said with a smile. Our Morgans Nairobi manager, Bill Wright, had told me this bit of chatter yesterday when he phoned the hotel after I got back from the doctor. He had hinted that this piece of news was the real purpose behind the chairman's journey.

"Yes." He gave a far-away look and coughed into his handkerchief. "One week from today Penelope gets married. She's my youngest, you know." He paused once more and proceeded to pull out a gold half-hunter watch that was secured to a waistcoat buttonhole by an embossed Albert chain. Then using the nail of his index finger, he clicked it open.

"It's getting on for ten o'clock,' he murmured. "Think I'll call it a day; my flight for South Africa leaves early tomorrow morning." He rose slowly from the chair, his tired eyes looking vaguely around. This strange environment was not giving him the recognition he was accustomed to in the London clubs, and together we wandered out into the lobby.

"Have you got your room key?" I asked solicitously.

"Yes," he smiled weakly, jangling the keys, waiting for the elevator to descend "and good luck Carter."

"Safe journey, Sir," I said quietly as he stepped into the confined space of the lift. There was a swish, and the automatic doors closed.

***

Rhythmic music drifted invitingly across the lounge. The young girl by the long curtains smiled as I made my way through the tight-fitting tables. "May I have this dance?" I asked, easing her chair back as she got up.

"My name's John," I began.

"Mine's Ann."

Within minutes of getting onto the dance floor I was reminded of my bad leg and had no alternative but to walk back to the table.

Her mother told me how they had flown down from Addis Abeba to taste the British atmosphere in Kenya and do some shopping. Ann's father was some kind of commercial consul who represented the United Kingdom's interests in Ethiopia.

An hour went by before we could drop the mother and go off on our own. After leaving the hotel, we walked one block to a coffee bar in York Street. I was more than aware that she would want a "fun time," but I felt hindered by my limp, which I did my best to hide. I tried to think of a good place to take her so that she could let her hair down. It was her first time in Kenya, and I was as determined as she was to turn this Saturday night into a success. Perhaps the Equator Club might be the answer; it was near enough in Queensway and had a lively New Orleans flavor.

"I know where to go," I said, sliding my hand into hers and looking into her almond-shaped eyes. "I'll take you to Hoppy's Bar on the Ngong Road."

We finished our coffee and grabbed an Archer's cab waiting for customers on the opposite side of the street. We motored up Sergeant Ellis Avenue, turning left onto Princess Elizabeth Way, and pressed onward in a southerly direction, picking up speed along an attractive four-lane road lined by flowering shrubs and jacaranda trees. The blueness of their fluorescent trumpet-shaped flowers shone warmly in the matching light of the curbside lamps. After half a mile, we curved to the right and passed through the early residential suburbs of Karen. The views became more extensive under the brightness of a clear tropical moon. Everything was green, spacious, and elitist as we started to climb up the gentle slopes with their detached villas, trim lawns, and gardens of hibiscus blossoms. The climb gradually steepened, and the wide-open views engulfed the gigantic flaw of the Rift Valley.

We were now out in the open, and the moon's brilliance had turned night into day. Over to the left we saw the Ngong Hills thrusting upward like the knuckles on a fist. They were the home of the Masais' first spiritual chief, or *laibon*. The word was that the hills were formed by a giant tripping over Kilimanjaro.

The land soon fell away on one side, and the steepness into the valley below was mind-boggling. The taxi driver dropped to second gear and pressed hard on the accelerator, but the cab continued to sway a little on the uncambered bends. Then, without notice, we came to a stretch of level ground and wheeled right onto a leveled parking lot.

Hoppy's Club was in full swing. The yellow glow from the windows gave depth to the large, sprawling building. The light from the bar spread out into the yard and outlined a concrete wall that ran the length of one side, and beyond was the flawed emptiness of the giant valley. This was the place to be on a Saturday night, and the young would make a beeline to this isolated club set on the rocky slopes of an escarpment. The British Army was still stationed in Kenya, and those men off duty at the weekend would also make their way here in preference to the nightspots in Nairobi. Privates, non-commissioned ranks, and junior officers would wear casual clothes, and therefore there no worries about anyone pulling rank. At the same time, the terrorist war that was waged against the Mau Mau was no longer a threat and was in steady decline. It was now time for everyone to relax, both the civilian and the military. The only people missing were the tourists, and that was another reason why people flocked to the club. Hoppy, a short, wiry man, could always be found darting from table to table, or holding court behind the angled bar at the top left corner of the enormous dance hall.

He was dubbed Hoppy because he walked with a limp—he had one leg shorter than the other. It was also said that he kept a loaded revolver on a shelf under the bar to use on anyone who might cause him displeasure. He certainly wasn't a man you would put to the test, because no one wanted to be thrown out of his club and banned from ever coming back. It occurred to me that he might not be amused if he thought I was trying to impersonate him with my own duff foot.

The music blared as people crowded the floor. Those who couldn't find space stayed at their tables and downed pints of lager and bitter. I danced cheek to cheek with Ann during one of the slow numbers, and her warm, sexy breath blew enticingly against my neck.

"Wow, what an evening," she gasped, her inviting pink lips slightly parted. "There's nothing like this in Addis, no fun places, so just imagine what I would have missed if I hadn't come to Kenya. My girlfriends will be really jealous," she cooed.

Two hours later we left the club and headed for the Montagu Hotel. We had already agreed to spend time together, and Anne had called her mother to tell her that we were at an all-night club that did breakfasts. "So don't worry, Mum," she had said, "I'm a big girl now and can look after myself."

"Well, if you're quite sure," her Mother agreed.

It was seven in the morning when I returned Ann to the Stanley Hotel. We stood outside on a chilly pavement having a final embrace. "It was fun, wasn't it, John?' she whispered huskily into my ear before turning to go inside. For a moment or two, she was framed against the doorway, and then she was gone.

***

At ten on Sunday morning, I sat down in the spacious dining hall of the Montagu Hotel and browsed through a Sunday paper.

A small, isolated group of BOAC aircrew was at the next table talking about flying—what else?—and the young, auburn-haired air hostess appeared to be staring into the middle distance, saying nothing. The trouble with a flight stayover in a foreign country for maybe two or three days is that things get boring. The crew had no transport and was stuck at the hotel, and besides this self-inflicted moratorium, they had no idea where to go or what to do should they've been given an opportunity to spread their wings. Those drawbacks no doubt contributed to their reputation of being dull and a wee bit tight-fisted, and that's why the hostesses grabbed at a chance of freedom when it came along.

After breakfast I went back to my room and wrote up an overdue sales report and completed the sales account, which included a list of my expenses, while making sure that my laundry bill was kept under £1 for the week—I put in for a cheeky nineteen shillings and eleven pence. Finally I typed out a covering letter confirming that I had had a successful meeting with the chairman, and as an afterthought put in a postscript informing the export department that I would soon be in a position to call on Mr. Crispin Netuwa.

My second letter to Carol I addressed to Nakasero to await arrival. I told her how much I missed her and how sorry I was to hear the sad news about her father. And for a moment my mind drifted away from the letter and I too wondered if her father's death could have been linked to the Witch Tree at Mubende. This was a prime example of how Africa rules ones thinking.

It was after one o'clock when I finished the paperwork and packed away the portable typewriter. I emerged from the bedroom and went outside to the beer garden. It was almost empty except for a family of four who were sitting at a white table on the lawn, and a couple of guys in deep conversation standing by a large automobile parked on the upper driveway.

"Where's everybody?"

"Soon fill up," the barman assured me as he poured my lager.

"That's OK by me," I said, glancing at the unoccupied stools circling the loggia bar.

Andy Savvides, the Greek owner, appeared from across the other side of the lounge. "Hey, John, how's it going?" He didn't wait for an answer. "I saw your name in the book," he said, "but the word had gone out that you were on one of your safari specials. Imagine my surprise when I saw your name. What brings you back to Nairobi?" He put an arm round my shoulders and smiled again. The barman broke open another beer and left us to talk. Slowly the room filled up with people and music drifted in from the gardens. "I must go," Andy said after a few minutes, gulping the last of his beer.

The British airline crew I had last seen at breakfast had now entered the bar and had settled down on the empty stools alongside me. It was by chance that the auburn-haired air hostess took the last empty stool right next to me. The crew, as usual with most crews, remained distant from the surroundings. They were still talking about flying while they ordered their soft drinks.

I couldn't pretend the pretty hostess wasn't there, so I smiled and said, "My name's John."

"Mine's Jennifer." She smiled back.

"Would you like to dance?"

"Yes, that would be great," she answered as she slipped off the bar stool.

For a moment I didn't know what had made me ask her for a dance, especially with my bad leg. I had done the same with Ann last night, but with the sound of island music ringing in my ears, it seemed the natural thing to do before anyone else got in first. And anyway, much to my satisfaction, the crew looked up in disapproval as though their ownership rights had been infringed.

In any event we hadn't been dancing for more than a couple of minutes—and by now I was getting used to the pain in my leg—when the lead musician announced that it was time to take five.

Back on our bar stools, I asked Jennifer if she would like to come for a drive along the Rift Valley and find some place to eat.

"Nothing I would like more," she said, "but I'm afraid I can't make it."

"Why's that?"

"I'm on a timetable," she said, "and our flight for Jo'burg leaves in three hours."

"That's too bad." I smiled.

The green-and-yellow flowers of the tulip tree hung decoratively over the smooth stones of the terrazzo dance floor. There were splashes of shade and light that made jigsaw patterns over the open patio. A few fallen leaves of bright emerald lay scattered over the dividing edge of concrete and grass.

"I've been here since Friday," she admitted, "and it's a shame we didn't bump into each other before." She tossed her head back so as to settle her long auburn hair, which had strayed across her lovely face.

"You win some, you lose some. That's life." I smiled.

The combo had by now returned to their spot under the tulip tree and picked up their instruments from the cases. The voice of the leader could be heard counting to two before the band came in with the lilting refrain of "Mona Lisa," and, in an instant, couples reemerged from the loggia bar and the garden tables that were dotted around the lawn to take their place on the parquet floor. It was difficult to think of this happening in other countries, it being lunchtime on Sunday.

"Maybe we could meet up in London sometime?" she suggested.

"That'll be great, and I'll take you to a show."

Jennifer then delved into her flight bag and pulled out a printed stick-on label. "Now you'll have to call me," she said with a laugh.

"We'll do a swap," I said and produced my business card.

We were happily having a chat about London things, and established that we had both lived in town at one time or another. I revealed that I had been born in Sussex Gardens, off the Edgware Road, when, at that moment, a uniformed BOAC crew member with two gold-braid rings on the cuffs of his blue jacket pushed between us and indicated to Jennifer that their early, pre-flight lunch had been laid out on the patio at the far end of the lawn.

"I guess it's time to go," she said.

"I'll ring you sometime in January," I said.

"Don't forget."

"No way," I said and laughed.

chapter

SEVENTEEN

The cabin of the aircraft was stifling hot as we waited at the far end of Nairobi's Embakasi Airport runway for permission to take off. Finally, after a twenty-minute delay, the engines thundered and we sped down the tarmac and lifted into a sharp climb, leveling off at five thousand feet above a trail of wispy white cloud. It appeared as though we were gliding as the craft set course south through the azure blue sky of springlike Kenya. This time the flight was direct to Tabora, except for a short stopover at Mwanza airport in order to unload cargo and let off a handful of passengers. The total journey of 385 miles was half that of going via Entebbe. This would eliminate the tedium of the outward flight.

I pushed a copy of the *East African Standard* across my lap. It was dated Monday, October 17. Then, with my head resting on an airline pillow, I shut my eyes and let my thoughts take control. It was a great relief to have had proper treatment for my leg. And I was pleased that the visit by Sir Frederick Bell went off all right, and I was also satisfied that he had been made suitably welcome. His trip would have been at the company's expense, and no doubt his report would have stated that he had met me and discussed various aspects of business. All this would hold up well under the scrutiny of our auditors when they noticed his African trip extended as far south as Johannesburg.

On reflection my time out of the bush had been well spent. My foot was now on the mend. I'd met two new friends and had had a worthwhile meeting with Sir Frederick at the Stanley. But it did cause me concern that in such a short time I had possibly reverted in character to being a "townie" and that I might find it difficult to settle down to being a safari salesman again. But when I thought of the unfinished work that had to be done in the bush, and the loyalty of my two colleagues waiting for my return, it soon dispelled any doubts that I might have harbored.

The airplane passed low over the Serengeti National Park, fifteen thousand square kilometers of yellow plains stretched endlessly below. The wild scenery, including the snow-tipped Kilimanjaro, was out of this world. At altitudes ranging from three thousand to six thousand feet, the passengers had a clear view of life below. I could see smoke coming from isolated settlements and children herding goats. It was a fantasyland with rivers, forests, swamps, and deserts—a spectacle—and beneath us was the greatest concentration of game in all Africa. From my cabin window I watched an enormous herd of Grevy's zebra run and scatter across the limitless savanna. This stampede created a cloud of billowing dust so that only occasionally was one able to pick out the narrow black-and-white stripes of that species.

My newspaper slipped slowly from my lap as the plane climbed and banked to the southwest. I stretched down to retrieve it from the carpeted floor, and, on lifting my head, I once more looked out of the window and caught sight of the metallic grays and blues of the southern gulf of Lake Victoria emerging on the right. The plane had angled on a wing tip to correct our approach for Mwanza airport. The leaden waters looked oppressive and melancholy under the sultry heat.

We were on the ground for less than thirty minutes. I took advantage of the stopover to phone Lal and ask him to arrange a further shipment of stock to be sent by rail to the halting place at Itigi. I explained to him that we would pick this up on our way east, and after that point, the burden of responsibility would then fall on our agents in Dar es Salaam. I also received confirmation that the consignment of Herbalex and Gripe Aid for Tabora, on which we had agreed earlier, had already been dispatched and should be there awaiting our collection. As I put the receiver back on the phone, it dawned on me that our links with Mwanza had now been cut for the rest of the safari, and I hadn't even said good-bye to Lal or thanked him for all his help.

Nearly two hours later we circled the grass runway at Tabora. The small, fourteen-seat plane glinted in the sky as we swooped downward, props whirring, and then leveled out for the final approach. With a flick of the eyes, I caught a glimpse of the cream-colored van parked to one side of the lonely airport building. The familiar twin speakers painted in deep green and bolted to the roof epitomized all the work we were doing in the bush, along with the large expanse of side paneling that was colorfully painted with advertising slogans under smiling faces. I realized that I was undeniably looking at my home for the next few weeks and in doing so was becoming sentimental. My mood soon changed to one of heightened expectancy and my daydreams were finally over. It was back to business, and the anticipation of getting back on the road was irresistible. I felt a jolt in my shoulders as the aircraft bumped onto the grassy runway, and then came the rush of air as the props reversed.

Thomas and Visavadia stood close to the van and waved as they saw me come off the plane. It was a baking hot day, and the temperature was well into the nineties, with high humidity to match. It was noticeably hotter than the congested streets of Nairobi.

"Hey, look at you," Thomas drawled in his usual way.

"What's the big joke?" I asked, slapping his hand.

"Well have a look at this." He laughed. "A new safari suit and a fancy haircut!"

Visavadia was hanging closely behind Thomas and I took his hand. "How are you?" I grinned as I pumped his arm.

"I'm fine."

"Are we ready to go tomorrow?"

"We've finished in Tabora," Thomas said with pride.

"That's great news." I grinned, turning my head to look at them. "It's good to be back again."

"How's the foot?" Visavadia asked.

"It's getting better, thanks," I said. "I saw a doctor in Nairobi and he's given me antibiotics and dressings. It's going to take a few days before the wound heals, but that's no problem."

I moved slowly toward the van and climbed into the cab. Immediately all my doubts were washed away. It felt good to be back among familiar surroundings. I reached forward and pulled out the ordnance survey map from the shelf under the dashboard. It detailed western Tanganyika and specifically included a street index of large towns.

Thomas started the engine and leaned sideways over the wheel. "Where to?" he asked.

"Let's start with the railway station."

The gentle residential streets of Tabora unrolled on each side of the road, a world apart from the bustle and energy of city dwellers in Kenya's capital. We cruised slowly along the main boulevard, curving left and dipping between rows of shops that led downhill toward the Gothic-styled railway station. We drove under the pointed arch of the main entrance and drew up outside the dusty-looking offices. It took another thirty minutes to present our documents and load the consignment of Herbalex and Gripe Aid.

Not long afterward Thomas dropped me off outside the Tabora Hotel in the middle of town. "Pick me up at nine tomorrow," I said, taking my suitcase from the back of the van.

"See you," Thomas shouted from the cab as he drove off with Visavadia.

***

The next morning, on Tuesday, October 18, we retraced the route north as far as the market town of Nzega, a straggling community of tin and timber shacks, twisted hoardings, and broken wire fences skirting empty fields. From this point we forked to the left and started working the roadside settlements, going due west to the township of Kahama, some sixty miles away.

By the time we arrived, the sky was dark blue and the light was beginning to go. Everything in the van was coated in dust. It was pure luck that we spotted a sign post for the rest house, and we immediately turned off the dirt road and went up a stony incline that leveled out in front of an isolated building. The garden was a wild tangle around a bare compound. We were surprised that the front door was unlocked, but decided it wasn't for us to worry about and went inside. There was no furniture in the house, and we spent the night camping on the floor.

From Kahama we went west on a low, looping road toward our next destination at a place called Nyaksnazi, exactly twice the distance of yesterday's journey. The road was lined on both sides with the tall, gray-leaved agave. Not only sisal can be obtained from this leathery, pyramid-shaped plant, which has a forty-foot flower stem, blooms about every eight years, and has as much as 250 gallons of sap—the genuine source of Mexican drinks—that can be siphoned from the spiky center of the leaf cluster.

We entered Nyakanazi at several minutes before four o'clock. There was nothing to be seen; only a small settlement of grass huts scattered about a hummocked field and criss-crossed with worn paths. Otherwise the place was empty. Once more it was solely a point on the map, a simple road junction for travelers turning south to the far-off lake town of Kigoma. The sound of dogs barking could be heard coming from the settlement. We saw a couple of bedraggled villagers making their way slowly toward us. The two old men supported themselves with dry wooden staves as they walked the last few yards toward our parked vehicle. *"Jambo, bwana."* They touched their heads with the tips of their fingers.

Thomas leaned from the driving seat, telling them that we were looking for a place to sleep the night. It took a little time for them to understand the Swahili dialect until we finally mimicked a sleeping person. Immediately, the two village elders went into a huddle, and after a minute, one of the men clasped Thomas's arm and pointed down the road. He spoke in short, rapid bursts and then dropped back into total silence.

"What did he say?" I asked Thomas.

"I think," Thomas began cautiously, "that there's some sort of place farther along the road."

"It's not in the guide book."

"That's just the point," Thomas said. "The old man was trying to tell me that there's a shamba built of stone. It was never completed because the government decided to abandon the building, saying that it was too remote and it was doubtful that any traveler would ever pass that way."

"Ask him if it's all right."

"Mzuri sana leo?" Thomas asked the two old men.

"Ndio," they said and nodded in unison.

We thanked them, gave samples, and pinned Herbalex badges on their old khaki jackets. It wasn't long afterward that we located the dilapidated stone house, half-hidden in tall elephant grass, thornbush, and burgeoning wild banana bushes. With difficulty we managed to park the van outside the front entrance. It was my guess that the original intention of building this bungalow was to cater for the needs of the visiting district commissioner when he was working up-country.

"It looks OK to me," Thomas surmised, adding, "there's even an adjoining garage on the far side with its doors wide open." He took a look inside and hastily retreated. "Bats," he exclaimed, and then began to choke. He hurried to the van to fetch his panga and immediately began hacking at the scrub in order to clear a pathway around the house. When he had finished with the pathway, he broke open the front door, which was already badly crinkled with dry rot. A strong smell of ammonia hung in the air, and we opened the four sash windows in different parts of the house to try to create a draft, leaving alone a large window at the back of the front room. It had neither glass nor a sliding frame.

The interior of the bungalow was basic. There was no connected water or electricity, and from what we saw as we tramped around, the building was divided into four sections, namely a front room, a bedroom, a kitchen, and a bathroom.

We took our time inspecting the property, each one of us intent on finding a place to sleep where we could lay out our blanket on a chosen spot and automatically make that particular space ours to keep for the duration of our stay. I noticed that Thomas had chosen an old iron bed frame—the only piece of furniture in the house—and had covered it with a double thickness of cardboard and his blanket. Visavadia selected the floor space alongside the bed frame, and I reserved the nook in the corner of the front room that led to the garage. That way I had protection on three sides, and any wildlife that might seek entrance through the broken door wouldn't immediately see me, let alone smell me, and I shut tight the connecting door to the garage.

It would be dark in less than hour, and it was time to prepare our supper. The meal itself would most likely be eaten during sunset, at which time we would light our paraffin lamp. I was in half a mind as to whether I should sleep in the van, but we had taken so much trouble to get to this place that it seemed churlish to change accommodation at this moment in time. I moved our kitchenware, foodstuffs, water, and bathroom items from the van, while Thomas did the cooking and Visavadia went outside with an ax to collect wood for the small, grated fireplace in the front room.

It wasn't long before we were sitting down on the floor of the front room eating our meal of spaghetti, brown beans, and bread. As usual, we were eating in silence until Visavadia touched upon an underlying problem. "You realize," he said, "that the rafters in the garage are riddled with bats, and also the trees and wild banana plants that ring this house?"

We peered uneasily around the room. "There's nothing here for them to hang on to," I said. "There's no beams, no rafters, no laths, nothing.'

However, Thomas, not to be outdone, was ready to answer Visavadia's Cassandra-like suggestion that doom might lie just around the corner. "I've checked out this problem," he said proudly, "and I'm able to confirm that the bats roosting in the garage are mainly the harmless leaf-nose variety. It's also possible that there's a lesser colony of large hammer-headed bats mixed in with the others, as I heard their distinctive *kwok-kwok* calls when I was hacking out a pathway. However, I agree with Vinoo that the banana plants were seriously littered with an endless swarm of fruit-eating bats."

"What's the point you are trying to make?" I asked.

"That all doors and windows should be shut."

"You two have made my evening," I said harshly as I banged my fork down onto the plastic plate.

"I wasn't going to say a word," Thomas shot back, "until Vinoo spoke up."

The smell of the bats' droppings had of course been there all the time. But as with so many things in Africa, one tends to overlook the obvious and get on with the task in hand. It was the fetid air that caused Visavadia to bring up the subject, something Thomas and I had tried to ignore.

"OK, let's talk about the swamp rats, cockroaches, and horseflies we've found in the kitchen," I boiled, "or shall we finish our meal in peace?"

"I expect Mr. Carter is undoubtedly aware of the problems in this house," Thomas said to Visavadia, ensuring that the conversation had switched away from him, "and I suspect that neither he, nor I, wish to talk about it anymore during the course of our meal." He looked away from Visavadia, and turned back to me for support. "Am I right?" he asked, and dug vigorously into his plate of food.

"Yes, you certainly are," I agreed.

My mood changed and I found it difficult to keep a straight face. I had been taken aback by Thomas's verbiage. "Let's forget the bats and the rest of animal life," I said, as I chewed on another mouthful of spaghetti.

No longer talking, we finished our meal in total silence. Afterward, we did the dishes and made the coffee in the kitchen and returned to our places in the front room. We watched the flames lick at the wood while we drank coffee and smoked cigarettes. Every now and then Thomas poked at the fiery embers with the toe of his boot. It was interesting to note that in spite of our mixed races, the three of us had adopted the African way of eating at night, and that was not to talk. Just the same, tonight had been an exception, and the pressure of late had weakened our resolve. Basically this was the only hot meal of the day, and in ordinary households it would have been prepared by the womenfolk. It was therefore a golden time of the day and too valuable to chatter one's way through.

"I'm turning in for the night," I said with a yawn. "We've got another big day tomorrow." I took my mug into the kitchen, washed it in a bowl of warm water, and returned to the front room. "Good night." I smiled and crossed the room to my bed space in the nook.

"It's early for you," Visavadia announced.

"It feels more like midnight," I answered.

I had laid my bed out on thick cardboard sheeting, topped with a reed mat. From there I picked up my toothbrush and paste, poured myself a mug of water from the jerrican, and opened the door to the bathroom. Not long afterward I wrapped my blanket around myself and settled into bed. I again made sure that the connecting doorway to the garage was shut tight.

Thinking back to when we first arrived, I had perhaps wrongly described the building as dilapidated, but now, on reflection, I would change that and call it "incompleted." For instance the iron grate where we lit a fire consisted of two brick shoulders protruding from the wall, which formed an alcove between the uprights. At the base there remained a two-foot gap in the stone work leading to the kitchen. It was plain that it was an incomplete chimney stack leading to a fireplace. The builders had either run out of brick or stone, or this was when the government threw the towel in and decided it had wasted enough money on a bungalow that was never going to be used.

Ten minutes later Thomas shouted a good-night from the bedroom and added, "I'm about to douse the lamp." I then heard Visavadia's voice saying good night.

It hadn't been dark long before the scratching sound of the bats through the thin wall noticeably increased. There was more activity as they shook off the coldness of their sleep and began to shuffle around, enjoying the fresh warmth of their circulatory blood, while at the same time quarreling among themselves.

Every now and then the dark sky was illuminated by the brightness of a three-quarter moon. But at times, the view from the window was restricted due to low-passing clouds. Then, without warning, the shuffling noises worsened, and there was a general air of agitation, shortly followed by a barrage of squealing and an ominous sound of whirring, bringing with it an unstoppable rush of air.

Now and then I was able to distinguish the blackness cast by the bats from that of the deep violet sky. It seemed that after the exodus from the garage, the bats had circled over the house, biding their time while the others caught up. Then, in one enormous cloud they turned northward, gained height, and temporarily eclipsed the moon. Their numbers, maybe a million or more, billowed out and flew off in search of feeding grounds of wild fruits, fleshy flowers, or even insects in flight.

For the next two hours I stayed awake. This was unusual. Normally I was a sound sleeper, but there was something different about tonight. It worried me that our safari was running late, and I was also annoyed that I hadn't bedded down in the van despite the limited space. For some unearthly reason, these simple things preyed on my mind before I finally drifted off to sleep.

It was several hours before I woke, and with the exception of the soft rhythmic breathing emanating from the adjoining bedroom, there was an eerie quietness. This peace lasted barely an hour before I became aware of rasping noises coming from somewhere behind my bed.

"My God, what's happening?" I shouted as a rush of cold, early morning air gusted across my face. My nose, mouth, and forehead were being touched, almost feather like, and I raised my hand in the hope that I could brush away the intruder. Almost at once I realized I was dealing with something more formidable, and I began to take hard swipes at my hidden enemy with the flat of my hand. But I no longer had control over the situation, as the space around my bed had quickly become thick with bats.

I rolled over and pressed my body against the reed mat and pulled the blanket over my head. This had an immediate domino effect. My legs now stuck out from the bottom end of the blanket, and in some crazy way I had managed to net a dozen of these unreal mammals. Their squealing and squawking become unbearable. They were at my face, pulling my hair, and flapping and raging between my legs. This was the fire and brimstone of my safari.

In the middle of this chaos, I searched my mind for the basic cause that had sparked off this invasion. My theorizing was cut short as hordes more descended into my nook, and this time I clearly sensed my heart, pumping wildly, inside my chest. I grabbed at one that was splayed out on my face. I prayed that it would neither sink its powerful teeth into my ear or into the back of my neck. Instead, I felt its soft, furry body pulsing with rage while a prisoner in my hand. It screamed, and at the same time another one clawed its way onto the top of my head. Like the one before, it shrieked furiously as I tore it off and hurled it onto the floor.

The bats seemed larger than the leaf-nosed ones that Thomas had earlier described. These ones were straw-colored, not black, with bigger membranes, and they were intent on coming blindly at me from all sides. It seemed to me that their navigational, or echo-locationary, skills stood for nothing.

All the while during the onslaught, I was being hit by slimy blobs of ammoniac shit, and there was little doubt in my mind that from now on I would become a true batophobic. I had had enough, and with my arms lashing out like Dutch windmills, I made my way to the bathroom. There was no water, but at least the room would afford protection—a bat-free zone, perhaps—that would give me a chance to regain my *compos mentis*. It appeared that I had been in occupation of their space, and yet, even at this stage, I failed to understand the root cause that had triggered this whole thing off. The stench on my body was overwhelming, and I began to retch uncontrollably into the sand-encrusted bath.

"Is anyone there?" I yelled and sank slowly to the floor.

"Mr. Carter, are you OK?" Visavadia shouted as he rushed from the bedroom.

"Yes, I think so," I gasped.

"What happened?" It was Thomas, who had arrived in hot pursuit of Vinoo.

I went into detail about the whole night.

"It's difficult to say what caused this situation," I ended, "but I feel sure it's something to do with the door leading to the garage. The bats that swamped me were larger than I expected, and weren't dark like the leaf-nose but…"

"Hang on a moment," Thomas said, and quickly turned around and dashed out of the bathroom.

A minute later he returned from his errand. "I've opened the connecting door, and guess what?"

"You tell us," Visavadia fielded his question.

"The bats have all gone!"

It occurred to me that the bats, because of their limitless numbers, had organized a one-way traffic system, whereby at dusk they joined the exodus through the garage doors and on return at dawn a number of them made their way back through the house.

"But how did they get into the house in the first place?" I asked.

"The answer's obvious," Thomas replied in a voice that lacked triumphalism. "They flew through the open window."

"But I checked the windows."

"You thought you checked the windows, but the one by your bed had no glass or sliding frame. We were all tired last night, and we forgot that the window was glassless. However, you were right about the different category of bats. It was the straw-colored ones that ganged up and came through the unglassed window; the same ones that perched at the back of the garage.

"I'm sorry to have been the cause of all this trouble."

"Don't let it worry you," Visavadia chipped in.

"At the end of the day," Thomas elaborated, "all you needed to have done was to leave things as they were, keep your head under the blanket, and let the bats fly over you. However, once you shut the door to the garage, you sealed your fate!"

"You're right," I said, "and maybe there's a lesson to be learned that we mustn't drop our guard at night when we are tired."

Thomas admitted that he had unknowingly heard muted sounds in the early morning but had dismissed them, arguing that we were traveling in deepest Africa and noises in the bush were normal. "Seriously," he said with a smile, "I thought you were having a bad dream."

"The same to you," I replied, "and if there's anything I can ever do for you..."

But before I could finish, there was a howl of laughter coming from both Thomas and Visavadia.

It was daylight now, and it felt cold. I set to and washed every square inch of my body with a bar of brown carbolic soap. It annoyed me that I had to use two gallons of our best drinking water, and when I'd finished I held a small jug of water over my head and took a shower. I felt great and thoughts of rabid infestation from mammals had gone from my mind. I changed into khaki shorts and a fresh T-shirt, and declared myself sanitized and ready to continue the safari.

It was colder than I thought, so I put on a V-neck sweater. We shook and folded our bedding, except for my blanket, which I stuffed into a box and chucked into the corner of the bathroom. We then unanimously voted to abandon this stopover point and take breakfast elsewhere.

The early morning dew clung to the greenness of the heavy vegetation. I noticed that the wild banana plants were covered with the dense blackness of hundreds of fruit-eating bats, all thankfully fast asleep in the half-open leaves, as well as those in the garage, which resembled the black hole of Calcutta.

"Let's get out of here," I growled as I climbed inside the van.

Three miles later we pulled over onto the side of the track and had our breakfast. We decided that nothing less than a full English breakfast was called for. However, the menu was limited to orange juice, one egg, a tomato, a sausage, and a slice of bread and marmalade. We sat around the small wood fire in total silence while we sipped at mugs of steaming-hot coffee.

It was Wednesday, October 19, and it had already proven to be a day that would stay firmly printed on my mind. It was ten o'clock, and we were running late. It was time to go to work. We washed and packed our breakfast things and stowed them away in the right place at the rear of the van. We were now ready to get under way.

"Where are we going to?" Thomas asked.

The roar of the van's engine pierced the quietness. The sun was rising into the clear, pale blue sky, and there were long wisps of unmoving cloud. The first warmth of the day filtered through the trees.

"There's a mission at a place called Kalengoe," I said, pointing a finger at the map. "It's about ten miles south of here, and I suggest we go and visit them, especially as it's en route to Kibondo, which by my calculations is about sixty miles from here."

"Isn't that the place where we have to deliver a chemical toilet?" Thomas stole a hurried glance at the map as he turned the van back onto the dirt road.

"Yes," I replied, "but much depends on whether we can find a Mr. Crispin Netuwa."

The journey to Kibondo lasted until four o'clock. We had checked out the mission at Kalengoe and sold ten gallons of pine disinfectant to them. We also did a dozen stops on the way, playing music, giving out leaflets, and selling products. At the end of the day we found accommodation at a properly run government rest house in the center of the township, and due to my broken sleep at Nyakanazi, I decided to call it a day.

The following morning, Thursday, October 20, we went to the police station to make inquiries about Crispin Netuwa. The only address we had was "near Kibondo," which could mean anything. The policeman listened with a certain amount of interest to our story and found it difficult to hide his amusement when we finally explained the nature of our business with our potential customer. "This Mr. Netuwa wants to buy some portable lavatories from you," the police officer repeated slowly. "Have I got that right?"

"That's correct," I said uneasily.

"And you've come all the way from London to see him?" The officer could barely disguise his amusement.

"You've got it again."

The policeman spread his hands on the desk and smiled. "Your company must take its export trade very seriously."

"We seem to," I admitted.

"All I can suggest is that you come back here after lunch, and I might by then have some information on this gentleman."

"Is it OK if we play some music around the town?" I pushed some samples of Herbalex and Gripe Aid across the top of the desk, along with one of our special brochures.

"Yes, that should be OK."

Over an hour later, we were busy giving a show to a large audience in the bazaar. After the first rush of cash selling was over, we were left with an audience of children. This was a good time for Visavadia and I to begin calls on Asian *dukas*, and as usual we left Thomas in charge of the cash sales from the van. While doing the rounds I took the opportunity of buying a new brown blanket, which Visavadia managed to get at cost price.

On our return to the van we got busy closing down for the day. However, we were interrupted by a police patrol officer on a bicycle. He had come pedaling down the road to inform us that his superior had managed to locate Mr. Netuwa, and if we would like to return to the police station he could give us the details relating to this matter.

"It was much easier than we first thought," the officer said as we re-entered the station. "As soon as you left, I put the word out in the market that we wanted this Mr. Netuwa. It wasn't long before we got a response. A rice grower with a farm near a place called Nyaviyumbu came forward and explained that he sometimes employs a Mr. Netuwa on a part-time basis, you know, helping load and unload grain sacks from his up-country warehouse onto trucks." The policeman paused to light a cigarette. "But what clinched this man's identity was the Christian name. It was Crispin."

"I'm very grateful for your help," I said.

"Not at all," he replied, extending his hand. "By the way, this settlement called Nyaviyumbu is ten miles to the east, and I'm pretty certain you'll not be able to take your truck beyond the village of Lutende. You'll have to walk the last three miles. There's a small pathway that leads directly through the swamp area. You can't miss it."

"Thanks again," I said, shaking his hand and adding, "We'll be leaving first thing tomorrow morning for Nyaviyumbu."

***

We arrived in Lutende early on Friday morning. The track from Kibondo, although narrow and lined by woodland savanna, ultimately emerged into the open, where villagers had bared land to build settlements of mud and wattle huts. The fields encircling the compounds were given over to subsistence crops, such as rice, maize, cassava, and bananas.

Before leaving the village for our onward march to Nyaviyumbu, we played music and handed out pamphlets. In addition we made arrangements with the *mzee,* or village elder, to take care of our motor vehicle while we were gone. The portable toilet that we would be obliged to demonstrate to Mr. Netuwa was removed from the rear of the van. A small group of boys watched with curiosity as we got our party under way. Thomas had already spent a good part of the previous evening at the rest house concocting a harness out of rope. The portable toilet itself was still packed in its box, and all that had to be done was to slip it into the harness. This left Visavadia free to carry two one-gallon tins of chemical fluid, which played an essential part in the treatment of feces; this fluid was used to break down the material into a soluble mix. As for myself, I carried eight pints of drinking water in a large can with a holder, and also my briefcase filled with samples and leaflets. As soon as we were ready, we waved good-bye to the excited villagers and began our march into the bush.

At the start of our trek, the worn pathway was reasonably easy to negotiate, but it wasn't long before the track was less discernible. This was of little consequence compared with the continuous pestering of large bush flies that pierced our skin with sharp, painful bites. The scrub stretched in every direction and seemed to end only with the hazy, reed-lined swamps. The deeper we penetrated the scrub, the narrower the path became, until it finally petered out. It was now basic bush conditions, and the safari took on a more serious edge. We had either been given wrong information by the police officer or we had veered off the track. It was time for Thomas to use his panga. The portable toilet was passed over to Visavadia.

These conditions would be testing enough under normal circumstances, but we were now in at the deep end and found our foray into the bush challenging. For instance, we were burdened with awkward-shaped loads of varying weights, and there was no protection from the unrelenting sun, not even a wisp of a cloud to break up the unshielded light.

After trekking for another mile, we calculated distances by reckoning that we traveled at an average of two miles an hour maximum. The conditions began to ease as banks of fleecy cloud temporally blotted the sun, while the circumstances at ground level were easier than before, given that there was less scrub to cut at our legs. We tramped past an unusual group of three flat-topped acacias before we noticed a pair of green pigeons swooping low from the seclusion of their platformed nest in the topmost branches of a solitary iroko tree.

"Look out," Thomas warned.

We stopped marching and waited while a multistriped, six-foot-long, hissing sand snake winded its way across the dusty path and disappeared into the long elephant grass. Again we pressed forward and little by little the acacias were left behind, and all that remained was a marshy area filled with tall layers of coarse grass and tawny sedge.

We came to the conclusion that we had covered at least four miles. We were exhausted, swimming in sweat, and plagued with mosquitoes. "Let's take five minutes," I shouted, and one by one we plonked our loads onto the pathway, passed round the water bottle, and lay down on an open area of ground.

"It'll be my turn with the toilet," I said to Thomas, who was wiping sweat from his neck.

"What about your foot?" he asked.

"It's fine," I replied, "and I've all but finished my tablets."

"Just the same, I don't think you should."

"I appreciate your concern, but I'm ready to give it a try."

I gave Thomas the water can and my briefcase, and once again we struggled to our feet and moved onward. The dull thump of feet and heavy breathing was barely audible in the still air. Another fifteen minutes passed—about half a mile—when Thomas turned around and pointed a forefinger. "There's something over there," he said.

Small plumes of smoke could be seen rising upward some hundred yards in front of our present position. We immediately slowed our pace. Still keeping to the worn pathway, we were soon able to identify the smoke. It was coming from a group of shambas set around a bare compound within a wider area of farmland. The huts with their thatched roofs and circular mud-brick walls portrayed a domestic and peaceful scene. We had at last arrived at our final destination, and I decided it was wise to take precautions and leave the toilet hidden behind some bushes. It would be a blow to our pride, having crossed hundreds of miles, if we had it forcibly taken from us at this stage, bearing in mind that London had placed such importance on this matter.

We resumed our advance and shortly began to see people on paths and heads leaning out from darkened doorways. A naked woman ran screaming from a nearby shamba, spilling water from a calabash that she carried on her head. A flock of scrawny chickens jumped into the air, clucking and squawking, and joined in the dash across the bare compound. All this pandemonium alerted three unkempt dogs that had been asleep in the long grass at the rear of the houses. They were now aroused, barking and ready to rampage, but luckily they were tethered by chains that clearly restricted their movements.

Thomas marched into the middle of the compound and took control. Everyone fell silent and with a broad grin he shouted *"Jambo,"* and in the pervading stillness his voice echoed throughout the hillsides and beyond.

Several more faces peered from the dark interiors of the surrounding huts; small children screamed and rushed behind the relative safety of a cactus fence. Then, unexpectedly, a tall man in a native shirt emerged from a larger shamba set in the center of the compound. He came forward brandishing a silver machete. The loose skin on his arms showed he was older than he looked. He seemed confused and for a few seconds he wavered, uncertain what to do next as his tribesmen gathered round him.

"This has got to be the village chief," Thomas said in a low voice as he turned toward me. "His shamba is smarter than the others, and take a look at the straw roofing. The overhang is also lower."

"I don't understand why you mention the overhang."

"It's designed so you have to bow down on entering the shamba and give him due respect," Thomas explained.

"It's gone quiet," I said, realizing that we had reached a standoff with the villagers, "and I think it's time that we explained the reason behind our visit."

"We've come to see Mr. Netuwa," Thomas declared in Swahili, "and we want to talk to him as friends."

The chief had stopped flashing his silver machete, and he looked uncertainly to his left and to his right. It clearly worried him to have this *muzungo* in his village. After all, to his way of thinking, I might well be a government man, here to collect taxes.

"Who are you and what do you want with Mr. Netuwa?"

"We have come a long way to see him, and he will be pleased when he hears what we have to tell him."

These words were followed by silence as the villagers looked to their chief and waited for his ruling. At least things remained quiet, and even the bony dogs could manage only the odd bark or two before being hit with a long, thin stick wielded by a little girl.

I thought this was a good time to build on the initial goodwill that Thomas had created. I slowly approached the chief, dipped my head, and pulled a pack of cigarettes out of my shirt pocket.

"Please take one," I said, and shook the pack in front of him. Slowly his face unwound as he handed his silver machete to another villager.

"Asante sana." He smiled gently and pulled out a cigarette. He was immediately joined by the man with the machete, who was dressed in a tattered army jacket and a pair of stained khaki shorts. He was more adventurous, and with a wide, open smile, he ferreted out three cigarettes from the pack that I still held in front of me.

Suddenly, everyone was smiling, and the children, who up to now had concealed themselves behind the hedgerow, were back in the open compound. It was hot, and the smoke from the cooking fires drifted across the dusty yard like a gray haze. I put what was left of the packet back into my jacket. The fleecy clouds had now lifted, and the sun was back again in full throttle.

"You'd better give out some samples and leaflets," I said to Visavadia, handing him my briefcase. Meanwhile, Thomas had gone back down the pathway to fetch the boxed toilet that we'd hidden behind a bush. Two minutes later he reemerged and placed the heavy package in the center of the compound.

The early tension had subsided, and the village elders, along with children, joined the scramble for the free samples of Herbalex. There was a group of young mothers on the far side of the stockade, and we made sure they each got a free Gripe Aid sample. They giggled among themselves and examined the miniature bottles. Some even began to read the words on the leaflets, even though they held them upside down. "It's for your babies when they get wind," Visavadia explained, but the mothers went on giggling. "It turns tears into sunshine," he persisted, but his words of jolliness were lost in the dust and clamor.

A slender, small-boned boy prodded my legs with the tips of his fingers, and his small brown eyes searched my face. But he said nothing.

"Would you like a badge?" I asked. He was naked, so I put the badge into his outstretched palm. "Next time you get a cough you tell your mummy you want Herbalex." I crouched on my knees and showed him the picture of the bottle on the leaflet, and how it was the same as that on the badge. I then gave him a barley sugar sweet from my jacket pocket, and with a trophy in each hand he raced across the compound toward where the women stood and grabbed his mother's leg. She was smiling all over her lovely face. It has to be remembered how brave this young lad had been to approach me, as it was a certainty that he had never seen a white man before.

"Does anyone know where I can find Mr. Netuwa?" Thomas shouted above the din.

"I am him," a man said, edging forward from the crowd. He was in baggy khaki shorts and a stained shirt. His sleeves were rolled up, and his face was glazed with tribal scars.

He came forward and shook hands with Thomas, who then as a matter of courtesy, introduced him to me by saying *"Iko hapa bwana mkubwa,"* or "here's my big boss."

I welcomed Mr. Netuwa, shook his hand, and gave him a thick illustrated brochure, which we had specifically kept aside for his perusal. It depicted in color the whole range of portable lavatories manufactured by Chemisan.

"Please come and see what we have for you." I led him over to the middle of the compound, where Thomas had cut the carton open with his sheath knife and was now occupied in unpacking the toilet. There was silence from the fifty or so villagers whose eyes were glued on the package; the suspense was almost unbearable until the moment Thomas unveiled the toilet. There was an immediate buzz of excited chatter and wreathes of smiles. At this moment Thomas took it upon himself to demonstrate the loo's use by flipping back the lid, sitting on it, and blowing out his cheeks. Then very slowly it dawned on the villagers exactly what the machine was used for and they began to howl with laughter. They started a kind of tribal dance, a *ngoma*, and went around and around in a series of tight circles making whooping noises. Mr. Netuwa was dumbfounded. He stood frozen to the spot while the villagers continued to shriek and howl with laughter. The dogs, which had originally returned to the darkened doorways of their huts, were once more raised off their haunches and joined in the jollity by barking and baying, but this time there was no small girl with a stick. She was too busy having a laugh.

It was sometime before the festivities died off. The crowds then became expectant and circled our potential customer, Mr. Netuwa, hoping that he might have something to say. Instead he remained silent and looked miserable as though he only wanted to disappear down a hole in the ground. Then, after more urging from the crowd, he finally took it upon himself to say something. In Swahili he said, *"Apana nataka wa sunduki,"* meaning he didn't hanker after this thing from the box.

"Tell him we've come all the way from London—King George's country—to bring him this box," I pressed Thomas.

The villagers knew at once that my reference to King George's country was England, and their reaction was instantaneous. They began hooting and trumpeting and jumping up and down. Once more they broke ranks and went into another dance routine, which entailed circling the compound in a rhythmic beat, rather like doing the conga, but with more oomph and less leg. It was ten minutes before the dust settled and the last bark of a dog was heard.

I held my hands wide above my head and smiled. I had asked the people to be sympathetic and understanding of Mr. Netuwa. I also told him that I would have to file a report to my bosses in London and, in turn, it would help me considerably to know why he wrote to them and showed a particular interest in purchasing a toilet or toilets.

"Well, I didn't really write a letter," Mr. Netuwa began softly. "You must understand that my two children are lonely here in Nyaviyumbu. I have been told that people who read newspapers can fill in coupons and receive gifts and letters from far away. A friend once brought me a newspaper, the *Daily News,* and I cut out one of those advertisements and asked an educated man to pen me a letter. You see," he explained proudly, "I wanted someone to write back from King George's country. My children would have been so happy to have a friend there. I paid the man two shillings to write to you, but I had no idea he asked for one of these machines from the big box."

"I'll tell you what," I said, reassuring him in front of his people. "When I get back to King George's country next year, I'll find someone to write to your children, you know, a penfriend."

I stopped for a moment and took a swig of water from our can. "In the meanwhile," I went on, "I strongly advise you to find a new penman to write your letters, and don't forget to put your full address on the paper."

***

It was Saturday, October 22, and we departed from Kibondo for the one-hundred-mile assault—and that's what it seemed like—south to the trading center of Kasulu. However, before leaving, we called at the police station to say good-bye, and also let the officer know about the outcome of our trip to Nyaviyumbu. He was still laughing when we climbed back in the van for the last time. "I nearly locked you all up," he roared, tapping his head with a finger. Three minutes later the town was past and the empty road began to run parallel with the Burundi border.

The savanna woodland with its spreading trees and dense shrubs formed a canopy of shade over the continuous layers of coarse grass. Every year the yard-high vegetation was systematically burned off, and yet, the trees stubbornly remained rooted to the soil, always able to withstand this annual cremation. Black drongo songbirds, with steel blue gloss on their plumage, stayed undetected as they perched on the scattered acacia and myrrh. Only when they darted from branches to chase insects could they be seen, and, if provoked, they would unhesitatingly attack crows and hawks in order to protect their young. Some distance ahead on the desolate track was a large troop of ambling baboons, or *nugu* in Swahili. We slowed to let them pass, and still unhurried, they wandered in front of the van, muttering and grunting and throwing surly glances in our direction.

We made several stops at isolated settlements along the route—names easily forgotten, such as Kangada, Makers, Mulenbera, and Mugombe. None of these places had so much as a local shop, and the few people we came across were scratching a meager living from parched-looking farms. Then, in one of those rare moments of fortune, we spotted movement high up in the soaring muvale trees. Thomas stopped the vehicle, and we peered upward through the open doors. "Do you see them?" Visavadia whispered over my shoulder.

Slowly we climbed from the van. Almost vertically above us was the heavy foliage of a solitary blackwood tree, and half-hidden among the branches, was a group of twelve to fifteen leaf-eating colobus monkeys. They could be clearly seen swinging their small twenty-five-pound bodies from bough to bough.

"They're really something," I responded, craning my neck upward.

I reckoned that the troop was part of the same family belonging to the spectacular black-and-white species, those with jet-black fur with white faces and long, bushy tails. Perhaps only the uhehe, or the red colobus, from neighboring Congo was rarer, with its black head, fine red limbs, and thumbless hands like all the others in the breed, but weighing no more than ten to twenty pounds.

It was nearly dark when we eventually arrived at the trading center of Kasulu, which was little more than a long, straggling village built around the sides of two dirt roads that led away from a central junction. We spent the night in the rundown government rest house, not far from the shops and screened from the roadside by a thin line of dusty jacarandas.

Early next morning we worked the main street in Kasulu before setting off in a southwesterly direction. The village was soon past, and the road became empty as we began our push toward the port of Kigoma some sixty miles away on a rough road. The land was reasonably flat until we got to the tiny township of Nkalinzi, and from there we began to climb, passing through the Manyovu Mountains. Soon afterward the road narrowed and dropped steeply away on one side. The curves and bends in the track were sharp, and every so often we came across faded road signs that simply stated Beware of Falling Rocks.

It was nine o'clock when we eventually pulled into Kigoma and stopped on the sloping road outside a two-story hotel near Lake Tanganyika.

The descent from the mountain had drained us, and our ears were aching. We had hardly taken notice of the Gombe parklands, with their cool highland meadows, and thick gallery of pine forests, which were the habitat for countless chimpanzees. And now, after snaking down the tortuous dirt road, we were enveloped in warmer air that ran off the lake. It seemed to be this mix of temperature change and lower height level that accentuated, rather than eased, our general feeling of exhaustion.

"I've got a helluva headache," Thomas complained as he climbed down from the vehicle.

"Do you want to share a room?" I asked. "It'll cost you nothing."

Visavadia had already extracted his wooden suitcase from the van and said he had friends in Kigoma; with that brief announcement he had taken off and headed down the steep roadway into the middle of town.

We went inside the hotel and stood by the desk in an almost bare lobby and for a few moments there wasn't a sound. Then we heard footsteps from the floor above. The patter of steps soon became more rapid as they started to drum down the carpetless wood staircase. A faint smell of mustiness hung across the hall.

"Good evening," a voice said. "How can I help you?"

"Do you happen to have a room?"

The man, an Arab, moved swiftly over the faded hall carpet and glanced briefly toward an old wall clock suspended from a dusty picture rail. He was dressed in a crumpled pin-stripe suit with an open-neck shirt.

"It's late now," he said less ceremoniously than before, "but I feel sure that something can be done for you. Most of my guests are already in their rooms....Now let me see." He hovered over a list of reservations, eyeing it closely.

I don't know why, but I felt uncomfortable, not really understanding the reason for the other patrons being in their rooms at this hour; everything was quiet. Perhaps the manager was uncertain or suspicious of our unexpected arrival and was playing for time while he made up his mind whether to offer us accommodation. "Do you want one room or two?" he asked.

Thomas gave me a nudge with his elbow. "I'll have the van," he whispered out of the side of his mouth.

"Are you sure?"

"I'm off," he affirmed, and spun round and fled.

The hotel manager was staring in my direction waiting for an answer. "Just one room."

"Certainly, sir," he said, more relaxed now, "but I should point out we don't do breakfast."

"That's not a problem," I responded.

"You pay cash now," he said unequivocally.

Safari Salesman

"Of course," I replied, and pulled some bank notes from the back of my trouser pocket.

"Now, if you will come with me, I'll show you to your room. Mind the third step up. I haven't yet had time to have it fixed." He jangled a bunch of keys from his hand.

"Nice place you've got here," I remarked.

"If you would wait here in the corridor." The manager pointed to a spot at the top of the staircase where the balustrade ended. Clearly preoccupied, he strode quickly across the passageway and unlocked an oak-stained door, opened it, and disappeared inside. I could hear some shouting in Arabic, and then the door swung open again, and about a dozen people in striped pajamas emerged, carrying mats, bedding, and a mixture of belongings. They trooped past me, seemingly half-asleep, and were soon lost in the dark shadows of the passageway. It wasn't long before the manager reappeared and said that the room was now ready for occupation. "Please come this way, sir." He bowed with a slight lowering of his head in my direction and led me into the recently vacated room.

I must have gotten the same feeling that cattle get when they are herded toward a pen and the gate is slammed behind them the second after they enter. I held on to the door frame and peered hesitantly into the room. "It looks nice," I said uneasily, and like a lamb to the slaughter I went in. The first thing that hit me was the smell.

"What time do you wish to be called, sir?" the manager asked with all the formality of a four-star service.

"About seven o'clock," I said, succumbing to the inevitable, and staring around at the bare, unfurnished room. I put my suitcase on the floor and turned back toward the manager.

"Good night," he breathed heavily.

"Yes, good night," I echoed the words, not really understanding what was going on and too tired to care.

"For reasons of security, I will have to lock the door until your call tomorrow. It's the policy of the hotel."

"Of course," I agreed, "whatever's best."

He backed out of the doorway, and I could hear the lock clicking into place. The room was over large, windowless, and had a strong odor of unwashed humanity hanging in the air. Not only was I hot, sweaty, thirsty, and hungry, and well aware that my own body was also adding to the smell, I also had an urgent need to urinate. It had never entered my head that I would be locked into this airless room for the next nine hours, and as the enormity of the situation slowly began to dawn on me, I cursed my luck and wondered how the hell, I, John Carter, could have wound up in this disgusting room. My stupidity was beyond all reasonable thought. I should have smelled something fishy when Thomas did a quick bunk. I thought of banging on the door but decided against it, as I had nowhere else to sleep, except in the street, but by no stretch of the imagination could I consider that. Thomas would be anywhere by now, and there was no hope of finding him so I could stake my claim to a bed space on the van. There was something final about the manager's "good night" when he left the room, and as my predicament slowly penetrated my mind, I realized I was hungry, waterless, and in need of a loo.

The first of those three things I needed to attend to was my urgent need to relieve myself, and I soon recognized I had no alternative but to urinate against the wall in the far corner of the room. My need for food and water was nothing but a daydream, and I was left with no choice but to curl up on the floor; my new blanket, of course, had been left in the van. For safety's sake I pressed my suitcase against the door, and then I waited for sleep to blot out my unrelenting dismay. I did manage to find some fitful sleep, but all the while I tossed and turned on my nonexistent bed. The only compensation came from the luminous dial of my wrist watch, which slowly ticked off the hours. Perhaps I could have wasted an hour by watching the dawn from a window, but there were no window, and all I had left was my own imagination. But somehow or other, at four a.m. or thereabouts, I at last fell into a deep sleep.

Then, precisely on time, I was woken by the click of the locking mechanism in the door. My body was cold and stiff, and I couldn't stop coughing, but nothing was going to stop me from getting out of this hellhole. The door slowly inched open, and a wave of semifresh air drifted in from the corridor. The manager looked disapprovingly at my suitcase lying on the bedroom floor.

"It's your Monday morning call, sir," he proclaimed, his voice echoing across the empty room. "You'll find the ablutions on the left, beyond the staircase."

I staggered to my feet and waited for my cramp to ease. Then, with bones creaking, I stepped forward and reached for my suitcase. I had, of course, overlooked the fact that the door to the room had opened outward, and my preemptive effort to set an alarm by having the case scrape the floor was valueless; however, on thinking about it, an intruder might well have fallen over it.

I picked up my razor, toothbrush, and soap, wrapped them in a small towel, and made my way to the washroom. There was already a large crowd of half-naked people jostling for an empty place at the enamel basins.

The first thing I did when I got downstairs was to ask the reception clerk for a glass of drinking water. It cost me four shillings but was worth every penny. Not only was my thirst quenched, but I also stopped coughing.

Twenty minutes later I was sitting at a table on the terrace of the hotel with my suitcase safely by my side, waiting patiently for Thomas to turn up in the van. The terracing jutted out into the road, giving me an unrestricted view of the town. The pavements were more or less deserted, and I watched as a cart loaded with bulging sacks of grain trundled past the hotel. An old man kept shouting at the donkey and asking for more. Its hooves slipped as it struggled to pull the heavy load up the sloping street. Every now and then the man brandished a long, dry stick and hit the animal hard over its bony hindquarters.

Kigoma region is very much an individualistic county or state, as Texas is to America. The sparsely populated region bears the same name as that of the capital, the largest urban zone.

From where I was sitting I could look down the rising street at the single row of tightly built houses, and on the opposite side there was another row running parallel. Likewise a double line of large ornamental trees—the African laburnum, with its bright yellow flowers—ran the same course as the houses and formed an attractive inland promenade.

The commercial life of the town was to be found in these houses, each possessing its own unique but rickety little front porch. There were banks, offices, and shops, starting from Station Square and finishing up six hundred yards farther on at Market Square. Everything I saw seemed beset by solitude and a general lack of communication in spite of the close atmosphere. The town gave off a dated appearance of earlier colonialism pioneered by the Kaiser Wilhelm. These characteristics still prevailed as I watched the first movements on the pavements of indigenous Africans walking silently to work.

It wasn't long before I heard the low hum of our transit van as it drew nearer. I got up from the table, lifted my case, and descended the dozen concrete steps onto the broken pavement.

"And how was the good life at the hotel, Mr. Carter?" Thomas asked in mordant tones.

"Don't talk to me about it."

"Why, what was wrong?"

"I'll tell you later," I said and gave him an uneasy smile as I turned to Visavadia in the rumble seat and exchanged another set of good morning greetings.

"Let's do the banking," I said.

"The bank it is," Thomas repeated positively as he released the handbrake.

I watched him out of the corner of my eye. He seemed very pleased with life, and his peaked cap was pointed almost straight upward on the back part of his head, a sure sign that he was in a jaunty mood. My guess was that he had probably met some friends in the town and had been to a party. He would also have possibly heard that my hotel was a non-starter. I only wanted to leave the place, but I felt that both Thomas and Visavadia were content to be here.

"We'll need two days to complete our work here in Kigoma and the surrounding district," I announced with difficulty.

After doing the banking, we went to the railway station to book a passage to Itigi, some four hundred miles away. There was no way we could go any farther east by road. It was impassable, and, for starters, the Ukumbi desert stood in the way. The clerk at the booking office of the East African Railway Company (EARC) gave us bad news—the loading ramp at Itigi had partially cracked due to an earlier shunting accident and was now undergoing repair. Apparently we could choose between going back to Tabora or go direct to Dodoma, the stop beyond Itigi. After poring over the maps, we finally decided to disembark at Tabora. We realized the bitter truth that no matter what place we chose, it would foul up our planned itinerary.

The clerk issued the boarding ticket and told us that we must report at 2:00 p.m. this coming Thursday. This would give us two full days before the stated departure time to complete formalities, including the loading of the van onto a flatcar.

The days went by reasonably quickly. The first thing we did after going to the bank and railway station was to get off the main road and park down a dusty side street. And while Thomas brewed a pot of coffee, I sent Visavadia off on an errand to buy a fresh loaf of bread and two pints of long-lasting cow's milk. I had already seen a bakery-cum-dairy on our way into town last night and was able to tell Visavadia the best route to take.

"And remember," I joked, "I don't want sheep's, goat's, or camel's milk, just plain cow!"

"There are no camels around here," Thomas quipped as he undid the lid of the coffee jar.

Forty minutes later we were into our breakfast, which consisted of orange juice, cornflakes, bread, and marmalade, and a second mugful of Thomas's steaming-hot coffee.

Then, when finished, we visited the many prosperous Kigoma traders, whose names we had obtained from a local handbook given to us by an assistant in the mayor's office. As we worked our way around, we were impressed with the positive reception we received for our products from the listed traders. We also secured a bunch of worthwhile orders in response to the promotional advertising campaign that we had carried out in the various districts of this large town. It was proof positive, if anything could be that people had listened to us, read our booklets, and decided to buy our products from retailers. It was satisfying to witness at close hand the excellent results that had been obtained here.

Eventually, at four o'clock, we completed our work and dropped Visavadia off at a large Asian store, and from there Thomas drove me on to my new accommodation at the Golden Lion Inn. The wide views of the main street leading down toward the lake were similar to that of last night's hotel, but that's where the similarity ended. Not only did I have my own room with running water, but there was a lounge and mock-Tudor dining room downstairs for patrons to enjoy.

Anyway, before dropping me off, Thomas was eager to tell me all about his new Kenyan friends, and how they had settled permanently in Kigoma. He said that they had invited him to stay at their house, and as he had no need for the van, we agreed to park it on the road outside the inn.

After a glass of beer at the hotel bar, I went for a short walk. The sun was beginning to turn down to the horizon and had already changed to burned yellow, and all around, the azure sky was splashed with gold and blue. I began to enjoy the freedom and loneliness of this walk. Every now and then I found it therapeutic to distance myself from all things safari. After a short while I started up a narrow road that twisted and climbed until it flattened out onto a grassy knoll. It was an oasis of tranquillity. From there I rambled onward and found a worn footpath that ran beside the edge of the cliff. I stopped for a few minutes and absorbed the spectacular panoramic view of Lake Tanganyika. Its blue waters stretched as wide as the horizon, indistinguishable from the sky that bounded the view, and behind my back beyond the town were the Manyovu Mountains. When I turned they looked faint against the sultry heat rising off the lower hills.

It was strange to think that the waters of Lake Tanganyika, covering 12,700 square miles, reached depths of 4,700 feet, making it the world's second-deepest lake. The main inlet along its 420-mile length is the Ruzizi River in the north, while the outlet is on the Rukuga River at Albertville in the Congo. *Tanganyika* in Swahili means a meeting place of waters; and within these fresh waters are many fish—the tilapia, tiger fish, the tiny sardine called *dagaa*, and the ever-present Nile perch—and in the dark of night, along the coastline, one could hear the beat of native drums as the fish huddled in terror and were easily netted—in fact, up to nine thousand tons were caught annually.

After having a cigarette, I continued my walk and went past luxury cliff-top villas. Dim lights were beginning to show from the upper windows of these fine residential houses belonging to the prosperous Indian traders. Finally I made my way back by going down the steep slopes that led into Kigoma. From there I went along the empty streets lined on both sides with those tightly built structures painted in avocado green, light blues, and faded yellows. The sun was now on the horizon beyond the far shores of the lake, and it was sending up a fiery ocherous sunset that spread in every direction across the dark blue sky. Twilight had begun and the multi-splashes of color that had bathed the town in warmth were no longer dominant. Everything had become diminished, and in so doing had created an optical illusion. The whole town appeared to lean inward, as though knitted together in grateful supplication. It was dusk when I turned into the entrance of the hotel.

Later, after supper, I returned to my room and began writing up a special report on our visit to Mr. Netuwa in the village of Nyaviyumbu.

***

The next day, Wednesday, October 26, we increased coverage to the suburban districts of Kigoma that we considered were in need of a second visit. I had told Thomas and Visavadia that we should step up our campaign, as I felt we had lately been adopting too much of an easy attitude. This was our last day here, in Kigoma, and I asked for a final intensive campaign to push the sales of our company's products.

It was midday when we agreed that the market had reached saturation point. We immediately switched coverage to the nearby, but no less important, villages of Simbo and Ujiji. We passed long groves of mango trees that ran down a grassy hillside into the lake. Then, without warning, the road dipped and we temporally lost the view, both in front and at back. There was nothing now but a hot wind and choking dust, and the air had lost its morning freshness. The reflection in our mirrors was diminished, and the view became nature's color chart of blurry shades of yellow, green, and orange. The afternoon sun was high in the sky, and its unending rays glinted onto the splattered insects that dotted the van's windshield. However, the sight of the mountains and the shimmering lake soon came into view and lent coolness to the landscape.

We turned south onto a narrow, dusty road that wound its way toward the tiny port of Ujiji. It was no more than a couple of miles away from the main track.

Ujiji is basically an unimportant fishing village separated from Kigoma by a broad headland sticking out into the lake waters. But it was at this very place that Henry Morton Stanley saw Livingstone sheltering under the dark, spreading shade of a mango tree by the lakeshore. Those immortal words spoken by Stanley still ring out as you tread the ground—"Dr. Livingstone, I presume?"

In actual fact, Stanley's journey had begun nearly eight months before in the island of Zanzibar in early 1871, and after delays in Tabora caused by a tribal war, he marched the final thousand miles to Ujiji, his caravan achieving its destination on November 10 of that same year. Today, a polished stone memorial stands on the site with the following inscription written on it in plain black letters: *Under the mango tree which stood here Henry Morton Stan-*

ley met David Livingstone 1871. Again, they weren't the first white people in this area, because thirteen years before the explorers Burton and Speke had entered Ujiji. The village port had a fearful reputation, as it used to be an important magnet for Arab slave traders.

According to some old manuscripts, the actual meeting place was set in a forest. We weren't too sure about this, so we decided to carry out our own exploration. We progressed slowly along a rough track that ran parallel to the course of a dried-up riverbed. However, we saw no trees of any consequence, only an occasional yellow-barked acacia tree with pinnated leaves. Just the same, it wasn't difficult to imagine that this narrow track was the original pathway taken by Stanley and his entourage. The surface was ribbed and rutted, and our progress was slow as we negotiated a steady incline with testing, angle-sharp bends. Every now and then we heard the spit and whine of stones as they shot out from under our tires. We drove carefully past a half a dozen mud and straw huts astride the pathway. Eventually we arrived at an open space, and Thomas brought the van to a halt. The hazy light was more yellow than before and the heat oppressive. Our eyes were led across the untidy compound to a mustard-colored monument of stone, shaped like a truncated pyramid. On one face was carved a map of Africa inscribed with a black cross. The place was dirty, strewn with scattered rubbish, and flies buzzed aggressively around our faces. We had no idea of the reason for the placement of this stone, as the written inscription had been effaced. However, I mentioned this anomaly in my note book and decided to take a photo. This was easier said than done. The three of us spent the next thirty minutes searching the van for my camera. We searched everywhere, but it seemed that we had lost it. I had probably already taken a dozen color photos, but for some reason or another, I would never to be able to show them to my grandchildren in the years to come.

We left this dreary place and motored slowly back to Kigoma, going via the small village of Simbo, after crossing a belt of cultivated land between the lake and the high plateau. There were vegetable gardens; unfenced fields of cassava, sorghum, and pulses; and wild flowers along the edges of the open woodland. It was good to be back on the road after the disillusionment of Ujiji.

"Don't forget to meet me tomorrow at the railway station," I said as I looked out of the van window from the driving seat. "Wherever the van is, that's where I'll be, and please, no later than two o'clock."

I watched as they sauntered down the road, Visavadia with his wooden case and Thomas empty-handed, having purposely left his leather case in the van. It was perhaps a wise decision on his part, as he had hinted that his Kenyan friends might be throwing a leaving party in his honor. And after all was said and done, he knew the van would be parked near the Lake Hotel, so he had a bed waiting for him should he get caught short.

After supper that night I sat out on the hotel veranda with a bottle of snow-capped Premier beer and idly watched the early evening promenaders strolling along the lakefront. Groups of bearded men in white, some plump, some stringy, were closely followed by younger men in cream tunics and button-down collars, while the women wore gossamery saris of blue and gray, and the whole scene made me feel sad that I was soon going.

chapter EIGHTEEN

I spent most of the next morning preparing for our departure from Kigoma. It was a perfect beginning to the day. The sky was blue and cloudless, and the air was warm with a spring-like freshness. From the small-paned windows of my bedroom there were clear views of the lake beyond the long concrete wall that bounded the boulevard with its green palm fronds. The low sound of the lake slapping and drumming against the parapet could be distinguished only when the road was empty of traffic. The lake was as wide as the horizon, more blue than yesterday, less claustrophobic with no clear line between the waters and the sky.

I had breakfast downstairs on the terracing and had a good view of the street. Last night's promenading had gone and was now replaced by street hawkers, office workers, and African women with babies strapped firmly to their backs on their way to market. I bought the morning newspaper from a boy who was circling the tables. I checked the date on the front page to make sure I hadn't been sold yesterday's copy, as sometimes the paperboys would try to pass an old edition, especially if you were a foreigner.

After breakfast, I strolled along the dusty pavements of the main street, first calling at the post office to mail my report on Mr. Netuwa and also to check if there was any *poste restante,* and then I went to the National Bank of Commerce to deposit the bulk of our cash.

Two hours later, past midday, I took a light lunch, paid my hotel bill, and motored down to the railway station, making sure that the van was loaded onto the correct flatcar for Tabora. It was not unknown in Africa for things to go badly wrong, despite having a paid-up reservation. It was a few minutes after two o'clock when the job of loading was finished, that I went looking for my colleagues. I was surprised that I hadn't bumped into either of them, and it was another ten minutes before I found Visavadia. He was sitting on an old wooden bench at the far end of the main platform near the engine sheds. His feet were firmly planted on his wooden case, and he had his head in a colorful Asian paperback.

"How's it going?" I asked, giving him a smile.

"Oh, it's you, Mr. Carter!"

He was startled by my sudden appearance, and he quickly bent the corner of the page before closing the book. "I didn't know what time you might come, so I thought it best to wait here."

"Not to worry," I said easily, looking up and down the platform on both sides. "Have you seen Thomas?"

"Not yet I haven't."

"I suppose there's still plenty of time." I walked to the end of the platform, hoping to catch sight of him. However, instead I noticed that our van had already been shunted from the yards.

Visavadia had now left the bench and caught up with me at the far end of the platform. "They've moved the van onto a siding." He pointed an index finger, and added, "It's behind the goods carriages."

"Yes, I know," I said.

For a moment I lost my bearings. My mind was focused on Thomas as I grappled with the possibility that he might not turn up. That would be a major disaster, and this irritation must have shown on my face as I stared down the empty platform.

"Mr. Carter." Visavadia's voice was edged with concern.

I quickly pulled myself together. "Look," I said, "we might as well move into the van and make ourselves at home." I explained that the station-master told me that we could board anytime we chose as long as we had our tickets.

The railway tracks were clear, and there was nothing coming, so we quickly jumped down from the platform and took the short cut to the open wagon. The van had been roped, and heavy wooden blocks were wedged under each of the wheels. There was nothing else for us to do except wait for the heavy jolting and jarring of a long trans-African journey that lay ahead.

Once on board, we sorted our luggage and arranged the cartons—each containing six dozen bottles—to give a flat surface for the beds, but at the same time leaving a small section vacant at the rear for use as a kitchen. It was snug and well planned, and, when we'd finished our work, I cracked open two cans of beer.

"Cheers," I said, and after making myself relatively comfortable, I asked Visavadia how he was, and about his family back in Nairobi. This was a private moment when we faced each other and had a tête-à-tête.

He told me how his wife was coping without him, and he showed me a recent photo of his two children playing in the garden. Visavadia wasn't a great talker. He was the silent kind, and he went on to ask me about the work opportunities that might be available in England for Asian people. I never got around to suggesting he contact the British Legation because our conversation was cut short by a sudden impact. We were hurled against the paneling of the van, and I clambered up and went over to the door. From the rolled-down window, I saw a huge shunter blocking the view, steam pouring noisily from the blackened funnel, its buffers straining on our wagon. The driver of the locomotive was busily coupling the two together.

"Watch what you're doing," I yelled over the hissing steam.

The driver raised a hand and shielded his eyes from the afternoon glare. "I didn't know there was anyone in the truck," he answered in a deadpan way.

"We've got a full load of glass bottles on board, and it won't help to have them broken."

I checked my wrist watch; it was nearly fifteen minutes past three. I glanced across at the driver, who was now climbing up the exterior metal ladder leading to his cab. "Are we going somewhere?" I called out, worried that an early departure might be on the cards.

"I'm linking you up with the Dar train," the man replied, and then he disappeared into the locomotive.

I was concerned now, unsure as to whether the driver had deliberately glossed over my question. "What time does it leave?" I shouted even louder. It seemed possible that the timetable might have indeed been altered and our departure was imminent.

The driver's head popped out of the cab. "Four o'clock," he yelled back. "It's printed on your ticket if you have a look."

We started to move down the lines. There was a loud blast of the whistle followed by a thunderous crescendo of steam. The engine then settled down to a meaningful rhythm.

"I don't like this." I turned from the window and looked at Visavadia. "What do you think had happened to Thomas?" The worry lines were now etched clearly across my face.

He gave serious consideration to my question and paused while he scratched his head. "I've no idea, Mr. Carter. He could be anywhere," he replied.

The flatcar gradually drew alongside the main platform. "I'm going to find him," I said, climbing down from the van. There was barely thirty minutes left.

"Whatever you do," I said, looking hard at Visavadia, "stay here and don't move an inch, and I'll be back before four o'clock." I leaped from the wagon and began a search up and down the station on both sides of the lengthy Kigoma terminal.

Failing to find him I rushed to the railway office of the EARC near the station entrance. The man in charge, a Sikh in a pink turban, checked with his ticket collector, but neither of them came up with an answer.

"If Mr. Mambui does turn up here," I said urgently, "please would you tell him to come to Tabora. We will wait there until he either arrives or gets a message to us." I could feel the minutes slipping away. It was boiling in the small office, and my jacket started to stick to my back.

"Yes, I'll make a note of it," he replied, and opened a pad on his desk and started to write. "What's your name?"

"My name is Carter, John Carter."

The man raised an eyebrow. "Where is Mr. Mambui staying in Kigoma? Perhaps it might be worthwhile trying to reach him there?"

"I'm sorry, but I haven't got a clue," I responded with a touch of impatience. It was a fact that I never really knew where Thomas went at night, even when taking the van. It was his business, and it was up to him if he wanted to tell me.

"He's of no fixed address then?"

"I wouldn't say that."

"Have you tried the police station?" the Sikh came back, adding, "You could check there." He got up from his desk, walked to the window, and pointed across the square. "It won't take you a minute to ask them about Mr. Mambui. If not, I suggest you try the hospital."

"I guess that makes sense." I nodded as I edged backward through the door, thanking them for their help, and raced across the open square.

Three minutes later I faced a police sergeant over a high and wide wood-polished counter that ran the width of the room. I was thankful that there was no one else in front of me.

"What can I do for you?" the officer asked.

I quickly repeated the story I had told the Sikh about losing my driver. There was an added urgency now, and I kept glancing at the clock on the wall that ticked away the seconds.

The officer listened, his head bowed over some papers. Occasionally he scratched his forehead with the blunt end of his pencil. "What's the man's name?" he asked without a change of expression.

In my hurry to explain the problem, I had overlooked the most important detail. "Thomas Mambui," I said. I was still breathing heavily from the run I had made across the square.

He smiled ruefully. "You should have told me his name when you first came in. We've got him here. We took him in early this morning for being drunk and disorderly...."

"I'm sorry for butting in," I said, "but I'm worried about the Tabora train. It goes in just fifteen minutes. Is it at all possible for you to release him?"

"That all depends," he said.

"On what?" I inquired.

"Will you accept responsibility for him?" The officer paused, then placed his pencil down on the counter and lifted his head. "And will you make sure he leaves town?"

The wall clock ticked off another minute, and his pencil began to roll across the counter. The officer then grabbed it with his hand before it toppled over the edge. "Well, what's your answer?" he asked. "Will you or won't you?"

"Yes, I will," I replied to both questions at once. I thought that at any moment the policeman would ask me if I would have Thomas for "better or for worse!" After the freedom of the bush, this situation seemed incongruous that I should be pleading for the release of my friend and driver.

The officer lowered his head once more and began writing across the top of a printed form. "If you sign here," he prodded the bottom line with the tip of his pencil "we won't press charges."

I signed it without hesitation and looked back at his face.

"Come with me and identify the prisoner," he said, as he pulled a bunch of keys from a hook on the wall. It was as though everybody I met in Kigoma was armed with keys. "Is this Mr. Mambui?" He tapped the bars of the cell with the edge of a large key.

Thomas was lying on a hard bench. He looked up and blinked as though waking from a long sleep. "Don't tell me if it isn't Mr. Carter?" he said in a slurred voice.

"That's him," I said.

"He's still boozed up," the policeman stated, unlocking the iron door. "If I was you, I would get him on that train before he goes looking for another drink."

I waited while Thomas rose unsteadily to his feet and lurched toward the entrance. "If you were an African like me," Thomas said with difficulty, "and not an *mzungu*, I doubt if this askari would let me out." He then jerked his head at the officer to emphasize his point.

"That's enough of that," the policeman snapped. "It makes no difference if this man is white or black. I have the authority to release you if the terms of the release have been met. Take my advice and go while the going's good."

***

The slow rumble of the train on the uneven track continued remorselessly through the night. Every so often we halted at unchartered stations along the remote Ilkumbi swamplands, which covered the first two hundred miles of the journey from Kigoma. It was dawn by the time we reached the town of Nguruke, where we took on more water and unloaded freight. From this point the track assumed the merest uphill gradient, and a few minutes later Lake Sagaru appeared briefly through the early morning haze. There were literally thousands of gray, white, and brown herons searching the tall reeds for crabs and fish. All the time the rattle and throb of the train powered itself up a rising track. The long-legged herons were now below us, and in one mass they took off skyward from the flatness of the lake, with heads up and legs trailing, like single-engine planes. Then they circled overhead, abiding their time while the train slowly steamed over the empty horizon toward the watery wastes of Ilsinge. Then at Kaliua we halted again. The track now divided, going south to Mpanda, while we pushed on due east toward the city of Tabora. The land was level once more, and the train increased speed as it crossed the scrub and flat woodland areas. We passed the Dar es Salaam train going west on the last section of its twelve-hundred-mile journey to Kigoma. It was in its third day, and Visavadia and I waved and exchanged greetings from the van as it trundled by.

Thomas was still suffering from the effects of his party in Kigoma. He was rolled up in his blanket and stretched out across the cartons. After leaving the police station, it had been a touch-and-go situation as to whether we would make it back to the train on time. Visavadia had witnessed the trouble I was having on the platform and came to help me. We only just made it. The station master had blown the whistle and waved a green flag the moment our legs left the platform. I dread to think what Head Office would have said if they heard we had lost the transit van. Fortunately it didn't happen, but it was close. Once on board Thomas continued to struggle and threatened to jump off the train. Finally, by sheer will power, we were able to calm him down and cajole him into drinking a cup of hot black coffee.

From the little I gathered he had been to an all-night party celebrating his departure from Kigoma with some old Kenyan friends. There was no way we were going to dig any further; he had too many drinks and that was that. I had already agreed with Visavadia that we wouldn't say anything about his temper, sparing him from any embarrassment. At the end of the day, we all needed to get on with each other.

A few minutes before midday, we steamed into Tabora's Gothic-styled station. It seemed that we were never going to get free of this place.

Eventually the flatcar was uncoupled and shunted into a deserted siding, and shortly afterward the locomotive belched clouds of dirty smoke and, with a loud rat-tat-tatting, rolled onward to the east. Then everything went deadly quiet. Visavadia and I had not only watched the train leave, but we were also aware that we had been abandoned by the shunter. "I expect he'll come back," I said, more in hope than expectation, and added, "Surely the man must know we're not on a ramp."

"Shall we wake Thomas?" Visavadia asked, as he sat down on the rumble seat and eyed him. "He's been more asleep than awake for the last eighteen hours."

"You wake him," I said.

"It's time to get up," Visavadia urged as he shook him by the shoulder.

"Where am I?" Thomas groaned, holding his head in both hands.

"We're in Tabora." Visavadia assured Thomas

"What the hell are we doing back here?" he said in a muffled voice as he stirred from his blanket.

"We're just going to fix lunch," I said. "Would you like some?"

"Yeah, that's great."

It took an hour to cook and eat the food. And then after coffee and a cigarette, we prepared the van for the next stage of the two-hundred-mile journey across the Swangala plains to Rungwa. This shortcut would bring us neatly back onto the scheduled route, something we would never have attempted had we not been forced into it by the original broken ramp at Itigi. The entire region would no doubt prove to be inhospitable and deserted and would offer little in the way of sales.

"It's two o'clock," Visavadia said gloomily as he folded the bedding. "Why do you think they're keeping us waiting?"

"I've no idea," I replied uneasily, "but it's time to find out."

Through no fault of ours, we had wasted a lot of time lately, and I was determined to right this wrong. The view I had from the flatcar was of empty tracks. There wasn't a single sign of life. I clambered down, crossed the lines, and vaulted onto the main platform of the station. At the far end there was a door marked "No admittance except on business." I knocked and went in.

The railway clerk was at his desk and was seemingly busy going through some papers. The EARC office was untidy and the floor in need of a sweep; various charts and timetables were pinned around the pock-marked walls.

"What do you want?'" the clerk said in an unfriendly manner as he leaned forward over his papers. His face was expressionless, and he was more than likely to have been upset by my unwarranted intrusion.

"It's about my transit van," I said.

"So what's the problem?" he asked, his pen poised in mid-air, as though ready to get on with his paperwork.

"We've been waiting for someone to come and operate the unloading ramp," I answered in a measured voice.

"That's not possible," he countered as he drummed the fingers of his left hand on the desktop.

"And why's that?" I asked, certain that I was being given the raw edge of bureaucracy.

"The driver of the shunter has gone home until tomorrow." He turned his head and looked at the printed columns on one of the wall charts. "Let me see." He paused once more while continuing to drum his fingers on the wooden desk as he consulted the roster. "Yes, that's correct." He smiled quickly in my direction. "There's no rail traffic coming through until the afternoon train from Kigoma. That's tomorrow, of course. I doubt if the driver of the shunter will report for duty much before five o'clock." He then laid his pen down and began drumming his fingers on the desk top.

"That's not how I see it," I responded sharply. "I've got a paid-up ticket that includes being off-loaded at Tabora. There must be someone you can phone in order to sort this whole matter out at a higher level."

"In that case I'll have to call the station master at his home."

For the first time, the clerk appeared conciliatory. It seemed he had misread my dusty, unshaven appearance for someone who could be easily brushed away.

He stretched forward, picked up the receiver, and began to dial a number. The moment the phone started to ring he cupped his hand over the mouthpiece, and in a quick change of mood said, "I'm doing my best for you, and it's not my fault the way things are."

I sat down on a rickety cane chair that was propped against the drab wall. I figured that his plea for understanding sounded similar to the reasons I offered to Sir Frederick Bell for not being able to visit Kibondo when I met him in Nairobi. I guess it depends on which side of the fence one is standing. I lit a cigarette and blew the smoke across the airless room.

After a few minutes' conversation, the railway clerk returned the phone to its cradle. "It's like this," he began cautiously, leaning forward, his elbows on the papered desk. "Apparently the driver was unaware that anyone was on board your vehicle. For this reason he shunted the flat car to the siding pending further official instructions. This was reported to the station master before he went off duty, and they jointly agreed to leave your van until the owners showed up with the keys to unlock the door and start the engine so it could be driven off the ramp."

"I was in the van all the time," I protested.

***

At five p.m. the next day, Saturday, October 29, we were pulled from the siding and shunted across shining rails to the loading ramp. A few minutes later we motored slowly down the cinder-strewn slope onto level ground. We were at last free. Our itinerary had been readjusted to meet the changed conditions—we now had to make a diagonal cut through the wild central plateau to reach the isolated halting place of Rungwa, a journey of nearly 240 miles to the south-southeast on a deserted dirt road of choking alkali dust and with temperatures in the low nineties.

We turned left from the railway yard and skirted the poor, broken-down areas on the southern edges of Tabora. There were colorful groups of women washing clothes by a street standpipe. They had their knees bent and backs hunched over as they scrubbed at their laundry with a hard brush that had been smeared with a thick block of carbolic soap. We also passed untidy mounds of scattered rubbish, the targets of pie dogs and little children, while on each side of the road ran tight rows of endless tin and wood-boarded shacks, then more slums, and an overpowering acrid smell that made one want to throw up. We slowed down for an unruly herd of frightened goats that had raced in front of our van. Gradually the road began to open and intermittent plots of land gave way to square-shaped farms, each with its own timbered dwelling. A sun-bleached board gave warning of a railway crossing, and the van jolted on the hard ridges as it skimmed the flat road.

Two boys ran quickly into the road, holding aloft green cabbages and cauliflowers taken from their roadside stalls that were piled high with fruits and other vegetables. Thomas leaned from the wheel and gave them a wave. They didn't have time to respond as a shower of Herbalex leaflets fluttered gently to the ground. They then put their vegetables on the soft, powdery shoulder and scooped up the falling paper. Without doubt their inborn inventiveness would lead them to make cone-shaped cups from the leaflets to sell lentils, beans, or groundnuts in measured quantities. The dirt road was empty and straight once more, and fields with corner posts slipped by on each side. The dry soils were intensely cultivated with crops of sesame, millet, and tall green maize. Gradually the subsistence crops gave way to groundnut estates. The stalks were bent over under the weight of clustered flowers, and their oil-seed runners were left to spread indiscriminately over the ground, burying their seed pods, which would doubtless ripen over the coming weeks and finish up being dug from the earth like a root crop.

An hour went by and the scenery changed. The scrub stretched all the way across the endless plains to the haze-filled horizon. We drove relentlessly onward past a place called Tutubu. There was nothing to see, just a tiny dot on the map forty miles south-southeast of our starting point, and weary and tired, we pulled off the sand-ridden track and camped for the night.

We got up late the next day. It was Sunday, and our morning breakfast was interrupted by a marching horde of safari ants. They turned over the soil as they drew closer, all the time growing in numbers as their large heads weaved endlessly on heavily armored bodies, searching and probing with deadly precision, able to kill rabbits and chickens. We swiftly moved back to the safety of the van, throwing food scraps on the ground in order to divert them from their present course.

Thirty minutes later we cleared the breakfast things away, packed the van, and got back onto the road. There was little to see and nothing to occupy us. We began to go through large tracts of Miombo woodlands. We lost the open view of the colorless horizon, and instead there was that stillness that comes from trees. The road was empty and looked as though it would remain empty for the rest of the day. The sun was now striking at the top of the fly-spattered windshield as we headed southeast and lowered the visors to fend off the unrelenting glare. Our first stop came after twenty miles, when we arrived at the desolate trading center of Ipole. But there was no one there, so we nailed up a few tin signs on the deserted timber shacks and pressed onward on the uneven dirt road. The van bumped and lurched, and at noon we made a second stop, this time for lunch. We had beans, boiled potatoes, and foul-smelling but delicious durian fruit.

Visavadia raised an arched eyebrow. "Do you realize we haven't sold a thing for three days?"

"That's nice of you to remind me. That fact makes me really happy." I paused for a moment and searched my memory. "You're wrong," I asserted. "I sold a bottle of Herbalex to a train driver at Kigoma station."

"Besides that one," Visavadia pressed.

"Fair enough." I nodded and walked over to the van and poured some water from a jerrican into a bowl. I drank part of it and splashed the remainder over my face.

"Tell you what," I went on, "I'll give you a guarantee that I'll sell six bottles within five miles of getting back on the road."

"I don't believe I've heard right," Thomas joined in the banter. "We haven't seen a living soul for over a hundred miles, and you're going to sell six bottles?"

My reputation as a salesman was now on the line, and I waited patiently until Thomas and Visavadia had stopped guffawing. "The proof is in the pudding," I said as I dried my face on a towel. "So do you want me to do it?"

"No tricks?"

"I've nothing up my sleeve."

"That's OK by us." Thomas said, and they nodded in agreement.

"My only condition is that you've got to assist, like any normal road show, and besides that there's no time limit."

We climbed back into the van and once again started down the empty track. For some time we didn't talk, and I was beginning to think that they might have either forgotten about the challenge or had not taken it seriously. But this glimmer of hope was short-lived when Thomas finally broke the silence. "Say when," he said with laugh. "We've already done four miles!"

"OK, let's pull in here by those bushes," I said pointing with my finger.

We climbed out of the vehicle, opened the rear doors, and as usual set up a few bottles on the floorboards of the van for the benefit of our customers. It might not have been up to the standard of the window displays along Delamere Avenue, but it was the best we could do. The turntable was switched on, and the raucous high-volume sound of a Latin mambo began to penetrate the bush and the woodlands beyond.

For the next twenty minutes we kept a steady watch on our immediate surroundings, and we became jittery at times when we imagined we had seen something. "Nothing yet," I remarked uneasily to Thomas, "although if anyone is out there, I suppose you must give them time to decide whether to ignore us or not."

"You might be right," Thomas said, but went on to warn that they may well be consulting the spirits of the forest before coming to any decision.

We'd been there almost thirty minutes under a baking sun that filtered through the tree tops. Thomas reckoned we should call it a day and get back on the road, but it was Visavadia with his suspicious nature who was the first to notice that we weren't alone. He frowned and his dark complexion appeared to pale around his face. "I think we have company." He shouted to overcome the deafening sound of the music. "There's something moving down there on the right, about two hundred yards." He didn't point, but just jerked his head in the general direction.

"Go and turn the volume down," I shouted. My adrenaline was flowing, and the back of my head began to prickle as I narrowed my eyes and peered down the road.

"There they are," he hissed.

The sound of the music was less abrupt than before as we waited for their next move.

For a fleeting moment we saw dark shapes moving through the tall elephant grass, using the yellow-barked trees as cover. Our visitors darted swiftly and silently from tree to tree, and each move brought them nearer. It was difficult to say at this stage as to how many of these people were hiding in the forest.

"I can't see them now," Thomas said breathlessly.

We continued to scan the right side of the trackway.

"I suspect they are waiting for us to make the next move," I said as I wiped the damp off my sun glasses. "Please go and tell Visavadia to put on an island calypso, and ask him to lower the volume even more."

On his return I suggested that he shout out some words of welcome to the people hidden in the trees.

"They are unlikely to understand Swahili," he cautioned as blobs of sweat beaded his forehead and dripped down his craggy face.

"Make's no difference," I came back, adding, "I very much doubt that many people speak their language. It's important that they hear the richness of an African voice. Tell them we come here as friends—that sort of thing!"

"If that's what you want..."

"Please," I urged.

He reached down and picked up the microphone. *"Jambo, habadi,"* he began, and his voice carried through the tunnel of trees that overhung the broad road. Then unexpectedly a group of tribesmen broke away from the dark edges of the forest and gathered hesitantly on one side of the dusty road. They were less than sixty yards from our position and were naked except for dark-colored loincloths. All the ones we caught sight of carried short bows. The arrows would almost certainly be poisonous and used to shoot down primates from the trees.

Thomas continued to talk on the loud speaker, and his deep resonant voice was both friendly and reassuring.

I tapped him on the shoulder and gestured him to switch off the microphone. "Let's go down there with a box of samples and leaflets," I said, and turned round and told Visavadia to stay with the van.

Thomas and I, with a certain amount of trepidation, walked down the center of the sandy road. At that moment I was struck by the actual reality of our situation, and I began to get seriously worried. I felt that it was a distinct possibility that each one of us might get a poisoned arrow in our chest.

The high afternoon sun filtered through the leafy foliage of the Miombo and muvale trees, and everything sparkled with flecks of brightness. It was quiet except for the snap of branches as a troop of red colobus monkeys swung from tree to tree.

"I don't like this," Thomas murmured out of the corner of his mouth. "These people are nothing more than *shenzis.*" He used the Swahili word meaning "wild men."

Only a few yards separated us from these forest tribesmen. They were small in height, perhaps a little less than five feet, and their dark, wiry bodies were covered in a thick film of white dust. They each had a colorful band of dried monkey skin wrapped around their tiny waists, and these were fashioned into a quiver to house their arrows. Besides this they wore a mix of necklaces made up of stones and seeds, and had tribal scars cut into their faces. The hard edges of their ears had been sliced open and filled with cork-shaped tubes of reedwood.

"I think you are being unfair to them about being *shenzis*. It's more likely that they are related to the Aki tribe who are from this area, but they are not warriors and just like to be left alone. It's all written down in my guide book," I responded. "Anyway, it's too late to do anything about it now."

The bows were lowered as we closed the gap and came face-to-face with the forest men. We took a final step forward and began distributing samples and leaflets. They began to chatter among themselves, and others who'd been lurking behind their compatriots came forward to receive their gifts. We smiled and joked, allowing the braver of them to prod and poke our bodies with the ends of their tiny fingers before they stepped aside to make room for their friends. One man, taller than the rest, had a ring of black eagle feathers swinging loosely between his legs to keep the flies off his private parts. He appeared to have more authority and showed greater restraint, not poking his fingers at Thomas or me. We beckoned him to follow us back to the van, and gradually the others overcame their earlier fears and tagged on behind.

They looked at the leaflets and then back at the display on the van and chattered more excitedly than before as they recognized the similar pictures of Herbalex and Gripe Aid. We decided to take them on a tour of the vehicle, pointing out the colorful paintings of coughing Africans and the smiling Madonna-like face of the young mother dosing her baby with a teaspoon of Gripe Aid. The tribesmen made gestures to each other and kept glancing at the pictures as we used simple sign language to explain the benefits of the two medicines. One of the more adventurous got inside the van and sat happily in the driving seat, smiling through the windshield at his friends. Then, without warning, he began banging the glass covers of the dashboard instruments with his knuckles and, at the same time, letting out sharp yelps from the corners of his mouth.

Not wanting things to get out of control, I asked Visavadia to change records and put on something less buoyant in order to calm things down. However, the minute the music started up and a crooner began to sing, the audience became visibly frightened and pointed at the green speakers on top of the van's roof, while the man inside went berserk and leaped wildly from the cab and raced across the track into the bush. I was left wondering why the change of music should have triggered off this sudden panic. All that we had done was replace the island lilt of a calypso for the softer, more melodic sound of a slow number. As far as I could make out, there was little there to have caused such alarm. But rather than risk another stampede, I asked Visavadia to switch off the record player. Perhaps the audience had been too close and had reeled back the moment they sensed a change in the style of music and took fright.

Thomas, however, came up with a more realistic theory. "When they heard the crooner," he said, "they'd probably thought it was the ghostly voice of one of their ancestors, and that's why they pointed at the speakers and ran."

When the turmoil had subsided, we once again persuaded the forest people to come out of the bush. This time we agreed to cancel all forms of sales pressure and leave it to our customers as to whether to buy a bottle or not.

The tribesmen again examined their one-ounce samples and compared them with the five-ounce bottle on sale. They chattered among themselves, possibly a tad confused by the different sizes, until the leader with the feathers took the tube out of his ear, unplugged the top, shook silver coins into his hand, and gave me a two-shilling piece.

Thomas handed him a bottle. "Is there anybody else who wants to buy one?" he asked quietly as he held another one up for viewing. There were about twenty-five people milling round the vehicle, and we soon sold seven bottles of Herbalex and one of Gripe Aid.

We ended the show and made the usual preparations to leave. It had been pleasant under the trees, and we were happy that everything had turned out all right.

"We ought to give these people something," Thomas suggested. "It's usual to exchange presents in these isolated places, especially after purchasing our products. This is their territory, and we are their guests."

"What do you suggest then?"

"Perhaps a bag of sugar or salt maybe?"

We stood with our backs to the vehicle and watched the tribesmen, who appeared reluctant to return to the bush. They lingered on the trackway, seemingly comfortable to be with us.

"That's a good idea," I said, "but make it a bag of salt, and tell their leader to share it with the whole tribe."

It never occurred to us that such a simple gift would cause so much activity. Almost instantaneously there was a conference in the middle of the track, and then we were earnestly requested not to go away until they had made their *hongo*, or tribute us. I asked Thomas to tell them that it wasn't necessary, as we had already been rewarded by meeting them.

"That stuff may be OK in England," Thomas said with a hint of a smile, "but out here, it would be dishonorable to turn down a promised gift!"

We waited another fifteen minutes while the tribesmen circled the van and chattered among themselves. Then from the side of the road three girls, naked except for a sash of green leaves hanging around their waists, emerged from the forest, each carrying a display of goods set out on large, wooden trays. This was the *hongo,* and, one by one, we were invited to take a gift. There were skins of monkey and zebra, wood carvings of animals, beadworks in papaya and apple seeds, herbs, and a glittering assortment of bead jewelry, mainly bangles, earrings, and necklaces. In addition they showed us an assortment of semi-precious stones of agates and amethysts, which they kept in the pouch of a goat-skin scrotum. However, the leader insisted that each of us take a green malachite stone to give to our wives. I thought it best not to mention I was unmarried, in case he tried to fix me up with an instant bride. If so, it would have been the height of rudeness not to have accepted her. Shortly before we left, we managed to persuade the tribe to accept a further gift of a packet of American cigarettes as a token of esteem for their generosity.

It was dusk when we said our good byes and headed back to the point near to the Kwasi tributary that flowed westward towards the Upugala River.

We were tired and pulled off the dirt road. It was Thomas who stumbled over some elephant droppings among the scarred trees when searching for wood to light a camp fire. I poked a stick into the different mounds, which were covered in a layer of forest dust. They were dry and crusty and had been ignored by the dung beetles. "They're a week old," I said.

"I agree," Thomas hummed before adding a cautionary word. "But there's no saying they won't come back. Just take a look at the fresh green leaves on top of the trees!"

It wasn't long before supper was ready. We had heated the tinned meat over the stove, keeping it warm in the glowing embers of a small wood fire while the rice took its turn on the stove. This was followed by fresh pineapple, a pot of coffee, and biscuits. We sat around the smoldering fire, saying little under the umbrella-shaped canopies of the taller woodland trees. Every now and then the moonlight found an opening through the soaring cedars, and little sparks of light flickered on the gray brushwood carpet beneath our feet. We smoked in silence, leaning forward from box seats, letting the fumes from the dying fire waft gently upward and keep the ever-present mosquitoes away from our skin. We spent about thirty minutes around the fire, intermittently yawning and stretching aching limbs until we finally made our way back to the van. It was going to be a severely cramped night, what with an almost full load and the three of us wanting body space. The last thing I did was pour the wastewater from washing up onto the hot cinders of the wood fire and watch as a pair of forest rats scuttled away into the tall grass.

We had been asleep for less than three hours before Visavadia woke me. "We're in danger of toppling over," he breathed urgently, "and it's a *tembo* again."

"Wake Thomas up," I instructed.

The essence of our safari was once again under threat and in danger of being terminated.

Thomas joined me at the passenger door, which I slid open. We peered cautiously out into the semi darkness. The lingering light from a quarter moon was sufficient for us to make out the hulking shape of a bull elephant with a pair of glistening white tusks. It appeared that he was busily engaged in rubbing his rear quarters against the paneling along the roof's edging. Each time the van synchronized with the elephant's movements, swaying backwards and forwards. The animal must have found this pleasurable, because his right eye—the one we could see from the doorway—would flicker open and then stay shut for ten seconds before opening again. He was definitely lost in a state of nirvana.

The to-and-fro motion of the van was similar to that of being thrown around in the cabin of an ocean liner while battling a force-nine gale. Thomas and I held on to the door frame while Visavadia was in the back trying to cope with the stock. The gallon tins of disinfectant were boxed and presented no immediate problem. The same applied to Herbalex and Gripe Aid. A dozen bottles were each packaged in separate boxes and then packed into damage-proof cartons of six boxes each. Visavadia's primary concern was for the three five-gallon jerricans—two of water and one of gasoline—which were running free. He was endeavoring to secure the three metal containers by running a rope through their handles and fastening them to the legs of the rumble seat. It was proving a difficult job under the abnormal circumstances, but he never lacked the gritty determination to get a job done and have that inner satisfaction on completion.

It was at the apex of one swing that the van finally lost balance and began to teeter over, but miraculously it held firm at an angle of forty-seven degrees. We heard nothing other than a soft crunching sound followed by deadly silence. It might mean that the elephant was uncertain what to do next, especially as he now had no sharp edge on which to press his backside. Whatever might happen, the fact remained that we were stuck at a dangerous angle.

Just the same, the elephant hadn't moved from his original position, and both Thomas and I kept watch, only feet away, hoping against hope that he would move back into the bush.

"What about using Vinoo's whip?" Thomas suggested.

"No, not that."

"What about using your flashlight?"

"That's it," I said.

After a hectic search in the rear cabin—and having got in the way of Visavadia, who was making use of the lull to tie the cans—I unearthed my suitcase, snapped the locks open, and ferreted out the flashlight among my belongings. I felt confident that its penetrating beam powered by three long-life batteries should do the trick.

"Hold tight," I shouted as I leaned from the door and clicked the light on. This time I targeted the elephant's flickering right eye, and the response was immediate. He let off an ear-splitting noise and lunged forward, and, for a moment, I feared he was going to attack us. But in a final act of defiance, he turned his head and once again trumpeted, even louder than before. Then, with his eyes rolling, he made off toward the trees. The bull was undoubtedly the herd leader and was soon joined by the others, which had been browsing the greenery of the topmost branches.

The moment they were gone from sight, we climbed down from the van and inspected the damage. It had been a stroke of luck that the right side of the vehicle had fallen against the huge stump of an old, dried-out baobab tree. I tried to avoid thinking about what might have happened had we turned over in this godforsaken spot. Instead I was preoccupied with my eardrums, which were hissing like a boiling kettle. It was Visavadia who brought me back to the real world and pointed out that a large bubble had appeared on the inside paneling where the van had fallen onto the stump.

"We'll hammer that out in the morning, "I told him, "but in the meantime we must get the van back onto its wheels."

I then turned to Thomas. "Is that OK with you?"

"No problem," He agreed, and with Visavadia's help he uncoiled what remained of the rope, some twenty feet in all, and threw it over the top of the van. Then together they pulled it tight, and knotted it onto the metal bar, which was there to support a roof rack. After several long minutes of tugging they managed to upright the van.

With that done, we went back to bed.

***

At seven the next morning, the sun was already rising swiftly into the pale blue sky, and deep shadows were forming against the forest floor by courtesy of the tall muvale trees. The tuneful, noisy singing of the dawn-loving green-and-brown bulbul could be heard as they flitted from their cup-shaped nests in search of berries and insects.

Before starting to check the van, we cooked breakfast over an open fire——maize porridge, egg sandwich, and coffee—and after clearing up and putting away the dishes, I asked Thomas to carry out a general inspection of the van.

Less than ten minutes later, he had made his survey. "There's not much to worry about," he reported. "Just light damage to the body work, and also one of the speakers has been twisted from its base."

"Can you fix these things without too much delay?"

"Give or take an hour."

"An hour?" I responded.

Thomas paused for a moment or two. There's also limited damage to the upper edge of the roof. It's where the elephant planted its bottom for a scratch, and as a result the paneling has buckled and caused minor ballooning on the inside."

"OK, do what you can, and we'll have it put right when we get to Dar es Salaam."

Thomas nodded and went straight to his tool kit.

I gave Visavadia the job of fixing the disconnected wiring on the van's roof and asked him to re-test the speakers. In addition he checked out our set of keys, and it was good news to learn that the locks on both doors and windows were still in working order.

Eighty minutes later we were back on the road. It was getting warmer by the second, touching 100 degrees Fahrenheit, and all the while hot air swished through the open doors. From where I sat I could see a group of small vervet monkeys. Their olive fur and black faces ringed in blue made them easily identifiable, and it was fascinating to watch as they played about in the trees that lined the scrubby banks of the Kwasi River.

I checked the calendar in my diary, and it was Monday, October 31. I thought about my friends in the London office. My mind drifted to those thousands upon thousands of people disgorging from the underground and trailing to work, many with recalcitrant footsteps that denied acknowledgement of that Monday morning feeling.

We pushed southward in silence, going a steady twenty mph, passing the lonely looking Mount Sumbo on our right. A few miles later we made a further successful crossing, this time at the Nkululu River, having followed an arrowed ford.

We were making steady progress until we encountered a larger-than-usual contingent of baboons, known as *nyani mkubwa* in Swahili. They were occupying the entire road and shoulders. Some were busy overturning large stones in a search for tasty morsels, while the main body of the group sat and stared vacantly at us; others cruised around, their teeth shining menacingly inside their long, hairy muzzles. Thomas had no alternative but to slow the van and ultimately apply the brakes. The freedom of our safari, not for the first time, was abruptly brought to a sudden standstill.

The unending muttering and grunting increased as a pair of large mandrills, both male with identical blue rumps, unearthed what appeared to be a king-sized scorpion with lobsterlike pincers from beneath a rock lying on the side of the road. This discovery was the green light to start a savage fight over who was to eat it.

Although the baboons appeared to show little regard for our presence, they were crafty enough to create a blockade across the track. Some ambled forward to give us a closer look. However, as far as I knew from reading a published guide, a direct attack on humans was unheard of. We, nonetheless, shut both our doors. A few of the baboons had now jumped onto the hood and were using it as trampoline, while the more adventurous of them leaped onto the roof. Thomas reacted to this invasion by hooting the horn, but this had little or no effect. Instead, those remaining on the dusty road stared harder than before, displayed a more menacing gridlock of white teeth, and barked in defiance. We were now unarguably impotent in face of this growing opposition, and Thomas had no alternative but to switch off the engine.

Meanwhile, those searching for tidbits along the edges of the road began to scrap and growl with each other, and they sprayed hot, vaporized air into their opponents' faces. The large scorpion that was the original cause of this developing brouhaha seized the moment and scuttled into the long grass.

The troop, or social group as some call them, consisted of about fifty or sixty animals, the majority of which began to show increasing signs of boredom and became restless as the stalemate took hold. The infants, however, were decidedly unsettled and found it difficult to interpret the change of mood their parents had adopted. The earlier atmosphere of indifference had transformed into one of turbulence, and for safety reasons the youngsters, one by one, rejoined their mothers, either clinging precariously to their furry undersides or riding jockey style on their backs.

The young males with tails held high patrolled the van, making tight circles, and every time they caught sight of us behind the windshield, they wrinkled their red-and-blue faces and barked before making a final derisive snort. The sound of this ruction echoed outward and was wafted away toward the dense Miombo woodlands.

This out-of-the-way parched track on which we were now stuck was hardly ever used as a throughway. In fact it wasn't inscribed on most maps. So to come this way we had gathered our information from talking to local people, and as a consequence, decided to use this unclassified route as a shortcut through an otherwise deserted region. Perhaps only two or three vehicles a day used this track. In earlier times it had been a lively river, an offshoot of the Nkululu that had threaded its way through the forest, stocked with fish and crocodiles.

The striding and tawdry showing off by the baboons had increased. They gave little or no indication that they might be prepared to consider a compromise and let us through. This outwardly unfriendly behavior clearly revealed that they were unaccustomed to humans, and they demonstrated their contempt by increasing the tempo of their activities. By this time many of the young males were pressing hostile faces against the windshield, snarling and thumping the hood with their knuckles. Their hot, foul breath, coming from gaping muzzles, was followed by a hiss of spittle, which congealed on the windshield, along with the mess of flies and other winged creatures. You could almost taste it. The message was obvious: "We're wild, this is our territory, we don't want you here, and we're not going to bend the rules for you."

"Move the van on slowly," I said quietly.

"Wouldn't it be better to stay where we are?" Thomas countered.

"Tell me why?"

"It's getting late and in two hours the baboons will have gone to ground for the night," he replied.

"Yes, no doubt you're right," I admitted, "but at the same time, our priority must also be to find a place for the night before it gets dark. This forest is not ideal. It's too wild and unpredictable, and we would end up as prisoners in our van. No, I'm sorry, but we have to move on."

"You're the boss." Thomas gave a smile and, after switching on the engine, began to inch forward.

The reaction was instantaneous. The main body of the baboons, which, up to that point, had been watching proceedings from each side of the road, were no longer neutral. They suddenly fired up, got off their haunches, and bared more teeth than before. They moved closer and stared uncompromisingly at us with their penetrating yellow-hooded eyes. All hope of atonement had gone out of the window.

I closed the window on my side.

"Awkward lot," Thomas growled as he turned off the ignition and shut his window. Then he added, "It's going to get mighty hot in here."

"You can say that again," Vinoo chipped in.

"All right," I conceded, "you can leave your window open a few inches at the top."

For safety's sake, several mothers with young had by now made their way onto the roof that Thomas had recently repaired.

He looked around from the driving seat and eyed the tiny minority of baboons, perhaps a dozen, who, despite everything, had remained squatting on the offside of the road. This lot hadn't moved since we arrived and was close to the spot where the fight over the scorpion had taken place. "Just take a look at the size of that baboon." He pointed toward the middle of the clique. "He's almost twice the size of the others. He has to be the leader."

"He seems quiet enough to me," I countered.

"That's the whole point," Thomas expanded. "He's the elder, the *mzee*, so to speak, and he's no fool. He's in charge here, and a single word from him and this harassment would cease, mark my words."

"Yes," Vinoo interjected, while looking over at Thomas, "and by that time the van will have taken even more of a battering."

The noise was unrelenting and blurred my mind. I found it difficult to maintain coherency. "There's got to be an answer to all this," I shouted as I wiped the sweat off my face with the back of my arm.

"You tell us," Thomas challenged. "You've already turned down my suggestion to wait for them to go."

It was at this juncture that I noticed Visavadia had got off his rumble seat and was busy searching among the boxes at the back. His doggedness soon paid off when he pulled his wooden case from under the cartons. Then, like a magician pulling a rabbit from his top hat, he produced his leather whip from inside the case, and without losing momentum he asked Thomas to change seats. I was taken aback when he acquiesced to this unusual request. Thomas was intensely proud of his position as a safari driver, although there were times, especially when he was tired, that he would hand the driving over to me.

The deafening noise continued without let up. This could have played a part in Thomas's decision to give up his seat, or, on the other hand, he might have detected a possible sign of panic in Visavadia's manner and decided it was preferable to give way. However, right or wrong, he relinquished the driving seat.

Visavadia wound down the window.

"Hey, that window should be shut," Thomas shouted, and added, "Go check it out with Mr. Carter."

But Visavadia was now on his own planet. His temperament had changed, and it seemed that for whatever bizarre reason he was ready to take on the pressure of the situation, despite the fact that we were a team, not individuals. He made his intention clear when he opened the window and leaned forward. There was a series of loud-sounding cracks as he lashed wildly out with his whip at any baboon that came within his range. Temporarily he failed to listen to the voice of reason that must have pulsed through his head.

There was now a private war going on: homo sapiens versus simians. Visavadia lost no time in hitting out against a mother and baby that were messing around with the side mirror. In the heat of the moment the infant became dislodged from its mother's back as she leaped onto the already crowded roof in an act of self-preservation. The little fellow whimpered and reached out as it grabbed Visavadia's head to stay its fall. The shock of having this creature glued to his face, suffocating him, peeing on him, caused Visavadia to drop back onto the cushioned seat. Vinoo was now seriously short of oxygen as he grappled to get the infant off his face.

Up to that point I had seen nothing and heard nothing of what was going on behind me. I was too busy warding off potential predators at my window, which I had opened a few inches in order to push and prod the baboons with a light bamboo stick. My reason for doing this was to try to keep as much weight as possible off the roof. My efforts were to no avail. The main part of the troop had now gained access to the already crowded roof.

Due to the racket and general confusion, I decided it was best to call off my activities. I was achieving nothing, and I had no option but to close my window. I then made a half turn and noticed that Thomas was sitting on the edge of the spare seat, leaning forward, and rummaging among the boxes in front of him.

"What are you looking for?" I shouted at him.

He neither looked up nor made any reply; this despite him being only a few feet from me.

The sustained noise had drowned my words, and it was now getting seriously hot in the van.

I then turned full circle to check on Visavadia and was aghast to see him slumped down in the driving seat. He was writhing in pain, and a baby baboon was lying on his face. I couldn't believe what I saw and realized that he was involved in a life-and-death struggle. It was a shock to my system that all this had been happening right behind my back for the past couple of minutes.

From this point everything began to fall apart and bedlam ensued.

I quickly bent down and pulled Visavadia into a sitting position, embraced him with my right arm, and reached forward with my left in order to rip off the quivering mask. Unfortunately the baby baboon was glued to his face. I knew at once that I needed help; otherwise, he might well succumb in my hands.

Thomas was still engaged in his search among the boxes. He seemed oblivious to the drama being played out in the front seats. It crossed my mind that he had some sort of fixation about finding his panga. After all, it had saved us before, so what else could he possibly want in this deepening crisis?

"Thomas," I screamed, "for God's sake, help me!"

This time he looked up.

"Come and help me," I bellowed again.

This safari was now teetering on the edge of disaster, all because a troop of baboons. Under normal conditions in the bush, they wouldn't have caused us the slightest problem. But because we were over considerate for their safety and their animal rights, we were reluctant to drive through them at the outset.

The incessant howls coming from the mother, who was sitting on the roof above the driver's window, were ear-piercing and blunted one's senses. It was at this particular moment, when I needed help to release Visavadia, that the mother made her own desperate attempt to rescue her infant from Visavadia's face. She leaned down, hanging with an arm around the speaker, stretched her free arm through the open window, and groped frantically for her baby.

I was totally unprepared for what happened next. I was busy pulling hard on the baby baboon that covered Visavadia's face when a young, one-hundred-pound, fully alert male baboon jumped onto the empty framework of the open window and wedged his upper torso and head inside the van. He had obviously heard the bawling and yelling going on and had taken it upon himself to mount a rescue.

Instantaneously I fell backward at the sight of this new arrival on the scene, and once more yelled for Thomas. The young male shot his right hand forward and plucked the baby off Visavadia's face. There was a dreadful sucking sound, similar to that of a bathroom plunger, as the tot was pulled free and dropped unceremoniously onto the road. The male then launched a vicious attack on Visavadia, who was seriously breathless and in a state of shock. The baboon reached forward and grabbed him around the neck, jerked his head forward, and sank his teeth into his shoulder.

Only seconds had elapsed since I first spotted Thomas on the edge of his seat searching for his panga. Thankfully, this time he heard me, and his response was clear and decisive.

"This one's mine," he shouted, looking up from his rumble seat, and in an instant the lost panga was no longer on his list of priorities.

Instead he scrambled over the boxes, pushed me out of the way, and reached for his sheath knife hidden behind the folds of his hot shirt. We all carried a knife—it would be impossible to launch a safari and step foot into the bush without one. However, the turn of events had suddenly taken on a dark, sinister element. The male baboon had gone berserk and was panting wildly. We had clearly lost control of the situation, and Visavadia's life was now at stake.

The stainless steel blade glinted momentarily in the light of the windshield before it was sunk deep into the coarse hair of the animal's ribcage. For one second there was total silence. The yellow eyes of the baboon turned red, and he glowered with hatred as blood spilled out of his doglike mouth. His head sunk slowly into his shoulders and he dropped back from the window onto the ocher track.

"That'll teach the bastard," Thomas seethed.

Together we pulled Visavadia from the driver's seat into the rear of the van and lay him down among the boxes.

"Check him over," I shouted.

"He's shaking with shock."

"Then wrap a blanket around him and let's get the hell out of here."

I slid into the driving seat, wound up the window, and started the engine. The windshield was splashed with filth, and I turned the wipers on and pumped a liberal amount of soapy water onto the glass. While waiting for the windshield to clear, I looked out the side window and watched as the remaining baboons on the roof and hood jumped down onto the hard ground and raced toward their leader, who was still occupying the roadside. It would seem that their will to fight had diminished, and while we may have lost the battle, we had undoubtedly won the war.

I watched as the wounded male pulled himself across the sandy road by digging his knuckles hard into the ground and pivoting around on them. There were splashes of blood everywhere as he used what was left of his strength to reach the far shoulder, where he turned around to have a look at his adversaries. He was disconsolate and stared first at the big drops of his blood that had spotted the ground and then raised his head and looked at me in the driver's seat.

I was uncertain if this was going to be a general capitulation by the troop. However, we had established that the so-called war of attrition was no longer a game. At this stage, I wanted to think that the old male baboon was wise enough to cut his losses and call off the remnants of his warrior army. After all, these cousins of ours were wild, and by their innate nature would automatically fight off any intruders that might trespass onto their territory. The main body of the baboons had now gathered in a semicircle around their leader, who was busy chattering to those around him. The young male looked shattered, and he again dipped his head to have a close look at the wound. He touched it with his fingers and sucked at the blood. Gradually the whole troop turned their attention to him and stared at the bright redness that glinted in the baking sun. Every now and then the young male would raise his head, look around in a bemused way, and then give me a vacant stare before being drawn back to his wound.

A gray swarm of cattle flies had descended from nowhere and were busy picking at the baboon's wound, but given time there's no saying that other more, serious contenders would zone in; perhaps a lone leopard on the prowl, a pack of wild dogs, or forest hyenas might happen by. The young male now had a serious price on his head, whether dead or alive. Above, in the cloudless sky, I heard an ominous squawk and spotted a flock of black-plumaged vultures, spanning all of eight feet, riding the thermals. They too would fancy their chances and would be on hand should the baboon die.

I turned in my seat and began to look at the road map.

"There's good news," I said. "Not twenty miles from here there's a mission. It's marked on the map at a place called Kitunda. I'll get there as fast as possible." I glanced at Visavadia lying in the back with his head cushioned on a folded towel.

"*Kwenda,*" Thomas said in a sharp voice.

I gunned the engine and headed straight down the track going south. The baboons were no longer an issue. They scattered from the roadside toward the woods, knowing full well that this time we meant business.

A couple of miles later, I pulled the van over to the side of the road in order for us to administer first aid.

It was here, in this semi-barren place at the southern end of the Swangala plains, that we were able to give time and assistance to our friend. We removed his blue jacket and examined where the teeth had pierced his shoulder. It was a clean wound, and wasting no time Thomas opened the first aid kit while I boiled water on the portable stove. We washed Visavadia's wound with a cotton swab, spread yellow antibiotic cream on a patch of gauze, and bound it down with surgical tape. The deep scratch marks on his face had more or less congealed, and we wiped them over with a disinfected cloth.

"How do you feel?" I asked as I offered him a cup of sweet tea. It pleased me that he was no longer shaking.

"I'll be all right," he answered quietly while he sipped slowly at his tea.

"We'll soon have you fixed up properly," Thomas assured. He moved into the driver's seat, and we pressed on silently, going westward toward Kitunda.

We wasted several minutes at the gated entrance of the mission before they allowed us through. The nurses were kind and showed Thomas and I into a small ante-room with simple African paintings and open bookshelves. It was strange to find ourselves in an enclosed room with four concrete walls, a proper ceiling, and fluorescent strip lighting shining down on us. This claustrophobic setting had unsettled Thomas after he had spent several unbroken months in the bush. I was all right, as I'd already had a break in Nairobi and was able to condition myself back into this environment. He hadn't had that advantage and began to pace up and down like a caged tiger.

"Mr. Carter," he began.

I moved toward him.

"Yes?" I said quietly.

"I owe you an explanation," he replied.

"I don't understand."

"I want you to know that I was fully aware of Vinoo's predicament, and it was for that reason that I searched for my panga. However, like you, I too had failed to release Vinoo's head from the baboon while you were occupied at your window. I should have called for help, but I felt that once I had the panga I could have shifted it on my own."

"I guessed that's what you were looking for," I said and nodded.

"I was going to strike the baboon with the flat of the blade. I reckoned the shock of being hit would be enough for it to loosen its limpet-like grip on Vinoo."

"That's not a problem anymore." I smiled, and added, "By the way I found your panga under the seat you were sitting on."

Thomas smiled back and we shook hands.

It suddenly went eerily silent in the ante-room while we glanced apprehensively at the door.

Twenty minutes later it sprung open and the doctor emerged from his surgery. He had good news for us. He had given Visavadia a thorough examination and treated his wound. Although he passed Visavadia as conditionally fit, he recommended that he take it easy for a week and limit himself to light work.

Both Thomas and I had thought the injury was far more serious, and to hear he had escaped any lasting damage was an immense relief.

"Once we cleaned the wound and saw the damage, we tidied it all up with fourteen sutures," the doctor informed. "It was a stroke of luck that the bite had missed the artery. My nurse has also cleaned the cuts to the face with an iodine solution and given him a tetanus shot."

"Thank you for all your help," I said.

"I'm glad you brought him here, because your colleague was certainly in need of professional attention. By the way, I have asked the nurse to give you painkillers, a spare bandage, lint, cotton wool, and a tube of antibiotic cream. It's my suggestion that the wound be changed every other day for the next eight days, and by then it should have healed."

"You've been very kind," I said, "and perhaps you could tell me what I owe you for this treatment?"

"It's on the house," he said with a smile, "but we're always willing to accept a donation for the mission's work."

I put my hand into the back pocket of my shorts and pulled out four notes totaling eighty shillings.

Ten minutes later we were back on the road going south.

chapter

NINETEEN

That night we made camp at Rungwa. It lay approximately twenty-seven miles to the east of Kitunda, amid the Miombo woodlands and rolling plains of the central plateau. It's in this region that rocky outcrops and ridges are frequently found.

Otherwise Rungwa had no reason at all to be on the map, as no one lived there. It was nothing more then a halting place between the towns of Itigi and Mbeya, a traveler's oasis, a junction in the soulless savanna of semi arid expanses where you need to carry your own water.

A herd of black forest buffalo, heavily cornuted, stood somberly facing in our direction. As we breakfasted, they grazed, while others waited their turn to wallow in the shallow pits of greasy mud. It was already overcrowded by a dark heaving mass that had got there earlier. This isolated spot was on the southwest corner of the Rungwa River Game Reserve. Besides buffalo in the water hole there were also spiral-horned and white-striped Kudos. They could be easily picked out as they moved along the rocky ridges that bordered the parched plains.

The game reserve covered 3,500 square miles of Tanganyika's heartland, spreading outward in a lopsided quadrangle as far as Dodoma, Itigi, and Iringa. Antelopes, both roan and sable, could be seen sprinting among the large herds of gray/brown African elephant that unceasingly roamed the muvale forests of the park.

Our destination was the town of Chunya, 137 miles directly south of Rungwa. We set off on this easier section with the knowledge that the most difficult part of the safari was over. After a thirty-mile stretch through empty, unbroken land, we drew to a halt at the tiny bush settlement of Mbogo. While Thomas and Visavadia gave a promotional show to the small group of villagers, I took the chance to do some paperwork, which included writing up my personal diary. The day's date was Tuesday, November 1, and the entry read, "Arrived Mbogo 10.30 hours; dry and sunny. No further problems."

We pushed on south through the leopard-hunting region near Makapi by the banks of the Lupa River, with its many shallow channels that meandered among numerous sandbanks. The wild animals in this area did not have the protection afforded in the reserves. We reached Chunya in the late afternoon, and it was on this leg that we set an all-time-best mileage record for a single day's run.

The route the next day from Chunya to Mbeya—a mere forty-five miles—was of great scenic beauty. This is the site of the original Lupa Goldfields, with the dark, leaden waters of Lake Rukwa to the northwest forming part of the inland drainage system.

We drove toward the escarpment, and with thirteen miles to go, pulled up on a stony plot of ground known as "World's End." From this precipice we had a limitless view of the Usangu Plains and the gigantically flawed Rift Valley. One mile farther down the road we passed a washed-out signboard. The faded black-and-red lettering said "Highest point of all the main roads in Tanganyika—Altitude 8050 feet." I felt disappointed that I had no camera to take a picture. The scrub on each side of the road appeared to stretch all the way back to the escarpment, which still bounded the view, but less abruptly, as we descended into Mbeya.

Mbeya was the regional headquarters for the entire district. It was originally founded in 1927 because of the interest shown in the Lupa gold fields. Today, the town is centered on a rich agricultural area and remains the last place of any size before entering northern Nyasaland. Some of the plant crops include cocoa, coffee, pyrethrum, tea, tobacco, and wheat. The many farmers and shamba owners grow fruit and vegetables on the strips of terraces cut along the sides of the mountains.

The backdrop to this beautiful town is formed by a horseshoe-shaped range of mountains topped by the Mbeya Peak at 9,272 feet and the Loleza Peak at 8,765 feet. It was strange to be confronted with a choice of accommodation after sleeping rough for the past few nights. There was the Mbeya Guest House sited on a hill overlooking the town or the Mbeya Hotel at the junction of the main boulevard, built around 1930 and forming six separate blocks surrounding a lawn and a bright flower garden. It gave off an air of part suburbia and part colonialism. In the end I checked in at the Mbeya Hotel, as it had a favored downtown position. Once again Thomas took the van and disappeared down the road with a chirpier Visavadia, who told me he had cousins in the town. I reminded him that it was time to change the dressing on his shoulder and he was to let me know tomorrow about his wound. Everything to do with our safari was now ticking over nicely, and we agreed that we deserved a break.

Because of the undoubted importance of this region with its many hillside villages tucked behind tall green plantations of maize and banana, I estimated that we would need a minimum of five days in order to engage the market and have sufficient time to launch a successful campaign of promotional coverage.

***

On our first day, Wednesday, November 2, we traveled south for fifty miles to the headquarters town of Tukuyu in the Rungwe District. On the way there, we crossed over the River Kiwira. A signpost gave the name of the crossing as God's Bridge. The simple explanation was because of the bridge itself, which was natural rather than being man-made. As we drove toward Tukuyu, we were encircled on both sides of the road by extensive tea and coffee estates. The vivid green leaves of the tea plantations contrasted with the paler green of the coffee shrubs—almost like the dark and light squares of a chessboard—both gleaming under the testing light of the afternoon sun.

Three hours later we took an alternative route back to Mbeya, bypassing the Mwakalali Catholic Mission. The towering Mount Rungwe at 9,713 feet slowly receded from the hazy view on our left side. From there we passed over a series of small streams lined with dark eucalyptus trees. The water flowed swiftly from high valleys and was awash with schools of freshwater trout. The road climbed and dropped and valleys became wider, but we kept going higher. The Poroto Mountains were faintly outlined in the distance, and at each village we were greeted by excited crowds of the Wanyakusa tribe. The planters in this lush region grew pyrethrum on the well-drained soils, which were protected from strong winds by the cooler highland ranges. The quick turnover of the crop, from root-stock to the harvesting of flowers, means the farmer has the advantage of several harvests per annum. It is from the daisy-like flowers that the insecticide oils are extracted and sent to Arusha for processing, and unlike many plants, pyrethrum does no harm to cattle or sheep. With the short dry season that is found in the highlands, no other cash crop enjoys such importance except for sisal, coffee, and cotton.

During the next three days, we maintained an intense advertising campaign in the hill villages and in the commercial areas of Mbeya. We concluded the sales program with an easy sixty-mile drive down the Great North Road toward the Rhodesian border and gave shows at Mlowa, Vwawa, Kasali, and at the custom post at Tunduma, where we were given permission to hand out leaflets on both sides of the border.

After lunch on Sunday, November 6, the day before we were due to leave, I found a deck chair and sat out on the green lawn of the hotel's garden to catch up with my reports and weekly accounts. It was a peaceful setting; the sun was out, and there was a zephyr breeze wafting across the lush, pink and blue flowerbeds that ringed the perimeter of the sloping lawn. Showy hibiscus shrubs softly waved in the summer air amid a profusion of angular-lobed mallows of hollyhock and okra. A lone flame tree gave shade to the flagstone path that ran parallel on one side of the hotel's concrete wall.

I was in the middle of addressing an envelope to Head Office in London when I was distracted. The sound of approaching feet came from a pebbled pathway that hugged the lawn and led off to the guest house. The rhythmic patter of shoes on stone was muffled the moment the stranger turned away from the path onto the short, thick grass behind my chair. There appeared to be a purpose in the steps, and at this juncture I was 90 percent certain I was the target.

An ineluctable voice of authority broke the peace. "I say, I want a word with you."

"Are you talking to me?" I said in puzzlement as I looked up from my writings.

"I don't see anybody else," the man responded, staring down at me in the chair. There was no way I was going to get up and shake hands. The rudeness in him had already settled that.

"Then how can I be of help to you?" I asked with a smile.

"My name is Bennett," he said by way of introduction, and with that done he began to clear his throat. "I am the chief medical officer of health for southern Tanganyika." His reddened skin seemed to indicate that he hadn't been up-country for more than a few days, and that he was probably on a short tour from the safety of his office in Dar es Salaam. He appeared uneasy, but at the same time was anxious to talk. Something was clearly bothering him, and he had most likely been watching me surreptitiously from the curtains of his room while I was sitting out on the lawn.

I changed my mind and got up from the low-slung chair, deciding that he had the physical advantage in looking down at me, and with a good deal of reluctance I shook his limp hand.

"What's the problem?"

"Am I right in assuming that you are the person who goes around in a truck selling medicines?"

"Yes, you could put it like that, although I prefer to call my motor a van." I shifted uneasily on my feet, wondering what he was going to come up with next, and went on, "I'm afraid I don't understand the point of this conversation, and I'm rather busy at the moment."

"You sell those patent medicines," he said accusingly, "called Herbalex and Gripe Aid." The deep flush of redness on his face began to change to a darker color.

"It's part of what I do," I admitted with a shrug of my shoulders.

"You know very well what I'm talking about," he rounded on me.

It was my guess that his growing ill temper showed that he wasn't used to handling anyone unless they were cowered by his presence.

"I haven't the vaguest idea what you're talking about, except you seem to me to be a very rude person."

He looked as though he was, at any moment, going to explode, so I decided it was time to grasp the bull by the horns.

"Is it that you want to buy a bottle of our cough medicine?"

"No, I don't want to buy a bottle," he spat out, his voice piping upward in indignation.

"What about Gripe Aid?"

He ignored my last question and proceeded to get the venom off his chest. "I came here to inform you that in my capacity as chief medical officer for the Rungwe District, I wholeheartedly disapprove of the methods you use to sell medicines in this country. I have been watching your activities in Mbeya and consider you are undoing all the good work done by my colleagues in the health department."

The doctor appeared relieved to have aired his views, and a flicker of triumph spread across his face.

"That's pretty strong stuff," I responded. "Not for one minute do I think that our customers in the bush would agree with you." I took a cigarette from my jacket pocket and lit it. "In my eyes your opinion counts for nothing." I blew the tobacco smoke into the air. "From the look of you," I said with sneer, "you've probably never got beyond the confines of a nice comfortable town in Hampshire. Your type knows nothing about the real Africa and the people who live in it."

"How dare you talk to me like that," he seethed.

"Look," I said as I tried to bring reason back into the argument, "don't you realize that we carry full licenses to conduct our business, and our work has been approved by the Nairobi Chamber of Commerce. So basically it doesn't matter a fig what you care to say, and, at the same time, I wholeheartedly dispute your uncalled-for comments."

"I'm going to report you." He trembled with rage.

"Be my guest," I said, "and no doubt you've already got my name and address. It's painted on the van, in case you haven't noticed." I moved closer to the doctor and poked him on the shoulder with my forefinger. "I feel sorry for you," I went on, "because in spite of your qualifications, you know nothing about the real people of this country. And anyway, all our paperwork is in order, so you are free to make your report."

"You wait," he stormed. "You'll be hearing from me."

And with those words ringing in my ears, he swept across the lawn and back onto the stony pathway.

I stared blankly for a few moments at the bright freesias that dotted the small rock garden; a pair of white-eye birds fluttered from their cup-shaped nest in the nearby flame tree in search of nectar amid the bounteous flowers. It seemed strange that after all the good friends we had made in East and Central Africa that I should have the first complaint leveled against me in such a pleasant setting.

Each and every show we had given had maintained the high standard that had been set out by management before we left Nairobi some eighteen weeks ago. As was our custom, we'd played endless rock, Latin, and highlife on our record player. The quality of the work that we carried out under this musical umbrella had been second to none. However, we were aware that it was possible to succumb to the pressures of life up-country. It can in certain cases lead to a general decline in one's mental health and the loss of being able to function at a normal level. Almost all travelers inside Africa have not only heard the stories but have personally known individuals who had "gone bush."

However, our health was fine—even Visavadia was on the mend—and our shows continued to draw large, enthusiastic crowds. The formula we used to stage a show had remained constant throughout the safari. Our contact with many thousands of people had always been on a very friendly basis, and wherever we went we were greeted with a sea of smiling faces. We gave away a mountain of Gripe Aid samples to pregnant women and Herbalex samples to those suffering from a bad cough—and to the poor and old who couldn't afford the price of a five-ounce bottle. We had also distributed leaflets, pinned on badges, and hammered up tin advertising plates, and for those people eager to buy, we operated a busy retail shop at the rear of the van. And as if that wasn't enough, we made endless visits to as many Asian shopkeepers as we could find.

***

The next morning, Monday, November 7, we left Mbeya and started on a 236 mile journey to the more northerly town of Iringa. We estimated that it would take us the best part of four days to reach our destination.

Beyond the main town area, the road began to open up. We passed a park that looked across the residential suburbs, negotiated a roundabout packed with pretty flowers, and then went straight ahead. There were more houses, white with red-tiled roofs, and farther on, in the hills, there were isolated African huts with vegetable plots and open compounds. All the time we climbed up a steepish road.

We waved and dropped leaflets as we motored by. At last we were free of the town and now pressed onward, climbing upward, as though heading toward a clear blue sky. We carried on past pyrethrum fields, and shortly afterward the road began to twist and rise relentlessly toward the Chimala escarpment with its fifty-two hairpin bends. At four we stopped at a place called Mwigi. We decided to pull over and spend the night in this beautiful area, and, within minutes, we had picked a spot with a fabulous view and settled down to having our tea.

The following morning, Tuesday, November 8, we pushed eastward, passing through an area of volcanic mountains. This time we traveled in a downward direction and dropped down to the floor of the Rift Valley. The enormity of this fault never disappointed the eye. We finally emerged at the township of Igawa at the lower level of 4,000 feet, and here we halted for a lunch break. After giving a show and before leaving town, we filled up with gasoline from a roadside garage. The place was more like a mortuary. It was dotted with old trucks and broken-down cars. Our journey now took us along the Mufundi Loop Roads. The whole area was centered on the endless Buhoro flats that dropped away to our left, and the view gave way to great plains that were webbed with countless rivers and streams. The wildlife population consisted of enormous herds of white giraffe, spotted zebra, and smooth-coated buffalo.

Several miles north of Igawa, we passed a narrow turn leading to the mission at a place called Makombw. We pulled onto the side of the road, keeping our right wheels on the hard-stoned track, and checked the map. It was soon evident that the mission lay on the fringes of the flats, and it was out of the question that we should contemplate taking our vehicle to such a remote place in the hope of securing a small order for pine disinfectants. Instead we drove on, and the land now began to flatten. The view became even more extensive as we entered the vast Wangingombe wastes. We saw another road sign that pointed to a second mission at a village called Llembula. It was less than four miles from the main road, and this time we set off down the stony track. On arriving there, we were given a warm welcome by two sisters who offered us tea and sponge cake with a raspberry filling while we talked about our products. We ended up with a useful order for ten gallons of pine disinfectant and ten more of coal tar, which we were able to supply from our stock in the van. It was worth noting that this call took us ninety minutes to complete—that is, from the time we started at the main road to the time we got back. However, we were glad that we called at Llembula, and it was nice to meet such good people.

Sometimes it was the pure inaccessibility that ruled out making a call, but as safari salesmen we hated to pass up any opportunity to sell. Still, there were times when we had to draw a line. It was now past five o'clock, and the light had started to dim. The road twisted downward and emerged from the bush. It now ran beside an almost-dry river toward the settlement of Kingolo, where we put on a fifteen-minute show.

"Let's stop somewhere here for the night," I said.

Thomas was concentrating on his driving and said nothing. The road drew away from the river and entered the bush again. The land was becoming broken, and there were more trees as the van bumped along the rutted track. Unexpectedly, he braked and pulled onto an open space.

"How about this spot?" he asked, and warned, "It'll soon be dark."

"Good as any," I confirmed, adding, "we'll get caught up in another village if we go any farther." And with that I raised my head through the open doorway and looked into the ever-changing African sky as the sun came down and began to set. It wasn't long before darkness began to seep across the savanna, turning dusk into night.

The next morning we worked the small nearby settlement of Makumbako, nothing more than two or three wooden shops with some faded advertisements on dry timber doors. A dusty collection of houses and huts ran on one side of the dirt road. It was chilly and smoke rose straight up from the huts. Then, after leaving the village, the road no longer followed an eastern course but changed direction and went northward to Iringa. We followed a shallow depression before climbing upward again, twisting and turning through the last of the loops, which gave us faint glimpses of the high plain that we had driven through yesterday afternoon. At noon we rested for an hour and then pushed onward, passing large hillside fields of pyrethrum and tea. We were traveling in the Sao Hills region. Not far ahead of us was a line of trees, some gray and almost leafless, that marked the course of a stream. Soon there were other streams—the Kigogo, Kibwele, and Kidofi—all teeming with trout.

We made steady headway for the next thirty miles. The road climbed and then dropped, and gradually we began to descend. Valley led to valley, and all the time we were aware of the declining sun. Eventually we arrived at a place called Ulete—like Rungwa, on the Itigi/Chunya Road. It was nothing more than a point on the map, just an EARC services halt, desolate and empty. It was here that we stopped for our third consecutive night in the bush since departing Mbeya.

The next morning, Thursday, we left Ulete and pushed onward over the forty miles that separated us from our destination at Iringa. We made about a dozen stopovers, including a mission center at Rungemba and other strange-sounding places, such as Tanangozi and Tosamaganga. This entire south highland region was dotted with roads, graves, and forts—a legacy from the Bantu people.

By late afternoon we had negotiated the rugged slopes of the Ruaha River escarpment and slowly made our way across the last miles that led to Iringa. On arrival we drove down the main boulevard, past the shopping center, and turned left onto Hill Street.

"Here you are," Thomas announced as he braked the van alongside the curb, outside the White Horse Inn.

My guidebook said that it was built in the middle thirties, partly colonial, partly suburban, and that the lounge and bar at night would be crowded with interesting settlers from the neighboring farms. It described Iringa as being an unusually attractive town and mentioned that the Hehe people—pronounced hay-hay—were the dominant tribe of the region, and that Iringa in their dialect stood for "a fence to stop wild animals."

"We'll stay here until Monday," I said, reaching for my case from the back of the vehicle.

***

With the long week-end behind us, we left Iringa and struck due north for the 164-mile journey to the town of Dodoma, situated on the central plateau in the very middle of Tanganyika. The moment we left the main tree-lined boulevard of the town, we turned onto the Great North Road and headed for Mapanda. To begin with the road followed the contour of the outlying hills, and then it climbed steadily across the ridge of the Ho-ho escarpment toward Isisi, a small village that had been built on one side of the Great North Road about a narrow dirt track.

At a place called Ntara, we bridged the Ruaha River and were no longer hedged in by the sight of overpowering mountains. Shortly, the highway opened up and ran straight for the next twenty miles. The escarpment in our rearview mirror still bounded the savanna, but less and less abruptly. Then, coming toward us at speed was a large gasoline tanker driven by an Asian. We surrendered the center of the road, having come out of the slotting, and were now both driving at about an eighteen-degree angle. The driver of the tanker gave us a friendly wave, which we returned, and then gave three short blasts on his horn as we thundered by each other. It was the first vehicle we had seen since leaving the hotel. After the village of Chipologo, we pulled off the road by a solitary acacia and made camp for the night.

On the morning of Tuesday, November 15, we pressed onward, leaving Mount Manangwe on our right and crossing over the Futu River. The sunlight and the scrub seemed to blur the vision as once again we met the rising ground. The Fu-fu escarpment finally gave way to the extensive plains of the Matumbulu Region. At long last we began to go down, and we sadly lost the fabulous view. On this side of the ridge the vegetation had changed. It was greener, and the light no longer hurt the eyes. Another three or four hours went by before we completed the hundred-mile safari from the village of Chipologo and arrived on the southern outskirts of Dodoma. We had left behind the wine-growing area of Bihawana, which had been transplanted from Kondoa in the north. It was started in 1950 by Italian missionaries, and it now produced a well-recommended rich, dry red wine.

Sometimes our safari seemed like a scenic travelogue and belied the fact that we were working all the areas we either passed through or deliberately went out of our way to check out. For instance, since the previous day, when we departed Iringa, we had given half-hour shows at each of the following places: Morogoro village, Mapanda, Mondomera, Asumani, Ikengaza, Machiusi, Nyangola, Isasi, Migole, Mkutubora, Ntara, Kisima, and Chipologo.

In Dodoma I found accommodation at a local hotel run by the EARC, the railroad company. It was all but empty, and during my stay I never saw more than two other guests. My room was large and airy, and the wood-paneled lounge had a quiet, well-worn look of earlier colonial times. Not only was Dodoma the headquarters town for the vast agricultural region, but it was also the main railway center on the sixty-three-hour rail journey from Kigoma to Dar es Salaam, which lies on the west coast of the Indian Ocean.

Three days later, on Friday, November 18, we left Dodoma and worked our way along the Great North Road, going upward and heading for the town of Babati, some 180 miles distant. We traveled by small suburban allotments that gave way to extensive acres of green maize on both sides of the dirt road. Every now and then we passed a patch of ground with stilted storage barns for their leafy husks. It is only when the grains are separated that the pests will attack the ripe cobs. The shut-in road suddenly broke free of arable land into open light. We now faced extensive swamplands that spanned out on each side, and a rush of warm air entered the cab.

The afternoon came and went, and by dusk we arrived at Kondoa, just over a hundred miles from our point of departure. It had been an exhausting day, and we were looking forward to a meal and bed.

The road was empty when we left the next morning, and after twenty miles, the land began to slope. The view soon became more extensive, and yet the emptiness of the road couldn't be taken for granted. It was warm in the van, and the sun rose swiftly into the sky. We were heading for the eight-hundred-foot escarpment at Kolo, a place of immense interest to anthropologists. It is here that the famous rock paintings in caverns were discovered. They depicted hunting scenes, wild animals, and human figures, all done in organic substances of red, yellow, purple, and black by mixing egg, arabic gum, lime, oil, honey, and earwax. It is said that the bushmen painted the animals because it would assist them in catching their quarry. From Kolo, we climbed the escarpment and continued along the high plateau to the tiny village of Bereku, stopping yet again to give a roadside show to a group of shamba owners. It was late afternoon when we arrived at Babati—another railway services road halt—and we soon discovered reasonable accommodation at the government rest house.

Saturday, November 19, was another brilliant day, and we spent two hours working the center of Babati. We carried on up the Great North Road and made good progress—we thought we might even be able to knock a couple of days off the two-week backlog that haunted us since first arriving in Kampala—and already we had Babiti thirty-one miles in our wake.

It was in this isolated sector that we went past a heavily loaded bus that had broken down on the side of the highway. The main group of passengers were sprawled out on the tufted roadsides, either asleep in blankets or busily cooking a meal. We stopped the van and reversed down the road, asking the driver if there was anything we could do to help.

"No, thanks," he said and grinned happily. "I've sent someone off to fetch a welder from Arusha."

"A welder?" Thomas repeated. "What's the problem?"

"The chassis cracked," he replied.

For the next thirty minutes we played music, handed out pamphlets, and pinned Herbalex badges. "See you around," we shouted to the passengers as we got back into the van.

At Madukani there were little shacks at crossroads. Here we turned left off the highway onto a narrow track and made for the township of Mbulu. From the open door of the van, we caught glimpses of Lake Manyara's southernmost shore. The water for the lake was fed by springs from the rift valley wall, and during the dry season it would shrink to mere sand and pebbles. The word *Manyara* comes from the Masai *emanyara,* meaning a thornbush for hedging stock. The lake is located only twenty miles southwest of the Ngorongoro Crater and is home for many water birds, including pelicans and flamingos.

The light became harder than before, and the air had lost its morning crispness. It was the openess of the plateau that surprised us when we left the relative safety of the main highway and drove down this narrow track. There was nothing now but billowing clouds of gritty smoke coming off fields and allotments. The problem was magnified when the track narrowed, so much so that we had difficulty in keeping our wheels from slipping into the guttering, and we started to bump up and down on the corrugated surface. The harsh sound of our approaching vehicle—we were in second gear—had unsettled the thousands of pink-plumaged flamingos with wings of red and black. They had been quietly occupied with filtering the lake's brackish water for organic matter and assorted shellfish with their lower beak. However, hundreds of others were nesting in muddy mounds along the lakeside, and in a sudden flurry, they rose upward and covered the cloudless sky in a blanket of pink.

The road soon began to twist and broaden, and fortunately we were at last free from the smoke, and could now see where we were going. We started to run parallel with Manyara's 150-square-mile game park and unexpectedly glimpsed a pride of lions sprawled under an acacia, some on low branches to escape the tormenting flies. Another hour went by before we arrived at the isolated trading center of Mbulu on the Eyasi Rift, located below the western wall of the Great Rift Valley. From here, beyond the Yaida Valley, was Lake Eyasi, imprisoned by its salt-and-soda waters. Living beside the lake the primitive Hadzaor bushmen hunt with poisoned arrows and live off plants. Their language is spoken in a series of clicks, like the Koison dialect, and they have small, dark, thick bodies. In fact this is the only place in the continent of Africa where you get four different linguistic groups, namely the Bantu, Hamatics, Nilotics, and the clickers of Koison.

We camped that night overlooking the walls of the valley, and in the morning we woke early and gave a sixty-minute show in Mbulu's only street. By ten o'clock we were winding our way back along the narrow, stony track toward the tiny settlement of Madukani. We passed a herd of klipspringers, a type of small antelope with yellow-gray coats, standing perilously close to the edge of rocky outcrops. Closer down, near the marshlands, were reedbuck, another type of antelope that made a whistling sound as they bounced and streaked across the flats.

Several miles later the track began to rise as it neared the high embankment of the Great North Road and joined at the place known as the Madukani crossroads. From there we turned sharp right and retraced the route back toward Babati. We were glad to be away from the flies. The people who had been stranded on the bus with the broken chassis were still sprawled out on the coarse grass, and we stopped once more and exchanged greetings. We gave them two gallons of drinking water to share among them. It was enough for a mugful to each person. Then, back at Babati, we turned right and left the Great North Road for good. In front of us was a 120-mile journey southwest to the township of Singida on the central plateau.

The single track swung below and around the dramatic volcanic slopes of Mount Hanang. It was covered all over in eye-catching blue-and-green scree. At the same time we had views of the piedmont of green forestation that surrounded its base, and this picture was spectacularly framed in the van's open doors. We had gone quiet and drove steadily westward, and the striking Mount Hanang that had for so long been reflected in our broad rearview mirrors had now diminished and was gone. All that was left was shimmering plain and hummocked fields in the distance.

At Llongero we had a crowd of more than three hundred, and it took more than two hours to complete our work before finally breaking off for lunch. In the afternoon we called at the Catholic mission of Itamuka and made more stops along the dusty road. It was past seven when we entered Singida, and although someone had gotten into the rest house first, we struck lucky with the Central Hotel on the north side of the main square.

Singida was an important town surrounded by a network of villages and served as a terminus for the EARC. We were informed that rogue lions were hunting down people who lived in the villages or worked in the fields.

Anyway, we spent the whole of the next day working the area. Then, on Wednesday, November 23, we drove seventy miles south—through Puma and Suna—to another railway halting place at Itigi. It was here that we had originally planned to disembark on the train from Kigoma, but due to the problems with the loading ramp we were forced to take a short cut to Tabora, where our safari nearly ended in disaster.

Once we had picked up our stock that had been waiting collection from EARC, as arranged by Lal Prasanna in Mwanza, and on the strength of having plenty of stock, we gave an impromptu show lasting an hour, and did brisk business before getting under way.

We turned eastward and the land was parched and more open. We pressed onward and stopped at three unremarkable settlements, until night began to fall. Earlier, we had agreed to work late. Otherwise another day would be lost, and that would seriously affect our chances of arriving in Nairobi by Christmas.

"Let's call it a day," I said, and glanced down at the luminous dial of my wristwatch, double-checking the time with that on the dashboard clock. It was six thirty p.m. and we were five miles short of the township of Manyoni. We were done in, and too tired to search for the rest house should we have gotten there. Instead we slowed to ten miles per hour and sought out a likely stopping point with our headlights.

"This'll do," I said, and Thomas braked to a stop as Visavadia climbed out of the cab onto the track with a stave in his hand. This night-time procedure had been rehearsed by us when in Nairobi. Every now and then Visavadia prodded the ground on the right side, then swept the stave to the left, and prodded again. And little by little we'd pick our way off the track onto a level patch of strawlike stubble. This was Africa's answer to the hard shoulder, and once off the track, we daren't penetrate any farther, in case of unseen ruts in the ground or, for that matter, any other unexpected danger.

An hour later we'd finished our meal, and after a welcome cup of tea, we washed, dried, and put the cooking utensils away. There was little room in the van due to the new consignment of stock, and we found it difficult to find a space to lie down as the cartons touched the ceiling. However, we shifted a dozen cartons onto the passenger side at the front of the van, which gave us enough room to lie down at the back.

Ten minutes later and without warning, there was a loud knocking noise on the paneling outside.

"Did you hear that?" Thomas said.

Instinctively in unison we both sat up in the darkness and hit our heads against the metal roofing.

"All this is beginning to get to me," I grumbled.

"Me too," Thomas echoed.

I put a restraining hand on Visavadia and told him to stay put while I squeezed over the top edge of the piled cartons and slid headfirst into the driver's seat. For a moment my neck got temporarily stuck beneath the steering wheel until I was able to struggle free by twisting my body around onto the seat.

I then heard more knocking.

"Is anyone there?" a voice asked.

Since first hearing the knocking, I was in two minds as to whether our night time visitor was animal or human. After all, I was half-asleep at the time of the interruption, but now that I knew it was human I pulled my knife out of its sheath.

"Who's there?" I hissed into the darkness as I unwound the window a couple of inches.

"Bwana," a voice came back. "I bring a message from my boss man. He wants you to come over and join him for a drink."

"Is this some sort of joke?"

"No, sir."

The voice was closer than before, and I peered out and saw the face of a young boy, about fourteen, framed in the light that fanned out from the window. "*Iko hapa,*" the boy said in Swahili, half turning and stepping back into the semi darkness. He raised his hands, beckoning, wanting me to follow him.

I slipped the knife back into its leather holder and turned around. There were beads of sweat on my mouth and forehead. "Come with me," I said quietly to Thomas. "I don't know if we can trust this guy."

We left Visavadia to guard the vehicle and clambered down onto the gritty surface dotted with coarse tussock grass. The boy was waiting a few paces from the van. There was a hint of a smile at the corner of his mouth, but there was no humor in it. We began to follow behind him, using the flashlight to illuminate the rough ground ahead. We had walked no more than one hundred and fifty yards before we recognized the yellow flush of a canvas tent, its give away shape made obvious by an inside light.

"In here, please," the young boy said, holding back a tattered flap.

"Good on you to come, sport," a voice boomed at us.

"Is this where the party is?" I joked.

"Saw you lot arrive earlier and thought I would give you a chance to settle down and have chow. My name's Tom Cooke, for the record."

"John Carter," I said, shaking his hand and introducing Thomas.

"You guys make yourselves at home." He waved a hand inviting us to sit down on the bedding.

"Is lager alright?"

"That'll be great."

We spent the next hour talking and drinking beer. Tom explained to us that he was prospecting in the region. He showed us samples of his finds, mainly beryls and zircons, but nothing to get excited about. "I had more luck in the Australian Outback," he jested. It was past one o'clock when we finally said our good-byes and left the tent.

Early the next morning, as the sun rose and spilled its warmth, I climbed from the vehicle and looked around. There was no sign of Tom's canvas tent, and the flat, open scrub gave no clue that he had been there. I raised a hand and shielded my eyes against the glare and tried to remember the direction we had taken on our short walk last night, but there was definitely nothing to see. I followed the footmarks for a short distance, but they led nowhere. And yet it puzzled me as to why a lone Australian had broken camp so early and hadn't come over to say good-bye. We had even extended an invitation for him to have breakfast with us, and he had replied that it would be dandy. It was almost as if I had dreamed the whole thing.

Without warning, a group of about a dozen warthogs came zipping across the stiff grass, tails vertical, hooves ripping and beating noisily on the tufted undergrowth, their faces made ugly by grotesque excrescences. Suddenly they swerved and turned back.

"*Ngiri,*" Thomas shouted disparagingly, using the Swahili word for ugly and foul.

An hour later, after breakfast, we resumed our journey eastward, keeping the speed down to twenty miles per hour in acknowledgment of the heavy load we had taken on board at Itigi.

It took us the best part of two days to reach the town of Kilosa. We covered the two hundred miles in a zig-zag fashion, repassing Dodoma and going via the trading center of Mpwapwa in order to complete our work schedule in Tanganyika's north-central region. It was late Friday night when we arrived at Kilosa, and we were left with no choice but to park in an open space on the fringes of this railway town.

At eleven o'clock the next morning, after completing two solid hours of promoting and selling our products, we left Kilosa and headed for the southerly regions of Tanganyika. The date was Saturday, November 26, and our next destination—which was marked on the map in black lettering—was the important market town of Ifakara. At the start we had to retrack through the center of Kilosa and were soon flagged down by a *duka* owner (shopkeeper) who wanted three dozen of Herbalex and of Gripe Aid. We had no option but to park in the center of the street while Visavadia and Thomas carried the six boxes into the man's shop. Meantime I made out a bill and went inside to collect the cash. The whole transaction had lasted less than two minutes, but in that time the traffic had built up, and one or two drivers had become upset. To calm things down, we handed out booklets and samples of Herbalex.

On the outskirts of town we crossed over a left-angled, narrow-gauged railroad track, and from there the road gradually opened up. However, we resisted increasing our speed, as the camber was greasy and dotted with water holes from the recent rains. It was these same conditions that had caused the accident at Gulu last October. It would appear that we had learned our lesson.

We made brief stops at roadside villages, such as Kisawasawa, Kiberege, and Solulu, and for part of the time motored parallel with the Mikumi National Park and in so doing passed through extensive plains and wooded hills. We were aware that we would have to return on this route next Monday in order to get to Morogoro and thence onto the road that would take us to Dar es Salaam on the eastern seaboard.

Mountains as high as eight thousand feet began to close in on us, and all the while the road climbed. There was stillness in the valley that signaled rain, and it became dark. Shadows disappeared and day was turning into night. It was usually hard to forecast the weather in these regions, although November was known as the month of short rains. After a while the road leveled off and we emerged from the mountains, which no longer bounded the uncertain view. It was less gloomy in spite of low clouds, and we slowly picked up speed as our confidence returned. We went by a thick row of trees that marked the course of a river, which was little more than a stream. Over to the left we had glimpses of East Africa's largest game reserve, nearly 16,000 square miles, named after its founder, Captain Frederick Selous, who was known to have hunted elephants from horseback. He was killed on January 4, 1917, during an attack on the German trenches by allied forces. Shortly, the road opened up again, and the wind became gusty as rain drummed on the roof of our van. We slid the doors shut, rolled up the windows, and dropped our speed.

The vegetation in this western region of Rufiji was typical of Miombo woodlands. The rolling hills were covered in mahogany, yellow woods, and iroko. And on the lower levels, intermittent patches of evergreen forests sloped toward open steppe lands with scattered acacia and myrrh trees. The Rufiji River forms the largest drainage system within East Africa, over 68,000 square miles, and has a huge delta with numerous mouths. The wreck of the German battle cruiser *Koenigsberg* from World War One can still be seen on the Konde River.

We spotted groups of workers sheltering from the tropical storm on improvised terraces. They had been laying track, extending the railway line toward the Nyasaland border in the south, primarily to move thousands of tons of copper to the international port of Dar es Salaam. Several miles farther on we drove past the old battlefields of 1905 to 1907. This was when 130,000 Africans died in the uprising against the German settlers. They objected to poor pay and bad living conditions. It was called the Maji Maji Rebellion, maji meaning water, because the Africans sincerely believed that the bullets targeted against them would turn to water. The end result of the uprising was a scorched-earth policy instigated by Governor Gotzen, which condemned the region to more than three years of famine.

At a place named Kidatu we bridged the Great Ruaha River for the third time, and in the openness, the rainwashed road could be seen for some distance ahead as it skimmed the tilted land. Then, without notice, the rain thinned, and with relief we rolled down the windows to rid ourselves of the smell of stagnation and allow in the fresh air.

The wide view began to go. There were more trees, mainly widegirthed baobabs, and every now and then we came across a circle of mud and wattle hutments with large compounds. Behind these structures were acres of sweet potatoes and beans with well-trodden paths zig-zagging into the distance. It had all the hallmarks of commercial farming.

Shortly we began to see groups of people, stray goats, roadside shops, cyclists, and squat concrete buildings scattered up and down both sides of the road. We had arrived in the market town of Ifakara, some 120 miles south of our departure point at Kilosa. It was dusk turning to night when we located a suitable camping spot—there was no accommodation here despite the heavy print marked on our road map—and after having a meal, we opened three cans of beer and had a chat around a wood fire.

We got up at nine o'clock and spent the morning giving shows from one end of the town to the other. After a midday meal, we concentrated on the large farms that employed and housed many workers as cotton pickers, the rich, deep, loamy soil of the area being ideal for the plants.

The following morning, Monday, November 28, we left Ifakara and back tracked northward for fifty miles to the village of Mikumi, heading northeast for Msongozi. The dirt road was no longer built on a high embankment, but it had dropped and narrowed and had begun to follow the level of the land. We were now transversing the Mikumi National Park with the Uluguru Mountains obscuring any view from our right. It was thickly covered in lush Miombo woodlands, still glistening from the recent rains. We caught glimpses of waterbuck and sable antelope drinking from sedge-lined pools.

It was night when we reached Morogoro. Thomas and Visavadia decided to camp out in the van and save their allowances while I checked into the Acropol Hotel.

A few miles out from Morogoro is the site of the *Simbamwene,* or Lion City, built by Zigua Chief Kisabeago. According to Stanley, while visiting the town in 1871, the perimeter had high stone walls and elaborately carved wooden gates. Today it is a bustling commercial center with rows of shops lined along an attractive boulevard adjacent to the main route stretching east to Dar es Salaam.

We left late the following day after completing our work in Morogoro and traveled due east for the 120-mile ride on a tarmac road leading to Dar es Salaam, the capital of Tanganyika, which lies on the palm-fringed coastline of the Indian Ocean. The wide, undulating road gave us an unusually smooth ride, and en route we passed extensive cashew nut plantations on the south side.

As we drew close to the port of Dar es Salaam, I checked the reading of the van's odometer. It showed 6,033 miles. The safari had so far taken 155 days, and this figure confirmed that we averaged thirty-nine miles per day, which was a decided improvement over earlier results.

Both Thomas and Visavadia wanted to make their own arrangements for accommodation during our estimated stay of one week in Dar es Salaam. I decided to avoid the city's dusty streets and high humidity, around 80 percent, and opted for the less congested and more beautiful areas along the ocean road. I checked in at the Sandhaven Hotel, some three miles north of Dar es Salaam. It was secluded and hidden behind a wide band of coconut palms that bordered the rich yellow sands of the blue ocean waters. A lone, large tulip tree with colorful flowers stood on the hotel's front lawn.

chapter

TWENTY

Dar es Salaam is Tanganyika's largest city. Its Arabic name stands for "Haven of Peace." This capital, with its mixture of German, Indian, and British buildings, was established in 1887 by the German East Africa Company, which structured a railway terminal with adequate port facilities.

Today, Dar still retains its old charm but is now blended with tall concrete buildings and extensive shopping complexes that can be found in any modern city of the world. There is everything for the tourist, and at the Tanganyika Trading Company on Changombe Road one can readily purchase items from the selection of famous ebony wood carvings done by the Zaramo and Makonde tribes. The carvings can be grotesque, showing a family tree of struggling humanity, or Picassoesque, with elongated and contorted limbs and bulging eyes. There are also many varieties of Masai beadwork used by their women for adornment and status that are on display in the windows of the many gift shops.

Climatic conditions for Tanganyika's coastal strip and the immediate hinterland are tropical at 80 Fahrenheit (26.6 Celsius) rising to 93 Fahrenheit (34 Celsius) with a 78 percent humidity count. The rainfall varies from around forty inches to a high of seventy-six inches. The climate controls what people wear. The women dress in almost see-through fabrics of bright colors and bold patterns called both khanga and kitenge, while the men are more conservative in their lightweight suits. In the many jewelry shops there is an extensive choice of items, from tanzanites, sapphires, diamonds, moonstones, garnets, topaz, and beryl, all the way along the spectrum to tiger's eyes, amethysts, agates, tourmalines, and zircons. All these stones are mined locally in Tanganyika.

The vegetation on this part of the coast was chiefly given over to coconut palms, although running the length of the country's eastern seaboard are extensive mangrove swamps, especially in the south around the Rufiji Delta.

The most important by-product of coconut is copra. This is obtained by splitting the actual nut into two parts and drying the white meat in the sun. When finally dry it provides the source of all coconut oil, which is used for cooking and for making soap and margarine. The residue can be utilized as food for livestock. The husks of brown fiber, known as coir, are made into ropes and mats. The trees themselves grow best on a rich loamy soil, but just the same, they do very well on the sand and salt of Tanganyika's coast line, especially around the waters of Dar es Salaam, where there is an abundance of big game fish, such as the marlin, tuna, shark, and sailfish.

The extensive mangrove swamps are made up of evergreen trees and shrubs and are located in sheltered bays, estuaries, and lagoons. The trees have special interlacing roots that grow upward, seeking oxygen, and are known as "stilt roots." Not only is the wood used for buildings and firewood, but the bark also contains tannin, used both in the preparation of leather and in medical products.

The first day in Dar we restricted our activities to the large area within the city's boundary. Our agenda included a courtesy call on Matthew Knott, the local manager of Morgans, who acted as our representative. I spent an hour with him, and we discussed the market relating to the vast region of southern and eastern Tanganyika. I was also introduced to members of his staff, all of whom asked interesting questions about the workings of our safari. It only goes to show that indigenous people have the same wonder about their own country as tourists do.

I mentioned to Matthew that we had no urgent need for stock replenishment, as we had recently picked up a consignment from the EARC in Itigi.

However, we did agree that he would set aside thirty gross each of Herbalex and Gripe Aid for collection at his warehouse before we left on the final leg of our journey to Nairobi. The map showed a distance of 631 miles, but it was likely to be over eight hundred miles due to our many off-track visits to villages and settlements. Considering this, I decided to change my mind and requested a further twenty gross each be shipped to the bus depot at Tanga.

"Nice to have met you," I said.

"I doubt I'll see you again before you go, so good luck."

We shook hands as I came out of his glass-walled office, and I made the rounds and said good-bye to his staff.

Once outside I asked Thomas to get the van serviced and washed down inside and out, and not to forget to restock essential items. I confirmed that we would need ten gallons of fresh water and five gallons of gasoline. I gave him some currency notes worth a hundred and fifty shillings, and a grocery list that included tins of beans, spaghetti, Spam, tomatoes, soups, a bag of rice, a pot of mustard, etc. I added a postscript on the list that he mustn't forget fresh bread and milk on the Monday morning before we leave Dar.

"I want you and Visavadia to come and pick me up at eight thirty tomorrow at the Sandhaven Hotel for our trip to Bagamoyo, OK?"

"No problem." Thomas smiled from the cab.

All these arrangements left Visavadia and I free for the remainder of the working day to make calls on the important African and Asian traders who resided in the bustling commercial district. We both wilted under the stifling heat in our search for potential buyers, and, without exception, we were given a friendly welcome—almost always offered cups of tea and biscuits—even though we had failed to make appointments.

While making these visits, I remembered to drop into the plush offices of the East African Airways in order to book an early flight to Zanzibar on the coming Saturday in response to London's request that I visit the island.

***

The following day, Friday, December 2, we motored northward along the coastal road to Bagamoyo, an attractive town with a historical past. It was a ninety-mile trip there and back, and we were informed that the coastal road might prove a challenge if the weather was to turn nasty. Anyway, on the way there, we stopped off at several villages, including Mbozi, Kunduchi, Buaju, Kereje, and Ktopeni.

Bagamoyo's past was linked to the old caravan porters who halted here and named the place after the Swahili word for "the place where the heart lays down its burden." In 1887 the Germans made it the capital of Tanganyika, and some of the original dwellings still stand today, including the district commissioner's office with its long Teutonic windows. However, it was the Arabs who left the legacy of the beautiful and traditionally carved doors on old houses. They were also responsible for conducting the slave trade with an iron fist.

For the best part of three hours we hugged the coastal road that ran alongside the Indian Ocean, until we approached the turn off for Bagamoyo. We forked left at a signpost and found ourselves on a narrow, sandy road that led away from the wooded area of mangrove trees. We slowed down and drove over a fifteen-foot paved bridge above the Mbweni River, which was nothing more than a shallow stream.

It was now exactly one o'clock, and we were fast approaching the outskirts of Bagamoyo. It was agreed that it was time to stop and have something to eat. We pulled off the road and found a likely place of leveled ground under the shade of a tamarind tree. It was a pleasant setting with green hills and rocky sides screening off the surrounds. Visavadia was soon warming up some baked beans on our portable stove, while Thomas was busy doing the odd kitchen chores, such as slicing fresh bread, fetching drinking water, and sharing out the contents of a tin of peaches into three plastic bowls. I took advantage of their activity and completed a weekly sales report along with the latest entries into my personal diary.

It was two o'clock when we got back on the road and headed for the town center, which was less than a mile away. We drove slowly through an avenue of coconut palms, which swayed in the warm breeze that spilled over from the Indian Ocean.

We spent three hours in this beautiful, historic town, and although we put on our customary show, we reduced the volume in order to ensure that our presentation was less flamboyant than usual and more in accord with these genteel surroundings.

We departed the town center by the same route and headed back through the splendid palms that straddled the sides of the sandy streets.

Besides the trees there was little else to be seen, but on the positive side, this emptiness generated a feeling of peace and calmness. Every now and then we caught glimpses of dhows, as well as the occasional felucca, with lateen sails, cresting the blue waves of the ocean beyond the palmy shoreline with its mangrove swamps.

Then, from nowhere, this tranquil picture changed. All at once the filtered sunlight started to fade and the wind became gusty, and without notice a blanket of darkened clouds raced across the sky. The town and its suburbs had within minutes turned gray. The final streaks of afternoon light disappeared, and in its place rain began to bucket down in big blobs. This sudden change in the weather took us by surprise, and we slid shut the doors and wound up the windows. We guessed that this variation in weather would be a foretaste of a heavier storm to come, and as if to corroborate our thoughts, the weather turned nastier. There was nothing now but the beating of rain on palm leaves and the crack of lightning as it streaked across the sodden sky, followed by a menacing rumble of thunder.

The thin road leading from the town center was no longer easy to negotiate. It had quickly become a narrow, greasy track of deep, wheel-swallowing potholes and sudden ruts. The van began to jump and jiggle as loose stones came bouncing off the surrounding hillside. We were almost shut in by bending palms and squally winds, and although there was no longer a view, we progressed slowly down the narrow track at little more than a walking pace. The eye of the storm seemed to be coming from the southeast and by our reckoning would soon head inland. It wouldn't be too long before we were caught in the center of a cyclone. At the moment we were dry and cozy inside the van.

Thomas's face had self-determination written all over it. He was hunched over the steering wheel and was steadfastly looking through the steamy windshield as the wipers cleared the driving rain. His eyes were searching for any sign of the coast road that linked with our trackway. And yet, despite everything, he was able to maintain a slow, snail-like pace. Then, without notice, the storm that had been uprooting trees and blowing people off their feet suddenly abated.

It was while we were savoring these new, easier conditions that our euphoria was swiftly interrupted by the sight of the swollen Mbweni River. No longer was it a harmless little trickle that we had disdainfully crossed before

Safari Salesman

taking our lunch break. It was now full of fury and had overflowed its banks. In layman's terms, it had become unbridgeable. The track began to dip as we approached, and Thomas teased the brake pedal with his foot, fearful that we might slide into the water. It was a mixture of good driving and good luck when we drew to a halt inches from the rolling waters.

The simple crossing of a pebble-and-sand riverbed had turned into a raging torrent, and somewhere under the swirling water was the paved bridge, the one we had crossed some four hours earlier.

We watched amazed as a man stepped forward from a small knot of people on the far bank, seemingly oblivious to the rush of water, and began to push his loaded bicycle the five yards to reach our side. However, despite placing himself in the center of where the bridge should have been, it was plain to those gathered on the opposite bank that his action was perilous. He'd got as far as midstream—at which point the flash flood reached his thighs—but despite his battle to stay upright, he lost his balance and was swept away. We all waited with bated breath, but there was next to nothing we could do to help him.

Moments later, at the point where the river widened, we stared in disbelief as a hand reached out from the swirling brown-colored water and clasped at a spread of upturned roots. Very slowly the man pulled himself upward onto the slippery bank, where he collapsed in a heap onto the marram grass above the bending river. Although we welcomed his survival and praised the fact that he would live to tell his grandchildren of this escape, we felt sorry that he had lost his bicycle and belongings. But this was soon resolved when we learned later that someone beyond the bend had grabbed the man's bike from the raging water and had returned it to him.

While this drama was unfolding, we felt a slight bump and quickly realized that a following vehicle had slid into us. It appeared that we were now boxed in on the greasy slope and there was no way out, as reversing was clearly out of the question. It was Thomas who pointed out to me that the water level was rising. Our front wheels were now fifty percent under water, but the wheel tracks on the opposite bank were still partially visible.

"What do you think of our chances?" I said to Thomas.

He surveyed the river. "Well, the way I see it," he began in a gloomy voice, "is that it's impossible to reverse. Both us and the fool behind us will end up in a ditch. However, if we wait long enough, we'll eventually slide into the river. We must also take into account that it's getting dark." He paused for a moment, removed his peak cap, lowered the window, and gave his head a good scratching with his fingers before going on. "The rushing water that's coming from the hills won't diminish for the next four hours, and that's providing it doesn't rain again. If it does, we'll have nothing to lose by trying to cross the river, but waiting here is not an answer."

He took a deep breath and looked hard at me. "Did you notice that man with the loaded bike? He got swept away when the water reached his thighs. That means if we get onto the bridge, the flood water will be no deeper than three feet. I reckon the van can cope with that, providing we have enough impetus at the start, you know, coming off the blocks like athletes do. However, the true depth of the water, if we miss the bridge, will be about eight feet, and that means we should be ready to jump out." Thomas then replaced his chauffeur's cap onto the back of his head, and strangely, in spite of our predicament, it dawned on me that he had just set something of a time record on being hatless, bearing in mind that he often slept with it on.

"Anyway, my vote is for going across," he announced.

"We'll stand no chance in that," Visavadia predicted.

"Well, we can't stay here, that's for sure," Thomas reiterated, "and remember I'm putting my job on the line. You'll be alright when you get back to Nairobi. You're a qualified salesman.'

"Right now you're the driver," I said in a loud voice, "so do I take it that your vote to cross this river is 'yes' and that this is your final decision?"

"It is," Thomas shouted back to me as the roar of the rushing water reached a new height, adding, "and as I've said before, we must get across as quickly as possible, otherwise we'll end up in it." He paused and wound up the window and wiped off the haze that had condensed on the inside of the glass. "You see the tire tracks on the far bank." He pointed, not wanting an answer. "I'm going to use them to guide us through the river and keep us in the center of the bridge. Is that OK by you?"

I nodded my agreement and then turned around toward Visavadia, who'd been sitting behind me, but he had moved and was hidden behind a wall of cartons.

Thomas had watched my movements from the corner of his eye, and as he was anxious to get started, he snapped, "Forget Vinoo. He's been outvoted anyway!"

"All right," I shouted, "let's go for it."

I leaned down and from a drawer under my seat pulled out a circlet of wiring, a pair of pliers, and a length of rubber hose. Without any delay I climbed out of the van and squelched my way to the rear. I noticed there was enough of a gap between the vehicles to get a leg through, which would enable me to carry out my task. I bent down and forced the two-inch hose over the exhaust and clipped off a length of wire, twisting it tight onto the pipe. From there I clipped off another length of wiring and fixed the rubber hose onto the rear door handle.

Once back in the van, I closed my door tight, raised my right arm and cupped a hand in a semi circle round my mouth and shouted, "Let's go."

"Then *kwenda* it is, Mr. Carter," Thomas shouted back as he turned his head toward me. His dark eyes glowed in the lights of the dashboard.

It was twilight, and it was becoming difficult to make out the tire tracks on the opposite bank. Thomas, however, had the best eyes of the three of us, and it was these tracks that would act as our lodestar and guide him into a central position on the unseen bridge. We watched in silence as a large chunk of sedge from the other bank tumbled slowly into the spate and was washed down the silt-thickened river.

"Hold tight," Thomas bawled as he clicked on the full-beam headlights and raced the engine.

"No," a young man protested from the far bank, holding a hand up as though directing Main Street traffic. But the crowd seized him by his clothes and pulled him back out of our way. Once it was clear, Thomas slipped the gear into first, gunning the engine, released the handbrake, and let the clutch out. He stared fixedly across the divide at the groove marks on the opposite bank. We then charged into the flooded channel, and the ominous sound of rushing water slapped against the paneling. It was scary to know that any deviation would end our second safari.

There was no other way out, and it was becoming obvious that we couldn't evade the issue. It had to be met head-on. Thomas had the most to lose should things go wrong. I empathized with him, knowing full well that his chance of pursuing a career as a professional driver would be dealt a severe blow should things go wrong. No prospective employer would want to employ someone who'd written off two new vehicles in the space of fourteen months.

I then heard Thomas give a gung-ho shout of "Let's go" above the roar of the engine. We were immediately blinded by a surge of water, and for what appeared to be an age, we wallowed, seemingly out of control, before we felt the thud as our front wheels came heavily down onto the paved bridge, bouncing both left and right as we raced forward and finally slotted into the deep furrows on the opposing bank. It was like a dream come true when we both felt the contact on each wheel, and we emerged from the water with the front wheels firmly slotted into the grooves on each side of the camber. We had accomplished the impossible and had safely crossed the fifteen-foot divide. The impetus had carried us safely onto the higher, drier ground beyond the waters. The crowd, larger than before, was ecstatic. They applauded and cheered our efforts, and strangely, it made us feel as though we had won a gold medal at the Olympics.

"What about that?" Thomas grinned from ear to ear and slid back the driver's door to acknowledge the applause.

"Not bad," I said with a smile.

He jerked his head sideways and jutted his chin. It was a meaningful gesture, and I followed the direction he indicated and saw that Visavadia was half-hidden behind a stack of cartons. He was kneeling and praying.

"Is everything all right?" I asked in a hushed voice.

"Yes," he replied quietly as he got off his knees.

We motored in silence back to Dar, passing the fashionable suburbs of Oyster Bay, and then turned right over the Selander Bridge.

"Don't forget to pick up that shipment at Morgans tomorrow," I reminded Thomas.

"It's on my list of things to do."

"See you both on Sunday morning," I said as I climbed from the cab outside the Sandhaven Hotel.

***

The following morning, Saturday, December 3, I got up early and went down to breakfast in the almost empty dining hall. The reason for the early start was to catch the 7:30 a.m. flight to Zanzibar.

It was here, at breakfast, that I met Marianne, the hotel owner's daughter. She was intrinsically an island girl. It showed in the way she smiled, went barefooted, and swayed her hips.

I'd seen her when I first arrived at the Sandhaven Hotel, but on that occasion our paths didn't cross. Today, however, we got to chatting as people do, and it wasn't long before she joined me at the table. She seemed quite interested in what I did, where I went, and how often I visited Africa. In between this string of questions and answers, she welcomed other guests who had entered the restaurant. She darted happily backward and forward from my table to the kitchen, making sure that everyone had full plates, toast and marmalade, and plenty of coffee before she came back to resume the conversation. It very much reminded me of the airline hostesses, who, having cared for every need of their passengers, would flop onto the next-door seat for an inspired chat about one's personal life. In Marianne's case I sensed she needed to communicate with the outside world, and any new face around the hotel, especially if male and under thirty-two, would spark her curiosity.

She suggested that she would welcome a lift to Nairobi in order to find work at one of the larger tourist hotels, mentioning that there was little future in working for her mother; she had higher ambitions. In response I told her that it was unlikely I could take her along, but I would think about it.

My taxi to the airport arrived right on time, and I made my excuses, grabbed my briefcase, and scrambled into the back seat. The flight on East African Airways had been knitted into my general itinerary. Apparently Head Office had already contacted Morgans in Dar and suggested I should cover the island's important wholesalers while I was in the area. They talked about an expanding market and how this was an ideal opportunity not to be missed to launch our products. It was no big deal, as the flight to Zanzibar was less than 30 minutes.

From the air the island appeared to be covered by a thick carpet of coconut palms broken by irregularly shaped plantations of coffee and cocoa, all of which was encircled by the green transparent waters of the Indian Ocean that sparkled under the morning sun. The fifty-mile flight was soon ended as we touched smoothly down on the short, rolling runway of Zanzibar's only airport. Minutes later I was being whisked by taxi to the town center. We passed underneath an unbroken archway of royal palms, their slim bare trunks of light brown, never vertical, leaning criss-crossed, with streaks of filtered sunlight slanting through the foliage. Under the trees there was emptiness except for a few scattered grass huts.

A motor vehicle hummed in the distance, and the taxi driver concentrated on the narrow roadway, half expecting to see an approaching vehicle around every curve of the shut-in road. And then it was in front of us, big and menacing, making low rattling sounds as it passed. It was the first vehicle we had seen since leaving the airport.

Soon we were out of the trees and in the openness, passing large estates of cinnamon, coffee, and cocoa that I had seen from the air. There were neatly lined orchards of gray-barked clove trees on one side of the road, and the pungent aroma from the ripening buds filled the sultry air. The land was becoming broken and we began to pass more vehicles, and suddenly the highway was full of cyclists and pedestrians. We slowed and went down narrow, tortuous streets, rarely penetrated by the sun and flanked by tall houses with galleried floors at the very top. They were shuttered from behind by perforated wood gratings so that you could see into the street without yourself being seen. The sound of car horns echoed off the walls, drowning other noises.

"You want to get off here?" the driver asked over his shoulder. He had drawn to a halt by the crowded fruit market.

"Yes, this will do," I agreed, and handed him a ten-shilling note, and rather grandly told him to keep the change. I suppose I felt human for a change without the van with its speakers to dent my feeling of well-being, although working on my own I felt vulnerable and missed my two colleagues.

I started to walk toward the narrow, cobbled lanes of the old city, with its tightly built shops running in parallel lines on both sides of the street. I went by the ancient slave market where they had their auctions, and, like any tourist, I began to look into the windows of the little shops. They offered ivory carvings, spiced pomanders, sculptured chests, and engraved silverwork seemingly unchanged since Livingstone made his home here some ninety years before. There was still the splendor of the old palaces of Maruhubi and Kibweni. On many of the Arab houses were massive front doors—African wood carved in floral and geometrical designs with great bronze locks and handles covered in decorative arabesques—and in the indirect reflected light you could feel the melancholy of this civilization cutting across the time barrier. Even the enormous dhows and smaller feluccas that were moored in the picturesque harbor, fresh from desert ports, brought a sense of permanency to the island.

It was sad to think that this was the world center for slavery until it was abolished in 1897. It was here that the chained and exhausted slaves arrived from their long treks across the African continent. They were then washed, perfumed, and adorned with gold necklaces, ostrich feathers, and turbans. Then, once sold, they would be stripped of ornaments and dragged away on ropes by their new masters. It should be remembered that the Arab merchants had actively collaborated with African chiefs who bartered their own people for beads, firearms, and copper wire.

I had difficulty making my calls on the retailers and wholesalers, not only because the streets were unlabeled, but all the time I was besieged by sellers of sweetmeats and coffee. It was while I was drinking a cup of Turkish coffee on a street corner that I was approached by a small boy, no more than ten, who offered to act as a guide. He also claimed the right to be my interpreter and keep other small boys and girls away from me while I made my visits. A price of twenty shillings was agreed, provided I kept him supplied with food and drink for the duration of the contract, in other words, until four o'clock in the afternoon. We spent the next two hours working the center of the city, and then we broke off for lunch. Enos, for that was his name, led me up a twisting stony alleyway, which emerged onto an open compound outside the walled garden of the Zanzibar Hotel.

"See you in one hour, mister," Enos said.

As I stepped through the doorway, I could hear the ringing tones of the lunch gong. I first went to the cloakroom and then headed for the darkened circular bar.

The hotel was of three stories and formed part of a one-time sultan's guesthouse. Inside, there was an attractive lounge, darkened by low ceilings spiked with ancient ant-proof mangrove poles. The Arab decor gave seclusion from the teeming, humid world outside its walls. I ordered a glass of iced beer, walked into the hallway, and crossed over to an adjoining dining room. It was long, narrow, and had facing tables on each side.

Exactly an hour later I stepped from the darkened interior of the hotel into the glare of the early afternoon sun.

"Hello, mister," Enos greeted me as he uncurled himself from the dusty stairway.

Our afternoon sales visits covered yet more ground as we slowly weaved our way through the maze of winding streets in the Arab quarter, and, at exactly four o'clock, we emerged onto a broad opening that lay between the edge of the town's buildings and the stretching line of the coast.

I thanked Enos for his help and paid him off in silver coins. I added an extra five shillings, as he had only soft drinks and no food.

"See you, mister." He smiled and was soon lost in the crowd.

I wandered across the road toward the white-sandy beach, where the sea lapped idly against the glistening rocks that lined the promenade. I watched some pink crabs scrambling among the stones while I sat by the water's edge and smoked a cigarette. It seemed odd that this idyllic island had no wildlife but its merchants had a thriving trade in elephant tusks, colobus skins, and heads of duiker antelopes to erect on the walls of tourists' drawing rooms.

***

It was dark by the time the DC3 landed back at Dar's International Airport. I took a taxi to the Sandhaven Hotel and spent the first hour filing a report on Zanzibar. I also included several confirmed orders for our medicines, toiletries, and disinfectants. It was always the same when I completed my paperwork—a huge sense of relief swept over me.

It was Saturday night, and I was ready to relax. After supper I went to the lounge bar and joined the Saturday night people. It was all happening—live music, laughter, drinking, and dancing.

I found an empty stool at the end of the bar. The large room had a worn look. The salt air had bleached the color of the furnishings, faded the curtains, and blanched the woodwork. However, nothing could detract from the party atmosphere.

"Hello, John." It was Marianne who popped up behind the bar. She gave me a large smile and asked if she could fix me a drink.

"I'll have a rum and ginger on the rocks, please."

"On the rocks?" she asked.

"What do you think?"

"I thought the English liked their drinks warm!"

"I'm one who doesn't," I explained with a laugh.

"What about tomorrow?" She leaned across the counter and put my drink on a coaster.

"You're talking about that lift to Nairobi. Well, I've given it a lot of thought, and I'm sorry but I can't do it. It's just not on. I've got another three weeks in the bush before I reach Nairobi." I paused to have a drink, swirling the ice cubes round the top of the glass with my forefinger. "Why can't you go by train?"

"Because I think it would be exciting to go with you," she cooed, reaching for my hand and laughing playfully. "I can make myself useful, you know."

"I know you would." I smiled back. "But we don't have enough room in the vehicle."

"I gave it my best shot," she said bravely. "It can't be said I didn't try." A look of disappointment crossed her lovely face.

"Let's have a dance," I suggested.

"Why not," she purred.

She slipped away from the bar and quickly joined me on the small parquet floor. It was less bright. The light bulbs on the four walls had been dimmed, and deep shadows no longer ran across the room. Marianne pressed her body against my chocolate-and-yellow native shirt. She wasn't wearing a bra.

"Can I come and see you tonight?" she asked, adding, "It's important, John."

I paused and said nothing. Instead I guided her from the dance floor to a cushioned sofa outside on the loggia. The blues music drifted from the bar and was clearly audible, and I could feel her shivering while I held her around the waist.

"What's wrong, Marianne?" I asked anxiously.

"I'm just being silly," she murmured into my ear. "It's because you are going tomorrow, and although I hardly know you, I wished I could come with you." She paused to catch her breath. "I'm all right really," she added wistfully.

"Why not come up to my room later and we'll have a chat?"

"Yes, I will," she said and smiled.

"I think you'd better go now," I said. "Your mother was giving us some worried glances when we were dancing."

We stood up and walked away from the sofa and reentered the lounge. By now the music had died away and there was a rush of people around the bar.

"See you," Marianne whispered.

It was past two o'clock when I heard the sound of muffled tapping on the bedroom door. There was a shaft of light from the corridor, and Marianne quickly tiptoed into the room and shut the door behind her. "It's me," she said in a low voice, throwing off her cotton pajamas and slipping soundlessly into the bed, her young body both warm and inviting as she pressed hard against me. I could feel her heart pounding.

We made love in the semi-darkness of the little room. The rustle of palm trees could be heard through the open slats of the Venetian blinds, but sometimes they were drowned by intermittent waves that lapped harmlessly against the sand bank of the lagoon that ran down the side of the hotel.

For a while we said nothing, content to lie in each other's arms. Then Marianne started to tell me about herself. She was born in the Seychelles. Her father, a British citizen, died in a boating accident when she was barely ten. And with the meager insurance money paid by his employers, her mother brought her and her sister to Tanganyika and took a twenty-year mortgage on the Sandhaven Hotel. "I can't stand it here much longer," Marianne pined. "Nothing interesting ever happens, and I can see my life draining away before it has ever got off the ground. I'll do anything to get away from this place."

"You've got plenty of time," I reassured. "I wouldn't be in too much of a hurry. There's your mother and sister to think about. Surely they need you here?"

She propped herself on a pillow and looked straight into my face. "My younger sister is happy here," she said, "and besides, my mother has always said that she wants me to be independent and free, so please, John, tell me what I should do?"

The intensity of her soul-searching made me feel that I held the responsibility of Marianne's future in the palm of my hand.

For an eternity we said nothing until I finally broke the silence. "I'll tell you what," I said, suddenly inspired. "I've got a friend, Andy Sevvides, who runs the Montagu Hotel in Nairobi. It's always full of interesting people from all over the world. I could put a word in for you when I get back to Kenya. How would that be?"

"Oh, would you do that for me?" She smiled as a tear streaked down her lovely face.

"Yes, of course I will," I replied.

"You're not just saying that, John?"

"The moment I get to Nairobi I'll call him. That's a promise."

Marianne rolled onto her back and stretched her arms. "I'll stay here until I hear from you," she said. Her head lay on the soft pillow, slightly angled, eyes watching. "You do mean it, don't you, John?"

"Of course I do," I repeated.

I leaned over her and kissed her again. Her lips were both inviting and demanding as I ran my hand over her curving body, the brown skin like coffee and cream, the breasts tantalizingly perfect, firm and pointed, as though carved in marble.

She stretched again, and I could feel her legs reaching out under the light cover, brushing against my body as she turned onto her side. Her glossy pink lips gradually parted and she ran her moist tongue under the rim of her white, even teeth. "John," she cooed, "may I ask one more question?"

"I don't see why not." I laughed, pulling her close and kissing her lovely searching mouth. Everything about her was a mixture of invitation and demand.

For several seconds she fell silent before finally opening her heart. "Please," she began, "spend New Year with me if I get to Nairobi."

"I'd love to, but I'll be in London getting ready for my next trip."

"John," she breathed quietly into my ear.

"Yes."

"Make love to me again...."

She pressed hard with her hips as her voice trailed away. Her breathing got heavier, and once again we found each other in this darkened room. Only the creaking bed and the slanting moonlight through half-closed curtains bore witness to our loving.

At ten a.m. the next morning, we stood outside the hotel in the shade of the lone tulip tree.

"You won't forget about your promise?"

"I give you my word."

The engine of the transit van pulsed in monotonous regularity a discreet distance away from the entrance. Marianne stood on her toes, with her arms around my neck and her head on my shoulders.

"I wished you weren't going," she implored.

"I must," I said, and ran my hand down her long auburn hair and kissed her for the last time. It was almost impossible for me to let her go. Everything about her was irresistible, all the way down to the very perfume she wore. Reluctantly, I released her and walked across the lawn toward the van. I climbed in, turned, and waved good-bye.

"Good-bye," she croaked, biting back tears. She stood alone under the tulip tree with its green and yellow flowers.

Thomas revved the motor and let the clutch out. "Where to?" He smiled as he turned from the driveway onto the road, shifting gears as he wrestled with the steering on loose gravel.

"Back to Morogoro," I said, "and then cut north to Mvomero."

"No problem."

"By the way, did you get the bread and milk this morning that I put down on the shopping list?"

"What do you think?" he said with a grin.

"What about the shipment from Morgans?"

"It's there right behind you."

chapter

TWENTY-ONE

The buzz of the van's engine droned remorselessly onward. The black-tarred road extended straight ahead to the distant horizon as it cut between two lakes. The lakes were magnificent, shimmering in the sunlight, mirroring the sky and lending coolness to the landscape, always an open invitation to those whose eyes took it in. But of course it wasn't real, just a verisimilitude, a mirage perhaps, for the traveler to enjoy. Only the sound of tires and the straight macadam road was real. Nonetheless, the play of sunlight on the open fields produced a feeling of well-being.

The highway was reasonably easy, and traffic was still light as our speed of fifty miles per hour remained constant. We covered the 120-mile journey to Morogoro in less than three hours. The town was considerably quieter than when we first arrived some six days earlier, and today's date, Sunday, December 4, was the reason for shops being closed. After a short break for a cup of tea and a beef sandwich each—by courtesy of Marianne—we pressed ahead with our journey, turning right at the top of town and forking northwest for the trading center of Mvomero, some forty-five miles farther on.

We began to make short stopovers at the villages that were located on each side of the dirt tracks that branched off the main road. These isolated settlements had corner posts to mark out their unfenced plots of land. Despite the poor soil that lacked nutrients, they still managed to produce the essential crops for struggling farmers, such as beans, maize, and cassava. It was difficult to get back into our stride after the comforts of the coast—discounting the flooded Mbweni River—and by the time we arrived in Mvomero, we had had enough. It wasn't yet four o'clock.

We found a camping site, not more than two hundred yards from the main road but hidden from view by a screen of wild pomegranate trees. It was a struggle to drive the van over the rough scrub that separated the road from trees. But when we pulled to a halt, it was worth the trouble. We were now totally secluded from the road, and everyone else for that matter.

Thomas cut down three golden pomegranates from a nearby tree, and, despite the tartness of its crimson pulp and many seeds, it made a good starter for our planned meal of minced beef and onions with rice. After we'd finished and had a mug of coffee, we spent an hour huddled around the open wood fire, chatting about our hopes for the future. Despite the banter, Thomas chipped away at one of our staves with his sheath knife, marking it out in feet and inches.

"What's that for?" I asked.

"Nothing really, but after the troubles we had at Bagamoyo, I thought it might come in handy should we need to measure the height of water again." For a moment he stopped working on the stave and chucked some wood on the fire. "After all," he added, "it was you who said that 'chance favors a prepared mind.'"

***

The next morning, Monday, December 5, we changed direction and headed northeast, toward a small town called Handeni. It was our day's destination and was clearly marked on the map as a ninety-mile journey. The land began to slope as we left Mvomero. The road twisted and turned, and the view gradually became more extensive. On our left was the 7,000-foot range of the Nguru Mountains, covered in thick layers of tropical forests. We noticed that the white-barked trunks were festooned with the funguslike liana plants, and not far ahead, on the other side the forest, the trees mapped out the course of the Rusange River. Three miles on, the road no longer twisted but ran beside the river, where water roared over stones. For some of the time we were close to the river, before turning away and then joining again. There were now people on terraced paths, and the mountains no longer bounded the view. Instead they were lost behind the haziness in the distance. Then there were more people within compounds, doing chores, such as fetching water and wood and tending small plots of vegetation that surrounded their mud-bricked houses from which smoke rose. We stopped often during our drive and gave as many shows as were needed at some strange-sounding places, such as Turian, Lusonge, Nega, Rugaga, and Mkonje.

"Leopard men operate in this area," Thomas cheerfully opened the conversation. The pressing heat and our unbroken activity at the villages had dulled our desire to talk. But now Thomas had dived into the deep end by referring to the murders of schoolchildren by men dressed in leopard skins. They'd imitate the animals and claw their victims to death and eat the warm livers to inherit power.

"Typical of Thomas," Visavadia commented as he raised his head from a book.

"Why is Vinoo always ready to pick to pieces anything I say?" Thomas growled and looked my way for an answer.

"I don't think he criticizes you any more than you do him," I said, "but anyway, let's drop this subject for the time being."

The afternoon sun struck the windshield, and an elongated shadow of our van stalked us on the right side. The light was yellow, and dust billowed upward as we skimmed the sandy road and passed farm houses that bordered unfenced pastures. For some time the land had been getting broken, and we now saw a cluster of huts and then the emergence of small concrete buildings where pathways began to meet the road and a simple road sign pointed to Handeni.

"We're here," Thomas announced, as he slowed to avoid groups of cyclists, and we headed into the main center of the town. Soon there were small pockets of children who waved at us from the roadside. We had noticed while driving along how observant children would become. They would single us out from a distance. Our vehicle was bright and sparkling and visually different from the usual humdrum traffic. We always had a crowd even before

Visavadia had stirred from his book and put a record on the turntable. Occasionally we entered a town with the music playing, and in such cases we would trawl half the population along with us. Whatever our methods, we would always, without exception, treat the people with utmost respect.

"Stop and ask someone if they know where the rest house is," I told Thomas.

And while he was busy trying to find out who'd gotten the keys to the rest house, I felt a tap on my shoulder. "What are our chances of getting back to Nairobi for Christmas?" The question had been on Visavadia's lips for some time, and he was anxious to keep his wife and children informed as to when he might be home. He'd been through a tough safari and had every right to have an honest answer to his question.

"I would say our chances are good," I reassured him, "but that's provided we don't get held up by any unexpected delay."

I too had a personal reason for wanting to get back before Christmas. I had an abscessed tooth that bothered me, and I was hoping to get an appointment with a dentist before the office closed down for the holiday period.

***

We left Handeni the next morning on completion of our promotional work, and headed in a northeasterly direction toward the important railway town of Korogwe. It was a short journey of forty-four miles, half of yesterday's distance, and we were on an easier road. This time we made no more than two stops en route, at the crossroad villages of Chanumbi and Sindeni, and arrived at Korogwe in the early afternoon. This left us sufficient time to mount a series of short shows throughout the commercial area of the town, including the customary calls on Asian and African retailers before dusk.

Because we had completed the whole of our work program in Korogwe by late afternoon, we were up early the next morning in readiness for the sixty-mile trip due east to the port of Tanga. The road we took was straight and, for a good part of the way, was lined on each side with tall, sharp-pointed sisal plants. The blue-green of their stiff leaves stretched to the horizon. Once again we made two stops, at the roadside villages of Mnyus and Muheza, before reaching our destination. We could hear Tanga's church clock chiming four as we motored through the center of the densely packed town.

We dropped Visavadia in front of a large concrete-and-timber store with the name Solkar and Company written on a board above the front entrance.

"He always seems to know who's going to have him," Thomas observed as Visavadia bounced off the van and disappeared into the dim interior of the building.

"I can't make it out either."

"Perhaps Vinoo's some sort of religious leader," Thomas aired. "If so, that would explain his acceptance wherever he goes."

"Don't look at me," I said with a smile. "I couldn't agree with you more. He's definitely something of a dark horse."

"Maybe he's a guru or something?"

"He's a good, decent man, and that's all I need to know."

"Where to now?" Thomas asked, switching the topic.

"The first hotel we come to," I responded.

We made a tight circle in the crowded street and drove along Hospital Road, eventually stopping outside the Palm Court Hotel. It had the long, gloomy windows of the German colonial days. There was no one in reception when I entered, and what with the cement floors and the minimum of furnishing in a bare lobby, I decided I wasn't going to stay. Luckily Thomas hadn't yet completed his three-point turn in the narrow street.

"What's up?" he asked as I hoisted myself back into the cab.

"It's one of those Spartan German places."

"You did say the first hotel," he reminded me, before adding, "I always thought that a roof over your head was good enough?" Thomas slapped the side of his leg and started to laugh, leaving me uncertain as to what the joke was about.

"Try the Tanga Hotel," I said, leafing through a guidebook. "It's on Eckenforde Avenue, which leads toward the sea." I looked straight ahead and pretended to ignore Thomas's laughter.

"Where's that?"

"Don't ask me," I said, turning my head and adding, "You're the driver!"

Ten minutes later we were outside the second hotel.

"How long are we going to stay in Tanga?"

"It's Wednesday today," I paused, studying a typed copy of the itinerary "and we'll leave next Sunday. That'll give us four nights here." I put the papers away and pulled my suitcase, typewriter, and briefcase out from the back seat. "Do you realize we are running exactly two weeks behind the schedule that we had worked out before leaving Nairobi?"

"They'll probably think we took a holiday."

"Before you pick me up tomorrow, I want you to get hold of Visavadia and load that shipment of twenty gross each of Herbalex and Gripe Aid from the bus depot. I also want you to check the post office for any mail. You can take an extra hour before we meet up tomorrow morning, OK?"

"Sure thing," Thomas agreed. "I'll see you at ten." He slipped the vehicle into low gear and drew quickly away from the curb.

I checked into the hotel, but before going to my room I sat out on the downstairs patio and had a cup of tea. The blueness of the sky was all pervading, stretching beyond the ornamental palms on the promenade and the ocean behind, as though waiting to gift wrap the wondrous scene. The gray shape of a British warship lay at anchor in the ampleness of the bay.

Tanga was the very heart of the vast sisal-growing region. But statistically it was also Tanganyika's second-largest town and port, outside Dar. The word *Tanga* in the Swahili language simply means "light." From the commercial point of view, the town is well situated and boasts a large number of African and Asian shops and small businesses.

Back in 1896 the Germans laid the first railway tracks from Tanga to connect with the important commercial center of Moshi, some 250 miles to the northwest. The Germans also constructed several spacious two-story buildings in the colonial style of the era, and in 1889 they erected a monument in the local park to commemorate the visit of *VSMS Leipzig* to the port of Tanga. Later, during World War One, *HMS Fox* arrived in the bay in November 1914 and demanded the surrender of the German garrison, but it was met with a rebuff. The thick bush, mosquitoes, leeches, and the persistence of the tse-tse fly proved too much for the incursive landing parties from the ship, and the invasion was subsequently called off.

While sitting in the hotel patio, I searched the esplanade with my eyes. It jogged my memory about other places and other times. The view was great and was equal to the walk along the promenade at Cannes. The baking sun was there, the palms, the lapping water, and the strolling crowds.

Some four years earlier, I had been staying at the Polano Hotel in Lourenco Marques on Africa's southeast coast. At that time I was on a whistle-stop sales tour of the southern region, trying to drum up business for our products. Anyway, I was having a drink in the hotel's cocktail bar when I got chatting with a Portuguese guy called Chris Douro. He was talking about life on his boat, a converted schooner, and how he plied his trade up and down the coastal ports that hugged the East African shoreline along the Indian Ocean.

Apparently he undertook some very lucrative commissions with Arab dhows moored at Zanzibar. Exactly what he bartered with them, I haven't a clue. It was safer not to ask. The long and the short of it was a casual invitation to a party he was throwing on his boat the following night. Chris drew a sketch on the back of a paper napkin as to where his boat was moored.

I went to the party and had a great time with a load of fun people. There was a live sextet that Chris had hired for the night from one of the city's ornate brothels. It was a wild night, and the partying went on until dawn.

When I left the ship, the sun had already climbed into the sky, and I searched for Chris to thank him for the invitation.

"Maybe we'll meet up again," he said, "and after all, we are both travelers."

We shook hands.

Unfortunately the story doesn't end there. I went back to Mozambique two years later and met up with his girlfriend. She told me he had gone off on one of his trips up the coast and had been reported missing by the harbor authorities.

"How do you mean *missing?*" I had said.

She went on to explain that he was last seen alive in Tanga. Apparently a friend of his had spotted him. He had been strolling down the very palm-lined promenade that fronted the sea where I was now. He had been in deep conversation with two bearded Arab men in djellbahs. But unusually for him, he looked stressed. A week later his schooner was scuttled off the island of Pemba. It was reported in the local paper that an internecine force of rival privateers had torched his boat because it was trading on their ground. The article stated that Chris and three crewmates were missing, presumed drowned.

***

Four day's after our arrival, on Sunday, December 11, we drove for the last time down the palm-lined promenade of Tanga, catching final glimpses of the white-spumed waters of the Indian Ocean. During our time here we had kept to our certified itinerary, which included about sixty visits to retailers and wholesalers, including a call at the coastal resort of Moa on the Kenyan border, some forty miles south of Mombasa.

We all felt sad to be leaving Tanga. It wasn't yet nine o'clock, and the boulevard was more or less empty of people. A long garden with friendly wooden benches separated the southern end of the boulevard from the sea. We slowed down to take a roundabout, covered with short grass and pretty flower beds, and from here the road curved away from the town. At the end of Market Street we turned left and cut inland, heading sixty miles due west, back tracking to Korogwe. We went past small groups of somberly dressed people on their way to the Anglican churches.

It was noon by the time we arrived in Korogwe. We broke off for an hour's luncheon and then pressed on with our journey, making a right turn at the main junction and going directly north, the next major destination being Moshi. Some two hundred miles of tortuous dirt roads lay ahead of us. The blinding openness of the sea was replaced by bright woodland, which extended to the distant Usambara Mountains that bounded the eastern horizon. This scenic view was hardly visible through the onset of a deepening haze and wispy clouds. Also gone was the heavy humidity of the coast, and that too was replaced by the milder, semitemperate conditions of the higher inland regions. From the doorway of the vehicle, we caught sight of the Usambara's highest point, the Chambolo Peak at 7,557 feet, referred to locally as *Jiwe wa Mungo*, or "Stone of God." This entire sixty-five-mile range of mountains is well-known as the Switzerland of Tanganyika. Some way on, hidden behind forests and sheltered from winds, were vast acres of tea, thriving on well drained acid soils amid the slopes and high valleys of the Usambaras. The vivid green bushes sparkled in these rainwashed areas.

We gave a show at the small railway town of Mombo, situated twenty-seven miles farther on from Korogwe. After closing down we turned right, heading toward our night stopover at a place called Lushoto. We couldn't avoid climbing the steep slopes that ran along the golden valleys, which were overgrown with a mix of cedars and eucalyptus trees on each side of the rocky track. Every so often we passed wide grassy fields that were being worked by the local Sambaa people. They looked up and responded to our waving by shouting friendly greetings. We noticed that the most primitive of tools were being used to cultivate the terraces, while on one occasion we saw a pair of water buffalo tilling a flat stretch of ground. Finally, after another twenty miles of narrow trackway, we emerged into the open countryside, with unlimited acres of wild colorful flowers.

Lushoto was spread across the floor of this high valley and was gateway to the Usambara Mountains. Lying twelve miles to the north were clear views of Chasbolo Peak, which was encircled, halfway down, by a belt of dense cedar forests.

Since leaving the highway at the crossroads town of Mombo, we had climbed over three thousand feet. The total distance we had traveled from our morning's starting point at Tanga was 107 miles. Lushoto was originally a German military outpost, and even today the Lawns Hotel with its musty smell, threadbare furnishings, and peeling walls retained some of the pioneer flavor from those earlier colonial days.

The next morning, Monday, December 12, we continued our journey to the north, and despite the distance we had traveled, we still had the Usambara Mountains bounding along on one side. Their panoramic view led the eye effortlessly upward. Since yesterday the road hadn't ceased its steady climb, and the entire time valley gave way to valley; the higher we went the lighter it became. Every so often we caught sight of dark trees lining out the course of rivers, and occasionally the road ran with the river and unexpectedly twisted across by means of a ford. Rivers, such as the Vuruni and the Mkumbara, with their multiple sidestreams teemed with brown and rainbow trout.

The view on the other side of the road was less abrupt. We passed gentle, open-wooded slopes of golden wattle trees. The farmers cultivated them from seed solely for the tannic substances of their bark. For would-be entrepreneurs, there's a waiting time of twelve years before they're ready for harvesting.

At a distance of thirty miles from Mombo the road swept right, curving around the southernmost reaches of the Pare Mountains, signifying that we were now out of the Usambara Range. Once again we stopped to give a show, this time at a place named Buikoi. There was a crowd of only twenty people, but this did not deter us from giving a full half-hour show, and we managed to sell thirteen bottles, which prompted Visavadia to make a gloomy prediction while writing up the sales ledger. He reckoned the poor sales since leaving Tanga was a sure sign that we would have to extend our arrival date in Nairobi until after Christmas. He based his theorizing on the fact that our sense of pride would prevent us from taking back unsold goods to Nairobi. Anyway, to allay his fears, we put on another record and reopened the rear doors. In the end it took us another ten minutes to sell two more bottles before he was satisfied that it was safe to continue the safari.

For several miles the road flattened and ran parallel with the semidesert regions of the Mkomazi Game Reserve, which, in turn, was linked with the Tsavo National Park across the border in Kenya. While we were having a break and something to eat, we spotted a family of brown mongooses furrowing under some thorny scrub searching for sand snakes or lizards. Apparently they kill snakes by biting their heads off. The extraordinary thing about them is that they make good pets. They were still busy working away under the bushes as we packed our plates and assorted kitchenware and climbed back into the van.

A few miles farther on we stopped at the village of Kisiwani, and launched a thirty-minute show to an audience of about sixty people. The sun was now on the horizon, and vast splashes of yellow light bathed the face of the mountains. Then, after closing down, we made tracks northward—some twenty miles—toward the important trading center of Same.

It was Thomas, our unpaid weatherman, who broke the silence by commenting that dark clouds, low in the sky, were racing inland from the east and that a cool wind was picking up. "It's a sure sign we're in for another storm," he warned.

We had by now bypassed the majestic South Pare Mountains over to the west, while at the same time we had said good-bye to the rolling hills and yellow deserts of the Mkomazi Game Reserve.

It was getting darker, and Thomas switched on the headlights.

chapter

TWENTY-TWO

Twilight had given way to dusk by the time we entered the trading center of Same, pronounced locally as Saa-May.

Above us, black cumulus clouds raced low in the sky, and the last of any light had faded from fields and houses. When the rain came, it was heavy, drowning the engine of the van. We drove straight into the center of the village and quickly located the police station. The bare compound outside was ringed with white-washed stones set at intervals. There was a tall flagpole. The Union Jack was no longer crisp, but limp and dark with rain. The freshly raked flower beds that ran parallel with the concrete building were dotted with yellow gardenia and cinchona shrubs. A solitary flame tree stood dripping gloomily by the perimeter fence. It seemed as though we had arrived in limbo land, and that Same was the frontier separating the rugged savanna of scrub and greasy cotton soil tracks from the more sophisticated cities in the north.

When the duty officer at the station desk handed over the key to the rest house, he asked for a signature in his rental book. He also issued a receipt for the fifteen shillings that we had to pay for one night's stay for the three of us. Even these petty formalities indicated that our days of freewheeling in the bush were numbered and that we had indeed reached the outer suburbs of civilization.

It didn't stop raining all night. The corrugated roof of the brick bungalow echoed to the storm, and, in spite of the drumming, which kept us awake, we were grateful to be in the dry. Strangely, after eventually falling asleep, we woke up to a brilliant day, with the sun climbing steeply into a clear blue sky. As soon as breakfast was over, we walked the hundred yards down the empty street to hand back the rest house key. We were anxious to be on our way to Moshi, some sixty-six miles to the northwest. It was already Tuesday, December 13, and I owed it to Thomas and Visavadia to get them back to their families by Christmas. They had been very loyal to me and had carried out all their duties without any real word of complaint. I also owed them a debt of gratitude after their help at Gulu on our first safari.

The village of Same was situated between the North and South sections of the Pare Mountains, which are divided by the Ngulu Pass. Since leaving Kisiwani yesterday afternoon we had driven past the South Pare Mountains and were now at this half-way point.

"I'm afraid you can't leave Same," the officer said as we trailed into his office to hand in the spare key. On hearing this startling bit of news, we automatically grouped around his desk.

"Why, what's the problem?" I responded.

"The rivers have flooded the savanna between here and Himo. The whole area is one big lake, and there's no way through for anyone journeying north to Moshi."

"How long do you expect this flooding to last?" I asked.

"Well," he said, shutting his eyes momentarily and sighing, "if it doesn't rain any more, it could be a week, could be two, your guess is as good as mine. The Public Works Department will inform us when it's safe to let traffic on the North Pare Road. We have already erected barriers across the highway, and they will stay there until the department advises us otherwise."

"Two weeks!" I said in disbelief.

"That's correct," the officer confirmed, his eyes once again open.

"In that case we'd better book for another night at the rest house," I said in an effort to pacify him, and suggested that by tomorrow we'll get a better idea of what's going on.

"You don't have a choice," the officer said dryly, handing back the key. "That'll be another fifteen shillings, please."

After leaving the police station, we turned left at the compound gates, having decided take a look at the floods. We walked to the end of the main street to the juncture where the road opened up, and now, without the restriction of a built-up area, we had a clear view. There was a wide borderland of scrub that stretched in every direction until it was swallowed up by the flat, endless floodwater. We were looking at one enormous lake that spread out toward the horizon and became indistinguishable from the sky. It was the light and the openness of the dark lake that surprised us. Some 150 yards away, we saw the red-and-white barrier that the policeman had talked about.

Sitting close to the barrier, on an upturned box, was an old man in a long khaki overcoat bearing a clasp of World War II medals. We exchanged greetings the African way and stared disconsolately down the road to the point where the sky dipped below the edge of the lake.

"How deep is it out there?" I said casually to the *mzee*.

"About two or three feet, I reckon."

There was stillness in the air. The sky was high and blue with the merest wisp of white cloud.

The old man, having given his answer, lapsed back into silence, almost comatose, and yet, every now and then, he punctuated the quietness with deep-throated humming sounds so often heard in the African bush.

"What about the road?" I pressed. "Isn't it built on an embankment?" I was aware that most roads in East Africa were strengthened in known swamp areas, either by a causeway or an embanked road. However, I needed some sort of confirmation on the route going to Moshi.

The *mzee* slowly lifted an arm to shield his eyes from the sun. "Yes," he agreed, "it's an embanked road." He gave off a deep hum, and then added, "I wouldn't think the water was more than two feet deep on the actual road." Once again he closed his eyes and lapsed into silence, although still communicating with us by using low humming sounds.

"Then we should be able to go through," I persisted. "Our vehicle is especially adapted for these conditions with a high chassis."

"Nothing is allowed through, whatever vehicle you drive," the old man countered, "and anyway, it's impossible to see the outline of the road beneath the murky water."

"Someone could walk ahead with a stick?"

"Not for the full fifty miles it takes to get to Himo," he said. "It's not a straight road and in some parts could be impassable."

We thanked the *mzee* and walked the two hundred yards back to the rest house, re-passing the police station on our right side. "There goes Christmas," Thomas grumbled.

Later, after an early lunch, we killed time by giving a series of shows up and down the main street. The high life music was played continuously. And regrettably the afternoon peace in Same was getting disturbed. We didn't like using our hardware to the disadvantage of local residents, but having taken a unanimous vote we decided it was worth the risk. It might prompt the police into letting us leave for Moshi, which was the next major stopping point on our itinerary should we first make it to Himo. Instead it had the opposite effect. We were approached by a constable and informed that unless we called off our activities, we would be arrested for disturbing the peace. All this was a strange phenomenon when compared with people in the countryside, who couldn't get enough of our music and listened attentively to all our announcements coming to them over the loud-speaker. However, Same was the head quarters of the Pare District, with the advantage of having its own police force, hospital, and rail junction, all of which went hand in hand with the self-importance of any satellite town. Anyway, this threat was an empty one, as it was getting dark and we were already playing our closing record.

***

"It's my guess that no one will be manning the exit barrier tonight," I told Thomas while we carried out a preliminary survey of the exit road leading north. For the second time, we started to walk toward the 150 yards to the red-and-white barrier.

Everything was silent, except for the distant barking of a lone dog and the hushed sound of our footsteps, which were muffled in thick trainers. The sky was clear, the moon bright, and the heavens dotted with stars, but this idyllic scene was soon to be tempered by a further gathering of low clouds approaching from the east.

We pressed on with our walk and stopped at the red-and-white barrier. This time the old man had gone, and there was no replacement. The unending blackness that had descended on the lake was ominous, and yet, despite the difficulties facing us, I felt in a positive mood. The luminous dial on my wrist watch showed the time at 12:45 a.m. and the date as Wednesday, December 14. We had now begun our third day in Same, a place that we would not normally have stopped in for more than an hour or two.

I turned away from the waters and looked deep into Thomas's face. "Are you willing to make a run for it?" I asked in a quiet voice. "The conditions are good, and I doubt we'll get the chance again. By the look of things, we could well be here for another three or four weeks."

"You mean now?" Thomas gasped.

"Yes, of course," I said. "It won't take us more than forty minutes to get ready and pack our things. What do you say?"

For several seconds he held his breath, giving himself time to absorb the enormity of my suggestion. "Well," he said, taking great care to measure his words, "if it means we get home before Christmas, then let's do it."

"That's good," I replied.

"And by the way, don't forget to attach the hose to the exhaust," Thomas smiled, adding, "I've got my stave ready."

We walked with purpose as we made our way back to the rest house. The sides of the road widened as we neared the outskirts of the town, and everywhere we looked was shrouded in semi-darkness. The only exception was a dim window light shining from a tarnished villa set within a tangled garden.

"Remember," I said, "don't use the van lights, and keep quiet when we leave. We'll have to push the van as far as the waterline before we risk starting the engine. OK?"

"Yes," Thomas hummed his agreement as he matched strides.

I took a last glance up and down the road before walking down the gritted driveway toward the rest house.

"What's Vinoo going to say to all this?"

"He's already agreed," I said.

"I don't believe you!" Thomas exclaimed.

"No, it's true," I murmured. "I had a chat with him earlier when you were having a shower, and he's champing at the bit to get started. However, he did add a word of caution and said he would come only if you voted yes."

"It shows he has faith in me," he commented.

Less than an hour later, at one thirty-five a.m., we were ready to go. The hollow howl of yet another dog sounded surreal when set against the quietness of the town. We pushed and shoved the van along the flat street, passing the uninhabited police station with its neat flower gardens and white blancoed stones. The tall flag pole was empty. There were a few more darkened shops, a set of tightly built houses, and the villa with the tangled garden, which no longer showed a light.

Gradually the road began to slope, and Thomas jumped into the driver's seat as the van picked up momentum. With relief we gave up the pushing and let it free wheel. We were soon out of town and on the narrow track that was bordered on each side with scuffed shoulders. Each second that passed we gathered speed, and Thomas touched the brake pedal as we neared the unmanned barrier.

The moon had unexpectantly broken free of the cumulus cloud, and the whole area suddenly lit up. It was as though we had come under a powerful spot light.

This worried Visavadia as he climbed down from the van. "Everyone's going to see me," he said.

"Of course they can't," Thomas said huskily. "Just stop worrying and get on with your job. Think of the family, Vinoo."

Visavadia went forward and lifted the thick red-and-white horizontal pole from its forked support. We quietly pushed the van through the opening and waited silently while Visavadia lowered the pole to its original position then quickly climbed back into the vehicle. Thomas released the handbrake and let it roll forward on the tilted land.

"Do you think there's any crocs in the water?" he asked, while drying his legs with a towel.

We said nothing. Our eyes were focused on the hugeness of the lake that spread across the endless savanna like a gigantic metal coffin, and we began to wonder what we had gotten ourselves into. It was plainly a journey of no return, and less than two hundred yards down the track we reached the water's edge and stopped.

This was the time to find out if the old man on the barrier had been correct about the depth of the water. I now used the stave that Thomas had notched with levels of feet and inches. It had been agreed that any measurement over thirty-three inches would be intolerable except on short stretches of the embanked road.

I waded into the leaden water.

Although we were uncertain of the direction the road would take, we did have the advantage of telegraph poles and sagging wires to give us a general guideline. After fifty yards the water rose above my knees and stayed at that level for another hundred yards; the depth was twenty-two inches on the central ridge and twenty-nine inches on each of the wheel tracks. I signaled to Thomas by waving a handkerchief that it was time to move forward. The sudden noise of the motor being started jarred the silence of the night, and I was immediately worried that someone living on the fringes of the town must have heard the noise. My reflex action was to look up and scan the scattered houses that circled the southernmost edges. We were about four hundred yards away, and it seemed improbable to me that the van's engine hadn't alerted someone. After all, people living in a country village are curious when strangers arrive, and yet no lights came on.

The van slowly came to rest by my feet.

"Mr. Carter," Thomas hissed, leaning sideways from the door. "I think this may be easier than we thought."

"Yes, I agree," I said, pleased to grab at any good news.

"The water levels are OK," Thomas continued, "and besides that, I can definitely see an outline of the road under the water. It's a lighter color than I expected."

I turned around in the middle of the road and faced northward. Thomas was right—a luminous ribbon of water curved into the distance, seemingly transparent under the moon, and running equi-distant from the course of the telegraph poles.

"What are we waiting for?" I asked. "All that needs to be done is to keep an eye on the paneling, and if the water rises too high, we'll have to get out and inspect the road." And with those words of encouragement, I climbed back into the vehicle and emptied the swamp water out of my pumps. "And while we're at it, keep an eye on those telegraph poles," I warned.

"Is there a problem with the poles that I don't know about?" Thomas questioned.

"It's possible that once we reach Lembeni Junction, the poles might start to follow the railway line rather then the road. It's something we'll need to watch out for, that's all."

We commenced our journey of no return and soon got our first taste of reality as we churned through the sluggish outer edges of the lake and past layers of assorted driftwood and islands of tufted grass.

Although Visavadia had earlier asked a genuine question about crocs—to which we had no answer—the only life we had actually seen to date was that of a long, multi-striped snake that had slithered into the water from the branch of a nearby tree. Having squirmed past us, it slowed down and, much to our amazement, raised its triangular head and stared straight at us. It was hard to tell whether it was just curious or was putting on an act of bravado.

***

"We've done ten miles," Thomas announced with pride, "and it's taken two hours. That's not too bad is it, Mr. Carter?"

"No, it's good," I agreed, and leaned forward to take a look at the clock on the dash. It pointed at a few minutes past four. "Let's keep going until dawn," I said.

Not long afterward we came on some higher ground, and the road emerged from the water. It was a great relief to be back on terra firma, but our happiness was short-lived. Less than a mile farther on our wheels partially disappeared into the dark waters. It was now Visavadia's turn to test the depth of the water. The light from the moon was gone, and the contrasting shades of dark had faded, making his work more difficult. It took ten minutes before he signaled that it was safe to proceed. We soon realized the reason for the delay. The water had risen alarmingly against the van's paneling.

"What's the reading on the stick?" I shouted from the cab door.

"It's thirty-one inches right across the width of the road," he replied. The water was lapping below his waist.

"That means the road isn't any longer built on an embankment," I shouted. "It's following the level of the land."

I turned to Thomas. "Is it possible to carry on?"

"Yes, but our speed will have to be reduced to no more than three miles per hour."

Safari Salesman

This was a shattering blow to our morale. At that rate it would take us two weeks to reach Himo. It just wasn't on.

"Whatever happens we will make our first stop at six o'clock."

We could now make out the immense outline of the North Pare Mountains to our right. They had already started to unveil themselves as the sky lightened, and it was their grandeur that bounded the view. As a consequence, the flat opaqueness of the lake spread in every direction, and no land could be seen except for occasional patches of green and brown. It was in this openness that the telegraph posts stood out like ghostly sentinels.

We were well aware that there was little or no chance that the plains would cope with additional rain, and drainage would take weeks, not days; we would be irrevocably cut off from getting back to Kenya. We weren't innocents abroad when we decided to make this trip across the flood waters, and neither could we forecast what was going to happen, but for the first time I questioned my sanity and asked myself what was I doing here, in the middle of a lake, in the middle of the night, pushing a loaded transit van full of cough medicine.

Everything was in slow motion and the minutes dragged by as the vehicle wallowed and swayed as we battled for each and every yard. The swell from the flood-water occasionally pushed us close to the edge of the unseen track. But Thomas was there, hunched over the steering, making corrections that were so important, his eyes swollen and exhausted from the bitter struggle to stay on track.

"I think we had better ease up," he murmured in the half-light.

"In that case let's find a high spot and hope that we'll be able to pull off the road."

Every now and then we passed low, isolated hillocks that formed the base of the mountains, and in the distance there was a copse of dank trees and their canopies. They gave off an optical illusion of being close to the ground, but it was the water level that made them stunted.

"How much land do you think is covered by water?" Thomas asked.

I was hoping that he didn't want an answer to that question and that he was only murmuring to himself. Unfortunately he was staring straight at me when I turned to look at him.

"I don't know," I began. "I've had a look at the ordnance map, but it's impossible to say, but I'll hazard a guess of say six hundred square miles."

"Some flood!" he said in wonderment as he whistled between his teeth.

"I agree," I said, "but if you put it in perspective, say with Lake Victoria, which is twenty-seven thousand square miles, it'll give you a clearer idea of the overall size."

Ten minutes later we had found a place to pull over. It was under a foot of water, but the risk entailed in trying to find a dry spot would rule out any likely advantage. It could be said that in trying to find higher ground it would take us farther from the security of the laterite track. It would also be necessary to take into account the treacherous gullies of deep water that separated the slopes. If the van got stuck that would be a clear signal that the safari had ended, and it would leave my friends without a job and me with a lot of hard explaining to do in London. I could see my curriculum vitae branded with the words "acts impetuously" in answer to a question about my character.

It was dawn now, and we were too tired to worry any more. It had been a grueling night, and we neither had the energy to prepare a meal nor to eat it. Instead we wrapped our blankets around ourselves, rolled into a ball, and fell fast asleep.

Three hours later we were woken by the yak-yak-yak-yak of a helicopter flying low. It could be clearly heard, and was, without doubt, targeting our encampment.

"The bastard is looking for somewhere to land," I shouted.

We scrambled out of our blankets, unlocked the doors, jumped into the twelve inches of water, and squinted into the glare of a noonday sun. We watched in stunned silence while the craft hovered closely overhead.

Suddenly it rose at a steep angle and circled us, and then, with its engine roaring, it swooped downward, flattened out, and landed onto a dry grassy knoll on the far side of the submerged track. As a consequence a series of three-foot waves rippled across the void and flooded the floor of our vehicle. We had totally forgotten to close the doors behind us. The African pilot, who wore silver mirrored sunglasses, clambered out of the cabin and stared threateningly across the water.

His companion, a European, quickly pulled an orange-colored package from the nose of the craft, and much to our astonishment pulled a yellow cord. There was a loud rush of air, and before we had time to give thought to these extraordinary developments, we gazed in growing disbelief while the white man paddled himself in his inflatable dinghy across the hundred yards that separated our positions. The scene was bizarre and bordered on the ridiculous.

"What the hell do you people think you're doing?" the man yelled as he rowed alongside the van.

"Are you talking to us?" I responded.

"Whom do you think I'm talking to," he snapped, and not waiting for an answer, climbed out of the dinghy and stood in the brown waters and stared at each of us in turn. "You were told by the police in Same not to leave the town without their permission. In addition you moved a red-and-white barrier belonging to the Public Works Department, which now means that you are trespassing on lands that were closed to the public by the authorities. What do you have to say?"

"And who are you?" I said.

"My name is Mr. Parker," he said crossly, "and I am under instructions from the district commissioner's office."

"Well, that's too bad," I said. "There's nothing we can do about it!"

"Oh yes there is, Mr. Carter," he crowed. "You can take this thing back to Same." He tapped the van with his knuckles.

"You must be joking. There's no way we can turn it around. It's absurd of you to ask us to do that."

"I can assure you I am not joking," he replied. "It's not my problem how you do it. You got it here. Now you can get it back." He stood with his arms on his hips and glared angrily into my face. "We'll be taking legal action against you anyway, but I would warn you that my report will now state that you are being uncooperative."

"I can't help that," I said. "It's still not possible to turn our van round, and anyway, we are nearly half-way to Himo."

"All right," he countered, "have it your way, but I now officially order you to stay here until as such time as we say otherwise."

"And how long will that be?" I asked.

"It could be a matter of two weeks, perhaps longer if it rains again."

"I don't have water or food for more than four days."

"As I said already," Mr. Parker spat, "that's not my problem. You should have thought about that before you left Same."

"You're a bastard."

"Call me what you like," he snarled. "It'll all go down on my report." He climbed back into the rubber dinghy and turned his head toward us. "Remember, you have two choices—stay here or return to Same, and that's an official order."

We stood in silence while Mr. Parker paddled himself unceremoniously back across the metallic water. He cut such a ridiculous figure in the yellow dinghy that we found it difficult not to laugh.

It was a boiling-hot day. The blades of the chopper whirred and the engine throbbed as it lifted off into the blue mackerel sky.

It was midday, and we set about cooking breakfast consisting of sausage, tinned tomatoes, an egg on bread, and a large pot of tea. I had by now noticed that it was always Visavadia who jumped forward and volunteered to make the tea or coffee on the portable stove without being asked. So I questioned him about this habit; he told me that he enjoyed doing it as it made life easy when compared with the wood fire he had at home. "It would be right up my wife's street if she had one these," he said with a big smile.

"It's time to go," I said as I glanced at my watch. It was 2:00 p.m.

Our position was still firmly fixed alongside the southern end of the North Pare Mountains. Their sheer size unwittingly led the eye upward. From where we were, we could just about distinguish the peak of Kindoroko, which at seven thousand feet rose proudly over the range, ruling it like a mother hen. The scene was like an earthly paradise, but as always, the flood waters brought us back to the real world.

Reluctantly, we climbed back into the van, dried our legs, and continued the journey northward. We kept a constant watch for the railway station at Lembini. It was possible that the platform was submerged, but it would help us immensely to get a fix on our exact position. I noticed that the altitude at Same was 2,815 feet while at Lembeni it was 3,123 feet. The difference of three hundred feet was encouraging and was perhaps an indication that the worst of our journey was over.

In fact it wasn't long before we sighted the station. It was, as we suspected, partially under water, and we noticed that the telegraph poles did indeed veer away from the course of the road. It would have been foolish of us to use them as a rough guide anymore. Otherwise we might well end up in the middle of the railway track.

"How far are we going today?" Visavadia asked as he leaned across from the back seat.

"It's not just a matter of distance," I said, doing my best to reassure him. "Much depends on whether the helicopter comes back to check on us before nightfall. But meanwhile we'll move on. I'm hoping that we can keep going until six, and then we'll take a break."

"Will we be traveling tonight?"

"I'm not sure at the moment," I said. "It's plain we'll be tired, and the last thing we want to do is make mistakes."

"We'll beat this in the end," Thomas said.

"I hope you're right," I said. "Anyway, what's our distance since leaving the campsite?"

He dipped his head away from the road and glanced at the odometer. "Four and a half miles," he answered.

"Make it five miles," I answered, "and we'll call it a day."

Thirty minutes later we found a good spot to make camp. It was situated on more or less dry ground and dotted with bushes.

***

The next morning, Thursday, December 15, we woke at seven o'clock. It was a bright, cloudless, cerulean day.

It was my turn to cook breakfast, and less than thirty minutes later we were sitting in our usual places, sipping mugs of hot Kigezi coffee and listening to the soft lilt of African music on the van's radio.

"They're coming back," Visavadia announced.

"What's the time?"

"It's past eight."

The clatter of the helicopter intensified as it flew close over the bushes and continued northward.

"Perhaps they haven't seen us," I said in a low voice.

"Maybe they're playing a waiting game," Visavadia said, "you know, the way a young lion juggles with a baby gazelle when he's got it in his clutches."

"I doubt that it's as simple as that," I answered. "It's more likely they can't find a patch of level ground on which to land as they did in the open countryside yesterday."

"I agree," Thomas chimed in.

We fell silent.

Not long afterward we once again heard the approaching clatter of the helicopter returning southward. It came in low over the bushes, and instead of flying past, it made a full circle above our position. The chopper then unexpectedly roared its engine and rose into the cerulean emptiness, momentarily dazzling our vision as the sharpness of the sun's rays struck its glass shield. We watched in silence as it sped southward back to base. All that remained was its clatter that soon became no more than a faint buzz.

"They're going home," I affirmed, "and it's my guess that once they reach Same they'll mark their map, hold a short discussion, contact their legal department, and get them to prepare committal papers, which in one way or another they will ultimately serve on us. Frankly it no longer matters whether they saw us just now or not, the point being that they have gone and we must play that to our advantage."

"What is it that you're suggesting?" Visavadia asked, clearly worried about being back with his family by Christmas, which was now fast becoming a day-dream.

"Well, I've got an ace or two up my sleeve."

"Such as?" Thomas said disbelievingly.

"All depends on us making an early start from here, which will automatically increase our traveling time. This move will hopefully give us an extra twenty miles before sunrise tomorrow."

"How's that going to change things?" Thomas persisted.

"Good question." I smiled. "It solely depends on us first completing those twenty miles." I looked across from my seat in the van and dared either of them to interrupt me for the third time.

"If we succeed," I went on, "we should find ourselves within twelve miles of Himo, which is outside the jurisdiction of the Pare District." I took a long breath and once more turned toward my colleagues. "As far as I can tell, the worst of the weather is over, according to the forecast on the radio, and I hazard a guess that the waters will be getting lower as we journey north."

"Are you suggesting that they won't follow us when we get into the Moshi District?" Thomas interrupted.

"I'm not suggesting anything," I replied. "I'm just saying that the farther we travel northward, the better. We will face any problems as we come to them. For instance the Pare police may have already advised their counterparts in Moshi, but at the same time the authorities there might prove reluctant to take this case on board. After all, it began outside their jurisdiction, and, when all is said and done, it is a relatively minor offense—hardly more than a traffic violation—and it certainly doesn't strike me as a cross-border crime. It seems to me that the Moshi authorities might well have more important things on their plates dealing with the repercussions of the flood."

I paused and took a long breath. "So let's vote on whether to travel nonstop and get outside the Pare District and within twelve miles of Himo. This will stretch us to our limits, but it's worth a try. We have nothing to lose and everything to gain, so how about it?"

My suggestion was greeted with silence.

"Well, do you want to get home for Christmas or not?" I pursued.

"I vote for going," Visavadia chipped in. "It's not them chasing us that worries me so much," he began, "but it's the thought that we'll have another broken safari on our hands."

"That's a good attitude," I commented.

"As far as I can see," Thomas waded in, "your plan is based on the sole fact that the authorities won't bother us again today?"

"Not so," I said, "and whether we like it or not, they've got the cards stacked in their favor. But by going forward toward Himo, we are giving ourselves a fighting chance of turning things to our advantage."

"I guess you're right," Thomas conceded.

"Then let's get cracking," I said with a smile.

We broke camp at nine o'clock.

It had been agreed beforehand that we must resist forcing the pace and that our maximum speed must be limited to no more than three miles per hour until conditions improved.

Some three hours later we had covered a distance of five miles. It was difficult work, and although there were a few fleecy clouds, they did little to ease the pain of a baking sun directly overhead.

We drove on in silence. Thomas and I took turns, each doing two-hour stints. We carried on with this rota throughout the day and at five o'clock in the afternoon pulled over for a three-hour break. The good news was that there was neither sight nor sound of the helicopter.

The air was less fresh than before, and bands of mosquitoes ascended from the lake. But like all tropical sunsets, the spectrum of color was breathtaking as the sun dipped behind the endless metallic waters.

At eight o'clock that night we were back on the road going relentlessly northward.

The conditions were near perfect. There was a little more cloud than before and yet it was neither menacing nor charged with storm, but just enough to darken the surface of the lake and dim the unseen road. The good news was about the depth of the water. The level had dropped to eighteen inches since we left our departure point this morning. As a consequence we were in safer waters and able to increase our average speed to four miles per hour.

Every now and then we caught sight of the road beneath the shallows. However, despite the good news, our journey north was slower than expected, and we had fallen behind the twenty-mile target that we'd set ourselves. It seemed that the early morning fly past by the 'copter had in some way dampened our urge to succeed.

"I know we're tired," I said, "but let's give it all we can."

I hammered home the plus side of today's journey, mentioning that there was little doubt that the latest depth readings we had taken had improved our expectations, besides which, there had been no further rain. However, we were still maintaining a regular check, and despite any intermittent opaqueness, the lake no longer presented a threat due to the shallowness of its water.

Eventually, after seven more hours of stressful driving, we decided to call it a day, and with great care we pulled off the road under Visavadia's guidance. He was meticulous in using the stave to search out good ground. It took time but was well worth the trouble. Eventually we parked in an orchard of wide-leafed raffia trees that spread across higher ground above the level of the lake.

We were at last within a twelve-mile radius of Himo.

By now I was getting worried about Visavadia, who had taken the brunt of jumping in and out of the van to check water levels so as to guide us through the watery stretches of road. I noticed as he climbed back into the van that he was shivering from cold, looked drawn, and had irregular breathing. Both Thomas and I thought he might well be suffering from a go of malarial fever. We immediately dosed him with aspirin, wrapped him in his blanket, and made him a steaming mug of hot soup. We then left him alone to sleep in the hope that he would recover. After all, he was physically strong and perhaps had only a mild case of shock syndrome. We would have to wait and see, knowing that each one of us was dependent on the others in order to keep the safari functioning.

Despite tiredness, Thomas and I set about camouflaging the van. We began by sloshing mud over the paneling to create a sunlit speckled effect. We then draped our two blankets over the roof to hide the doors and windshield and secured them with cord. We put in brushwood at ground level to ensure the wheels and hubcaps were glint-proof. On completion of the basic work we added an extra coating of mud, which we finally topped off with lengths of trunk and branches that we'd hacked from nearby trees. These were placed carefully on the roof and hood to provide bulk weight to counteract any downdraft from the helicopter should it fly by.

Once we had done the final touches, we took a slow walk around the vehicle, both close up and about fifty feet away. We agreed that it was well-nigh impossible to discern any change in the ground. The van had literally become invisible, and any sign of its contours had gone. We also reckoned that it was unseeable from above—Thomas having shuffled up the short trunk of a neighboring tree—and in a final act of professionalism, he got the rake out and went over the disturbed ground, getting rid of any telltale traces of habitation. After that we got inside our invisible home and slowly eased the door shut, putting on the interior lights.

It was getting on for five a.m., some twenty-one hours since we had been visited by the officials from Same. It was now time to get something to eat. I was pleased to see that Visavadia was sound asleep; his breathing appeared normal, and the shivering had ceased. Later, while I took his pulse, he stirred; I used the opportunity to ask him if he wanted anything to eat, to which he replied, "Yes, please."

He struggled upward into a sitting position and gave me a big smile. He was bathed in sweat, so I quickly handed him a spare towel. Besides being lucid he now dried himself off. He had indeed made a remarkable recovery, and it was good to see him back to normality.

I left Thomas to prepare breakfast, which freed me to get on with my written work. I found a place to sit down on the cartons and lost no time in typing out the daily sales report, which bore today's date as Friday, December 16. It wasn't easy to record "nil returns," which undoubtedly would have to be repeated today. I explained to London that we were held up by unseasonal rains, and included a sum of two pounds ten shillings on my overnight expenses, with an apology for having mislaid the relevant receipt. However, I said nothing with regard to Thomas and Visavadia, as they would automatically get credited for each and every night they were listed as being on safari.

After breakfast I moved up front to the passenger seat, and once I was settled, Thomas passed my mug of coffee to me. It was while I tinkered with the radio dial, searching for the popular station that played records from Kenya's top-ten hit list, that Visavadia questioned me about our next move. He'd been out of the picture for the last couple of hours and had no idea of the work we had carried out on the van, let alone the informative chit-chat that had been going on between Thomas and me.

"As I see it," I began, "we're going to stay here right now and await developments. I'm as certain as I can be that the helicopter will come this way sometime today. We've covered the van in camouflage, and we are now within striking distance of Himo. It's possible the measures we have taken will confuse them, and they will reckon we've reached Himo—which will certainly puzzle them—or they've missed us on the way up. You must remember that they stand to lose a lot of face if they fail to find us, but hopefully with the lead-up to Christmas they will find more pressing matters that will need their attention. Anyway, in answer to your question, I plan to make the final push for Himo tonight. It'll most likely be daylight by the time we get there."

I pulled a packet of cigarettes from my shirt pocket, lit one, and inhaled deeply. For the next ten minutes I listened to the easy music coming from Radio Nairobi, while my mind wandered back to our present position. I felt sure the water level would reduce to twelve inches overnight, and what with the camouflage we put up and the improving conditions, there was every chance that we would leave all this behind us by tomorrow.

I switched off the radio and stubbed out my cigarette in the metal ashtray.

"Anyone mind if I turn off the light?" I asked, but there was no answer. They were already asleep.

Five hours later I was woken by Visavadia.

"Listen," he hissed in my ear, "they're back."
"What's the time?"
"It's ten."

I was cold and had little proper sleep. However, the moment I heard the news, I sat bolt upright and slowly turned my head until I locked on to the familiar yak-yak-yak of the chopper. It was approaching swiftly from the south and was louder than usual, seemingly angrier than before.

We remained quiet inside the cabin and waited. The craft came low and swept over the shallow waters around our wooded area. We could feel the tremble of the van, but the helicopter kept on course, not making its usual circle, and, seconds later, its giveaway crackle faded as it continued to journey northward.

"He hasn't seen us," I said as I glanced at the luminous dial on my watch. "The real test will come any minute, so keep your fingers crossed."

We stayed silent and waited for the craft to make a second sweep of the area. It took less than four minutes before it raced past going south. This time I could somehow or another sense the pent-up hatred the crew had for us. It was almost tangible, and it wouldn't have been a surprise if they did another sweep.

It was after midday when we inched open both passenger doors to take in some fresh air. For a moment the sunlight filtered through the protective brush, catching the passenger-side window and making sparkles inside the van. Then, after ten minutes we carefully closed the doors.

It seemed plausible that whatever was the result of this venture I would end up with a summons, and the longer I thought about it the more certain I became that all this was going to cost me my job.

We spent the rest of a long day enclosed in the van. However, it gave us the chance to relax and read books. Visavadia was reading another of his mysterious eastern dramas, and every so often he paused, put it down, and took a rest. Thomas, however, was engrossed in a travel novel covering the Caribbean, while I made a start on the second of my paperbacks, titled *Something of Value,* written by Robert Ruark.

It was only when the light began to fade that we ventured outside. It was relaxing to breathe in the cool nighttime air.

After stretching our legs, we returned to the van and set about preparing a hot meal of spaghetti and chopped tomatoes with a sprig of wild basil in the pot. This was followed by a tin of sliced peaches. Later, after coffee, we chatted for a while before making ourselves comfortable and going to sleep.

Then, sharp at midnight—a full twelve hours since we last breathed in fresh air—we got ready for our final assault on Himo. An hour later we were again back on the road. I checked my watch which showed that the date was Saturday, December 17.

The lake had diminished, and there was now less than fifteen inches of depth across the flat swamps. This meant that the embanked trackway was all but clear of the water. We could now upgrade our speed to a maximum of five miles per hour, and there was no further need for one of us to go out front should we lose sight of the track.

There was a perfect moon, and gradually we lost the dark outline of the North Pare Mountains. It was replaced by the rolling hills of Teita, and unknowingly we passed over a tributary of the Pangani River. We carried on in silence for another hour and slowly the water gave way to stretches of mushy track.

"I'd like to drop back to three miles per hour," Thomas requested, breaking the silence. "I am finding it difficult to control the steering, and we're starting to yaw on the mud and slime."

"No problem," I responded.

The van had carried a heavy load all the way from Same, and at times it was prone to becoming unwieldy. It was better to be safe than sorry.

Four hours later it began to rain. Large blobs of water dotted the windshield, but it no longer mattered. We were driving on good-to-soft ground, and dawn had arrived. We had driven through the night without let or hindrance.

Shortly the sun emerged, and despite the rain overhead, it lit up the eastern horizon in a mix of orange and yellow. Miraculously the track began to climb and we fell silent, almost breathless, unable to grasp the significance of this development after the many setbacks we had endured since leaving Same. It was then that we spotted a black-and-white barrier across the road. It was to be our last obstacle before entering the busy trading center of Himo. The sound of our vehicle laboring up the final slope attracted the attention of a growing crowd on the far side of the barrier. In fact it caused something of a stir, as from where the people were standing, it appeared that we were rising out of the lake, very much like a submarine breaking surface.

"Where have you come from?" a soldier asked.

"We've been stuck in the bush for the past three days," I said, "and we got caught out by the rains."

"You're lucky to have made it here," he responded.

"You're dead right." I grinned from the van's window. "It's been a difficult trip.'

A large crowd had assembled on each side of the road, and it was not only the soldier but all the others who knew that it was our lucky day. No one had spotted anything illegal by our unexpected arrival. Instead, thunderous clapping broke out, and there were smiles all round. It was incongruous that we had been hounded across the flood waters by all the might that the district officer of Pare could muster, and yet here we had entered another world of peace and friendliness.

"Well, anyway, I'm glad you made it." The soldier smiled and lifted the black-and-white barrier, signaling us through.

We moved forward in second gear, quite a change from grunting along in first, and passed a line of trucks, vans, and cars. The people were smiling and waving, the majority of whom had been waiting here for three days to go south to Same. Other groups stood uneasily around wood fires on which cooking pots were suspended, waiting their turn to have breakfast. It worried us that these tolerant people were now witnessing the fall of new rain and the awful fact that it was coming down in buckets. It looked like a long wait for them, and it was probable that the goods they transported would perish. It was a sad situation. Every now and then, we stopped to give out leaflets and pin Herbalex badges. The applause was still ringing in our ears as we pushed forward along the track and slowly climbed the rising embankment toward the highway.

At the town of Himo we gave our first roadside show in three days. We ignored the rain and moved forward into the bazaar area, which was crowded with wives of workers from the surrounding sisal plantations. We did swift trading in Gripe Aid.

"We'll move on now," I said to Visavadia after having completed our calls on both African and Asian shops.

"It's nice to be back on dry land," he remarked. "Those fifty-five miles from Same were a nightmare." His face broke into a rare smile.

On the straight road going west to Moshi, we drove through the middle of three-thousand-acre sisal estates, each one having its own roads and railway systems, besides workshops, factories, shopping centers, and churches. Block upon block of land was given over to the cultivation of sisal's sharp-pointed blue-green leaves that would eventually end up in a giant crushing machine. The fibers would then be made into bags, paper, twine, and matting. For nearly twenty miles the unfenced fields came and went, replicating until the eye blurred against the uniformity. It was nearly dark when we arrived in Moshi, and we dropped Visavadia off with his wooden case alongside a string of concrete-and-iron Asian stores. Some of the street lamps had already come on, and the yellow fluorescent light fell across the neatly signposted streets. The windows of houses and flats showed off more dim lights in the growing darkness.

We drove silently through the city center and emerged on the western side. It was a short ride to the next stop, and I was half-asleep when Thomas braked in front of the extraordinary Livingstone Hotel with its white columns fronting the entrance. It was like one of those palatial mansions you see illustrated in travel magazines in America's Deep South. I clambered down from the mud-coated van and unloaded my three pieces of luggage. My final request to Thomas was to get the van cleaned, send our blankets to a laundry service, and pick me up at midday.

"It's Sunday tomorrow," he reminded me.

"So what?" I laughed. "Everyone will be open. Haven't you heard it's Christmas week?"

He grinned back and flashed the headlamps before disappearing into the night.

My room in the hotel was a welcome sight. I took a hot shower, changed into clean clothes, and went downstairs. I walked through an enormous but empty ballroom that opened out onto the dining room. The menu included such choice dishes as filleted black bass, Wiener schnitzel, and steak diane sautéed in brandy. This was another world. It was strange to be seated at a table and served food by a waiter. And finally when dinner was over, I was seized by exhaustion and went straight to bed.

chapter

TWENTY-THREE

The sound of repetitive knocking on the bedroom door eventually woke me up.

"Come in," I called out.

I heard the jangle of keys, and the door slowly open. A steward dressed in a white tunic and trousers, topped by a green fez, walked into the bedroom. "It's nine a.m., sir," he informed, striding the length of the room and pulling open the curtains.

"What day is it?" I blinked uneasily against the hard light.

"It's Sunday," he said quietly and crossed back to the door. He poured a cup of coffee from the top of a trolley that he had parked outside my doorway. "Anything else?" he inquired as he placed the coffee on the bedside table.

"No thanks," I said.

For several moments I stared at the white ceiling. I felt disoriented, as though making a real effort to remember where exactly I was. Still half-asleep I climbed out of bed and showered. I had almost finished shaving when I remembered that the steward had left the cup of coffee on the bedside table, and not wanting it to get cold, I went back to fetch it. I was halfway from the bathroom when I stopped in mid-stride and looked through the large plate glass window. The view from the room was overwhelming and compelling—it was the mighty spectacle of Mount Kilimanjaro in cinemascope, with its snow-capped peaks and glaciers rising to almost twenty thousand feet, the jagged rims of gleaming snow-covered craters set against the thin blue sky.

The Swahili word *kilima* means "mountain," and *jaro* simply stands for "caravan," which translates as "a place where caravans meet."

From the tiny village of Marangu, on the lower southeastern slope of the mountain, it's possible to climb past the shambas and enter the domain of the Chugga people, who grow high-quality coffee on the rich, moist soils. Then farther up the trail lies a broad belt of thick rain forest alive with the chatter of the silky-furred colobus and blue monkeys. Finally the ascent through the alpine forests opens out onto the heather moorlands at an altitude of 13,000 feet, giving way to the wide alpine deserts. It is now time to negotiate the saddle, which in turn leads to the snow line at 15,000 feet with its distinctive rock faces and screes. Then at 19,565 feet, you reach the top of Africa.

After breakfast I put a call through to Bill Wright at his home address in Nairobi and requested a final shipment of Herbalex and Gripe Aid to be bused to Arusha to await our arrival. On the map Arusha was some fifty miles west of our present position at Moshi, which lies on the southern slope of Mount Kilimanjaro.

Moshi is an important commercial and agricultural center, linked by road not only with Nairobi in the north but with the international ports of Mombasa and Dar es Salaam to the east and south.

The whole of our day was taken up giving advertising shows in the bazaar and market areas of this very attractive town, concluding with our usual run of visits to the many Asian retailers, from whom we obtained worthwhile orders.

Once again it was dark by the time Thomas dropped me off at the hotel. It was strange to see the glow of lamps along the boulevard, a sure sign that our safari was slowly emerging from the bush, and with any luck we should arrive in Nairobi in about a week's time.

The next morning, Monday, December 19, we left Moshi before nine o'clock and made our way down the western boulevard heading toward Arusha. The streets were quiet, and on one side of the road were large villas set in their own gardens, full of flowers and ornamental trees. We heard the menacing bark of a dog at one of the garden gates, a low repetitive sound setting off other dogs from other villas, some of whom came bounding into the road, barking and running parallel with our van. We slid the doors shut and increased speed as the pack grew in numbers. Shortly we emerged from the residential area, and the road was once more empty. We could still hear the barking in the distance but saw nothing in our rearview mirrors. We slid the doors open and let the warm air rush into the cab.

We continued past a line of office buildings, each with large iron gates attended by police. Thomas reckoned they were the Kilimanjaro Regional Offices that were much talked about in the press. "All this is new," he commented with a broad smile. "The people are getting ready for independence."

"It's possible that those offices will house a growing army of bureaucrats that will be needed to govern the newly formed states," I said.

"But we need our freedom whatever the price."

"Of course," I agreed.

For several miles we stayed on tarmac, and then, without warning, we were on a rough road and back in the openness. Large arabica coffee fields stood out, the bright green shrubs flourishing in the moist climate, part of Tanganyika's thirty-million-pound trade in coffee exports. As we neared our destination, I looked up at the haze-clouded peaks of Mount Meru. They loomed through the top of the sun-struck windshield as though they were about to crush us. This high range of precipitous mountainside—clocking in at 15,000 feet—virtually sealed off one side of the road and blocked all view of the sky. There was stillness in the air, and all that could be heard was the hum of the van's engine and the threatening sound of approaching traffic. In Swahili the word *meru* means "that which makes no noise." The inhabitants of these mountain areas are tribal and of Bantu extraction. They keep cattle, while for crops they grow coffee, maize, and pyrethrum.

On arrival at Arusha, we turned away from the Great North Road and circled the clock tower sited in the center of Bona Junction. It gave the time as three minutes before noon. We swung right and drew up in front of the New Safari Hotel. From the outside it looked old and shabby, but the manager on the front desk was very quick to dispel any negative thoughts by pointing out with just pride that John Wayne had recently stayed there when checking out the countryside in search of a location for a movie to be made called *Hatari,* which roughly translated would mean "look out, here comes danger!"

"The entire film crew will be back sometime next year to make the movie," he said enthusiastically.

Instead of the film people, it was us who booked in for two nights.

Immediately after lunch we got back on the road and made a fifty-one-mile drive southwest to the township of Makuyuni, and by doing this we completed the vital link up on the highway running southwest to Dodoma. It was exactly four weeks to the day, on Sunday, November 20, that we had camped at Mbulu on the rift wall near the southern shore of Lake Manyara. We were now back at this saline lake, but this time on the northern shores, and we were reluctant to cross the road barrier that would have carried us beyond Makuyuni, as we would have been delayed by the long line at the tsetse fly control station. Anyway, it was pointless continuing south as there was little in the way of settlements—and there was nothing on the map—until we reached the link up spot at the crossroads with Madukani. After an hour in Makuyuni, we started on our return journey to Arusha, hoping to get back before dark. The route we traveled on the Great North Road gave access to the Ngorongoro Crater some twenty miles west, down a dirt road. The crater itself forms an enormous twelve-mile-wide caldera and is some two thousand feet in depth, second only in size to the Mono Craters in America.

The mountains that surrounded the rim of the crater bounded the view in every direction, except for those parts wrapped in cloud. The ranges include the Oldeani, the Loomalasin, the Olomoti, and Lemagrut. This entire area is officially protected because of the interesting archeological discoveries. Among the many finds was one made by a German butterfly collector Professor Kattwinkel, who, on the western edges of the Lemagrut Mountain near the fringes of the Serengeti Plains, stumbled on the world's most famous pre-historic site. Here in the year 1911, at the dry-river gorge of Olduwai, he discovered hundreds of Pleistocene fossils.

And in 1959, Mary Leakey found an almost complete skull of the Zinjanthropus boisei—a million and a half years old and known to be the world's first toolmaker. This was followed two years afterward by the unearthing of skeletal fragments of an adult and child buried together. On the edge of the Olduvai Gorge one can see the different-colored earths that abound on the original shoreline of the lava lake, having been disturbed by movements in the tectonic plates of the earth's crust some thirty thousand years earlier.

Beyond this fossil-yielding region are the 5,700 square miles of the Serengeti Plains. This treeless expanse runs from the Masai lands in the east to the banks of Lake Victoria in the west. The limitless terrain is broken by occasional groups of shade-giving thorny acacias. There are also gray, rocky outposts known as kopjes that litter the flat landscape, while water from streams, swamps, and worn lakes provide drinking places for the greatest remaining concentration of wildlife that roam these vast plains. The word *Serengeti* comes from the Swahili *siringet,* which means "extended area."

***

After yesterday's return trip to Makuyuni, we spent Tuesday covering the commercial and bazaar sectors of Arusha. We also found time to pick up the consignment of Herbalex and Gripe Aid waiting for us at the bus depot. Following that we proceeded to make a further batch of non-stop calls on the all-important Asian wholesalers and finally departed the town early on Wednesday, December 21, for the north. The last destination of the six-month safari lay only 173 miles up a straight dirt road. During the passage of time, Nairobi had very much become the cynosure for weary travelers coming in from the bush. Nothing really mattered except the ending of the journey. We too had become obsessed with reaching Nairobi, which we had also made into a race against time.

On leaving Arusha we got our final glimpse of the snow-capped peak of Kilimanjaro before it faded from view in the eastern sky. We pressed onward, through the lush farmland areas with fields of maize, beans, wheat, and potatoes. Some thirty miles farther along the dirt road, at a place called Lariboro, we stopped to pick up two young Masai warriors who were hitching a lift to the trading center of Longido. They were high on pombe and sat down clumsily on a few half-empty cartons behind the front seats. Their brown bodies were coated in an ocher dye of oils. They wore conical hats and iron red sarongs, decorating themselves in the traditional Masai jewelry of copper bangles and bead necklaces. Unfortunately the van hit a bump, and the jolt caused their spears to slide down the side of the paneling and somehow end up between the seats. The metal barbs were hardly an inch from my legs. "Don't touch their spears," Thomas warned. "It's an insult if you do."

I slowly moved my hand away.

Twenty miles later we pulled up at the village of Longido. There were many young Masai warriors gathered near some grass huts beyond a thorn hedgerow. Others were waiting by the road, standing on one leg, leaning against their spears; their tall thin bodies were draped in rust-red cloth, their faces finely sculpted with intricately plaited hair. Some of them had ostrich feathers banded tightly to their shaven heads, forming part of the complex initiation rites.

Visavadia woke our passengers. They clambered slowly down from the van, clutching their spears, and meandered across the road, collapsing wearily on the dusty shoulders of the road. Moments afterward they picked themselves up and walked unsteadily toward the settlement, half-hidden behind a thorn fence, their spears now balanced nonchalantly over their shoulders. We spent a few minutes passing out leaflets before continuing up the straight and narrow road. The smell of cattle dung and urine attracted the attention of some dusty-gray cattle flies, forcing us to open the rear doors to create a draft strong enough to remove the insects and the smell.

Dirt roads began to meet the narrow highway, and simple road signs kept pointing north to Kenya. We glimpsed the 8,625-foot Mount Longido to the right; it seemed small after Meru and the snow-capped Kilimanjaro. The word *Longido* is a translation of the Masai word *oloonkito,* meaning "a place of stone for sharpening knives." The dirt highway now once again changed back to tarmac.

"We'll soon be back in civilization," Thomas commented.

I turned in my seat, looking at the scrub stretching into the boundless distance.

"I'll be sad to leave Tanganyika," I said. "It has a bookful of memories that'll stick in my mind for the rest of my life."

The tires of the transit van hissed gently over the smooth road. The miles came and went. The eye lost itself in the endless wastelands. Every now and then there were clusters of timber shacks, grassed-over huts, and then more open spaces.

"Here's Namanga," Thomas said triumphantly. There were more Masai leaning on spears. An askari belonging to the Kenyan police stood alone in his open-sided sentry box. He waved in answer to our blast on the van's horn. We had crossed from one great country into another, and it was all done with a smile and a honk of the horn.

"We're home," Thomas persisted, a rictus grin creasing his face.

"We'll have to have passports the next time we go to Tanganyika once independence is declared," I said with a smile. "That's provided they'll give us a visa to operate a safari."

"I hadn't thought of that," Thomas answered quietly.

"Don't let it worry you," I said. "It's my guess that this is not only the first sales safari to operate across borders but also the last."

"By the way," I said, changing the subject, "did that policeman get a leaflet?" I turned clockwise in my seat and looked over at Visavadia.

"I put one out of the door," he answered, before checking the rear window, "and he's picking it up now."

A half mile farther up the road we entered the actual village of Namanga, entry point to the 1,259 square miles of the Amboseli National Park, named after a dry lake bed seven miles east, beyond the Ol Tukai Safari Lodge. The park included the usual heavy concentration of protected wildlife with water holes and marsh areas at the center. The heat haze on the white, powdery plains formed a watery mirage, and for a few moments it seemed we were back in the flooded regions of the Pare Mountains and the dividing flats.

Over an hour later, we finished our work in Namanga, and, by way of a celebration, I bought three warm orange sodas from a roadside stall.

"Are we staying here tonight?" Thomas asked anxiously.

"No, not here," I said. "The lodges are full of rich tourists, and it's not us." The sweat ran in streaks down our faces. "It's only a little more than a hundred miles to Nairobi."

Thomas took a gulp from his soda bottle. "We could drive there now," he added hopefully.

"I know," I said. "But we must work this safari to the very end, not taking any short cuts. What we'll do is to get to the north end of this game reserve and pull in for the night at a place called Bissel."

We finished the sodas in the half-light and climbed back into the van. There was now no regular traffic in either direction. We passed the odd road sign warning about wildlife. However, a heavily laden truck thundered past us with inches to spare, with lights blazing and a plaintive blast of its horn, which we acknowledged with a not-so-loud blast from our van.

It was dark. The sky was inky black and the moon was covered by a blanket of trailing cloud. There were no signs of people. All we saw was bush on both sides of the road, other than the solitary ruins of a rusted shed and a weathered signpost giving the name of Nairobi eighty-one miles away. Beyond that was the empty wilderness filled with unseen acacias.

I took the road map out of the glove compartment and flicked the button on the overhead passenger light. The darkness was everywhere except in and around the van. The camber of yellow earth and gritty sand was spread all over the road and extended beyond the unseen shoulders of scrub and overgrown ditches on each side. Everything was blended into a single-colored surface. The danger of veering off onto a minor road was ever present. It was essential that we stay slotted into the parallel furrows and remain alert for any change in the driving conditions.

Then, without any warning, the van began to lurch sideways.

Thomas was bowed over the steering wheel, his head pressed forward to avoid the reflected glare from the dashboard. The sound of screeching as the footbrake was pumped broke the silence. We slewed across the sand-covered tarmac, jumped a shallow ditch, and landed four-square onto patchy scrub. It was the last thing we expected—ending up in the bush at night.

"What's the problem?" I asked.

Thomas and Visavadia were already standing on the road and were stooped over the front passenger-side wheel. "Flat tire," I heard Thomas growl in the dark.

I put everything back in place before I picked up the flashlight and got down from the cab. "These setbacks always seem to happen when we push too hard," I groused, adding, "at least this is no one's fault; it's just one of those things." I raised the flashlight and shined it around the immediate area.

"We're in the middle of a game park," I warned.

"There's nothing we can do about that." Thomas stood up with his arms akimbo.

"I agree," I said with a nod.

Once again I flashed the light around.

"Let me give you a hand," I said.

I passed the flashlight to Visavadia and told him to stand with his back to us and keep a sharp eye out.

"That way Vinoo will be first on the menu," Thomas said and chuckled.

"Give it a rest," he snapped back.

"Be quiet," I urged.

Thomas went to the rear of the van and removed the jack and tool kit, while I undid the tape that held the spanner to the side of the spare wheel and began unscrewing the nuts that secured it to an iron cradle under the floor. The job took less than three minutes.

Thomas was working flat out, and it showed. Beads of sweat dripped off his face onto the ground while he wrestled the wheel off the brake drum and replaced it with the spare.

It was tiring work, and the only sounds that could be heard were the clink of metal on metal, intermittent gasps of exertion, and the shuffling of trainers on a gritty surface.

The first drops of light rain began to spatter.

"Mr. Carter?" Visavadia's hushed voice was coated with fear.

I didn't wait to hear more. My name was enough. I instantaneously followed the beam of the flashlight that he held in his outstretched hand.

"It's a lion," I gasped.

A pair of yellow stars glowed in the surrounding blackness. The deep rumble of breathing and the twitching of furry ears were unmistakeable. I took a handful of Visavadia's clothes and yanked him backward, while Thomas, not waiting for any further prompting, scrambled under the van.

"Thomas," I hissed from the passenger-side window, "are you OK?"

"I'm here, under the chassis," he countered in muffled tones.

"Listen," I began, "when you are ready, give me a shout and roll out on the passenger side. I'll have the door open the minute you surface."

"That's OK by me," Thomas answered. "I'm easing my way over there now."

Visavadia shined the flashlight from the half-open window in the direction of where we had last seen the lion, but there was nothing there anymore. He then repeated the maneuver on the other three sides, opening the door at the rear, and reported back that it was all clear.

"Are you ready?" I shouted down to Thomas.

"Yes, whenever you are."

Visavadia flashed the light once more and ran the beam along the length of the grassy shoulder beyond the dust-laden road before switching to the passenger-side window so as to take a final look at the ground where the lion had been originally been seen. There was still nothing there. "It's all clear," he repeated quietly.

"OK," I called out, "you can come out now."

In one quick movement, Thomas rolled out from underneath the chassis and climbed through the open door.

"I don't want to do that again." He grinned, banging the dust from his clothes with the palms of his hands.

"We'll stay here the night," I said, "and deal with the wheel in the morning."

I reached behind the seat for the box that housed the portable stove. "Let's have something to eat. I'm famished."

We ate our meal in silence until the moment I bit on something hard. Maybe it was a piece of chicken bone, but the pain jerked my head backward. It was worse than before.

Visavadia noticed me flinch. "You all right?" he asked.

"It's an abscessed tooth."

"You'd better get it fixed in Nairobi."

"It's top of my list."

"There's a cottage hospital at Kajiado," Thomas interrupted. He had finished his meal and was sitting on a pile of cartons in the rear and was busy scratching out plaque from between his teeth with the top edge of his knife. "They'll be sure to give you some pain killers for it."

"Thanks for the advice." I smiled.

After a mug of coffee we bedded down, each one of us searching for a place to sleep, moving cartons about, pushing suitcases, heaving drums, and exercising care with our food box and camping stove. In my case, having found a perfect spot, I wrapped my blanket around me, lay down, and used my briefcase for a pillow. It made me think of dogs turning circles in their basket or chickens doing similar things on straw before laying an egg.

"Goodnight," I said, and switched off the interior lights. It was pitch-black, and I waited for an answer. There wasn't any.

They were already asleep.

Safari Salesman

***

"As soon as the sun rose in the sky, we got up, had breakfast and completed the wheel change." These few terse words were written down in my diary on Thursday, December 22, 1960.

It was hot by the time we headed directly north on the dusty yellow road. There were deep furrows on each side of the central ridge, and we were soon lulled by the steady drone of the engine. Saying nothing, we progressed northward along the empty highway.

Some miles farther on we entered the lower section of the Kajiado game reserve, and like its southern neighbor, the Ambolesi National Park, it too was brimming with wildlife. We decided to stop for a midmorning break of tea and biscuits, and took time out to watch a pair of black rhinos wallowing in a water-filled pool left from last night's rains. Some fifteen minutes later we re-started the van's engine, by which time the rhinos had surfaced from the water hole and were browsing in nearby shrub, while being groomed by a flight of tickbirds. It was an idyllic setting until the moment they heard us. They at once looked blindly around and crashed forward in our general direction. The unpredictability of the animal is well-known, and this pair, caked in mud and dripping water, meant business. Thomas needed no prodding and immediately put his foot down on the accelerator to draw away. In fact we were touching forty miles per hour, faster than a racehorse, before the rhinos called off the chase. Seemingly bewildered, they sniffed the air and probed defensively with their horns. Within seconds of this turmoil, the tickbirds were back again pecking at their food source.

It was Thomas, ever alert, who soon spotted a leopard lying astride the shady branch of a solitary fig tree. It was blissfully asleep with its legs, tail, and head dangling. Only its ears were upright and twitching. I'm certain if we had had the time and got closer, we would have heard this beautiful animal snoring away.

The game reserve certainly lived up to its name. Next was a herd of mature elephants with young, which lumbered across the road in front of the van, heading for open woodland a mile distant. In view of our earlier misfortunes, we remained quiet and kept a respectful distance. And similar to rhinos, these enormous mammals were trailed attentively by another set of house-guests, in this case a flight of many-splendored white egrets—similar in looks to river swans—which were occupied searching for insects among the large piles of dung.

On reaching Kajiado we turned from the main highway and drove slowly into the center of the town. There was no way our promotion could have been completed effectively unless we agreed to make this place an overnight stop. The bazaar and market area were filled with Christmas shoppers.

The general clamor for our two leading products in standard five-ounce bottles was overwhelming. A long line had also formed for plastic badges, and it wasn't long before three policemen, armed with black batons, arrived on the scene to take control of the impatient crowd of Masai who had by now surrounded the van.

The Masai themselves have a traditional life that depends on their livestock—such as cattle, sheep, and goats—which they move about according to the seasons so as to find good pastures around the Rift Valley, southern Kenya, and northern Tanganyika. They live in huts encircled by thorn bushes and divide themselves into age groups. Their enemies are the Kikuyu tribe, although intermarriage does occur.

When we finished our initial advertising show in the rutted streets of Kajiado, we drove the van down to the cottage hospital. Here again there were large crowds of people, and they were either sitting on the hard ground or standing in a raggedy line. I joined those standing in a line. It was two hours before I worked my way to the front and explained my problem to an Asian doctor. I asked him for some painkillers to tide me over until I found a dentist in Nairobi.

"That tooth needs to come out now," he said, slapping at a fly that had landed on his arm. He appeared to have ignored my request for pills.

"In that case I'll wait until I get to Nairobi."

"You won't have to." He smiled laconically. "We have a mobile dental surgery visiting here today. It comes every Thursday, so you're in luck." He began to write something on a scrap of paper and called a nurse. "Take this man to the dentist," he boomed and handed her the slip of paper.

I followed the nurse across the bare compound, like a lamb to the slaughter, heading toward a huge white-painted trailer, drawn up under the shade of a green-leaved cotton tree. She turned and asked me to wait outside. I noticed that Thomas was busy distributing leaflets to an orderly line of

Masai, which left Visavadia free to deal with the retail sales at the back of the van.

Shortly afterward the nurse reappeared from the trailer, closely followed by a man in a gray, loose-fitting smock. "My name is Sam Ngowo." He smiled easily. "The nurse tells me that you have a problem with a tooth?"

"Yes, that's right." I answered.

We shook hands.

"Would you open your mouth, please?" We stood in the middle of the muddy compound while he probed each of my teeth with a dental prodder. He was shorter than I was, so I had to bend my legs. "You've definitely got an abscessed tooth," he confirmed and stepped back a couple of paces. "It'll have to come out."

"I'll be back in Nairobi tomorrow...." I repeated to no avail.

"No, no," Sam Ngowo interrupted, "it must come out now. In fact you couldn't have chosen a better time." The dentist paused for effect, adding as an aside, "Don't you think so, Nurse?"

"Yes, definitely," she said and smiled back at him.

"What's going on?" I asked in bafflement.

"It's like this," Sam began as he took a pace closer and leaned toward me, adding conspiratorially, "We've got a bit of a tricky situation here at the moment."

"That's nothing to do with me."

"That's where you're wrong," he countered in sharp tones, "so please hear me out!"

I nodded in silent agreement.

"These fellows," he gestured with a low sweep of his hand at the Masai, sitting in irregular rows around the edge of the unfenced compound "have refused to have any work done on their teeth. Several of them urgently need extractions because they have serious gum infections, like you yourself might have, but their spiritual leader, or *oloiboni,* has warned them against any treatment that means using the white man's gas. They believe they won't ever wake up again." The dentist paused, took a handkerchief from underneath his gown, and mopped his brow. "All I ask from you," he went on, "is that you agree to let me demonstrate the gas on you, and I'll do it for free."

"I'm not sure about that," I said cautiously, "and anyway, it's been raining and I don't fancy being operated on in the damp."

Sam slapped his hands together enthusiastically. "Good," he said and grinned, "I'll take that for a yes."

"Hang on a minute," I said. "This is all happening too fast. I need time to think."

"This is the breakthrough I've been waiting for," Sam Ngowo said in positive tones, "and I can't let it go. I'll have a word with the *oloiboni,* and hopefully this will change his attitude toward the use of gas on the Masai. You see, by using gas on you, it will prove beyond doubt that it is a safe means of dealing with their ailments."

"Now, Nurse, if you would see that the sofa in reception is placed in the middle of this compound." He paused as he tapped his chin with a forefinger. "I'll also need my tray of instruments and a gas cylinder, and then everyone can form a circle to get a clear view of what I am doing. I think that about takes care of everything."

Ten minutes later the preparations had been completed, and I reluctantly lay down on the couch in the open compound while the dentist placed a vile-smelling mask over my mouth. He then asked me to count slowly to twenty.

It seemed as though I had hardly drifted into unconsciousness before the nurse was shaking me awake.

"You'll soon feel better, Mr. Carter," she said enthusiastically as I staggered uncertainly to my feet. "Please try and smile for the Masai. They need to be reassured that everything is all right." I dabbed at the blood seeping from the corner of my mouth with my handkerchief and smiled at the throng of tribesmen squatting on the dirt. The dentist was standing in the middle, triumphantly displaying my tooth aloft, holding it between his thumb and forefinger. Then with the urgings of the nurse, the crowd formed a tight circle around the couch to make room for the others who wanted to see what all the commotion was about. She led the applause. There followed a banging of spears on the stony ground and more enthusiastic applause, and I thought that at any minute I would get a standing ovation.

After all that had happened, we agreed it was preferable to spend the final night of our safari right here in Kajiado. It would have been wrong to have hurried the ultimate fifty miles back to Nairobi and arrive in the dark. It wouldn't have been like us to have taken a shortcut after traveling for six months, and anyway, we wanted the chance to work the settlements to the very end.

We found a small African hotel with a double room available at a rent of twenty shillings for the night. Unfortunately it had no proper facilities. The room measured less than ten by twelve feet and was crammed with two old-fashioned iron bedsteads. This would mean that one of us would have to sleep crosswise on the floor at the bottom end of the beds. Otherwise, the only feasible alternative would be to sleep on the hard floor of the van, although we did have a good supply of cardboard to cushion our bones. We reckoned that a night spent in the van would encourage young children to wake us up at any hour and beg for samples and badges. So we decided that the hotel was a better bet.

However, the hotel had the look of a tumbledown shack. We weren't innocents abroad by any means and were well aware of the limitations of local hotels—all you get is a place to sleep and the rest is up to you. One by one we dipped our heads as we entered the room to avoid the sharp corrugated sheeting that overhung the wooden roof rack on which it was fastened. Once inside, I found myself looking at a line of wattle sticks that were embedded into the adobe clay wall. It was uncanny how the structure resembled an elongated ribcage of a brontosaurus dinosaur. The conditions were plainly primitive, but at the end of the day this was the real Africa, and like it or not, life was raw.

Thomas wasn't slow to point out that there was a sizable gap in the roofing, and when we showed this deficiency to the manager, he explained that it was the result of yesterday's surprise storm and he hadn't yet found time to have it fixed.

"We ought to have a discount off our bill for running repairs," Thomas said sarcastically some minutes later when he nailed half a dozen Herbalex plates over the offending hole.

However, attention was also needed to deal with a soggy patch of mud at the bottom end of the beds, and when I asked Visavadia to lift up his wooden case so I could lay cardboard flooring, a group of four large rats scurried off through the open door. The sight of them dashing away was enough for Visavadia, who then retreated back to the van.

By now, we were starving and lost little time in joining Visavadia in order to cook an evening meal. The menu consisted of a meat curry stew with rice, followed by melon and three cans of lager. We decided to eat our meal on the floor of the van, away from the rodents. After washing up we sat on the few remaining cartons with our usual mugs of hot coffee. These were precious moments when we sat back, chatted, and were free of any work.

A short while later, Thomas and I returned to the room, and while he read yesterday's newspaper, I decided it was a good time to catch up with my written work, which I needed to clear up before tomorrow's arrival in Nairobi. I opened my briefcase and pulled out different colored files; the green one for accounts, the yellow for invoices and stock audits, and the blue for my correspondence. It was while I was sorting out the letters in date order and making sure that all the points made by London had received a reply that I came across one of those flimsy blue airmail letters that I had failed to acknowledge. I had gotten it from Thomas after he had checked the *poste restante* on our first morning in Tanga. It seems I must have tucked it into the blue file and forgotten all about it. I quickly pinned an urgent note to the top of the letter file alongside another note that I had already written to remind me to call Andy Savvides of the Montagu Hotel and ask him that should a vacancy occur on his staff at junior level, would he be kind enough to consider a young girl called Marianne who had work experience at the Sandhaven Hotel outside Dar. I then typed in her phone number for easy reference.

Anyway, the unanswered letter was from London. It informed me that my next assignment was to be Venezuela. Apparently our Caraquenian agents wanted me out there to assist in the launch of our new line in toiletries, which, if successful, would open up the markets in other Central and South American countries.

Before turning off the light, and being careful not to wake Thomas, who was partially covered in the newspaper he'd been reading, I slipped outside to take a last look at the van and see if everything was OK. To my surprise Visavadia was still reading one of his paperbacks. After saying good night, I made my way back to the room.

For a brief moment I stopped and took a last look at the immensity of the night sky. It was lit by a three-quarter moon and a billion stars. I then slowly lowered my gaze and found myself staring at the high edges of the distant southern mountains from which we had recently departed. Without knowing it I became hypnotized by the repetitive streaks of lightning that cracked furiously against its sharply rising flanks. This marvel portrayed no grand finale to my six months in the bush. Instead it made me feel sad at having to leave this wonderful, powerful, and savage continent. I took a long breath, shrugged my shoulders in resignation, and dipped my head downward as I re-entered my room.

Our safari had generated a lot of goodwill with the public, who had unceasingly given us a warm welcome throughout the length and breadth of East Africa. It was fitting that we should have our last night in an African hotel in an up-country African township.

We had traveled to all four points of the compass. As far north as Nimule in the Sudan; as far west as Kisoro in Rwanda; as far south as Tunduma on the Rhodesian border; and as far east as Tanga on the edge of the Indian Ocean.

***

Early the next morning, Friday, December 23, we left for the last part of our safari. It was nothing more a fifty-mile journey along a straight, smooth road, thrusting northward through the Kapiti Plains to Nairobi. Buoyant herds of dark-cornuted wildebeest, with flying tails of silk, cantered carelessly across the flat savanna.

In the earlier rains, the colors had been milder, but now, in the bright sun, the softer greens and yellows were harsher against the eyes. We spent only a short time at the settlements we passed by. It was a disappointment to witness that they were no more than a hodgepodge of shabby gray shelters standing in compounds of trampled mud. The inhabitants had lost their friendly countrifiedness and had become a dependent satellite to Nairobi.

Farther down the road we spotted a herd of nonchalant giraffes gathered around a high-spreading acacia, consuming spiky green foliage with their long, black, leathery tongues. It was their favorite diet. These animals, called *twiga* in Swahili, always astounded me. Their "horns" or protuberances are covered with skin and vary in number from three to five between their ears. Their height alone is overpowering—a big bull would reach 18 feet above ground level—and I couldn't take my eyes off them as they slowly slipped from sight as we advanced northward toward our goal.

No sooner had they had gone when we came across a nervous, tail-twitching herd of Thompson gazelles, known as Tommies, which were jammed together in the shade cast by a copsewood of flame trees. They were easily identifiable by their red upper bodies, white underparts and small black tails. Then suddenly we witnessed the rare sight of a cheetah on the hunt. It was running at full speed and soon brought down a young, unthinking Tommie. It was all over in a matter of seconds.

Farther afield, in the hazy middle distance, was a herd of several hundred common zebra. They're usually found in these parts of East Africa where there is suitable grazing. The unusual thing about them is that they always look sleek and well fed, even in the most adverse conditions. However, there is a rarer breed known as Grevy's zebra in the more northern parts. It has narrower black-and-white stripes, is of taller stature, and has large, donkey-like ears. Anyway, something must have seriously disturbed them, probably a lion, because they suddenly broke ranks and raced across the Kapiti plains, blotting themselves out in an endless cloud of billowing dust.

We'd been silent since the kill of the Tommie, and it was Thomas who broke the quiet.

"How do you feel?" Thomas grinned, looking at me.

"I'm fine," I replied.

"Well, we're back in time for Christmas," he said triumphantly.

"We only just made it," I replied.

"By the skin of our teeth," he countered.

"My teeth, you mean," I said.

We all had a good laugh.

I turned sideways in the passenger seat and looked across at Visavadia. "How's the family?"

"Last time I heard from my wife was when we were in Tanga. They're all doing well but are anxious for me to come home."

"How's the bite?"

"That's all right too." Visavadia smiled.

We halted at the Athi River Township for our final show.

"We only have four dozen Herbalex and twenty-nine bottles of Gripe Aid left," Visavadia informed.

"Then that's a perfect ending," I said.

I was pleased that I had arranged a pick-up at Arusha. Otherwise we would have run out of stock before reaching Kajiado, and that would have put the kibosh on having a final show here at Athi River. It was a matter of professional pride that, despite working deep in the African bush, we always had stock to sell.

We started to hand out the leaflets, and a line soon formed. Thomas got out a boxful of badges and began to pin them on the shirts of little children or give them out to the many parents who were also keen to have a keepsake.

The retail sales were going exceptionally well, and I asked Visavadia to go and put on another record, perhaps a Trinidadian calypso, something with the pleasant rhythm of steel drums. It seemed that island music would suit the friendly atmosphere.

The dust was rising as more people thronged the van. You could feel the heat from their bodies floating through the hot air. The music came on, and I smiled to myself as I watched Thomas kneel on the ground to fix a badge on a little tot of two years. There were only a few bottles left now, and I knew from experience that they would soon be gobbled up when we got ready to close down.

I sold the last bottle of Gripe Aid. This was the dreaded moment when I asked Visavadia to put on the big band sound of "American Patrol." I stayed close by and watched while he placed the record on the turntable for the very last time. It was a foregone conclusion that he would turn up the volume.

The loud sound broke out across the dusty compound, and not only did shopkeepers come to doorways, but gaily dressed women attending food stalls shaded their eyes against the sun and looked over in our direction. An air of excitement took hold, and at the rear of the van we were besieged with customers clamoring for attention and brandishing East African notes and silver shillings. But our stock had run out, and we could no longer meet the demand.

I nodded to Visavadia to open the last of our samples boxes and distribute them. The whole scene was deadly familiar. I stole looks at Thomas, who was, as always, crouched on the ground busily pinning badges on children, chatting with them, and getting them to roar with laughter. Visavadia was now being besieged as the word got around that we were giving away free samples.

It took several minutes for the pressure to simmer down. The ending of the show was different today. There was an air of finality this time as we set about cleaning up and closing down the van. Usually we kept a spare box of each product in front with us for late customers. This time we had to brush away those who wanted to buy a bottle and refer them to the pharmacists in Nairobi. I found it difficult to take my eyes off my two colleagues and deep inside I felt a hollow sickness, knowing that we would never work together again as a team. I only wished I had a camera so someone could have taken our picture, the three of us together, but it wasn't to be.

It had been a hard six months, and this was the moment I dreaded most of all. I walked across the compound and stood alone under a nearby avocado tree.

"Are you ready, Mr. Carter?" Thomas shouted from the van some minutes later.

"Yes, I guess so," I said and smiled.

"*Kwenda.*" He laughed, knowing full well that he had stolen my own valediction of "let's go."

The sun was gleaming off the black road. We passed a tourist bus parked on the dusty shoulder. Some Masai were posing for pictures with the white people; dollar bills and sticks of chewing gum were the inducements. Subtle changes were happening in Africa, and I wondered, with the coming independence, if the days of traveling freely might be numbered. It didn't matter now; we had done our safari. It had been the first and last of its kind. It was unique.

We continued alongside the Nairobi National Park and passed a large herd of waterbuck, with thick hairy coats and flicking tails, which were busy drinking from a murky-looking water hole. They scattered nervously in our wake, a mass of *V*-shaped horns on slim, attractive heads galloping into the shimmering haze of the noonday sun.

Overhead, in the blue unbroken sky, I heard the muffled sound of an approaching aircraft. I leaned from the cab and looked up. The four-engine plane, propellers gently whirring, flaps down, was making a slow descent toward the airport at Embakasi over to our right. The wheels from the undercarriage were already lowered for the landing, and the BOAC markings could be easily seen on the glinting fuselage. It was a Britannia—the whispering giant of the airways—and I thought about how the aircrew would be relaxing at the Montagu Hotel tonight.

The scrub of the open lands had now gone. We passed wide billboards on tall poles that showed ever-smiling Africans smoking, shaving, and drinking. We went past small farms and patchy allotments that gave way to the suburban gardens with their jasmine shrubs, gardenias, and scented cassia plants. The sharp-edged shadows from bright flame trees fell lovingly across sloping green lawns, pleasantly guarded by lines of dark privet hedgerows. Lonesome-looking potato saplings stood in line fronting school fields, and the traffic on the outer streets gradually thickened and then opened onto Princes Elizabeth Way.

We were heading into the center of the city. The broad Delamere Avenue was divided along the middle by an earthy strip of herbaceous plants. We caught glimpses of modern glass-faced shops catering to up-market customers. The sidewalks thronged with all races. There were raucous knots of excited tourists gathered outside the New Stanley Hotel boarding single-decker buses for an afternoon's safari to the local game park. At the bottom end of the dual carriageway we circled the grass-covered roundabout and left the boulevard, curving westward past elegant hair salons, gift shops, bookstands, and coffee houses. We made a sharp, right-angled turn away from Harry Thuku Road and ran downhill behind the Norfolk Hotel.

The clock on the dashboard registered 1,115 miles since leaving Dar. This gave a total for the whole safari—Nairobi to Nairobi—of 7,148 miles (11,501 kilometers) in 180 days, or an average of forty miles per day.

"We're here." Thomas grinned, pulling hard on the steering as we swung off the gradient and entered Grogan Road.

We pushed onward and went left at the bottom of the slope and parked behind a large concrete-and-tiled warehouse that overlooked Morgans' head office. There was no one to be seen, and there was only a flicker of lights from a darkened storeroom. The padlocks on the doors signaled that all was closed for Christmas.

"Yes, we're here," I agreed.

The engine of the van was still ticking as I climbed down from the passenger seat and stretched out my arms.

Thomas switched off the motor and went around the back to fetch his case and bedding. He was joined by Visavadia, who pulled his wooden suitcase from the almost empty van. All that remained was my suitcase, briefcase, portable typewriter, the portable cooker in its box, and a scattering of cardboard.

Seconds later Thomas and Visavadia reappeared. They placed their baggage on the ground and looked into my eyes. It was as though they had rehearsed some kind of ceremony, but it wasn't that. They felt as I felt—that it was time to say good-bye, and it hurt.

"Would you do me a favor and make a swap, Mr. Carter?" Thomas asked sheepishly.

"It depends on what kind of a swap you're talking about." I smiled in puzzlement.

He looked down at his feet. "It's what footballers do at the end of a game. They swap shirts."

"He doesn't want your shirt," Visavadia interjected. "He wants your knife."

"Sure, why not." I smiled. "I'd like to do that."

I put a hand behind my back, loosened the belt, and slid the sheathed knife free of my body. We then made the exchange.

"It's something to remember you by," Thomas said slowly, and added, "Have a Happy Christmas."

"And same to you." I grinned, and shook his hand the African way, looking straight into his finely chiseled face.

"Hang on a second," I said, looking around at Visavadia.

I went back to the van and took out the box with the stove. "Here's something for your wife." I grinned and handed it over to him.

"Happy Christmas." Visavadia smiled back and clasped my hand before picking up his heavy wooden case and the box that housed the portable cooker.

"Good luck," I said with a smile.

This "saying good-bye" was a bigger wrench than I had expected, and a mood of sadness took hold of me. I watched in silence as my two friends wound their way up the twisted driveway. But before they were swallowed up by Christmas shoppers, I swore I'd heard Thomas's rich hum. I recognized the deep resonance of his voice. He was signaling the end of our long journey together and the parting of ways.

THE END

Made in the USA
Charleston, SC
12 June 2013